Uncensored

SRLT

Uncensored

Samizdat Novels and the Quest for Autonomy in Soviet Dissidence

Ann Komaromi

NORTHWESTERN UNIVERSITY PRESS / EVANSTON, ILLINOIS

Northwestern University Press
www.nupress.northwestern.edu

Printed in the United States of America

10 9 8 7 6 5 4 3 2 1

Library of Congress Cataloging-in-Publication Data

Komaromi, Ann, author.
Uncensored : Samizdat novels and the quest for autonomy in Soviet dissidence / Ann Komaromi.
pages cm. — (Northwestern University Press studies in Russian literature and theory)
ISBN 978-0-8101-3123-1 (cloth : alk. paper) — ISBN 978-0-8101-3124-8 (ebook) — ISBN 978-0-8101-3186-6 (pbk. : alk. paper)
1. Underground literature—Soviet Union—History and criticism. 2. Underground press publications—Soviet Union. 3. Russian fiction—20th century—History and criticism. 4. Russian fiction—20th century—Political aspects. I. Title. II. Series: Studies in Russian literature and theory.
PG3026.U5.K65 2015
891.709'0044—dc23

2015004446

This book is dedicated to the memory of my father, Imre Joseph Komaromi.

Contents

Acknowledgments

This work has long been in gestation and I have benefited from the feedback, advice, and example of many generous colleagues and teachers. My dissertation advisor Yuri Shcheglov sparked my interest in the language of late Soviet culture and the strategies of Soviet parody. Gary Saul Morson taught me to think about subjectivity and moral responsibility in the context of Russian literature and thought. David Bethea and Alexander Dolinin helped me appreciate the author and reinforced the message not to succumb to ready-made terms or fashionable critical discourses without a fight. Halina Filipowicz taught me to find my own voice. Judith Kornblatt modeled for me a sociological approach to late Soviet culture built on respect for the voices of participants in it.

Among historian colleagues Benjamin Nathan's work on dissidents has been particularly inspiring to me. In Moscow, scholars at the Memorial Society, including Arsenii Roginskii, Aleksandr Daniel, Tatiana Bakhmina-Khromova, and Boris Belenkin, provided invaluable materials and insights. Gennadii Kuzovkin has been a constant source of support and dialogue for my study of Soviet dissidence. I am grateful to all of them for access to materials, and for their collegial support and willingness to share their firsthand knowledge of dissidence and samizdat. The opportunity to collaborate with the History of Dissidence project at the Memorial Society has been one of the most exciting and fruitful aspects of my work for over a decade.

Similarly, I owe an enormous debt to Gabriel Superfin for his expert advice and help guiding me through the outstanding collection of samizdat and dissident materials at the Forschunggstelle Osteuropa at the University of Bremen. The support of Wolfgang Eichwede and Susanne Schattenberg of the Forschunggstelle Osteuropa has been crucial to my research and the shape of my projects.

I am grateful to Olga Zaslavskaia and the IS[R]A initiative she initiated to facilitate communication and collaboration among researchers of samizdat. The Radio Liberty samizdat collection she curates at the Open Society in Budapest provided an important foundation for my work, as it has for other researchers of samizdat.

In Michigan, Janet Crayne and Kathleen Dow were among those at the Hatcher Graduate Library who provided access to and stimulating conversation about Ardis materials.

An earlier version of parts of chapter 1 appeared as "The Unofficial Field of Late Soviet Culture," *Slavic Review* 67, no. 4 (2007): 605–28. Parts of chapter 3 appeared as "Andrei Bitov's *Pushkin House*: A Critical Analysis of the Late Soviet Hero," *The Russian Review* 72 (2013): 390–408. A somewhat different version of the analysis of *Moscow Stations* appeared as "Venedikt Erofeev's *Moscow Stations*: Performance and Performativity in the Late Soviet Text," *Slavic and East European Journal* 55, no. 3 (2011): 418–38. A version of chapter 5 appeared as "Samizdat as Extra-Gutenberg Phenomenon," *Poetics Today* 29, no. 4 (2008): 629–67.

My work benefited from the anonymous reviews and editorial process of all those articles. I wish to thank also Michael Beizer, Ellen Chances, Catherine Ciepiela, Barbara Falk, Lazar Fleishman, Sibelan Forrester, Anatoly Gribanov, Gerald Janecek, Yelena Kalinsky, Friederike Kind-Kovacs, Edward Kline, Yuli Kosharovsky, Jessie Labov, Priscilla Meyer, Gary Saul Morson, Catherine Nepomnyashchy, Ellendea Proffer, Peter Reddaway, Yaacov Ro'i, Joshua Rubenstein, Ekaterina Sukhanova, Aba Taratuta, Rimma Volynska, Lisa Wakamiya, Enid Wurtman, and Sarah Young for ideas, useful information, and constructive feedback on various parts of this work over the years. Generous colleagues at the University of Toronto who have shared their time and insights with me include Kate Holland, Ksenya Kiebuzinski, Donna Orwin, and Alexandra Gillespie.

Students and research assistants including Anna Chukur, Maggie Gruszczynska, Anastassia Kostrioukova, Nina Kouprianova, Victoria Lyasota, Luba Shmygol, Roman Tashlitskyy, and Brett Winestock brought practical support and helpful insights to my research.

My debt to my husband and colleague Leonid Livak is of an entirely different order: I thank him for enriching all aspects of my life. Our daughters Josephine and Isabelle have inspired my work and also made my time away from the computer extraordinarily meaningful.

I acknowledge with gratitude the generous financial support I received from the Swarthmore Faculty Research fund, the Coburn Award at Victoria College in the University of Toronto, and the Social Sciences and Humanities Research Council of Canada.

Uncensored

Introduction

Writing the Free Self: Cultural Autonomy and the Dissident Subject in the Late Soviet Era

WHEN VENICHKA, the feckless narrator of Venedikt Erofeev's samizdat novel *Moscow Stations* (*Moskva–Petushki*, 1969), visits the Sorbonne to request admission, the authorities tell him, "If you want to study for a baccalaureat, you need some sort of inherent phenomenon. What've you got in the way of an inherent phenomenon?" "I'm an orphan, for God's sake," Venichka replies. "What, from Siberia?" ask his interviewers. "Yes, Siberia," Venichka tells them. "Oh well, if you're from Siberia, there must be some sort of inherent distinction about your psyche. So, what is it?" The story of Venichka's adventures at the Sorbonne is being told to an audience of passengers on the electric train. Venichka explains to them what happens next:

> Well, I had a think. I mean, this isn't Khrapunovo, this is the Sorbonne, I've got to say something really clever. Anyway, after a bit of thought I said, "Okay—as an inherent phenomenon, I am a freely accelerating Logos." But while I was thinking up something smart, the Director of the Sorbonne had been creeping up behind me, and he suddenly wallops me on the back of the neck. "You're an idiot," he says. "You aren't any kind of Logos! Get out, Yerofeev!" he shouts. "Go on, get the hell out of our glorious Sorbonne!"[1]

The humorous tension of Venichka's story at this point depends on the patent improbability of a lowly Soviet alcoholic petitioning for admission to the Sorbonne in Paris. The violent blow he receives releases that tension. The energy of the scene and the motivation for the audience to suspend their disbelief come from Venichka's engaging storytelling. Venichka's tale exemplifies the "freely accelerating logos" (*samovozrastaiushchii logos*) of which he speaks. We as readers value that logos much more highly than does the character of the Sorbonne director. Venichka's fanciful tale strikes readers as both poignant and funny, given the actual circumstances: a regular Soviet citizen like Venichka would not be able to travel to Western Europe. Indeed, author Venedikt Erofeev failed to get permission to go to France for needed surgery even after his writing brought him fame, financial means, and invitations for treatment from doctors in the West.[2]

Erofeev's uncensored samizdat novel—like Venichka's story—exemplifies the freedom of creative imagination soaring above the real constraints of life in the U.S.S.R. in the late Soviet period. A couple of generations earlier, the poet Osip Mandelshtam had suggested that real literature comes from the voice.[3] Venichka embodies that voice in the uncensored work: *Moscow Stations* circulated first in the unofficial system of samizdat (self-publishing), passed in typescript copies from hand to hand, before it was published abroad. Erofeev seemed particularly compelling as an author because of his marginal status—he was, in fact, from Siberia, and he lived in an orphanage for some time. As an adult, he managed to get himself expelled from several institutions of higher education, and his employment consisted of a series of odd jobs and manual labor, fictionally represented in the novel.[4]

For all the flights of fancy and ironic humor of *Moscow Stations*, readers understood Erofeev to be saying something both authentically independent and profoundly true about life in the Soviet Union. In one well-known passage, Venichka wishes somebody would "just show me a corner of [the world] where there's not always room for heroics."[5] One of the most perceptive and articulate of critics to address Erofeev's novel, Andrei Zorin, suggested that *Moscow Stations* occupies a particular, privileged place in the pantheon of uncensored works of this period: "When they call us up for some kind of judgment, we will testify about the time in which we lived with a hand on *Moskva–Petushki*."[6] Foreign readers also felt that Venichka was special, that he somehow "gets to the heart of the matter."[7]

Erofeev and his novel exemplify the powerful belief in autonomy associated with Soviet dissidence and nonconformist literature and art, much of which circulated in the samizdat system of uncensored publication in the 1960s–1980s in the Soviet Union. In this book, I explore how this system came into existence, and what kind of belief in autonomy it supported. One of the most striking aspects of the samizdat system and uncensored cultural production was the degree to which it was embedded in the system and forms of Soviet expression from which we imagine it to be independent. For example, Venichka's "sacramental" wine is fortified rosé at a ruble thirty a bottle, and the sense of authenticity of his work comes from recognition of this typical Soviet product, as well as Erofeev's unconventional way of referring to it in literature. Erofeev and other uncensored writers and artists took Soviet products and forms and transformed them through art into the stuff of life not beholden to official values or control. Similarly, Soviet dissidents transformed relations among Soviet citizens and between Soviets and Western audiences by speaking out on behalf of independent moral and social commitments. Samizdat and tamizdat (Western publication of uncensored Soviet texts) provided the lifeblood for this activity.

A scholarly evaluation of culture of this period should involve critical questions about the kind of alternative incentives available—in terms of both cultural prestige and Western markets for dissident literature. To help set up that kind of inquiry I appeal to Pierre Bourdieu's notions of capital, the field of cultural production,[8] and the "interest in disinterest" that autonomous cultural activity implies.[9] I also appeal to theory of the avant-garde to help explain the radical reimagination of the relationship between writers and readers in the samizdat text. My intent is not to expose avant-garde or autonomous positions suspiciously as part of a concealed ploy for economic or social domination.[10] In fact, transposing Bourdieu's theory from his own modern French context to that of late socialism in the Soviet Union can help us appreciate the continued potential of autonomy as a necessary condition for critique.[11] Similarly, the shift of avant-garde tactics and ambitions to the latter half of the twentieth century show expanded possibilities for radical critique, the persistence of the political and economic systems they challenge, notwithstanding.[12] Bourdieu defined the avant-garde portion of the field of cultural production to be that area where authors and artists worked toward a future in which they could be recognized and consecrated. All the autonomous writers considered here aimed for future transformation of their social collective based on a new imagination of active, critical subjects and relations among them.

THE DISSIDENT SUBJECT—A DRIVE TO CONNECT

Zorin's image of holding Erofeev's book when called up for judgment echoed Jean-Jacques Rousseau's declaration from the beginning of his *Confessions*: "Let the trumpet of the Day of Judgement sound when it will, I will present myself before the Sovereign Judge with this book in my hand. I will say boldly: 'This is what I have done, what I have thought, what I was.'"[13] By bringing to mind Rousseau, Zorin helped underscore a connection between late Soviet autonomous activity and the reimagination of the self in the modern era. Rousseau's *Confessions*, appearing in the late eighteenth century, pioneered the expression of the individual subject in the context of a varied and changing French society. Two centuries later in Soviet Russia, Erofeev's protagonist Venichka, an alter ego of the author, expresses the voice of the individual whose personality and changing world seem similarly complex and compelling.

Questions about Soviet subjectivity have occupied scholars for some time. In his influential work on the formation of the self under Stalin, Jochen Hellbeck cautioned scholars not to cast Stalinist actors as "liberal subjects" in the Western mold; that is, as "individuals in pursuit of autonomy who cherished privacy as a sphere of free self-determination."[14] Stalin-era individuals sought rather to merge with the collective through teleological self-fashioning. What Hellbeck described in the Stalin era suggests the promotion on a mass scale of the type of self-fashioning members of the Russian intelligentsia pursued in an earlier era. The longing to join something greater than oneself informed the self-conception of educated readers of Russian literary works in the nineteenth century. Based on her analysis of the debt owed by major Russian writers including Fyodor Dostoevsky, Leo Tolstoy, and Ivan Turgenev to German Romanticism, Donna Tussing Orwin submitted, "One may conceive modern Russian culture and within it the Russian understanding of the psyche, as the desire for wholeness and various attempts to achieve it."[15] In Stalin-era diaries, Hellbeck found that individuals sought an "integrated selfhood in which the personal would be raised to the level of the social." They sought to escape an "atomized existence," to see themselves as "part of a collective movement." That integration could be achieved by becoming conscious adherents to a Soviet ideology including faith in the socialist utopian future and a merging with the collective in step with the Hegelian laws of history.[16]

We can draw a line from that modern Russian literary self-conception through the Stalin era to the post-Stalin era and Soviet dissidents. There, too, the drive for wholeness informs attempts to fashion a viable self. However, Benjamin Nathans argued against the wholesale transfer of Bolshevik or Stalinist models of forming subjectivity onto Soviet dissidents. Ideological self-fashioning did not persist unchanged into the post-Stalin era. Nathans warned likewise against psychologizing dissent; that is, treating dissidence exclusively in terms of the inner psychological needs of the personality.[17] Soviet officials exploited their own kind of psychological reductionism when they defined dissidents as mentally ill in some of the most shocking instances of post-Stalin abuse.[18] Soviet authorities also liked to ascribe dissidence to exclusively external factors, in particular the influence of Western propaganda and the covert operation of Western and Russian émigré groups aiming to undermine the Soviet system.[19] Such diagnoses greatly distort the picture. While there are lines of affiliation to prerevolutionary experience and given that a variety of Western influences should be borne in mind, it is important to emphasize that the dissident self developed organically out of the post-Stalin context and Soviet experience.

Oleg Kharkhordin explained the distinctiveness of Russian and Soviet subjectivity established on the basis of regulation by the collective, as opposed to Western subjectivity, which situates individuals around a single, elevated authority.[20] Kharkhordin reminded readers that the notion of a "private world," so familiar and important for the idea of selfhood in the modern West, was not natural but created. The influence of German and English Romanticism on aristocratic authors in Russia produced some remarkable instances of private selves (here we might think of the inscrutable motivations of Eugene and Tatiana in Aleksandr Pushkin's *Eugene Onegin*), but the idea of a private self hardly penetrated into the self-consciousness of the popular masses or even among the mixed-class intelligentsia (*raznochintsy*), from whose ranks Russian realists of the more radical stripe came.[21] Kharkhordin made the interesting claim that a private sphere came into being precisely in the Stalin era on the basis of "dissimulation." Dissimulation in Soviet society did not arise as a way to protect a preexisting private world, as some Western scholars seem to believe; rather, dissimulation itself constituted the split between a public and a private sphere.[22]

In this case, dissidents of the late Soviet era may have understood a covert "private" sphere in precisely these terms, as characteristic of a Stalin-era mentality. Splitting the private from the public in order to protect it was not the goal. Rather, dissidents aimed to forge a new type of public that would authentically reflect the concerns and aspirations of a variety of constituents. Support for this shift away from a strict dichotomy of private vs. public can be found in the recent account by Viktor Voronkov and Jan Wielgohs of a mixed "private-public" sphere in post-Stalin Soviet society.[23] Indeed, members of the democratic movement, the loosely organized activists who struggled to protect the human rights of Soviet citizens, spoke out against the mythology and mentality of the "underground."[24] Dissident Vladimir Bukovskii noted the influence of revolutionary romanticism as propaganda and popular Soviet culture. Stories about Bolsheviks founding a secret political movement and and going underground to distribute incendiary literature caught the imagination of children and young adults in the Soviet Union. Such popular books and films based loosely on the history of the Communist Party were exciting, Bukovskii acknowledged, but real dissidence required maturity: "How can grown-up people seriously believe that revolutions are the result of the activities of some underground organisations?" Bukovskii wrote.[25] Democratic dissidents did not want to perpetuate dissimulation of a hidden sphere because of its associations with revolutionary mythology and the mentality of the Stalin era. Along these lines, literary dissidence, of the kind promoted by Andrei Siniavskii, did not create a separate, individual poetic world. Instead, such dissident works tended to thicken the medium of literary language as a way to accommodate negotiations between the individual and society, private identities and public issues—two linked halves that required far more elaboration and negotiation than official Soviet culture allowed.[26]

Jerome McGann wrote about a "mode of resistance" in the literary work that impedes the efficacious transmission of information. With all its "noise," the literary work provides a special site for exploring the exchanges inherent in interactions that occur at the site of the text.[27] To refer this insight to Bourdieu's theory, the literary work functions like the field of culture does—it refracts like a prism forces external to its own logic. When understood this way, the work or cultural field can be analyzed to reveal something about those autonomous structures as well as something about the external determinants defining their context.[28] Bourdieu indeed took this approach when he elaborated the model of the social field and its exchanges as viewed through Gustave Flaubert's point of view in his novel *Sentimental Education*.[29] Soviet dissident writers used literature as a space for exploring new images of the self and society. Critical analysis can thus find in uncensored works of poetry and fiction mediated reflections of the changing social context.

THE BREAK: THE EMERGENCE OF DISSIDENCE AND SAMIZDAT

The late 1960s marked a major turning point for the Soviet intelligentsia. Attempts to work with the regime had failed in spectacular ways. Two key events of the late 1960s epitomize the changing climate and evolving attitudes and strategies of the Soviet intelligentsia. The first was the case of Iulii Daniel and Andrei Siniavskii, arrested for anti-Soviet propaganda in late 1965, and tried in early 1966. Authorities aggressively pursued a case against these writers who published fictional works abroad without official permission. The writers' wives and friends began a campaign of open letters that circulated in early samizdat networks, which were used also to summon people to the demonstration that took place on December 5, 1965, in Moscow's Pushkin Square to demand openness in the proceedings. These events caught the attention of the Western press and helped inaugurate new, more direct and independent communications between Soviet citizens and Western journalists.[30] They inspired Aleksandr Ginzburg to compile his *White Book* (*Belaia kniga*), an independent account of the case against the two writers. Ginzburg and his collaborators were arrested and tried in the 1968 Trial of the Four, a trial reported independently in the first issue of what would become a major samizdat bulletin, the *Chronicle of Current Events* (*Khronika tekushchikh sobytii*, Moscow).[31] Thus, as the period of official liberalization came to an end, independent dissident activity began to flourish.

The dramatic break with the regime and official Soviet culture came with the invasion of Czechoslovakia by Soviet tanks to crush a peaceful movement calling for "Socialism with a Human Face." The poet Joseph Brodsky, a Nobel Prize winner whose verses circulated initially as samizdat,[32] wrote in December 1969 about "The End of a Beautiful Era" ("Konets prekrasnoi epokhi"): "but the widened horizons should narrow somewhere, and here— / here's the end of perspective" (*no razdvinutyi mir dolzhen gde-to suzhat'sia, i tut— / tut konets perspektivy*).[33] The end of perspective suggests both the loss of hope for the future (as in "*net perspektivy*") and the loss of one way of looking at the world, a way that involved romantic ideas about the possibility of finally realizing an ideal socialist society. Indeed, many memoirists and cultural historians report a shared sense of a caesura, a major social break, around this time.[34] Noted rights activist and historian of Soviet dissidence Liudmila Alekseeva articulated this sense strongly and specifically: "The Soviet invasion of Czechoslovakia dealt a heavy blow to the moral attractiveness of socialism. It destroyed the hope in a possibility of the Soviet leadership moving in the direction of democratization. At the same time as the invasion of Czechoslovakia, a tendency of Soviet leaders to embrace re-Stalinization grew more sharply defined."[35] The latter trend provoked mobilization on the part of a small number of democratic activists. It prompted others to drop out of engagement with official Soviet institutions and life.

In the spirit of dropping out, the 1970s saw the rise of what Soviet rock musician Boris Grebenshchikov called the "Generation of Janitors and Doormen" ("Pokolenie dvornikov i storozhei").[36] People with higher education began to avoid work they felt would be compromising and to take jobs as boiler-room attendants and night guards. In some cases this was done out of necessity, as in the case of Jewish refuseniks and other dissidents forced out of their jobs for nonconformist behavior. However, in many cases poets and others chose to drop out. Not unlike their counterparts in the West,[37] these Soviet dropouts refused the social benefits associated with working for established institutions. Bourdieu distinguished a more general "social capital" from the more autonomous "symbolic capital" whose value depended on the fact it could *not* be converted easily into monetary gain, or social power in the larger field.[38] The new symbolic capital in the emerging field of dissidence and nonconformism made it attractive for people to define themselves in new ways through activities independent of established Soviet institutions.

The divide cannot always be drawn as neatly as it might in the case of Venedikt Erofeev. Many nonconformist artists supported themselves with book illustration and official union membership, for example. However, a significant number of Soviet intelligentsia felt motivated to venture occasionally or entirely outside regular jobs and educational institutions in order to devote themselves to activities like music and art, writing, informal socialization, and rights advocacy. These dissidents believed that such activities connected them more meaningfully to a greater social or cultural whole.

AUTONOMY, DISSIDENCE, AND THE AVANT-GARDE

With the term "dissident," we tread on contentious terminological territory. Most people engaged in independent activity, even among human rights advocates of the democratic movement, rejected the label "dissident" at that time.[39] The word undoubtedly had inflammatory implications in the context of the Cold War, when Soviet authorities tended to demonize dissidents as mentally unstable or agents of foreign powers. "Dissidents" appeared most often in the Western press as selfless heroes fighting the repressive regime. This constituted an obvious and potentially harmful oversimplification.[40] Nevertheless, from a retrospective point of view, it can be useful to apply the term "dissident" to people engaged in a wide range of independent activity in order to emphasize the common quest for social autonomy. The Latin etymology of the term reveals that *dis-sidere* means literally "to sit apart," a sense employed metaphorically to signify disagreement. The notion of sitting in a space apart resonates with Bourdieu's spatial model of the field of autonomous cultural production as a distinct area more or less separate from the general social field with its prevailing economic and political forces. In the socialist economy and one-party structure of the Soviet Union, all cultural production, like all public debate,[41] had been folded into the domain of state institutions. We can use Bourdieu's model of the autonomous cultural field to examine critically the notion of dissident separation as a response to particular Soviet conditions and in light of broader modern ideas about the relationship of public critique and culture.[42]

Many will also recognize the "avant-garde" as another hotly contested term. Groys effectively denounced the Russian and early Soviet avant-garde in his well-known monograph on the subject by linking that avant-garde art in terms of ambition to Stalin's totalitarian control over Soviet life.[43] The need to break free from the imposing legacy of the historical avant-garde, and the awareness of different historical and social challenges for their late Soviet art motivated many nonconformist artists to mark their difference from predecessors like Kazimir Malevich. Elsewhere, the animus toward Vladimir Maiakovskii went hand-in-hand with recovery of the repressed Silver Age portion of Russian Modernism.[44] Indeed, the avant-garde poet Maiakovskii collaborated with the early postrevolutionary regime and achieved unparalleled canonical status in the official Soviet pantheon conferred by Stalin himself. As John E. Bowlt and Mark Konecny recalled, Stalin rehabilitated Maiakovskii after his 1930 suicide with an editorial in *Pravda* published on December 5, 1935. Stalin's pronouncement that Maiakvoskii was "the best, most talented poet of our Soviet epoch" provoked "an intense scholarly revision of the role of Maiakovsky in Russian literature. Now recast as a Bolshevist sloganeer, Maiakovsky was distanced from Futurism, forgiven his youthful digression, and promoted to hero of the Soviet State."[45] If Stalin made study of Maiakovskii compulsory, the "Silver Age" of Russian poetry seemed, by contrast, to be the "stolen air" of which Mandelshtam had spoken.[46] Anna Akhmatova promoted this alternative heritage of modernism to the young literati of Leningrad, including Joseph Brodsky, whom she consecrated as the leading new poet, "Our Premier."[47] The Silver Age poets, separated in this mythology from the avant-garde ambitions they had abandoned or never really possessed, appeared to be surrounded by an aura of loss and longing for "world culture,"[48] ties to which were broken in the twilight of culture brought on by the Revolution.[49]

We need to see beyond these powerful "anti-avant-garde" lenses for a more balanced perspective on the dynamics of late Soviet nonconformist culture and to recover some analytic tools that can be helpful in examining it. Siniavskii, who described his dissidence as "stylistic," talked about encountering his dissident *prise de conscience* when he saw modernist culture being stamped out under Stalin. He depicted his knowledge of and enthusiasm for modernist culture as coming out of his participation in Vsevolod Duvakin's seminar at Moscow State University in the late 1940s. There he learned that all kinds of modernist and international characters who made a mark in culture could be studied under cover of Maiakovskii.[50] Lev Losev also testified to the crucial importance of Maiakovskii in the early and mid-1950s. Maiakovskii created a "hole in the wall" through which one could access Futurism and other modernist authors like Mandelshtam, Akhmatova, those associated with the OBERIU and others not represented in official Soviet publications.[51] Maiakovskii's poetry represented a vigorous current of culture that remained available under Stalin and which had the potential to lead to less controlled perspectives on modernist culture and the radical possibilities of literary art. Siniavskii became interested in the "Maiakovskii Brigade," a group begun in the 1930s to read Maiakovskii verses in factories and club settings. Many young people became acquainted with Maiakovskii in this para-official setting.[52] After the opening of the monument to Maiakovskii in Moscow in 1957, youth began to gather spontaneously around the monument to declaim poetry and share manuscript items and handmade collections of texts. These readings happened between 1958 and 1961. A few years later, in 1964, the group SMOG (*Samoe molodoe obshchestvo geniev*, The Youngest Society of Geniuses) met regularly at the monument.[53] Over the course of the 1960s, Nikolai Khardzhiev and Gennadii Aigi mounted exhibits at the Maiakovskii Museum in Moscow.[54] These exhibits helped acquaint many dissident artists and writers with the Russian avant-garde heritage.

For methodological purposes, the notion of the avant-garde helps bring the historical and social specificity of the late Soviet context into a dynamic relationship with theoretical considerations. The turn to modernism has enormous general relevance for the establishment of dissident culture in terms of the links to the past and the West. The specifically avant-garde impulses expressed in uncensored works of this period also establish a critical artistic relationship to the present Soviet context and a thrust toward the future.[55] For Bourdieu, the "avant-garde" designates those trends or groups within the field of culture production that contest established positions and values.[56] In the culture of Soviet dissidence, this includes a critical relationship to the official Socialist Realist canon. Within the more limited field of liberal intelligentsia culture, it also may manifest in terms of resistance to consecrated dissident modernism.[57] Bourdieu explained that the avant-garde essentially produces a cultural future by creating new positions beyond established ones; that is, by introducing difference and the possibility of changing tastes and means of expression.[58] As parts of the cultural heritage are rediscovered or reclaimed, the cultural work of the avant-garde involves activating that heritage in the present for the sake of the future. Late Soviet avant-garde artists and writers, like their forebears and Western counterparts, critically engaged their context, passing back and forth across the boundary between art and life. They artistically embraced their present environment (however hostile or degraded it may seem to be), rather than trying to escape from it. They did so for the sake of a different future.

The influential Marxist theorist of the avant-garde Peter Bürger denied the possibility of an authentic neo-avant-garde.[59] While this position today seems dubious, to say the least,[60] Bürger's insights continue to inspire analyses of both historical and newer avant-garde works, and they can help us formulate an approach to late Soviet experimental culture. In particular, we will turn to Bürger's description of the ways in which avant-garde artists dismantle the complacent subjectivity associated with a stable representation of the world in the artwork. Avant-garde autonomy in dissident culture means a creative relationship to the forms and conditions of Soviet life and independence from liberal pieties as well as official ideology.

SAMIZDAT NOVELS

The core of the present study comprises a close examination of three uncensored novels written on the cusp of the 1960s and 1970s. I treat these novels in terms of their autonomous samizdat status and their avant-garde approach to the status of the work of art and the construction of subjectivity. Vasilii Aksenov's *The Burn* (*Ozhog*, written 1969–75), Andrei Bitov's *Pushkin House* (*Pushkinskii dom*, 1964–71), and Venedikt Erofeev's *Moscow Stations* (*Moskva–Petushki*, 1969), demonstrate the maturity and viability of an unofficial field of culture at this time. All portray the late Soviet context critically, projecting their authorial personae into the work for critical reconstruction. In *The Burn*, Aksenov took a searing look at his generation of creative intelligentsia in Moscow. He portrayed a collective of five adult protagonists, with common roots embodied in a single teenage youth whose life they seem to share as memory. The story of that youth appears to be drawn largely from Aksenov's own experiences. These protagonists suffer from a structural dependence on the authorities and the repressed trauma of a childhood spent with parents imprisoned in Stalinist camps. Aksenov used grotesque and fantastic images to draw out the violence that persists from the Stalinist era into the late Soviet period, and to convey the frustrated aspirations of his generation. Bitov focused in *Pushkin House* on a single character, his alter ego Lyova, whose problematic formation and integration into Soviet society he probed in a sharp way. The psychological analysis to which Bitov subjected his protagonist corresponds to the formal structure of the book, which is something like a deconstructive "analysis" of the genre of the novel and its evolution through Russian and Soviet history. Erofeev's *Moscow Stations* takes us on a wild ride through one day in the life of alcoholic protagonist Venichka. While Venichka appears in some ways most conventionally engaging thanks to the author's sympathetic portrayal of him, the character ultimately draws readers into a risky, radical reimagination of what the text can mean for writer and reader.

Aksenov and Bitov both turned away from successful careers in official Soviet publications as authors of "Young Prose," a mildly avant-garde trend in official letters. In the 1960s, Young Prose and other developments like "mauvism"[61] responded to the greater cultural freedom afforded by Khrushchev's Thaw and the influence of debates about Western movements such as the new novel (*nouveau roman*), which became a topic of heated discussion at a UNESCO conference on the novel held in Leningrad in August 1963.[62] In works associated with these trends, writers attempted to push against the boundaries of permissible language, character, and narrative possibilities in Soviet literature. In an officially published essay from around that time, Aksenov referred to young novelists, including Georgii Vladimov, Vladimir Voinovich, Anatolii Gladilin, and Iurii Kazakov as interesting new writers. He defended their use of techniques of "deepened psychology, dynamic narrative construction, concentration of time and internal monologue" as susceptible to reading according to the principles Soviet critics usually found in more classic realist works.[63] Official attitudes from the right of the Soviet literary establishment about "bourgeois formalism" and the degenerate influence of the West competed with a growing appreciation of the distinguished modernist heritage of Russian culture and exciting new developments in contemporary literature and cinema around the world.[64] Stimulated by such developments in their early careers, Aksenov and Bitov became frustrated by the retarded rate of liberalization of Soviet culture in the Brezhnev era beginning in the late 1960s. Meanwhile, the samizdat/tamizdat system began to flourish. As a result of that new uncensored venue, Aksenov and Bitov each found it possible to conceive of longer and more formally challenging literary works to engage the critical issues of their generation. For his part, Venedikt Erofeev's choice to bypass the official system altogether and make his literary debut with an uncensored manuscript might—given the great success *Moscow Stations* enjoyed—serve as an even more striking indicator of the perceived viability and stimulating effects of the new samizdat system.

The fact that all three authors embraced the genre of the novel (however deconstructed or qualified) for their uncensored debuts suggests the scope of their ambitions: the genre of the novel possessed great weight in the Russian and Soviet literary traditions. Therefore, re-conceiving it in independent literature signaled a serious bid to establish new terrain. These highly experimental novels implicitly skewered the formulaic and codified nature of official Socialist Realism on the grounds of its own privileged genre.[65] They also answered an unofficial desire to see culture revived and developed anew. Bukovskii described the process of starting over after Stalin:

> Throughout Moscow, office typewriters worked overtime, clicking out—for the pleasure of the typists or for their friends—the poetry of Gumilyov, Mandelstam, Akhmatova, and Pasternak. It felt as if everyone were gingerly straightening numbed limbs after ages of sitting still, of people trying to twiddle their fingers and toes and shift position as their bodies pricked with pins and needles. It seemed there was nothing to keep them sitting still any longer, but they had lost the habit of moving and had forgotten how to stand on their own two legs.
>
> The rebirth of culture in the Soviet Union after half a century of plague recapitulated all the stages in the development of world culture: folklore, epic, tales passed from mouth to mouth and from generation to generation, songs by troubadours and minstrels, and finally prose—novels, dissertations, philosophical treatises, topical articles, open letters and appeals, journalism.[66]

Bukovskii and others imagined a complete destruction of culture under Stalin. His narrative about nascent dissident culture after that catastrophe mimics the Hegelian progression, recapitulated on a short time line.[67] According to this view, the appearance of independent prose meant the maturity of dissident culture.[68] Moreover, the novel, heroicized by Mikhail Bakhtin, managed despite its prominence in the canon of Socialist Realism to occupy a special place in liberal Soviet thought: the novel remained a site for looking from the ground of the present toward the future.[69] Bakhtin's ideas exerted tremendous influence on intellectuals in the Soviet Union beginning in the

1960s, and these novels are among the many works that reflect directly or indirectly Bakhtin's impact. In *Problems of Dostoevsky's Poetics*, a manuscript originally written in 1929 and revised for publication in 1963,[70] and in the book *Rabelais and His World*, based on thesis work originally submitted in 1940 but also revised for publication in the 1960s,[71] Bakhtin offered a fresh evaluation of the crucial importance of novels rooted in a tradition of laughter and associated with human freedom, as opposed to the rigid didacticism of official Socialist Realism.

The three uncensored novels by Aksenov, Bitov, and Erofeev exemplify better than other works of the time the avant-garde desire to exploit the potentials of the novel genre in a way that captures the dynamism of a dissident cultural field. They exhibit precise sensitivity to the changing cultural landscape, evoking the regenerative power of carnivalesque laughter. At the same time, they exemplify the doubt felt by members of the Soviet intelligentsia who embraced those attractive ideas rather too enthusiastically in the run-up to 1968. Looking back, Maia Kaganskaia described Soviet intellectuals' relationship to Bakhtin in the following way:

> Our relation to Bakhtin was not disinterested; his texts, already so packed, were overloaded with a subtext, and the criticism of the monologic form of artistic expression we took as the negation of monolithic ideology in general, and of the one that occupied us in particular (or, more exactly, that occupied itself with us); we read *The Problems of Dostoevsky's Poetics* like a novel: in L. N. Tolstoy, for example, we divined an allegory of Soviet power (which, speaking honestly, is not such a strained interpretation, if one keeps in view a structure whose basic categories, not political but aesthetic, are "the people," "simplicity," and "moral benefit"). Dostoevsky was our positive hero (a symbol of spiritual freedom), and a personage by the name of "Polyphony" stepped forward as an allegory for "pluralism" and "democracy." Ridiculous?—Well, ridiculous. Painful?—Yes, painful.[72]

Although Kaganskaia talked here about ideas in the Dostoevsky book, her point applied equally to Bakhtin's book on Rabelais and the carnival, which Soviet liberals embraced with similar ardor in the 1960s. This initial enthusiasm for Bakhtin's ideas, superficially understood and assimilated directly to life, gave way to regrets in light of the disillusionment of 1968.

Aksenov's statements about his literary art most obviously justify the application of an avant-garde analysis to these novels. Aksenov described his preferred aesthetic as the "avant-garde," a style he contended was more true to popular roots of literary art in the Russian tradition than Socialist Realism, because of the avant-garde's connection with the grotesque and fantastic elements of popular fairy tales.[73] Aksenov also explicitly contested the "carnivalesque" ethos of his 1960s bohemian milieu.[74] *The Burn* represents a sober and painful evaluation of the false sense of romantic enthusiasm and illusory independence to which Aksenov's generation fell prey.

Bitov's *Pushkin House* represents this critical turn with irony and a relatively light touch. The scenes of the November 7 holiday late in the book evoke a carnivalesque atmosphere and pose serious questions about how people yield the right to distinct subjective judgments and moral responsibility in the context of mass celebration. In this, Bitov's novel resembles *The Burn*. Although begun a few years before *The Burn*, Bitov's *Pushkin House* demonstrates that author's resistance to dominant mythologies of liberal Soviet intelligentsia already in the mid-1960s. Like *The Burn*, Bitov's novel exemplifies a desire to break through barriers constraining topics and techniques in Soviet literature.[75] Bitov, however, undertook a more specifically literary—and thus more autonomous—approach to these issues in *Pushkin House*. If Aksenov treated at length the illusory freedom of the carnival, apparently independent but actually reinforcing official control, Bitov concerned himself with the possibility of an authentic critical subjectivity. He did this by directly challenging the liberal self-consciousness of his generation. Bitov's deconstruction of the form of the novel provides the readers with the tools to build the kind of critical and creative awareness Bitov's protagonist Lyova strives to achieve, even if we do not see Lyova realize that goal within the novel.

Venedikt Erofeev's *Moscow Stations* deliberately straddles generic classifications. Subtitled "An Epic Poem" (*poema*), Venichka's picaresque journey brings to mind Nikolai Gogol's similarly subtitled novel *Dead Souls*. The world depicted by Erofeev is even more obviously haunted by fantastic specters and demons. The mix of genres and carnivalesque whirl of intertexual referents in *Moscow Stations* suggests the ossified and crumbling totality of a Soviet culture that has lost its foundations. Erofeev's reference to Gogol's novelistic epic poem likewise makes the reader think that his satire of the present points toward a redeemed future, although in an ironically lowered key: Gogol's speeding troika at the end of *Dead Souls* possesses a late Soviet counterpart in Venichka's electric train (*elektrichka*).

All three novels demonstrate the recuperation and creative reinterpretation of modernist models in late Soviet uncensored fiction. If Aksenov's novel refers most obviously to Andrei Belyi's symbolist novel *Petersburg*, Bitov's evokes the self-conscious engagement of literary tradition found in Vladimir Nabokov's novel *The Gift*. Erofeev's precedents, less generically specific, include the poetry of Aleksandr Blok and the small prose works and drama of Daniil Kharms and the OBERIU. Within this neo-modernist engagement of artistic autonomy, Erofeev's slim work distils the avant-garde potentials of the samizdat field. Erofeev's depiction of his protagonist Venichka's attempts to reach paradise in the town of Petushki shows him ultimately spun back into the violent heart of the Soviet state. The urge toward freedom, independence, and the realization of oneself and human desires expresses itself in a spatial trajectory away from the center of power. However, that centrifugal force collapses in the end back onto the center in Moscow's Kremlin. Erofeev's novel suggests the impulse to autonomy cannot be realized in a removed space, but only in time, within the unfolding of history.

All three novels can be called "avant-garde" in part thanks to their experimental and provocative qualities as uncensored works that challenged both Soviet authorities and readers. Bourdieu described avant-garde works created on the limited field of cultural production as maximally resistant to integration and consecration within existing culture. These novels tend to disassemble previous forms and they aggressively assault even samizdat readers' expectations. All three writers also clearly aimed to help forge a new artistic language expressive of their time and historical moment. In one way or another, each of these uncensored novels attempted to shatter illusory ideas about existing Soviet society and to establish anew the relationship between the individual and society more constructively for the future.

SAMIZDAT NOVELS AND THE AVANT-GARDE USE OF LANGUAGE

Siniavskii's attitude to language reveals much about how the new artistic use of language in uncensored works worked to destroy the charm of official use of language and harness it for new artistic purposes. Siniavskii's keen ear, honed in his work as literary critic, led him to protest with exasperation in 1975: "We can't understand why the 'masters,' the 'bosses' endlessly repeat phrases that everyone, including the 'bosses' themselves, are fed up with, of the sort: 'Socialist Realism,' 'cult of personality,' the 'anti-party group of Malenkov, Molotov, Kaganovich and Shepilov, who attached himself to them (*i primknuvshii k nim Shepilov*).'"[76] Change the phrase, at least move that Shepilov, Siniavskii pleaded. He compared the ideological-political education of men to the training of dogs: both are based on rote repetition.[77]

Siniavskii refused to submit to the clichés and forced ideological formulations of official Soviet print. At the same time, he sought to construct a critical and creative relationship to his contemporary moment: that meant engaging the language that was current. Although Aksenov did not cite Siniavskii as a specific mentor or source, important affinities exist in this regard. Aksenov shared Siniavskii's love for avant-garde poetry, his close attention to language, and his desire to develop new expressive means and critical potentials in contemporary speech. Aksenov made use of the same ridiculous and ubiquitous journalistic phrase cited above by Siniavskii in one scene in *The Burn*. In that episode, a train arrives inside the supermarket where the protagonist and his friend Pat have been hiding out. The train rolls in festooned with garlands and a portrait of "Vyacheslav Moiseyevich Bulganin and the ears attached to him" (*portret Viacheslava Moiseevicha Bulganina s primknuvshimi k nemu ushami*). The narrator, identified here with the protagonist, observes, "The locomotive headed straight for us, crunching melons as it came."[78] When Siniavskii cited this phrase about the "anti-party group," endlessly repeated in exactly the same strained form, he despaired of the possibility of release from this kind of discursive rigidity in official Soviet print.[79] Aksenov similarly sensed that this language expressed the ossified and oppressive character of a post-Stalin system incapable of real reform. In *The Burn*, he portrayed fantastically that political language's crushing mechanical force.

The work of Andrei Bitov and Venedikt Erofeev differs stylistically from that of Siniavskii and Aksenov, but it likewise shows the authors' critical attitude to contemporary language. Bitov spoke explicitly about language in his essay on fellow writer Iuz Aleshkovskii. Bitov noted Aleshkovskii's ability to mimic folk and popular oral styles.[80] When Aleshkovskii applied that ability to the clichés of Soviet propaganda, he revealed their similarity to profanity. Russian profanity features endless combinations based on just a few semantic roots. The "folk art" of profanity depends on the expressive potential of creative combinations entirely divorced from referential meaning. Profanity expresses emotion, and in some cases wit, or even improvisational art.[81] Aleshkovskii used Soviet clichés like profanity, that is, he made their lack of connection to the real world obvious. Against that void, the wit and emotion of the speaker's performance come to the fore.[82]

Although Bitov expressed delight at Aleshkovskii's creative facility with Soviet language, he also appreciated its critical edge. Bitov termed what had happened to language in the Soviet era a "linguistic genocide."[83] He employed a gastronomical metaphor to explain it: imagine, Bitov wrote, a table with the full range of drinks developed and refined over centuries, from beer to fine wines, champagne and liqueurs. Then consider the result when they are all poured together into one barrel from which people drink. This would be like the mixed-up Russian language of the Soviet era.[84] Bitov's metaphor emphasizes the consequences of such a situation: people imbibe this nauseating swill, it goes into them, it changes and shapes them, intoxicating and confusing them about reality and culture. While it may be disgusting, there is no way to separate the different sorts of culture mixed together. Likewise, it is impossible to separate oneself from the discursive environment that has shaped one, forming one from the inside, as it were. Purifying that language through the filter of independent literature might help begin a cure, however.

Venedikt Erofeev wrote in similar terms. In an essay on writer Vasilii Rozanov, Erofeev's narrator says:

> Everything poured into me since adolescence kept splashing about inside me, like slops, overflowing my belly and my soul, seeking a way out, and the one course of action remaining to me was that most tried and trusted of methods: to spew it all up using two fingers. One of these fingers turned out to be the New Testament, the other, Russian poetry, that is, all the Russian poetry from Gavrila Derzhavin to Marina Tsvetaeva.[85]

Here Erofeev suggested that the power of authentic culture, found in spiritual or poetic traditions, might purge this ersatz culture. Previously, however, in *Moscow Stations*, the Bible and poetry did *not* save Venichka. For the late Soviet person, the kind of spiritual and literary autonomy represented by these sources was simply not accessible: people had been cut off from them. Moreover, as in Bitov's remarks, the metaphor of consumption undercuts the plausibility of a simple solution: if a person has fed on this "slop" all one's life, it has become part of that person.

In their uncensored novels, Aksenov, Bitov, and Erofeev did not seek a realm of culture free from contemporary Soviet use of language, abominable as it seemed to them to be. Instead they made use of apparently alien as well as more ideologically congenial bits of discourse in a bewildering collage of intertexts and referents. For example, in Aksenov's *The Burn*, the incidental character Professor Abbas in the Congo reads from a newspaper that "progressive public opinion throughout the world angrily condemns the bandit-like attack by imperialist hirelings on the United Nations hospital in Katanga." Readers of the time would easily perceive the ideological clichés of Soviet propaganda exposed here by the author. However, the crowd listening to Professor Abbas, which includes Aksenov's protagonist, bursts into "stormy, unceasing applause that grew into an ovation." The phrase about the ovation is not set off in the novel by quotation marks, although it is recognizable as a formula from transcripts of official Soviet meetings. We readers suspect the falsification of enthusiasm but are not sure exactly where the critique is directed. Should we indict the crowd that goes along with this kind of artificial representation? If the transcript of the event is false, then what is the author doing by incorporating it into his apparently direct description? The lines between the protagonists and the faceless Soviet crowd get blurred, just as the line between those protagonists and the evil mercenaries becomes disturbingly indistinct in Aksenov's fanciful scenes.[86]

Bitov's quotations create discomfiting ambiguity somewhat differently. His narrator tells us with suspect joy about the return of a family friend from the camps: "'Justice' triumphed further—Uncle Mitya had been the first swallow—they permitted themselves to remember Grandfather in the family. All these years, Grandfather had been alive!" Uncle Mitya's return from exile after the camps had helped initiate the Thaw era for the family of Bitov's protagonist Lyova. While not so specifically traceable as the literary quotations embedded in the titles of sections of the novel, such as "Fathers and Sons" (which readers immediately recognize as the title of the famous novel by Ivan Turgenev), the word "justice" here, because it remains in quotation marks, retains the character of a foreign element in the text. Again, however, we suspect that Bitov does not critique simply the falseness of official rhetoric that labels the emancipation "justice." Lyova's family has been culpable in its suppression of what happened to Grandfather.[87] Although not directly involved in the initial betrayal, Lyova shows traces of his own corruption when he attempts to forge a new relationship with Grandfather and his work. Lyova is one alter ego of the author, while the narrator is another stand-in for Bitov. The narrator's slippery tone gives the reader little purchase for stabilizing a conception of the author beyond the rings of complicity that join his protagonist to the crimes of his family and those of his society.[88] Bitov's exploration of the complex issues attending quotation provide a framework for considering the problems of post-Stalin society in which people sought to create their own meaning using language contaminated by official abuse and haunted by the repressed meanings of the past.[89]

Erofeev distilled the problem down to its essence: the witty and irreverent manipulation of bits of discourse early in the novel *Moscow Stations* evokes via their obviously abstracted character the state of ossified language in late Soviet society as a whole. These formulas come back later to prey on Venichka in demonic guise.[90] Venichka's "Maksim Gorky" on Capri, his "Mussorgskii and Rimskii-Korsakov," together with his "revolution" in Petushki, to name just a few examples, help make this text a vibrant and motley weave of cultural references. These references reflect not only Soviet propaganda. Their flattened and ready-made character evokes a whole world in rigor mortis. Erofeev's savvy satire of Soviet culture encourages readers to reappropriate the cultural detritus like Venichka does. However, by the end of the journey we understand that such simulacra also fill Venichka and the reader with horror at the void they reveal. Venichka plaintively appeals for shelter and response: "Go on, try any house in Petushki, knock on any door and ask them, 'What's my heart mean to you?' . . . I knocked, shivering with cold, and waited for them to open up."[91] Renewed communication, and community, will depend on establishing bonds between real human interlocutors, not simply manipulation of empty communicative shells.

The intertextuality of these samizdat novels, into which "foreign" elements have been introduced, recalls the principle of montage, with the unsettling implications for self, society, and the work of art that montage entails. Bürger characterized montage as "the fundamental principle of avant-gardiste art."[92] The difference between montage and collage can help us understand the satirical point these samizdat novelists make about Soviet discourse. As opposed to collage, which depends on the introduction of heterogeneous real materials from outside the text, such as a piece of newsprint or the cane weaving of a chair seat, montage means the juxtaposition of images, a technique familiar from cinema or photomontage. The bits of discourse evoked by these samizdat novelists (like those appearing in Soviet conceptualist works later) resemble images. These verbal elements no longer bear any substantial connection to exterior reality. Their ability to speak to any real human concerns is called into question by their use in the artistic composition.

Bürger contrasted the work of montage to the traditional "organic" work that produced the impression of a self-contained whole. The organic work corresponded to the unified subjectivity of the artist who created it. By appearing to reflect the world (even as it offered escape or release from the stresses the real world exerted on audience members), it affirmed the organic totality of audience member and world in a harmonious relationship. By contrast, the inorganic work, that is, the avant-gardist work, broke apart the illusion of a seamless whole. The organic impression of wholeness, unity, and integrity at the level of the work confirmed those qualities in the subject of artist and viewer alike, while it subtly promoted their harmonious or reconciled relationship to the world whose wholeness and integrity appeared also in the integrated character of the work. However, the inorganic work created a sense of the world as disharmoniously disjunctive.[93] In an analysis of varying uses of photomontage, K. Michael Hays described photomontage's destructive capabilities in terms that recalled Bürger's: "Ordinarily, we discover meaning by claiming some sense from the outside world and constructing a unified, integral image of reality on the pictorial surface, as if in service of the self, as a metaphor for the integral self." By contrast, Dada photomontage emphasized the fissures and gaps separating disparate images, artistic representation of the "absolute incompatibility" between the outside world and the self.[94]

Comparing these examples of historical avant-garde montage to the technique and effects of dissident writers and artists, we might identify an element of Dada negation as well as hints of hope for the possibility of artistic reconstruction. Soviet dissident writers and artists who employed a montage principle, whether verbally or in other ways, emphasized the alien character of those inserted elements. However, the arrangement of those elements on the page or canvas suggests a tentative promise for remaking the self and the world. The neo-avant-garde artistic reconstruction does not resemble the utopian dreams of the historical avant-garde. These dissident artists do not fancy themselves like Lissitzky, a conscious engineer, out of whose Constructivist head the new utopian order will come. Instead of a new scientific consciousness, based on supposed laws of history and the just society, these samizdat novelists propose a new consciousness that is dialogic by artistic design and practical necessity. As opposed to the phantoms that populate Venichka's world, Venichka appeals to readers to respond in a real human dialogue. The provocation aims at making writer and reader partners: this ideological goal corresponds to the reality of samizdat texts, which required of readers far more personal investment and active collaboration than printed works.

PLAN OF THIS BOOK

The chapters that follow consider dissident writing and the alternative construction of an individual subject in late Soviet society as part of an autonomous cultural field that emerged and began to develop during the late 1960s and early 1970s. The treatment of dissidence and samizdat writing in terms of a "field" draws on Bourdieu's sociological analysis, where the field designates a social space united by a common belief. The dissident belief implies an initial rejection of the false belief holding Soviet society together into one whole on the basis of lies, half-truths, or delegitimized ideology. As Bourdieu explained it, the restricted field of cultural production coalesces around a belief in its own autonomy, which involves negation of the political and economic forces structuring the larger social field in which it is embedded. Bourdieu's "field" is part of a triad of central concepts that include also *habitus* and capital.[95] These terms of reference will provide a framework for critical analysis of the autonomous culture of Soviet dissidence. Insofar as they imply a subject (Bourdieu often calls this an "agent") who embodies the knowledge of the field and pursues the symbolic capital of that field, these Bourdieusian concepts will also set up the analysis of authors and the images of dissident subjects they develop in uncensored works. While the societies examined by Bourdieu, especially modern French society, differ from the late Soviet instance, his terms can be applied flexibly to highlight the particular characteristics of the Soviet context manifesting in dissident cultural autonomy at this time.

Thus, in chapter 1, I take up Bourdieu's description of the field of culture to describe the dynamics leading to the emergence of dissident activity and the generative tensions that drive further development. In particular, I explore the dissident subject through the examples of Andrei Siniavskii and Aleksandr Esenin-Volpin, two outstanding figures in the history of dissidence endowed with the vision to perceive and the courage to pursue new possibilities for independent activity in the late Soviet period. Siniavskii and Volpin, coming from different perspectives, helped establish the basis for complementary directions dissidence might go, oriented on the one hand to autonomous literary and artistic work, and on the other hand to independent public interventions. Juxtaposing these two pioneers highlights the ambivalent role of literature for the dissident field: literature for dissidents represents a consecrated canon of transcendent values to be defended, but it also becomes an active site of contestation for renewing values by asserting their autonomy from material gain and, particularly, political forces. We seek to understand here the structural relationship between autonomous literature and independent public interventions as an engine driving development of the dissident field.

Chapters 2 through 4 consider in depth and in context three uncensored novels that demonstrate the inorganic deconstruction of the conventional Soviet subject and the construction of dissident autonomy in literature. Chapter 2 profiles Vasilii Aksenov and his first major uncensored novel, *The Burn*. In his angry exposé, Aksenov reflected on his own past and present as an allegory of what happened to Soviet society. The result is a fascinating and provocative fictionalization of his youth in Magadan, Siberia, with his mother Evgeniia Ginzburg, who became known in the 1960s for her own uncensored memoirs. That repressed past breaks through into the glittering life of the elite intelligentsia living and working in Moscow after Stalin. Critical analysis of what Bourdieu would call Aksenov's *habitus*, his social position and feel for the game of Soviet letters, shows intriguing ambivalence. Aksenov exposed his past and reflected critically on his present position as part of a bid to assert his dissident independence in *The Burn*. Nevertheless, he aimed to use his established fame as a Soviet author to produce an immediate and significant impact on the literary field. Bourdieu's model helps us perceive some of the contradictions of Aksenov's position. We begin to see in this case the features of historical discontinuity and international penetration of the dissident field that inform the particular character of Soviet dissident autonomy.

Bitov's *Pushkin House*, the novel explored in chapter 3, exemplifies a more purely literary character and thus amasses more of the symbolic capital associated with the space of restricted cultural production on the dissident field. Like Aksenov, Bitov examined what Bourdieu would call the *habitus* of intellectuals of his generation, that is, their social position and cultivated feel for the game of Soviet life. Bitov also suggested parallels to his own biography, although he eschewed the public drama and specific autobiographical references employed by Aksenov. Bitov deconstructed the Soviet intellectual with a literary scalpel, revealing his smug but fragile integrity to be a mass of contradictions. The discontinuities of the psychological portrait and narrative presentation in *Pushkin House* speak to Bitov's avant-garde intentions, which are similar to Aksenov's: he aimed to provoke readers out of unthinking conformity to Soviet or liberal values into a more creative engagement with the reality of their Soviet world. Such discontinuities also reflected the state of the social and cultural context as perceived by dissidents, riven by the trauma of the Stalinist era and the break in cultural continuity associated with it. The fragmentation of this revolutionary society distinguishes the Soviet field from that described by Bourdieu. Oriented to the model of radical change characterizing a revolutionary society, Bitov and other dissident authors remain, somewhat paradoxically, distinctly Soviet in their autonomous literary works. At the same time, Bourdieu's critical question applies here, too: the scene of the reconstruction of the *Pushkin House* museum at the end of Bitov's novel forces us to ask, what can really change? Does a literary revolt mean changing the structures of consciousness and thus the bases for an authentic self and society, or is it simply a concealed gesture of defiance (*figa v karmane*), the kind of carnivalesque interlude that can be hidden or covered over when the authorities return?

Bitov's work suggests a new type of subjectivity that corresponds to these discontinuities and doubts without trying to resolve them into a seamless whole: the author recognizes the partial character of a human perspective, refusing the godlike perspective of romantic lyrical subjectivity and scientific ideology alike. The individual subject of a post-totalitarian world can creatively express a unique position by acknowledging the irreducible difference of others. Such a change of consciousness could furnish the building blocks of a new society.

In chapter 4, Venedikt Erofeev's protagonist Venichka in *Moscow Stations* exemplifies the kind of consciously incomplete individual subjectivity suggested by Bitov, in a performance self-consciously staged for the response of others. Erofeev's novel most successfully represents a specifically dissident form of cultural autonomy. A consummate outsider, Erofeev, unlike Aksenov and Bitov, never enjoyed any elevated social station in the Soviet system, and in part for this reason, Erofeev and his protagonist Venichka appeal to readers as particularly compelling. Perhaps because he had no professional standing or connections, Erofeev produced a work that materially and poetically corresponds best to the samizdat system in which it circulated: slim and full of aphoristic phrases, this work invites and models the participatory role of reader-publishers, who could re-voice Venichka's sayings and bring them to life in their own renditions. The avant-garde character of Erofeev's work consists of this theatricality, part of the tautly drawn tensions of the autonomous cultural field as reflected by Erofeev in the book. Readers apprehend Erofeev's novel as a powerful mechanism for transforming Soviet reality and experience into universally translatable elements of world culture.

Chapter 5 examines the kind of discontinuous or eclectic temporality materialized by the samizdat system and the "extra-Gutenberg" culture associated with it. This culture entails epistemological uncertainty and it depends on networks of trust as well as the juxtaposition of irreducibly different points of view both to establish what is true and valuable and to support the life of texts. The samizdat text, not fixed in print, features a more obviously pluralized form, realized across different material reproductions that may vary and carry the traces of different types of investment and endorsement. As such, the work, apprehended as a collection of its different realizations, corresponds to the pluralized character of an intersubjective and far from homogeneous community. At the same time, the text links people in cross-border exchanges that facilitate the performance of individual identities negotiated at the site of the text. Mauss's theory of gift exchange helps us integrate this more "traditional" model of exchange into the modern economic system disrupted by samizdat.

In the conclusion I review the critical framework for analyzing Soviet dissidence and samizdat made possible by Bourdieu's model with its critique of the belief in autonomy. Bourdieu's analysis proves particularly useful for the way it allows us to position subjects and groups relative to one another on the field of dissidence. We find limitations in the possibility of conducting a Bourdieusian critique in part because of the lack of full data about the market for samizdat and tamizdat texts. Soviet dissidence also exceeds the Bourdieusian model by being embedded in a trans-national set of interlocking markets and social contexts: samizdat travels across the Soviet border for tamizdat publication, and texts printed abroad enter the U.S.S.R. for informal circulation. Bourdieu's book on *The Field of Art* ends with a renewed commitment to intellectual autonomy as the grounds for meaningful critique and this fact, combined with other statements by Bourdieu regarding the varied manifestations of a legitimate intention to autonomy might suggest we should view Soviet dissidence as one potentially instructive realization of the ideal of autonomy.

Finally, Soviet dissidence viewed in its manifestation in samizdat texts provides an intriguing analogy to our current global digital culture, which is also full of international and local networks that exist parallel to established institutions of authority and print culture as part of an extra-Gutenberg condition. Samizdat with its low-tech character helps put the focus on the human element of new media culture. Familiar problems with information consumption and civic activism can be considered through the lens of the kind of quotidian resistance samizdat meant for most Soviet citizens engaged in it. In this way the voice of samizdat still resounds today.

Chapter One

Literature and the Field of Dissidence

IN HIS HIGHLY READABLE memoirs,[1] dissident Andrei Amalrik described the room he and his wife Gusel shared in a communal apartment in Moscow in the late 1960s. Amalrik had inherited a huge piano from his aunt, which amounted to a sort of white elephant for the impecunious pair. Neither he nor Gusel could play the massive instrument, which dominated the room and often confounded visitors. Amalrik wrote:

> Some people—especially foreigners—used to laugh at us, because while we didn't even have a table to eat at, half the room was occupied by a useless grand piano. But its very uselessness and beauty, together with the paintings, the old books, the grandfather clock, and the withered, spidery plants on the sideboard, made our room look like something out of a fairy tale.[2]

The useless grand piano represents in a delightfully literal way the commitment to autonomous culture that constituted a core belief for those involved in unofficial culture and social dissidence in the late Soviet period. Amalrik socialized with Western visitors,[3] and they might indeed have been confused. The value of such an object depended on the specific context of an official Soviet culture that instrumentalized literature and art as the means of educating its Soviet citizens: it forced culture to have a use. Authorities implemented control of culture by the State through the doctrine of Socialist Realism, by establishing a Soviet canon of realist works that emphasized the tradition's progressive teleology toward a proper revolutionary consciousness, and with the help of a network of institutions that administered the proper interpretation of existing literature and art, and ordered and censored new works.

Reading against the grain of official interpretations of canonical works, Amalrik described a dissident impulse to reassert subjectivity coming from Russian literature of the nineteenth century. Famous literary works, including those by Tolstoy and Dostoevsky, comprised a literature "passionate in its defense of the individual against the system," as Amalrik put it. His dissident turn meant mobilizing this defense against the current system, in which the sense of an individual "I" had been lost. Comparing the dissident idea of selfhood to that of opposition in a previous era, he said:

> One of the dominant ideas of the prerevolutionary opposition was the readiness to sacrifice one's "I" for the sake of the general public; and in that way everything was lost. But how to replace that senseless sacrifice, not with the idea of narrow selfishness, but with the value of one's "I" in the universal sense . . . to live not for oneself alone and not just for others but with all and for all—that was the search that underlay our Movement, and it created real bonds among human beings.[4]

For the democratic dissidents with whom Amalrik identified, but also among the nonconformist artists he knew and the budding original uncensored writers of whom he himself was one,[5] uncensored activity meant reestablishing the "I" in the context of a different social compact, one that would be more humane and authentic than the corrupt official Soviet order. Literature served as a key point of reference and guarantor of these more humane and authentic values.

Official culture in the Soviet Union allowed for no distinction between cultural activity and established ideology, and therefore there could be no dissenting opinions outside of the official line. Dissidents had to establish their autonomy against the insistently propagated vision of perfect public unity. In 1977, for example, the head of the KGB, Iurii Andropov, proclaimed, "We rightly consider out greatest victory to be the ideological-political unity of Soviet society. There never was in history a social system similar to ours, able to knit together in a unified, close family all classes and social groups of society, all nations and peoples of the country."[6] For Amalrik and many others, literature provided a logical sphere of reference for challenging this false public unity: in the nineteenth century the construction of the identity of the Russian intelligentsia had been tied to literature in ways that borrowed from Western models.[7] However, the Russian context featured specificities including the belated emergence of modern secular literature and the repressive environment of an authoritarian tsarist regime. For these reasons, literature might serve as a substitute for debates in the press. Literature also more readily embodied a spiritual authority distinct from and in some sense analogous to, but not directly challenging, State authority.[8] Could literature provide the foundation for robust public debate and real influence on governance? The answer seemed less than clear in both tsarist and Soviet times. Literature and art of the modernist period concentrated debates about autonomy and social relevance in the revolutionary context. In retrospect, as maintained in the mythology of the Silver Age and a martyred avant-garde, the regime bureaucrats won this battle at the expense of poets and artists. People in the late Soviet period sought to reconnect with true art and its independent store of cultural values. Whether those values could be mobilized by dissidents to provide any real check on the actions of the State remained unknown.

Pierre Bourdieu's account of the establishment of a field of literary art in the late nineteenth and early twentieth centuries in France provides a model for a functional relationship between cultural autonomy and intellectual interventions in public discussion.[9] We can use this model as a starting point for an analysis of Soviet dissidence, keeping in mind important differences: the autonomy of the public collapsed under Stalin. Dissidents hoped that through samizdat and other independent means of communicating with a Western audience, they might achieve status as an independent public. This hope entailed the reestablishment of a distinction between "pure" culture and political interventions. In practice, as the Soviet intelligentsia learned through bitter experiences in the late 1960s, especially the suppression of reform movements in Czechoslovakia in 1968 (the shock of which amplified previous traumas including Moscow's response to Polish agitation and to the Hungarian uprising in 1956), the regime would continue to act with terrible violence and flagrant disregard of its own citizens' views whenever it deemed such measures necessary. Perhaps real political pressure might be brought to bear by foreigners. Thus, for strategic reasons specific to the late Soviet context, but also by the logic of the phenomenon of modern intellectuals, Soviet dissidents felt constrained to establish a sphere of pure culture independent of politics and to disavow the political nature of even social activity and commentary. This proved to be as true of democratic dissidents and national groups as of nonconforming literati and artists.

In this chapter I begin by outlining the emergence of a "field" of dissident culture that involves autonomous literature and dissident social interventions.[10] Unofficial literature has not commonly been described as "dissident," and dissident social activity has not usually been treated as a "culture," but the uneasy relationship between these terms reflects the tension that mutually constitutes the two types of activity (one purely cultural and the other sociopolitical) and charges the field they share. A dynamic of productive competition can be found, for example, among uncensored poets and democratic dissidents in the late 1970s. Both groups understand the value of their activities to be the inverse of values determined by the regime in official Soviet culture, though they compete with one another to define the character of that independence.

Two figures illustrate the position-takings that came to seem like opposing points within the developed dissident field, although they looked closer together at the beginning. Andrei Siniavskii's role in the important

1966 trial of Siniavskii and fellow writer Iulii Daniel for supposedly "anti-Soviet" works published abroad without permission is well known. In this chapter I will focus on the struggle Siniavskii engaged in with his editorial board over an introductory article in a posthumous collection of Boris Pasternak's poetry. This wrangling behind the scenes demonstrates Siniavskii's efforts to stake out a new autonomous sphere of literary culture in the late Soviet era. Aleksandr Esenin-Volpin, a mathematician, developed a highly influential strategy of legal dissidence first employed in demonstrations related to the case against the two writers.[11] Siniavskii and Volpin stand therefore as two related but distinct figures in the emerging field of dissident culture. Bourdieu treats such figures as "agents" in the field, whose perception of the range of possibilities depends on the knowledge about the field they have accumulated through their social position over time.[12] His method will underpin my own critical approach to claims of autonomy and dissident agency.

I use this survey of the activity of two key figures to consider the construction of dissident subjectivity. I will consider dissident subjectivity from a critical analytic perspective, and from the point of view of those who constructed it, finding in many cases resonance between the representation and the analytic model. Toward the end of the chapter I will return to neo-avant-garde literary strategies as a special case of dissident self-perception that exposes persistent forms of dependence and pursues new forms of autonomous expression not through pure separation from the late Soviet context but in critical engagement. This inquiry will set up more detailed exploration of the provocative literary imaginations of dissident subjectivity in the uncensored novels of Vasilii Aksenov, Andrei Bitov, and Venedikt Erofeev. The critical perspective on the dissident field and notions of autonomy operating within it will lead to an analysis of the conditioning context of these writers and their own response to a new field of possibilities: what notions of autonomy did they reflect from within their own social contexts? How much did their own explorations of a dissident voice and possible agency depend on moving their audience—what was this audience and how did they reach it?

THE EMERGENCE OF A DISSIDENT FIELD, I: ANDREI SINIAVSKII AND AUTONOMOUS LITERATURE

Siniavskii stands out as one of those rare uncensored writers in the late Soviet era who did not shun the term "dissident," even though he emphasized that his heterodoxy manifested primarily in his writing, writing that was esoteric, stylistically obscure, and not calculated to evoke broad political resonance.[13] While his role in the landmark trial of literary writers that helped launch Soviet dissidence at home and abroad helps us recognize Siniavskii as a dissident, Siniavskii never took a public stand like the writer Aleksandr Solzhenitsyn did. On the other hand, he never appeared as marginal to the Soviet establishment as someone like the poet Joseph Brodsky. Siniavskii occupied a place within the official Soviet literary establishment. Thanks to this position he became aware of the possibility of doing things differently—of bending the rules.

Although they occurred out of the public eye, Siniavskii's debates with the editorial board of the prestigious Library of the Poet (Biblioteka poeta), publishing series in letters spanning the years from 1962 to 1965, offer a window into the way Siniavskii attempted to open up a sphere for autonomous literary expression from inside the Soviet system. The editors considered Siniavskii's introductory article to the collection of Boris Pasternak's poetry they were preparing for publication to be insufficiently political.[14] The correspondence of Siniavskii with these editors shows how deeply Siniavskii's conviction regarding the autonomy of literature informed his professional activity. Siniavskii's statements in letters and memoirs suggest that the eruption of unofficial activity came, not from outside, but from within Soviet society as a result of its own tensions and forces.

Siniavskii himself maintained the idea that dissidence proceeded from the Soviet experience itself. Born in the 1920s like his counterpart Aleksandr Solzhenitsyn, Siniavskii described dissidence as the experience of a generation born and bred within the Soviet state. Dissidence arose out of a loss of absolute faith in the system. It resulted in Siniavskii's experience from encountering what he called a "stumbling block," which caused him to begin to think and act independently. Repressed modernist masters Pasternak, Anna Akhmatova, and Osip Mandelshtam might be considered "heretics" of Russian literature, but they were not "dissidents," Siniavskii asserted: "one cannot call them dissidents for the simple reason that their roots go back to bygone, prerevolutionary traditions of Russian culture." Dissidents, by contrast, were part of a generation formed within the Soviet order. They experienced a crisis or realization from a position inside the system. This dissident "stumbling block" was essentially an individual experience, one provoking a sense of moral responsibility to "think, speak and write independently, without regard for the norms and prescriptions of the state," as Siniavskii put it.[15] For Siniavskii, this stumbling block was seeing modernism being rooted out of Soviet culture. Unlike his coeval Solzhenitsyn, Siniavskii defined his dissidence as aesthetic—his independent action was to write differently. "In the internal conflict between politics and art, I opted for art and rejected politics," Siniavskii said.[16]

Siniavskii's critical essays and fantastic fictional writing as Abram Terts obviously represent aesthetic dissidence. But Siniavskii's subversive emphasis on the aesthetic was also clear in his work as an official Soviet critic. Prior to his arrest, Siniavskii enjoyed a promising career as a young liberal literary critic working within the establishment. In official publications of the late 1950s and early 1960s, Siniavskii broke new ground by emphasizing the autonomy of literature. His position relative to the context was provocative enough to cause sharp polemics. Surveying Siniavskii's career, Catharine Nepomnyashchy divided Siniavskii's ten articles for *Novyi mir* (written alone and with his colleague Andrei Menshutin) into three related rubrics—those that reconsidered literary figures formerly banned or marginalized (Pasternak, Robert Frost, Akhmatova), those that emphasized literary as opposed to political evaluation of contemporary Soviet works, and those that criticized establishment writers for hackneyed, politically tainted work.[17]

Siniavskii's critical attitudes and methods as a literary professional fit naturally into Thaw-era developments after Stalin's demise. Writers tried almost immediately to reassert autonomy in literature. As early as 1953, Vladimir Pomerantsev had caused a sensation with his article "On Sincerity in Literature."[18] Pomerantsev attributed the insincere "varnishing" of reality in literature to an attempt to present a desired reality in contrast to the existing reality. He thereby went to the heart of the paradoxical logic of Socialist Realist doctrine, which "demands from the author the truthful, historically concrete representation of reality in its revolutionary development."[19] Pomerantsev called on the individual author to be more sincere and truthful. Siniavskii's approach to literature several years later was more sophisticated, and it claimed greater autonomy for literature from life: Siniavskii, with his love of modernism, returned to a method of critique based on formal poetic characteristics. For example, the success of Olga Berggolts's poetry about the Leningrad blockade depended not primarily on her personal integrity and not only on the power of her tragic subject, Siniavskii argued: rather, Berggolts's expert handling of specifically poetic techniques, her minimalist poetic form, her lyrical prose, and her avoidance of political or sentimental clichés made her writing powerful.[20] When Siniavskii and Menshutin criticized the upsurge of romantic poetry at the beginning of the 1960s for being longer on enthusiasm than technique, they raised the ire of their colleagues. In response to a spate of heated responses, Siniavskii and Menshutin pointed out that, in fact, being able to chop wood does not guarantee that one can write good poetry about it.[21]

Siniavskii's attention to language and his focus on specifically artistic language made him stand out. He shared an aversion to clichés with other liberal critics of Soviet literature—Siniavskii greatly appreciated Pasternak's convictions on this score, and he analyzed Pasternak's poetry from this point of view in the article for the Library of the Poet edition. The point Siniavskii made was rather subtle: Pasternak used common phrases from everyday and popular speech. These common phrases were called in Russian *shtampy*, and Siniavskii compared this technique to Maiakovskii's deliberate vulgarisms and street jargon, though the register and effect in Pasternak's case were rather different. In Pasternak's poetry, however, these common oral *shtampy* represented a way of combating worn-out literary and rhetorical models (*shablony*).[22] From Siniavskii's single meeting with Pasternak at the end of 1957, he seized on Pasternak's provocative approach to ideological cliché:

> For Pasternak, radical changes in the consciousness of society were the concern of tomorrow, a process that could not be reversed and would be all-encompassing. But the first front in this process appeared to him to be the liberation of language from the forms of ideology, not so much from ideology itself as from its restricted character, its formalization, its nauseatingly familiar phrases, which caught in one's throat.[23]

Thus, even though cliché was a target of Pomerantsev's critique as well, Pasternak and Siniavskii in private conversation showed concern for specifically political cliché as a symptom of a tired ideology. They both saw the struggle against that type of language as part of a larger process of changing the consciousness of Soviet society. If for Pasternak, this battle belonged to tomorrow, that tomorrow was dawning with Siniavskii's generation.

Steeped in culture of the revolutionary period, Siniavskii might have been more ready than others to believe in the possibility of radical change in the structure of society. For Bourdieu, the *habitus*, or perception of structural possibilities, tends toward conservation of the field, even in the case of agents on the literary field, who imagine their activity to be more or less autonomous of the laws obtaining in society at large.[24] On the other hand, Siniavskii knew well the fate of poets like Maiakovskii and Pasternak in a revolutionary society: his belief in the power of their work had to do with its potential for changing modes of perception within language. All indications are that Siniavskii intended precisely this kind of "revolution," one from within Soviet language that might stir winds of change in the minds of Soviet readers, without directly challenging the regime or its institutions.

However, it remained far from certain that these grounds for change could be made available to Soviet readers. Siniavskii had sent his writing under the pseudonym Abram Terts abroad for publication: he counted on help from outside the Soviet system. He also expected to be arrested. Thus, the struggle over Siniavskii's article for the volume of Pasternak's poetry occurred just as the battle over control of Soviet culture was about to break into the open. Social changes, notably the emergence of the phenomenon of "dissidence" and samizdat, remained just in the offing, too, as we know now with hindsight. Siniavskii continued to be obliged to play the game according to the roles that obtained on the Soviet field. His struggle with the editorial board hinged on the common practice of using a few phrases of standardized political critique to appease the ideological watchdogs, thereby making it possible to present Pasternak's work as integrally as possible. Siniavskii had played this game in his review of the first posthumous collection of Pasternak's poetry, a slimmer volume from 1961: "Pasternak's creative path was uneven, complicated. To a greater or lesser degree Pasternak was drawn to the attitudes of the old, prerevolutionary intelligentsia, to ideas of abstractly conceptualized humanism," he wrote.[25] The phrase "abstract humanism" constituted one of those expected, unflattering ideological clichés. In this review, Siniavskii set the stage for his own work with the Library of the Poet edition. It was strange, Siniavskii wrote, given the negative attitude to Pasternak in recent years, that there was no introductory article or commentary. The edition on which he would collaborate would, with his own 53-page introduction, weigh in at a substantial 732 pages. It would be almost twice as long as the 1961 collection, and far more significant for the establishment of Pasternak's position in Soviet culture.

The negative official attitude to Pasternak resulted in large part from the unauthorized 1957 publication of Pasternak's novel *Doctor Zhivago* abroad and the subsequent awarding of the Nobel Prize in Literature to Pasternak. Soviet authorities pressured Pasternak to refuse the prize. This official Soviet opprobrium dogged Pasternak to his grave and beyond, creating the problem with posthumous editions of his verse. The vicious campaign of vilification not only exacerbated Pasternak's health problems, it created a social problem—even liberal members of the Moscow Writers' Union did not dare openly challenge the official line during the 1958 vote calling for Pasternak's expulsion. There existed no effective support at that time for a real challenge, since unofficial circulation and alternative publicity were neither automatic nor systematic.[26] The legacy of this official attitude toward Pasternak posed a problem for the editors of the Library of the Poet edition after Pasternak's death in 1960. A volume in the prestigious grand series (*bol'shaia seriia*) of the publishing house Library of the Poet, founded by Maksim Gorkii in the 1930s, promised to represent a significant posthumous rehabilitation of Pasternak. The uncertainty of Khrushchev's cultural thaw made it possible—but far from certain—that this might be done.

Liberals had to be careful, especially after the conservative revanche of late 1962, which began with the scandal at the Manège art exhibit in December.[27] Those circumstances appear to have directly impacted work on the edition. The preserved correspondence between the editorial board of the Library of the Poet publishing house and Siniavskii shows that he was officially invited to write the article in June 1962. At that point editors expected the volume to appear in 1963, and Siniavskii was urged to submit his article quickly, before the end of 1962. A long hiatus followed, with the next letter to Siniavskii in the collection dating from September 1963. At that time the editors let Siniavskii know that changes that would have to be made.[28]

Chief editor Vladimir Orlov himself wrote a detailed commentary on Siniavskii's manuscript in which he chastised Siniavskii for his unacceptable silence on political issues. The publication of the volume in question would rehabilitate Pasternak as a mainstream Soviet author. But Pasternak's work was known to be uneven from an ideological standpoint: Orlov asked in his letter, how was it possible to think that one could pass over this in silence? Given that "the dramatic events associated with the widely recognized crude political mistake Pasternak made toward the end have become popularly known, we simply do not have the right to be silent about this," he said. Orlov made the case to Siniavskii this way: "Of course it is not a question of once again 'working over' [*prorabatyvat'*] Pasternak for his 'mistakes.' . . . But we must give an exact and objective characterization of the ideological bases of Pasternak's work and his literary career. In what tone this is done depends on the tact of the article's author." Orlov both demanded and encouraged Siniavskii: "It is simply impossible to get by without posing the question about the philosophical roots of this poetry. Don't be afraid to call things by their names—idealism is idealism and neo-Kantianism is neo-Kantianism."[29] Concepts like "idealism" and "neo-Kantianism" carried a clearly negative political load in Soviet discourse.

Bourdieu used the metaphor of a game to describe cultural activity: the action takes place on a common field of endeavor, and it is competitive. Players observe the rules of the game, occasionally bending those rules or creating new variants on them. If we think of Orlov's comments in terms of what Bourdieu described as a feel for the game,[30] then Orlov pointed out to Siniavskii what he should not have needed to say to a professional critic who understood the stakes of this edition: the use of clichéd ideological pronouncements amounted to a necessary strategy, an enabling performance of rhetoric required for publication of the Pasternak volume. Liberals could finesse this performance as they played the game in Soviet letters. Such finesse represented in fact the only leeway writers had as they tried to satisfy the vague and ever-changing demands of censorship and political correctness. When Orlov encouraged Siniavskii simply to tell it like it is, however, he glossed over the capricious nature of constantly modifiable expectations. Orlov as editor in chief of a major Soviet publishing house accepted the rules insofar as they could be known. Siniavskii had different ideas. He refused to play this game this way: "I do not consider it correct or possible for me to write about Pasternak's political and philosophical mistakes," he insisted.[31]

Thus, members of the editorial board and Siniavskii, who began as collaborators in the endeavor to publish this volume of Pasternak, moved apart as the climate and expectations changed. The conservative crackdown in 1962–63 made the editors bend right, while Siniavskii moved (or the shifting ground makes it seem as if he moved) into a more radical position. Siniavskii refused to accept the rules of the game. His attitude foreshadowed what would become common later at the end of the 1960s when alternative possibilities had been created by the introduction of new forces and outlets: the most liberal or free-thinking of Soviet students and intelligentsia would become so frustrated by the administration's renewed hard line that many would eventually drop out of the game, perhaps to create their own game on the side, creating spaces of cultural autonomy and what Bourdieu described as a "restricted" field of cultural production.[32] Others would continue to play but would insist on more stringent and fair observation of the rules of the game. These would be the rights activists and their allies.

In his critical commentary on Siniavskii's article manuscript, Orlov acknowledged Siniavskii's work as the first serious scholarly attention to Pasternak's lyric poetry. Yet he found Siniavskii's treatment to be insufficiently politically informed. In general, lyric subjectivity of the type Pasternak developed seemed dubious from the standpoint of a proper historical materialist analysis as required by Soviet ideological standards. By contrast, Pasternak's particular lyric subjectivity emerges in Siniavskii's analysis as one of the richest and most striking aspects of his poetry. Pasternak, unlike Aleksandr Blok, Sergei Esenin, Maiakovskii, or Marina Tsvetaeva, did not often express his "I" directly. Instead Pasternak frequently allowed nature to testify to the resonance of the poet's emotion in the world.[33] Having posed the problem of Pasternak's apparent disconnection from historical events at the beginning of the article, Siniavskii developed an argument about Pasternak's unique poetic communion with the world of nature, history, and, ultimately, humanity. Pasternak was sensitive to the time of revolution, as in the summer of 1917, when he wrote the collection *My Sister—My Life* (*Sestra moia zhizn'*): "Pasternak called art 'the extremity of the age' (and not its equal partner) and he related the creation of art to historical events as two congenial phenomena taking place on different levels," Siniavskii wrote.[34] With this argument Siniavskii attempted to answer Soviet ideological concerns, but he did so with terms and logic not fully predetermined by the political discourse. Siniavskii read poetic subjectivity through Pasternak's verses in terms decidedly distant from those describing traditional lyrical individualism and closer to the connection between subject and history developed in Marxist thought; nonetheless, Siniavskii insisted on the freshness or even the strangeness (to recall the Formalists' technique of "making strange" [*ostranenie*]) of the way in which Pasternak might express such subjectivity and in which Siniavskii could analyze it.[35]

Siniavskii's description of Pasternak's poetic relationship to the world in terms of morality and humanity, rather than in orthodox ideological terms, caused problems, too. Comments in the correspondence regarding the Gospel-themed poems from *Doctor Zhivago* are especially revealing. Orlov complained that Siniavskii did not criticize Pasternak for resorting to weak allegory (that is, the Gospels) and an "artificially narrow, ahistorical" treatment of moral issues. These poems, and Siniavskii's commentary on them, did not appear in the edition as finally published: the back-and-forth in the correspondence about whether they could be included highlights the capriciously shifting boundaries of what was permitted in Soviet print.[36]

The final published edition shows that Siniavskii made changes to the article. He attempted to satisfy certain demands. He augmented his analysis of the lyrical poetry with more attention to the epic works Pasternak wrote in the 1920s: *A Sublime Malady* (*Vysokaia bolezn'*), *Lieutenant Shmidt* (*Leitenant Shmidt*), and *Spektorskii*. Regarding *A Sublime Malady*, Siniavskii addressed Pasternak's portrait of Vladimir Lenin at the end, as he was asked to do:

> These stanzas, which re-create the irrepressible energy of Lenin's thought, are among the best representations of the leader of the revolution in Soviet literature. The poet's language, dense and slow at the beginning, becomes especially hard-hitting toward the end of the work. The language becomes full of strength and tenseness of will, as though transferred into verse directly from Lenin's rostrum.[37]

Siniavskii analyzed the strength of Pasternak's portrayal of Lenin in poetic terms, as a function of the way the poem is put together. Siniavskii said of the novel in verse *Spektorskii* that Pasternak there entered more into the world of epic form. In that poem Pasternak paid less attention to individual humans than to "the spirit of the time against the backdrop of the broad historical panorama." Siniavskii wrote, "For Pasternak the important thing was the breadth of the reach, the general perspective, not Spektorskii, but a specter."[38] Even as Siniavskii keyed his remarks to the expected orientation toward the historical at the expense of the individual, his remark about the specter sounds less like an obedient reiteration of the metaphor from the opening of the Communist Manifesto and more like a spook sneaking in from the fantastic world of Abram Terts.

Tracing Pasternak's development through the epic poems of the 1920s and beyond, Siniavskii found that, in later verses, Pasternak's efforts proved most successful when he pursued his own indirect method. Those poems "in the form of direct and loud response to the contemporary ("A Terrible Tale," "The Victor" ["Strashnaia skazka," "Pobeditel'"]) fall noticeably short in artistic quality of verses on the same theme written . . . in his own long-established key of landscape description or intimate lyricism ("The Gates," "Winter Is Coming On" ["Zastava," "Zima priblizhaetsia"] and others)." Siniavskii continued to say that Pasternak's best poems, "shot through with the feeling of history and contemporary time, often sound like an introduction or a foreword to the future and in the main they convey the condition of the era through imperceptible movements of nature or the soul of the poet, through everyday details, and signs of the flow of everyday life." As an example, Siniavskii cited the lovely beginning of the poem "Spring" ("Vesna," 1944):

> This spring renders all things particular.
> The noise of sparrows is more vivid.
> I will not even try to say
> How light and calm it is for the soul.
> One thinks, one writes differently,
> And loud octavos in the chorus
> Are how one hears the powerful earthy voice
> Of the freed territories.[39]

Thus, Siniavskii played the game by conceding that an argument for Pasternak's connection to history must be made, but he established that connection in a nonstandard way, sensitive to the particularity of Pasternak's poetry. Siniavskii argued with imagination and at length for Pasternak's intimate connection to historical events in response to the criticism of Pasternak as a poet estranged from revolutionary processes. Siniavskii was not willing, however, to speak in ready-made terms about Pasternak's mistakes as judged from the orthodox political point of view. The vicissitudes of constraint and relaxation from the side of the regime do not constitute the primary interest of the game as reflected in this correspondence. The more interesting tension occured between Siniavskii and the editorial board. They pushed him to write what was necessary for an acceptable volume, while he persistently insisted on his own authorial autonomy in writing about poetry that exceeded the categories and standard terms of Soviet criticism.

This "game" had serious implications. In late 1963, assistant editor Galina Tsurikova wrote Siniavskii to express sympathy and exert pressure: "You understand that the firmness of your position, praiseworthy in itself, has in fact jeopardized the Pasternak edition?" In February 1964, Orlov confirmed the danger that the edition would be derailed.[40] One finds little correspondence from Siniavskii's side in this collection, and Siniavskii likely would have avoided speaking about this directly in any case, but he must have felt the professional and moral pressure regarding a volume in which he was at least as heavily invested personally and professionally as the editors. This was not all, however. Siniavskii's payment for the article depended on successful completion of the volume. This became a particularly urgent matter as the edition dragged on through negotiations. Siniavskii's son Egor was born at the beginning of 1965, and his family was attempting to move into a new apartment. To put it bluntly, Siniavskii needed the money.

Siniavskii agreed at last to a couple of minor political concessions, adding the word "unengaged" (*otvlechennye*) to the phrase "unengaged ideals of moral perfectibility" and inserting quotation marks around the word "eternal" in the phrase "'eternal' categories of goodness, love, and human justice" in the opening pages of the article. Siniavskii fretted greatly over these additions when speaking to Pasternak's son and daughter-in-law. They assured him that such "minimal" damage did no real harm to the success of the edition.[41] For their part, the editorial board at last agreed to append their own collective foreword to include the requisite evaluation of Pasternak's political shortcomings. Although there is no letter to this effect preserved in the collection, Siniavskii must have suggested at some point after Orlov's critique that the editors write a separate foreword. Tsurikova conveyed a categorical rejection of this idea, which Orlov separately refused.[42] Nevertheless, the edition appeared with this separate insertion. The foreword by the editors describes Pasternak as a poet who "came of age in the prerevolutionary period, in the depths of bourgeois culture." He was influenced by neo-Kantianism, the idealistic philosophy "fashionable at the time." Thus we see, say the editors, Pasternak's "extreme subjectivism" and the paucity of social content in his early lyrics. Although at times, wrote the editors, one senses Pasternak's revolt against the "moral poverty, the smug vulgarity and falseness of the bourgeois and petit bourgeois world," this protest did not take an active or direct form but was expressed rather as a desire "to escape from 'unpleasant' reality into solitary concentration on personal feelings and spiritual strivings." Pasternak did not become an "active fighter for socialism." That is certainly true enough, and these pronouncements, delivered in the expected rhetorical turns of phrase, satisfied the requirement for a sensible Soviet evaluation of Pasternak.[43]

Siniavskii's article, which remained almost entirely free of such language, appeared in the official edition as a space of relative artistic autonomy. If we think of Siniavskii as trying to stake out a new separate space for artistic literature within Soviet culture, then this edition graphically depicts that effort, with Siniavskii's article placed as a kind of bulwark in between Pasternak's poetry and the editors' politicized foreword. Of course, Pasternak's poetic texts, too, represent remarkable freedom from the expected language of Soviet political commitments. What the paratextual apparatus reflects about the changing situation in the 1960s, however, is the new battle to reassert literary autonomy, with Siniavskii standing apart from the editors. The autonomy for which Siniavskii stands is not simply derived from a prerevolutionary freedom, nor does it come from somewhere outside Soviet culture: it wells up from within the very heart of Soviet culture itself.

The consequence of seeing the emergence of the unofficial field of culture in these terms is that the boundaries do not necessarily appear clear, and the identities of actors in the field are often not neatly defined. This messiness coincides with new aesthetics of Siniavskii's type, even as he re-asserts the familiar principle of aesthetic autonomy. Pasternak adopted the noble universality of the poetic Jew-turned-Christian (a poetic identity consummately revealed in *Doctor Zhivago*). Siniavskii went the other direction, an Orthodox Russian Christian who played at being the criminal Jew Abram Terts in his creative writing.[44] Siniavskii is both scholarly critic and imaginary jester-transgressor; he is a writer within the establishment and one who fights for aesthetic autonomy. His roles complement one another and cannot be neatly divided. Pasternak was an important touchstone for Siniavskii and others, a poetic heretic in Soviet culture, someone whose worldview originated in the culture preceding Soviet culture. As such, he mediated culture from a realm beyond the Soviet world, a sphere like the highly serious and ultimately transcendent world of Zhivago's poetry. That space apart became, with Siniavskii's parodic and playful Terts, a less serious and less pure alternative space within Soviet culture itself. Siniavskii's challenges came out of the Soviet context, but they were not aimed simply at the regime, as though at some power that existed separately from Russian people and Russian culture. Precisely because Terts took aim at paradigms undergirding Russian culture more fundamentally, rather than at the superficial trappings of Soviet power, Siniavskii-Terts managed to provoke scandal also among dissidents and Russian émigrés.[45]

Siniavskii never set himself directly against the regime in some kind of binary opposition. Instead, he struggled with his fellow literati in official literature and took aim at the sacred cows of the general Russian readership. Resistance *within* the cultural field became key to opening up the field of dissidence from within Soviet Russian culture. That field expanded out to include the heterogeneous types of dissident writing and activity found in the 1970s and 1980s in samizdat. Siniavskii's feeling for the avant-garde preceded the emergence of the dissident field, but the impulse it represented, of pushing forward on the basis of internal tensions in the field of culture, corresponds to the avant-garde engine for cultural development described by Bourdieu.[46]

We may trace this development in retrospect, but the outlines of a dissident field as such were not apparent in August 1965, when the volume of Pasternak's poetry with Siniavskii's introductory article appeared. Publication of the book had been an uncertain affair up to the period of relative freedom during the interregnum following Khrushchev's fall in October 1964. Shortly after the volume came out, on September 8, 1965, authorities arrested Siniavskii. They ordered the Pasternak volume with his article be yanked from library shelves, although they were not fast enough to retract them from booksellers, since the edition sold out almost immediately.

THE EMERGENCE OF A DISSIDENT FIELD, II: ALEKSANDR ESENIN-VOLPIN AND LEGALISM

Aleksandr Esenin-Volpin, mathematician, was born in 1924, the son of poet Sergei Esenin and Nadezhda Volpin. Esenin-Volpin organized the "Meeting of Openness" ("Miting glasnosti") on December 5, 1965, to demand transparency in the proceedings against Iulii Daniel and Andrei Siniavskii. Not only did he perceive the possibility of new types of activity that would be crucial to civic dissidents in their claims against the regime, but Volpin, like Siniavskii, pushed off against others on the field to develop his distinctive, and subsequently highly productive, strategy.

The case of Daniel and Siniavskii helped spark the systematic social activity that would become known as dissidence. The wives of the defendants, Larisa Bogoraz and Mariia Rozanova, wrote open letters proclaiming their husbands' innocence. The technique of writing open letters, to be circulated in samizdat and printed abroad, became quite popular. The fact that, during this scandal (unlike during Pasternak's), 60 of the 80 people who signed a collective letter in support of Siniavskii and Daniel were members of the Moscow Writers' Union suggests that a much greater sense of collective autonomy had been created. At the same time, the support of the accused by Union members also demonstrates the permeability of the border between official and unofficial.

The case proved to be particularly important for the international attention it attracted: articles in the *New York Times* and *Le Monde* as early as October 1965 shone a light on the murky proceedings against the two writers. Foreign correspondents waited outside the courtroom with Soviet citizens during the trial in February 1966. Following the trial, the *White Book* assembled by Aleksandr Ginzburg and containing comprehensive materials about the case circulated in samizdat and was published in tamizdat.[47] The *White Book* contained Siniavskii's last word at the trial, where he, like Daniel, refused to admit his guilt (something almost entirely new and quite striking for a Soviet trial). In this speech, Siniavskii said, "The position of the prosecution is that artistic literature is a form of agitation and propaganda . . . if it is not [pro-] Soviet, then that means it is anti-Soviet." Yet this, argued Siniavskii, was a false equivalence: for judicial purposes, the narrower a word, the more precise it is; conversely, the broader an artistic figure's significance, the better. Here Siniavskii articulated his critical aesthetic position publicly.[48] This made no difference to his judicial fate: Siniavskii was sentenced to seven years of hard labor, and Daniel to five, for anti-Soviet propaganda. For the *White Book*, Aleksandr Ginzburg and three of his associates were put on trial in the notorious "Trial of the Four" in 1968. That trial would, in turn, be covered by another *White Book*. By that time, both unofficial activity and contact among dissidents with the foreign press had developed further.[49] Thus, despite officials' attempts at judicial repression, the Siniavskii-Daniel case initiated the high-profile struggles of the early human rights movement.

The "Meeting of Openness" was the first spontaneously organized public demonstration in the Soviet Union after Stalin's death. It appears to have possessed more symbolic importance than political impact. A few dozen people participated in this demonstration at 6 p.m. on December 5, 1965, Constitution Day, on Pushkin Square in Moscow. They held signs reading: "We demand transparency [*glasnost'*] in the case against Siniavskii and Daniel!" and "Respect the Constitution." The meeting did not elicit the demanded judicial transparency. Moreover, the technique of public demonstration, though tried a few more times, did not prove to be a feasible or effective tactic (at the time of the August 21, 1968, invasion of Czechoslovakia, for example, just 8 people showed up on Red Square to demonstrate in protest). In important ways, however, this meeting showed the public emergence of an autonomous field of activity. The spontaneous, uncensored production and circulation of the "Civic Appeal" ("Grazhdanskoe obrashchenie") in 1965 was one of the first uses of informal networks of text-sharing (it was not yet called "samizdat") for political purposes. Vladimir Bukovskii recalled that he and other youths distributed the "Civic Appeal" using such informal channels, which represented relationships of trust established over the course of the preceding decade through the circulation of copied and original literary collections and the verses of Mandelshtam and Pasternak. Interviews show that the leaflet circulated relatively widely and by a variety of inventive means: for example, it was left on the back steps of Moscow State University and brought disingenuously into a university seminar for discussion.[50] Evgenii Kushev, editor of a short-lived uncensored journal called *Russkoe slovo*, said,

> We did not know who composed the call or who first passed it around. It did not really matter, however. The important thing was that it appeared, and also the tone in which it was written: simple, composed, without challenges and provocations, making exact references to relevant paragraphs of Soviet law. There was not the slightest hint of an attack on the state order or power in the text. . . . I had one amusing meeting with one young poet, already a member of the Writers' Union. We bumped into each other on the street, got to talk-

ing, even had a beer together, and as we parted, we each extended a copy of the "Appeal" to the other.[51]

The "Appeal" was unofficial, but it was effective precisely because it did not actively seek to oppose the regime. The action of passing the text was spontaneous and informal. Nonetheless, Soviet authorities did crack down on the activity—Bukovskii and young students Iuliia Vishnevskaia and Leonid Gubanov were arrested and sent to psychiatric hospitals for distributing the leaflets. However, those who passed it around hardly qualified as underground agents.

Several dozen people gathered at the square, and a group of approximately forty students held placards. Of these, about twenty were arrested, held for a few hours, and subsequently expelled from their educational institutions. In retrospect, this meeting—which did not seem so significant at the time—became known as the birthday of a rights movement in the Soviet Union. Looking back, we can likewise recognize that the organizers' innovative use of informal means for social mobilization helped establish an autonomous field of action, which in the repressive context of the Soviet Union would play out most often in samizdat texts, and very rarely on public squares.

Initially, little information was available about exactly why Siniavskii and Daniel had been arrested. Among the intelligentsia speculation and even suspicion of the writers abounded. Volpin's attitude was extraordinary on a couple of counts. First, he said that it did not matter who they were, and it did not matter what they wrote—it was worth fighting for transparency in their case.[52] Volpin declared he had not read their stories and would not read them before the meeting. "Literature does not concern me," he insisted. At issue was the judicial process and transparency. The defendants need not be writers to have this demonstration: "These ideas provoked great surprise," remembered Volpin.[53]

The second aspect of Volpin's way of thinking that stands out is his insistence on strict legality, as reflected in the placards calling on authorities to "Respect the Constitution." Volpin's concept of legal dissidence depended on meticulous observation of the law. His strategy of legal dissent would prove to be a very powerful idea that later became the norm for many Soviet groups, including the democratic movement and Jewish activists. What kind of autonomy does this idea represent? Volpin's legal dissent came out of his search for purely rational and logical principles to oppose the way things were done in practice, in arbitrary and often unjust ways. Volpin's personal search for rational principles to guide social interaction, his mathematical training and extensive reading in logic and philosophy, and his own experience of arrest (in 1949 for alleged anti-Soviet agitation on the basis of his uncensored poetry) contributed to the development of his interest in strict legality and transparency as expressed in the materials for the Meeting of Openness.[54] Volpin's insistence on the transcendent character of the law represents a sort of autonomy of pure principle, if one may so put it, from the notoriously capricious and autocratic application of the law common in the Soviet Union. Such a principle does not imply separation from the official Soviet system, however. On the contrary, Volpin's strategy depended completely on the immanent structures of the system—he always worked with the constitution, referencing the laws on the Soviet books. This is in large measure why the strategy proved particularly viable and effective in the circumstances of the Soviet Union at that time. Volpin's view also reflected a conviction about the independence of the law from issues of personal reputation or literary value. The contamination of the two did not proceed from official Soviet culture as such; rather, the problem went to the heart of longstanding traditions within the Russian intelligentsia at large to ascribe authority to literary writers and to tie this authority to personal morality and exemplary characteristics.[55] Volpin's insistence on strict legality resembled Siniavskii's principle of aesthetic autonomy in that both insisted on a strict separation of discourses and systems of value. At the time, it seemed especially striking that Volpin insisted on this point. Everyone else believed that Siniavskii and Daniel had to be defended because they were writers, maintaining as a consequence that the quality of their works mattered. The creative tension of Volpin's conception depended on innovatively stepping back from questions of literature as such, even as Siniavskii and many others saw those questions as exactly the site of resistance. Volpin's conception arose out of his perception of problems within Russian society at large—the problem of a traditional literaturocentrism. Thus, he reacted not simply to official abuses. Volpin's legal theory contributed to the significant dynamism within the unofficial field itself that helped open up that field for autonomous cultural activity on the one hand, and autonomous legal reasoning on the other.

The demonstration would not have taken place without Volpin's unique vision: his peers thought he was insane to try to organize an unauthorized public demonstration. Liudmila Alekseeva described the fear she and Natalia Sadomskaia felt when Volpin told them about planning a demonstration. They tried to dissuade him.[56] The boisterous young people who agreed to distribute leaflets and hold placards would not have lasted long without the discipline Volpin imposed.[57]

In this way, then, Volpin's personal vision was decisive. It did not, however, fully determine the way things played out. In the cases of both the autonomy of art propounded by Siniavskii, and the transcendence of the law as upheld by Volpin, the idea provides the impetus for new spaces for social activity. But the realization of unofficial social activity always challenges the purity of conception, demonstrating the messy, contingent, and malleable nature of this unofficial autonomy. Volpin's exceptional idea could not be perfectly implemented. Volpin knew that he would have to surrender some aspects of his idea in order to distribute an effective call to action. He reduced the original twelve pages of the "Civic Appeal" to two. At the bottom of the "Appeal," which contained both discussion of the motivation for the meeting and information about where and when the meeting was to take place, the reader was instructed to copy the text and invite two other people. This was a new technique: "We were curious how this would work," Volpin recalled. As frequently happens with samizdat, some corruption of the original text occurred in copying. For this reason, the copy included in the *White Book*, and the one most frequently cited subsequently, contained a mistake. It read:

> Some months ago, the KGB arrested two citizens: the writers A. Siniavskii and Iu. Daniel. There is reason to suspect the law is being broken regarding transparency in the judicial process. It is widely acknowledged that any kind of illegality is possible in closed proceedings, and that the violation of the law regarding transparency (art. 3 of the Constitution of the USSR and art. 18 of the Criminal Code of the RSFSR) already in and of itself constitutes illegality. It seems improbable that the work of the writers could comprise a state crime.

In place of "state crime," Volpin had originally written "state secret." This mistake illuminates the common lack of understanding of the fundamentals underlying Volpin's legal philosophy: Volpin meant to say that only in the case of a state secret might the process legally be kept from public view, while those who (consciously or not) changed the wording held to the more common view that the works in principle could not constitute a crime.[58] Volpin's conception was altered in the transmission and reception. Samizdat, like the telephone in a telephone game, indeed, like any medium, introduced some noise into the message. This medium also made participation by a relatively large group possible. As opposed to the perfectly reproduced copies of a printed book, the samizdat text can vary among its spontaneously reproduced copies. This characteristic also implies that the text must resonate with a public in order to live, even if the ideas will be received somewhat differently by those mobilized. In this material realization of unofficial activity, we see a challenge to the modernist conception of autonomy insofar as it implies the individual idea in a fixed and inviolable print form. Dissident autonomy differs.

Volpin made the decision to hold the demonstration on Pushkin Square in Moscow in consultation with his co-organizers, physicist Valerii Nikolskii and artist Iurii Titov and Titov's wife Elena Stroeva. Stroeva suggested that the meeting should occur "closer to the poet," that is, to the statue of Pushkin on the square. The monument to Pushkin had been erected in 1880 through the efforts of a liberal intelligentsia striving to establish itself on the basis of values embodied in literature, aiming to be a salutary counterpublic in Russian society on the Western European model.[59] Volpin ignored the specific literary associations, claiming that the square itself was appropriate because it was located across from the offices of the newspaper *Izvestiia*, which was "supposedly the mouthpiece of openness," as Volpin put it. Volpin in fact showed greater sensitivity to the specificity of his own, present Soviet context.[60]

The Pushkin Square, and the different ways in which people understood the space, might serve as a metaphor for the field of dissidence at the time of its emergence in late Soviet society. Looking back at the literary tradition and the aspirations of the Russian intelligentsia, budding dissidents strove like their forebears to respond to their current circumstances. This field did not represent some transcendent space constructed in an ideal sphere beyond the real society and the dynamics of economic and political power that crossed it, even if a core and unifying belief of the field consisted of the idea that it was somehow possible to judge and act in ways independent of official dictates. As Bourdieu outlined it, the field of culture in its modern autonomous variant represented a rejection of the false *illusio*, in favor of the true illusion, the illusion that recognizes itself as such, an artistic representation (or other codified abstraction), which will provide truer insight.[61] Having rejected the official illusion of a unified populace sharing with its government established conceptions about the world and society, dissidents chose other "illusions," literary truths or strict legalism.

Once present on the field of dissidence, participants sought to express the particular ways in which they saw autonomy—some were "closer to the poet," constructing it through literature or art that, like Pushkin's own work, did not make direct public challenges. Others oriented themselves to the contemporary public outlets, such as *Izvestiia*, setting up an alternative public forum. Bourdieu's model of the field provides a way to understand these various dissident activities in terms of relations, not only to the regime and official culture, but to each other, as players on the field, competing for the symbolic capital, seeking to amass what exists or to produce a new, refined version of it. Bourdieu's original critical insight about nonmaterial forms of capital draws attention to the specificity of symbolic capital on any given field.[62] In the case of the late Soviet field, the repression of a cultural heritage and suppression of independent readings of the canon played a key role in the constitution of a restricted field of cultural production after samizdat. A crucial function was also served by the Western audience for Soviet dissidence. First a foreign press and then also a foreign market—not devoid of its own pretensions to autonomous cultural values—constituted the exogenous elements that made Soviet dissidence possible.

One of the wonderful aspects of Bourdieu's sociological analysis is his careful and imaginative reading of Gustave Flaubert's novel *Sentimental Education* for insights into the relations among an autonomous cultural field and the larger social field whose material exchanges and power relations it denies. I aim to do something similar here—subsequent chapters will look closely at the uncensored novels by Aksenov, Bitov, and Erofeev. How did they perceive their social position and possibilities for change? What new means of expression did they forge in uncensored literature for an independent reflection of the late Soviet era?

Chapter Two

Aksenov's *The Burn*: Searing the Hearts of Men

> The only people for me are the mad ones,
> the ones who are mad to live, mad to talk,
> mad to be saved, desirous of everything at the
> same time, the ones who never yawn or say a
> commonplace thing, but burn, burn, burn like
> fabulous yellow roman candles.
> —Jack Kerouac, *On the Road*, part 1, chapter 1

VASILII AKSENOV knew his uncensored novel *The Burn* (*Ozhog*), written between 1969 and 1975, would be far more incendiary than anything else he had written to that point. Aksenov kept the manuscript close, knowing how dangerous it was, but a couple of years after he finished it, officers of the KGB came to him to warn him about it, saying they would overlook other publications abroad and even the uncensored compilation *Metropol* if only *Ozhog* would not appear in print. This novel about the disillusionment of Soviet intelligentsia following the invasion of Czechoslovakia in August 1968 combined fictionalized episodes based on real events and fantastic and symbolic characters with some identifiable prototypes. One of these characters proved all too easy for the KGB to recognize: the name of Cheptsov, the grotesque father-rapist in the book, resembles that of his prototype Chentsov, who had been one of two security officers involved in the second arrest of Aksenov's mother Evgeniia Ginzburg, in 1949, in Magadan, Siberia. Aksenov lived in Magadan at that time with his mother, who had been released from the camps not long previously. He fictionalized in Cheptsov a person who played a dark role in this traumatic event from his teenage years. While Cheptsov represented a symbolic figure more than a real person, the names were close. Chentsov's role, described briefly in Ginzburg's memoirs, made the connection to Aksenov's character clear. Chentsov, of course, had no desire to see his name blackened this way.[1]

Aksenov at last authorized publication of *Ozhog*, knowing it would mean his emigration. The book appeared in print in 1980.[2] This large and angry novel, weighing in at over 400 pages, did not circulate widely in samizdat prior to its tamizdat publication.[3] To a great degree this must have been because Aksenov wanted to choose his time for emigration. It seems fair to think Aksenov also hoped a judicious release of the book would enhance its bombshell impact: his frank, critical and formally experimental novel would challenge the friendly and accessible image of him many Soviet readers harbored. Moreover, Aksenov aimed to change the landscape of late Soviet letters for readers at home and abroad. No longer would there be strict if unspoken divisions between fathers and sons, authorities and rebels, official and unofficial writers, with repressed modernism and Western art kept outside the realm of Socialist Realism—all would be "swirled together" in a great spiral that would take off from the earth in Aksenov's transcendent perspective.[4] As a result, people would recognize in the Soviet past and present a dramatic human experience.

The way Aksenov saw his literary landscape and the model Pierre Bourdieu offered for the modern field of literary art can be juxtaposed for productive analytic tension: Aksenov created energy in *The Burn* by crossing over boundaries between what could be said and what could not, between officially acceptable realist representation and "degenerate" formal experimentation. As he did so, he exposed the way Soviet people had allowed the Soviet regime to trample on human dignity and decency. Aksenov modeled for Soviet readers the recovery of memory and selfhood needed to put a stop to boundless humiliation and violence. He also imagined that his own power as a writer to bring together cultural forces that had been divided might create a field beyond political boundaries in which people would communicate about themselves and their lives on a human basis. Aksenov projected a cultural field like a kingdom of the human spirit separate from and even broader than the Soviet Union. Aksenov's sweeping panorama in *The Burn* suggests a literary vision designed to bring together American and Soviet readers and different generations in productive dialogue.

Bourdieu's model underscores a conflict in this vision: Aksenov's avant-garde methods for treating his material suggest he forewent his mass readership when he undertook provocative artistic experimentation in samizdat. However, Aksenov aimed in fact to broaden the scope of his art to appeal to both Western and Soviet readers. Aksenov's novel is a book of breathtaking ambition and reach incommensurate with the real possibilities at that time for readership and influence.

SAMIZDAT: AKSENOV CROSSES OVER

The emergence of the uncensored system of samizdat made it possible for Aksenov to believe he could write differently and address his audience more directly. Aksenov's mother, Evgeniia Ginzburg, had written one of the most popular works to circulate in samizdat in the late 1960s. A former Communist Party official, Ginzburg had been arrested when Aksenov was just four years old (Aksenov was born in 1932), and she spent eighteen years in the Gulag camps and Siberian exile. Her memoirs about the experience enjoyed remarkably high circulation at the time.[5] In 1967, the first volume of those memoirs appeared in print in English translation in the West. The success of Aksenov's mother as an independent writer helped pave the way for his own uncensored work.

Aksenov, however, already enjoyed a successful career as a popular Soviet author. He had trained as a medical doctor on the advice of his mother and stepfather: in their day, children of political prisoners were liable to become prisoners themselves, and it was a good profession to have in prison and the camps.[6] Under Khrushchev, however, Aksenov not only avoided arrest—he achieved fame in the Soviet literary establishment as a writer of so-called Young Prose.[7] Thus, Aksenov became another in a distinguished line of medical doctors-turned-writers in Russia that included Anton Chekhov and Mikhail Bulgakov, whose works he explored as intertexts in *The Burn*. Aksenov's novellas in the early 1960s won him a broad and appreciative following among Soviet readers.

Mildly controversial, Aksenov's official novellas portraying his generation's search for self featured laconic and ironic young people who distrust high-flown rhetoric and clichés.[8] Oleg Kharkhordin outlined Aksenov's achievement as an influential author who adjusted the typical Socialist Realist narrative in a couple of significant ways. For example, in his well-loved novella *Ticket to the Stars* (*Zvezdnyi bilet*, 1961), Aksenov subtly reimagined the Socialist Realist struggle with remnants of the past. Invoking the typical Socialist Realist fight with vestiges of the capitalist and bourgeois period of history, Aksenov implied that the more relevant struggle for his generation had to do with the legacy of Stalinism, a past that continued to manifest itself in the post-Stalin era in people's inability to make independent decisions. The hard-won independence (*samostoiatel'nost'*) of Aksenov's protagonist Victor in that story wins the respect of his elders. The head of Victor's lab says, "For four years, I've watched you and your like with mixed feelings, I could not understand you too well. What are they after, I wondered? Is it just to take everything to pieces, to reject everything? But now I believe I can see what you are after and I believe it is the same thing that I am after myself."[9] Aksenov affirmed a basic continuity between generations, despite the changed form of the struggle and their different ways of expressing themselves in it. Kharkhordin identified Aksenov's other important development in this novella in the portrait of Victor's younger brother Dmitrii, who fails to choose a vocation by the end of the novel. The rejection of the choice of a vocation *is* his choice. Although one Soviet critic complained that Dmitrii amounts to an empty shell, Kharkhordin argued that this lack of definite choice resonated as an option for a generation that had lost faith in lying words and high rhetoric and sought a new chance to replace them with real experience and deeds.[10]

Aksenov's Dmitrii resembles Flaubert's Frédéric Moreau, who as Bourdieu explains it cannot commit to any of the social games people play because of the unacknowledged illusions they entail.[11] In contrast to Flaubert's Frédéric, Aksenov's Dmitrii implies that authentic work can suture the rift that opened between generations and between young people and their society in the wake of revelations of Stalin's crimes. Later Aksenov will portray this rift in terms of a much less reparable discontinuity.

Already in the middle 1960s, Aksenov played with the possibility of addressing the festering problems inherited from the Stalinist era in his fiction. The jazzy prose of his novella *The Steel Bird* (*Stal'naia ptitsa*, 1966) previewed the ornamental effects Aksenov would employ later in *The Burn*, while the fantastic quality of the Steel Bird character suggested its allegorical potential as a grotesque representation of the spirit of Stalin. Aksenov tried to get this work by the censors, spinning it as a satire on bourgeois values.[12] Although *The Steel Bird* did not manage to get passed for publication at that time in the Soviet Union, it caused nothing like the furor *The Burn* would raise more than a decade later.

Aksenov's novella *Surplussed Barrelware* (*Zatovarennaia bochkotara*) also offered readers more than the standard-issue Socialist Realist satire. It appeared in print in the official Soviet journal *Youth* (*Iunost'*) in March 1968. Despite its formal and linguistic flourishes and its relatively daring message about the need to recover a sense of common humanity and shared values, it passed the censors. Aksenov managed to slip in a satire on lingering Stalinist tendencies, embodied in the old man Mochenkin, as he advocated for a renewal of humanist values. Stylistically, the work is a tour de force, with different characters embodying various more or less recognizable patterns of speech and behavior. In addition to the Stalinist Mochenkin, a former Colorado beetle inspector who still keeps a sharp eye out for destructive elements, the cast of characters features the hapless Volodia Teleskopov, a lover of Esenin who expresses himself in garbled poetic quotes.[13] Other characters include the scholar Vadim Afanasievich, the lovelorn and unmarried schoolteacher Irina Selezneva, and the sailor Gleb Shustikov. Aksenov brought this motley crew together for a journey to town that turns out to be a quest for a more unified humane collective as they shed their accustomed roles. Aksenov used an abundance of popular and literary cultural references, including familiar songs and poems, in what was for Soviet prose a very fresh style.[14] While Aksenov used elements from the popular cultural imagination of his day to animate specific characters and situations, he also used fantasy and archetypal plots—notably in the dream sequences of *Surplussed Barrelware*—to suggest a higher unity. This work remains like earlier novellas essentially affirmative: the characters by the end achieve positive, if not wholly unambiguous, fulfillment in their shared love for the barrelware and the worn humanistic values it represents.

The shock of August 1968, when Soviet Russian tanks rolled into Prague to crush the peaceful movement for reform there marked a turning point for Aksenov, as it did for many in the Soviet intelligentsia of that time. The 1960s had been a heady era. Aksenov reflected back on it later in an interview: "A new generation came into literature—daring, a bit hooliganish, and defiant. It was such a provocative generation—there was a Renaissance-like, carnival spirit." However, in 1968, it was all over and "the hangover began."[15] Aksenov associated the carnival spirit with youthful inspiration and idealism: intellectuals enthused over Mikhail Bakhtin's study of popular culture and the democratic renewal of humanistic values.[16] The 1968 invasion marked the end of those illusions.

Aksenov could no longer believe in the system and its susceptibility to reform. In *The Burn* he conveyed how he had come to see the character of Soviet authorities. At the same time, he indicted his own generation for silence and complicity. That very day he heard the news of the invasion, on August 21, he turned indignantly to his fellow citizens: Evgenii Evtushenko recalled Aksenov jumping up on a table to castigate indifferent vacationers standing in line at a local cafe.[17] Like Mikhail Lermontov after the death of Pushkin, Aksenov indicted not just the rulers, but the society that aided and abetted their murderous regime.[18] Recalling Pushkin's lyrical persona in the poem that marked his turning point, "The Prophet" ("Prorok," 1826), Aksenov broke with his earlier, more light-hearted work to heed the divine charge, and "with [one's] word sear the hearts of men" (*glagolom zhgi serdtsa liudei*).

The Burn revolves around the painful wound of 1968. Book 1 of Aksenov's novel features a collective protagonist. The five adult intellectuals, whose symbolic kinship Aksenov underscores with the common patronymic Apollinarevich (sons of Apollo) appear together early in the novel in a scene set in the Crimea in 1968. They are sculptor Radii Khvastischev, surgeon Gennadii Malkolmov, writer Pantelei Pantelei, saxophone player Samson Sabler, and scientist Aristarkh Kunitser.[19] Also present at this significant gathering is Tolya von Steinbock, a character who represents their common teenage past, as we learn from subsequent scenes. One of the group in the Crimea castigates the other campers standing in line for water as belonging to some mass entity called "Unanimous Approval" ("Edinodushnoe Odobrenie"); that is, he indicts them as complicit in the invasion. The protagonists' drinking and ironic belting out of battle songs make them stand out from the other campers. Nevertheless, they hardly mount effective resistance, as the narrator knows. At the end of the passage, the narrator laments, "All of us, dirty pigs, were to blame for what happened" (29; 26).

The theme of Sixty-Eight recurs throughout the novel. In book 2, Sabler the saxophonist burns his back while playing an inspired riff on "The Fateful Questions of Nineteen Sixty-Eight." Sabler leans up against an exposed hot water pipe like those common to the boiler rooms where marginalized artists and poets commonly found work space in this period (409; 345). Finally, in book 3, Major Koltun, an odious bridegroom for the protagonist's beloved Nina, recalls leading troops into Prague and shooting a woman carrying an umbrella they mistook for a gun. Significantly, the narrator recalls being in Prague at that time and coming across a tank crew at rest, reading an issue of the journal *Youth* with Aksenov's novella *Surplussed Barrelware* (477–80; 399–401). The detailed material reality of the "yellow-covered issue" in the hands of the tank men with their weapons beside them suggests the compromising purposes for which cultural products can be employed. It does not matter that Aksenov's intention was to reaffirm humane values: official culture provides a diversion that covers over the violence and inhumanity of the system. This scene suggests that the affirmative character of the work grated on Aksenov's conscience after the Sixty-Eight invasion and helped prompt him to write an incendiary work that resisted assimilation.

The narrator of this scene foregrounds the problem of memory: "What indeed are our blurred, faded memories worth at all? What price our whole past life? And did it ever happen at all if we remember so little about it?" (480; 401). The violence of the August 1968 invasion recalls the violence of Stalinism as a repressed trauma in the collective psyche. The expected linear narrative logic gives way in *The Burn* to the mixed-up chronology and repetition of trauma, where the past breaks through into the present and suppressed memories resurface at unexpected moments. Most strikingly, the past of the adult protagonists breaks through as scenes of the life of teenager Tolya in Magadan. This fictional rendering of Aksenov's own life with his mother in Siberian exile mirrors scenes from her memoirs but alters them according to the needs of Aksenov's own writing.[20]

Shortly after his mother's arrest, Aksenov's father, a high-ranking Party official in Kazan, was also arrested and became a prisoner in the camp system. Subsequently Aksenov spent his childhood with his aunt's family. As a teenager, he went to live with his mother at the place of her exile for a year and a half. In her memoirs, Ginzburg described in extremely affecting terms the arrival in Magadan and extended stay of her son Vasya (Aksenov) with her in Siberia.[21] She portrayed the long and emotional struggle to bring Vasya out to see her after many years apart. As Ginzburg described it, when Vasya arrives, he puts on a dignified and stoic front, advising his mother, "Don't cry in front of them." Aksenov's own account emphasizes on the contrary his uncontrollable emotion, particularly during his mother's second arrest for unspecified reasons, in 1949. Aksenov portrayed feelings that break through the controlled surface of realistic representation, creating a whole landscape of shame (*pozor*) that combines the embarrassment he feels as the son of a prisoner and the personal discomfort of his own unregulated emotions. Upon being told of his mother's arrest, with the opportunity to see her briefly before she is taken away, Tolya emerges from the school building and sees: "Shame—clean, snowy, and sunlit—stretched out in front of him. The expanse of shame was crisscrossed with wooden, raised sidewalks . . . The backdrop to shame was the Palace of Culture. The sharp, cubist geometry of shadows decorated the background of shame" (297; 252). Tolya finds the "center of shame" in the black *Emka*, the official car driven by security agents who arrested his mother (298; 252). This "cubist" landscape conveys the discontinuity of trauma as perceived by the mature and artistic perspective. Aksenov's narrator embodies the adult awareness of the way his mother's second arrest shattered his already fragile teenage world. The sense of fragmentation created by events like these occurred in millions of families. That trauma remained largely unaddressed by society and official culture even after Stalin, and therefore it rises up in Aksenov's work to tear apart conventional realistic novelistic representation. Aksenov projected the lack of social coherence and the lost integrity of the shattered self at that moment onto the landscape in this passage. That artistic decision appears indeed to affect the whole novelistic structure where past and present often lose their coherent relationship and the depth of time gets flattened into a disjointed swirl. To put it in broad terms of ideology and temporality, Aksenov renounces the official propaganda about a progressive march to a bright and just future: with no adequate memory of the traumatic past, no coherent present is possible and there is no promising future. The novel loses its expected linear trajectory.

Aksenov's task in writing differed from that of his mother. Natalya Kolchevska wrote about Ginzburg's mission to "promote a cultural and moral vision" to a society that had lost it. She did so in part by tracing her own trajectory from being a member of the intelligentsia by virtue of social status, to being one on the strength of inner substance and insight acquired through long years of imprisonment and exile.[22] Ginzburg also showed herself to be a sophisticated realistic writer. Kolchevska pointed out that "*Whirlwind* reads like a novel, has a polished narrative exposition, a strong authorial voice alternating with dialogue that is staged and characters who perform, a grasp of the difference between 'real' and narrative time, and a wealth of literary and cultural references."[23] Aksenov shared his mother's humanistic values.[24] However, he could not assume the same type of authority his mother possessed. His writing in *The Burn* in particular resembles what Marianne Hirsch described as post-generational writing. While Hirsch analyzed the art of a generation that succeeded survivors of the Holocaust, the dilemmas and techniques she outlined seem applicable to the generation that succeeded Stalinist camp survivors as well. These dilemmas include forging an authority distinct from that of the survivor and witness to be able to speak about their own lives and the different trauma and concerns they have. Art of the generation of post-memory characteristically involves citation and critical interrogation of media and the means of expression, features we find easily in Aksenov's writing.[25]

In *The Burn*, Aksenov treated this part of his personal biography as something emblematic of his generation's experience for the first time. On the one hand, his relationship with his mother, their shared history, known and respected by samizdat readers, provided Aksenov with entrée to an alternative venue and means of reaching readers through uncensored writing. On the other hand, as Aksenov entered the realm of samizdat/tamizdat in which her name was already known, he staked out his own position.

Of course, Aksenov and his mother could not be in direct competition as writers: he was already a famous and accomplished literary professional. The sophistication of his technique underscores his experience and demonstrates his trajectory from a basically conformist, if relatively independent, young official writer to a powerfully critical Soviet satirist. Like Siniavskii, Aksenov came to embrace a grotesque and avant-garde literary art more suited to exposing the absurd reality of his late Soviet society and more authentically rooted, as he believed, in folk culture than realism.[26] Aksenov explained his turn toward a more experimental style he called "avant-garde" based on experiences with the authorities and their repressive measures in the early 1960s. Already then, said Aksenov, "I realized that we live in a totally absurd world. That reality is so absurd that a writer who makes use of the absurd or the surreal is not coloring his work. Rather he is trying to make some sort of harmony out of this reality, which falls down around him like garbage into a dump."[27]

Aksenov portrayed the event that sparked his turn toward a grotesque, absurd style in book 1 of *The Burn*. In the section titled "The Occasion on Which His Youth Came to an End," writer Pantelei tells about a public meeting between creative intelligentsia and authorities. Aksenov depicted the scene in wildly fantastic ways—instead of Premier Khrushchev, "the Boss" (Glava) also called Nikita Kornponevich (Kukita Kuseevich) leads the event (115–22; 101–07), and the Chair of the Ideological Commission L. F. Ilichev becomes the "High Priest" (Verkhovnyi Zhrets), described as a weird anteater creature with sucker appendages (118; 102).Contemporary readers would have easily recognized the prototypes. Many would have known about the real event on which the scene was based, a meeting held on March 7–8, 1963, with over 600 members of the young creative elite summoned to hear from the leaders about their responsibilities. During that meeting, Khrushchev took Aksenov to task for an interview he and the poet Andrei Voznesenskii had given to the Polish paper *Polityka*. In that interview the writers touched on the theme of "fathers and sons." Voznesenskii claimed the present literary "fathers" were no good. He explained that he looked further back for spiritual predecessors in poetry. Aksenov treated the theme more personally. His father had been a victim of Stalin, but he also blamed his father's generation: "How could they have allowed the year 1937 to happen?" he asked, referring to the height of Stalin's purges.[28]

In the book, Pantelei, crazed with fear at being brought up for scrutiny at the meeting, starts singing the "Song of the Varangian Guest," from the opera *Sadko* (121; 105). All these weird details possess their own logic. The name Nikita Kornponovich reflects Khrushchev's excessive enthusiasm for corn crops. The High Priest with his sucker appendages elsewhere tries to suck Pantelei into an uncomfortable relationship with the authorities (161–63; 140–44). Pantelei's singing has its logic, too: it realizes a threatening metaphor from official discourse, "to sing to someone's tune," as in "to sing to the tune of the imperialists" (*pet' pod dudku imperialistov*). The Boss's language, wild as it is in this scene, also seems to be a slightly exaggerated version of the kind of outbursts Khrushchev was known for producing in real life. Khrushchev denounced formally renegade artists as "pederasts and abstractionists," threatening, "we'll grind [them] into powder!" (*my [ikh] sotrem v poroshok!*), as Aksenov has the Boss say here (121; 105).[29] Also in real life, subsequent to this event, Aksenov published a statement in the official newspaper *Pravda* acknowledging the "just" criticism and pledging to do better, a sentiment he felt compelled to express.[30] The shattering impact of this kind of pressure and forced capitulation appeared in retrospect to foreshadow the shared sense of betrayal experienced in 1968, as the portrayal of both moments in the novel suggests. Aksenov's use of avant-garde techniques in *The Burn* conveys a destruction of subjective integrity and harmonious coexistence with the existing social order. Peter Bürger described such destruction as characteristic of the challenge avant-garde artists mount to their society.[31]

Aksenov depicted representatives of the regime, including the Stalinist "fathers," in the most disturbing of forms. Nina Efimova, who noted the relationship of Aksenov's grotesque to folklore, observed that Aksenov regularly presented supernatural demonic figures as allegories of Soviet power, while his ideal unity of spirituality and creativity appears in Christ-like figures.[32] Certainly, one could describe the monstrous Metro attendant of early scenes (13; 13), the judge in the Crimea (202–3; 175) and Cheptsov as demonic.

Cheptsov appears in a variety of hypostases encountered by the adult protagonists, including the cloakroom attendant and Theodore the mercenary. On the other side of the spectrum, the character Sanya Gurchenko, who is beaten by Security officers (195–97; 169–70) and later becomes a Catholic priest initiating the protagonist into the mysteries of the "Third Model" (266; 227), suggests the Christ-like spirit of humility and sacrifice.[33] Sanya, we learn toward the end of the book, has been irradiated during his work as a prisoner in a uranium mine (486; 406), a realistic, and politically sensitive explanation for his superhuman asceticism. However, as a fighting, race-car driving European man of the cloth, Sanya embodies various characteristics associated with the representations of masculinity familiar to Tolya as a young person. Sanya is "the bold Ringo Kid himself, the jaunty, cheerful Jewish deportee, the 'paladin of Jesus Christ' who had bummed his way around Europe" (196; 170). Worldly Sanya transcends the barriers and boundaries that confuse and constrain Tolya. Sanya knows everything about Magadan's system of prisoners and jailors. In overturning the official dichotomy of "us" vs. "them" he displays to Tolya a refreshing independence of judgment and begins to liberate Tolya from his debilitating shame: "So you're one of us!" Sanya announces with a cheerful laugh, asking "Fifty-eight?" in reference to the article under which most political prisoners, including Tolya's mother, were arrested (238–39, 243; 203–4, 209). Sanya is the one who manages to cross the Bering Strait, which seems like the "borderline between two worlds that no one could cross" (484; 404). Normal people like the protagonist stand between the divine forces that sometimes get channeled into people they meet. The ideal answer is not always comprehensible or feasible for them: "But Sanya!" cries the protagonist, "What should I do if I am shaking from anger, disdain and shame?" "Keep shaking," says Sanya, adding, "You can't imitate God" (481; 402).

Aksenov conveyed the many manifestations of Stalinist violence through grotesque and perverse scenes, including that of Lyuda Guly's evil father, who experiences arousal as he whips his daughter to the tune of a song from 1948, "We don't need—one! The shores of Turkey—two! And what is Africa to us—three! We don't need it, don't need it, don't need it!" (241; 205–6).[34] The incestuous character of this scene suggests the closed nature of a Soviet Russia under Stalin with tight boundaries to seal out the rest of the world and unbounded violence within its borders. It recalls also the chauvinistic emphasis on great Russian superiority that grew in strength during World War II and after. In another scene, the retired security officer Cheptsov rapes his stepdaughter Nina, who calls him "Bloodsucker, toad . . . I swear that everything about you is monstrous, inhuman!" (341–44; 288–91). The incendiary scene was sure to offend readers, including the character's prototype Chentsov. Aksenov treated real events and people with phantasmagoric artistic licence. This scene does not seem to be based on any actual rape, although Aksenov hinted with the prisoner Alisa at the real but little-discussed problem of sexual violence in the camps (234; 199). The graphic rape of Nina by Cheptsov seems to underscore the message about a still potent violence of Stalinist "fathers" along with the perverse character of an inwardly turned culture associated with them.

As bitter as his indictment of the Stalinist fathers was, Aksenov did not spare the "sons." He showed the adult protagonists of his generation seeking inspiration in the wrong places and settling for temporary forgetfulness and empty escape in carnivalesque carousing. Each of the five protagonists has an American friend, Patrick Thunderjet, who drives an Impala car, and an émigré girlfriend, Masha, both of whom we see in formulaically repeated scenes in the ABCDE section (50–63; 44–55). The repetition helps link the protagonists as variations on a generational type who ignores systemic problems and focuses on personal friendships and lifestyle, portrayed here as an empty escape. In another set of scenes connecting the protagonists gathered under the heading "One Day in 197 . . .", a child in Kensington Gardens sees a satellite and asks whether it could be a Russian bomb (249; 213). The scene recalls the story of scientist Kunitser, one of the protagonists with a loose connection to his prototype, the nuclear physicist Andrei Sakharov. Kunitser had already recognized that as soon as he made his scientific discovery, it no longer belonged to him and might be used for deadly weaponry (53; 46). While the "bomb" is not used at this point, the reader realizes the threat and the implications for Soviet intelligentsia—the fruit of inspired labor can be put to terrible purposes. Pantelei the writer drives home the point about their lack of independence: "Alas, we are not free agents, we're not genuine personalities, not gods, and not giants. We just let Moscow churn us around at will in its meat grinder" (445; 374).

STRANGER IN THE NIGHT: AKSENOV'S CHALLENGE TO THE AUTONOMY OF CULTURE

People in the world of *The Burn* compensate for their humiliation with things that make them feel good and free. These things include Western goods, slang, and even a bit of repressed poetry—in his novella *Colleagues* (*Kollegi*, 1960), Aksenov managed to pass off as his own a stanza from Pasternak's "Ballad," 1930, at a time when Pasternak's name was still officially anathema. Such indulgences probably struck the authorities as relatively harmless gestures toward independence among young people in Aksenov's early works. True, official Soviet critics had objected to the enthusiasm in the Young Prose of the 1960s for "jeans, jargon and motorbikes." Official critics denounced this fetishization of foreign items as a "surrogate emancipation of the self,"[35] but the basically affirmative character of the early works helped them pass muster with the authorities. Later, Aksenov's early champion, the Soviet critic Stanislav Rassadin, reviewed with skepticism the long list of consumer goods enumerated by Aksenov's character Luchnikov in *The Island of Crimea* (*Ostrov Krym*, 1979). The list shows Luchnikov's Soviet mentality, argued Rassadin—a sated American imagination simply could not hold in mind such a long and specific list.[36] Neither in his early official nor his later uncensored works did Aksenov celebrate consumerism. At the same time, he did not critique it in the same way a Western writer would. Aksenov showed that for the Soviet person Western goods meant more than material gratification because they signified Western values—including respect for the individual, quality, and professionalism—as well as status for those who could obtain such goods. In this spirit, Aksenov treated such items for their ability to signify, like elements of a language.[37]

While not critiquing consumerism as such, Aksenov drew attention to the fetishistic quality of Western and other scarce or elite goods and culture in the Soviet imagination. Drawing on his knowledge of the privileged classes, Aksenov exposed the use of luxury items to signify a compromising closeness with the regime: thus, for example, the impresario Blazer, rival of the protagonist for Alisa's affections, drives a fast car, knows foreign artists, and gives off the "full playboy bouquet" (*polnyi pleiboiskii buket*) of cognac, Yardley's lotion, and Kent cigarettes, along with the smell of sex (423; 356). Blazer's name and other references to him (such as "Four Brass Buttons" [288; 245]) indicate he is a grotesque figure, a stuffed suit, inflated by money and privilege, and lacking substantial values. This "self-satisfied son of a bitch" is one of the "gilded offspring of the Party élite."[38] Yet, the attachment of Soviet *stiliagi* to Western fashions, and later of hippies to English phrases and musical styles, speaks to a different phenomenon: these Western imports also functioned to mark out a space of freedom and independence within Soviet society. Such idealism and the assertion of status could come together in the use of Western goods, producing an uncomfortable mix.[39]

Aksenov showed that when objects, whether consumer goods or cultural products, begin to function merely as signs of affiliation, status, or even illusionistic idealism, that is, when they become fetishes—they belie a spiritual deficiency. Aksenov exposed the affectation by members of the Soviet intelligentsia of independence in tastes and values as too often lacking substance. Sabler's friend Silvester corresponds with jazz celebrities including pianist Thelonious Monk, broadcaster Willis Conover, and jazz historian and journalist Leonard Feather, who sends Silvester the jazz magazine *Down Beat*. The names signify international influences and connections (30; 26–27).[40] This group of jazz lovers comports itself "like playboys" (*pleiboiski*).

Their circles include "flower children" (*deti tsvetov*) described as being like those in London. However, these trappings of cosmopolitan and free culture mask the real situation in the Soviet Union. Aksenov's narrator relates a fantastic story of Sabler arriving from *Wellen* (Belgium) by way of *Wrangel Island*, where he received a saxophone sent by *Stan Getz* on an *Oil Alaska snowcat* (all terms in italics signify exotic foreignness). This story, we learn, circulated among friends and added to Sabler's mysterious and hip aura. Aksenov's narrator comments on the fact that such fantasy crowds out the names of less exotic places, like Berlin, Poznan, Warsaw, Budapest and Novocherkassk, all sites of crushed uprisings of the post-Stalin era. Aksenov's ironic choice of words in describing the arrival of Silvester's correspondence by "stagecoach" and "dangerous roads" resonates with the cinematic heroism portrayed elsewhere in the novel. Teenage Tolya watches the 1939 American film with John Wayne *Stagecoach* (a trophy film brought back from World War II by Soviet troops and known to Soviet audiences as *The Journey Will Be Dangerous*) many times. Aksenov undercut the suggestion of Sabler's "heroism," noting that state officials have examined and allowed the mail (29–30; 26–27). Similarly, Aksenov showed the daring use of English words to be part of a strategy to affect freedom while avoiding open confrontation: when he goes to meet the High Priest, the writer Pantelei wears the pin saying in clumsy English, "I fuck censorship" (*Ai fak sensorship*)[41] on the *inside* of his jacket (160; 139). This is the ineffectual mode of resistance with a "fuck you" gesture kept concealed inside the pocket, a"figa v karmane," as the Russian phrase goes.

Aksenov exposed Soviet intellectuals clinging to Western culture as a way of concealing their real dependence on the Soviet system and avoiding uncomfortable realizations. In an early scene of *The Burn*, the sight of a man dragging scrap metal and carrying a spoon, as a prisoner would, threatens to bring to Kunitser's mind the painful memories of abandonment and the camps that the protagonist would rather not recall (12; 12). He seeks solace at home in familiar things, including *The Plays of T. S. Eliot*, the picture of a cowboy, a key from the Vatican with a portrait of Pope John XXIII, and the steering wheel of a car smashed in his youth. These souvenirs provoke no difficult memories. The protagonist thinks of the girlfriends who have contributed mementos to his collection of bric-a-brac, tokens of events and entanglements without lasting consequences (11; 11). Near the end, similarly, the narrator describes the "cosmopolitan riot" of the protagonist's apartment, dubbed the "sympathetic den of an intellectual" (434–35; 520).[42] That description closes with a stanza from Innokentii Annenskii's poem "September" that speaks significantly of "those whose lips have tasted of the lotus flower," as though the objects enumerated have a comfortably narcotic effect on their owner.

Like the interior of the self, where inspiration and memory have been corrupted by official appropriation and control, the private space of the home in Aksenov's novel has no integrity or sanctity. In the opening scene, the protagonist's feeling of comfort at home is disturbed by the TV blaring in his apartment. Near the end, the protagonist jumps through the "eye" glued to the window of the room he shares with Alisa. Apparently the eye is part of a propaganda poster. The protagonist thinks of this as tearing through the "web of lies" that this oversized poster represents. It also brings to mind the grotesque metaphors of Vladimir Maiakovskii's *Cloud in Trousers* (*Oblako v shtanakh*, 1914–15), including Burliuk crawling out of his own eye, and Maiakovskii's lyrical hero trying to jump out of his own burning chest. Ultimately, that which burns him is inside of him, it is part of him.

Aksenov spoke about Russian Futurists betrayed by or even having submitted willingly to a corrupted revolutionary society.[43] For his late Soviet generation, the Futurists and particularly Stalin's favorite Maiakovskii represented an ambivalent heritage: they represented at once a core of freedom and inspiration within Soviet society, and a lesson about how the revolutionary society would consume its own talent. Aksenov talked about learning modernist poetry from his mother. She taught him Symbolist and Acmeist poetry, including "miles of Pasternak," as well as early Futurist verse by Maiakovskii and Khlebnikov that he could not get from his schoolbooks.[44] This poetry had a tremendous influence on the young Aksenov. After returning to the city of Kazan, as a young university student, Aksenov and his friends set up a bohemian household which he described as a Futurist commune. Their commune coincided with the final months of Stalin's life: it was only by good fortune that Aksenov and his friends did not get arrested for their unorthodox behavior before Stalin died.[45]

In *The Burn*, Aksenov associated Maiakovskii with Tolya's youthful aspirations. Maiakovskii serves as template for Tolya's romantic and heroic image of the self, with a "black top-hat and cape with upturned collar, challenging look, sensitive lips" (224; 191). Lines from Maiakovskii's poem *A Cloud in Trousers* ring in Tolya's ears: "Remember, you said, Jack London, money, love, passion" (229; 196). The frustrated eroticism of the outsize lyric hero in that poem fits the emotion of Tolya, who desperately longs to fit in with his class at school and hopes to win the love of the local officer's daughter, Lyuda Guly, before realizing that is impossible. In a larger sense, Maiakovskii represents the romantic longing to integrate oneself and one's talents into society, and to bring together the sundered parts of Soviet society into a real unity. The protagonist Sabler is surprised and touched to find, for example, that Kriushkin, a member of the citizen's brigade, and his enemy in other respects, knows and loves Maiakovskii like he does (39; 35). Pantelei refers to Maiakovskii "his teacher" in a desperate attempt to appease the authorities at the Kremlin meeting (119; 104). Finally, the monument to Maiakovskii, erected in the middle of Moscow in 1958, attracts poets, artists and civically minded youth, although for this reason it also merits surveillance and control by the authorities (439; 369).[46]

For Aksenov's protagonists, the integration to which Soviets aspire through Maiakovskii, the "rebellious young European" (439; 369), also involves an erotic desire to be reunited with the world culture from which Russians had become cut off in the Soviet era. The "Silver Age" in Aksenov's novel represents the feminine complement to Maikovskii's virile Futurism.[47] Aksenov summoned up the spirit of the Silver Age in an early scene of the protagonist wandering through Leningrad:

> Oh, God, oh, God, is there no end to loneliness? Even then, in that spring, when the slush of the Nevsky Prospect was seeping through the worn-out soles of my shoes, in the twenty-fourth year of my life, when I wandered, a romantic masturbator, among the silent monuments of the Silver Age and read the appeals to join the ranks of the blood donors and thought of the donors of Budapest, even when I was penniless and abandoned on Aptekarsky Island on the night of the flood, I was not alone and could feel behind me the presence of mother Europe. She did not leave me, a European youth; silent, great, nocturnal, she was there. Where are you?
>
> Bozhe, Bozhe, est' li konets odinochestvu? Ved' dazhe togda v tu vesnu, kogda nevskaia sliakot' prosachivalas' skvoz' stertye podoshvy, v tu dvadtast' chetvertuiu vesnu zhizni, kogda romanticheskim onanistom ia brodil sredi molchashchikh pamiatnikov 'serebrianogo veka' ia chital prizyvy vstupat' v riady donorov i dumal o donorakh Budapeshta, dazhe togda bezdenezhnyi i broshennyi v noch' navodneniia na Aptekarskom ostrove, ia byl ne odinok i chuvsvtvoval za svoei spinoi mat'-Evropu, i ona ne ostavliala menia, iunoshu-evropeitsa, i byla ona, nochna, velika i molchala. Gde ty? (21; 19).

The paragraph is stylistically compelling, evoking Andrei Belyi's prose and particularly his novel *Petersburg*. Like the narrator of *Petersburg*, Aksenov's narrator proves tricky, sometimes identified with a character, other times apparently omniscient, seeing with a perspective that crosses over boundaries of time and locale. As in Belyi's work, the prose here is rhythmic and musical: the repetition of "b" in "*Bozhe, Bozhe*," echoes later in the characterization of the lyrical self as "*bezdenezhnyi i broshennyi*." The tripartite syntax used to describe "mother Europe" as "silent, great, nocturnal" (*nochna, velika i molchala*) recalls the use of triple repetitions and other structures of three that Belyi used to ornament his prose, a trick he acknowledged deriving from the prose of Nikolai Gogol.[48]

Aksenov transferred these tokens of the Symbolist heritage to the Soviet capital Moscow and his time.[49] The references to posters calling for blood donors, reminding the protagonist of the "blood donors" of Budapest, help us locate this scene in 1956. The information that this is the twenty-fourth spring of the narrator's life helps us fix the narrator's year of birth as 1932, the same as Aksenov's own. Belyi and Blok employed autobiographical associations and current events, too, but their trajectory ran overall "*a realibus ad realiora*," that is, from contingent or everyday reality to the truer reality art may reveal.[50] Belyi promoted the primacy of creation and artworks as the symbols of human creation over cognition and a bare empirical knowledge of reality.[51] Aksenov revived the Silver Age orientation to spiritual values, but he also, importantly, suggested that people must bring those ideals back down from the heights to critical engagement with the social and political realities of the contemporary time. One of the questions Aksenov seems to be asking by encoding himself and his experience into this novel is whether the connections to the past and the West that seemed so promising to him as a youth possess the power on their own to redeem him, his art and his society. *The Burn* suggests the promise of such ideals continues to be elusive at best and possibly misleading.

The narrator's desire for an abstracted feminine entity ("Where are you?" [*Gde ty*?]) suggests to the reader the image of the Divine Feminine (*Hagia Sophia*).[52] Vladimir Solov'ev had evoked that Divine Feminine as his mysterious friend in the seminal poem "Three Encounters" ("Tri svidaniia," 1898). Blok and Belyi picked up and developed Solov'ev's orientation to the Divine Feminine in works that also reimagined the fantastic and demonic aspects of literary Petersburg for the "Silver Age." Aksenov echoed the ambivalence of Blok's portrayals of the Divine Feminine as a desired "You" (*Ty*) and her alter ego the Stranger (as in the poem "The Stranger" ["Neznakomka"]). The Stranger is a prostitute, an alluring but deceptive hypostasis of the Divine Feminine principle. Aksenov's Alisa, the closest to an ideal figure inspiring the protagonists' longing, is also the most promiscuous with other characters, suggesting the betrayal of ideals the protagonist feels.[53]

The poetic bifurcation of Symbolist ideals—as divine Hagia Sophia on the one hand, and degraded prostitute on the other—could not resonate in Aksenov's time quite the way it didfor the Symbolists. He and readers of his time would have had in mind the denunciation by Stalin's cultural policeman Andrei Zhdanov of poet Anna Akhmatova as "half-nun, half-whore" in 1946, an event widely reported and with unpleasant consequences for the poet.[54] Aksenov explored this poetic binary as symptomatic of the kind of thinking that divides people into "us" and "them," and justifies violence. The protagonist has fallen prey to this kind of pattern. In one segment early in the novel, the doctor protagonist Gennadii Malkolmov and Pat are working at a

U.N. hospital in the Congo where they meet and make the acquaintance of Masha.[55] Masha is Marianne Coulagot, daughter of white Russian émigrés in Geneva. When the mercenaries come to take the wounded from the hospital where the protagonists are working—they get paid for delivering bodies, and the patients are easy pickings—Malkolmov sees a resemblance of one of them to Cheptsov, whose name and role in arresting his mother and beating his friend Sanya he does not yet quite remember. One of the other mercenaries, Jan Strudelmacher, turns out to be another version of an erstwhile companion of the protagonist, Alik Neyarky, usually seen when the protagonist and Pat are together. As Malkolmov struggles to bring past events to mind, he appears to enter a kind of trance: "One more moment, one more moment . . . and I will never be avenged, avenged, avenged . . . that's what I remembered, that's what I remembered, that's what I remembered" (72; 63). The poetic repetition suggests the unresolved plots in his head that interfere with clear perception of the present situation. Masha, on the other hand, springs into action, effectively distracting the mercenaries from their vicious mission with a promise of sexual favors. Malkolmov prays for a "holy insanity, a searing fury," or even just "ordinary courage" to save her, but he feels paralyzed (73; 65). He pictures to himself Masha's gang rape, reflecting, "How you do imagine that at length, how long your wonderful imagination keeps working!" (73; 65).[56]

The protagonist seems dimly aware of his own pathological preoccupation with scenes of sexual oppression. Such acts represent in his mind the violation he feels at once called to avenge and helpless to address. Malkolmov painfully imagines Masha's voluptuous pleasure during the gang rape and wallows in his own consuming shame at having failed to prevent it. Then he realizes how solipsistic his imagination of the situation is. Her reality has nothing to do with him. Masha is the active subject, using her wiles to save the wounded. He becomes stunned as he realizes the extent of her altruism, compassion, and readiness to act. Malkolmov suddenly sees her as she is, rather than how she might figure into his fantasy of saving her (or failing to do so), only once the tension of the scene is released and she returns, upset, but apparently untouched. Malkolmov and Pat subsequently dispatch the mercenaries in a moment of farcically exaggerated cinematic heroism.[57]

Oddly, when the dust settles, Malkolmov and Pat join the mercenaries for fraternal drinking of methyl spirits. What looked like a case of villains and heroes turns out to be another version of the "Men's Club."[58] The "Men's Club" of the title of book 1 and the beer kiosk of the same name refer to a group of drinkers united by chauvinism and alcohol abuse. The odd turn of events suggests the complicity of the "heroes" with the wretched mercenaries, both used by the regime. The fact that Pat and Malkolmov join the band of men here and at the kiosk named the "Men's Club" suggests they can easily be led astray—by the intoxication of alcohol, or by movie plots, or by poetic and mythological patterns.

Aksenov subjected to critical scrutiny the force of erotic longing that propels his young Tolya into a confusing world in which his options for social integration and fulfillment seem slim. Alisa, Lyuda Guly, and Nina all at various times inspire the protagonist to want to save them, suggesting an archetypal plot about the bad father and the lovely daughter whom the young man must steal. That plot animates the romance of Lorenzo and Jessica, united against the wishes of her bad father Shylock, as well as the stories of Jason and Medea, Theseus and Ariadne, and even Jacob and Rachel in the Bible.[59] While not necessarily evoking these subtexts specifically, the invariant nature of the archetype suggests a sort of mythological machine that draws the protagonist into a fixed role with the very agents of oppression and violence he would oppose. In his case, the protagonist can only imagine, in excruciating detail, the abuse of these women: he cannot as an individual hero save them, and his imagination, insofar as it makes the women players in his story, rather than real people or partners, participates in their dehumanization.

Aksenov also examined critically the modernist belief in the power of art to transcend or redeem the reality of his historical moment. The multimedia show "The Battle of Gods and Giants" near the end of book 2 brings together all the players and forces in an artistic effort to transcend current conflicts and merge with the higher order of things. The planned show synthesizes the talents of various protagonists—Pantelei wrote the script, Khvastishchev did the set design, and Sabler wrote the music—into a total work of art. Like the modernists, Aksenov's artists take inspiration from the classics. Typically for Aksenov, the synthesis he imagines is specifically contemporary even as it refers to a classic cultural framework: "We'll unite two generations, the forty-year-olds and the twenty-year-olds, jazz and rock! . . . We shall rebel against Cronus and fill in the gaps in the Pergamum frieze!" (407; 343).[60] The union suggests the fraternity of younger generations: "They were enemies in the Phlegrean marshes on the peninsula of Pellene, yet they became allies in Pergamum . . . In the Pergamum marble, both gods and giants fought together against Cronus" (422; 355).[61] Cronus is the bad father. He also stands for Time that eats away at marble,[62] an artistic material used for monuments for its supposed ability to withstand time. Aksenov, like Pushkin in his poem "Exegi monumentum" and like Horace before them, set verbal art against marble monument as a more flexible and more enduring medium.

Aksenov addressed the desire for and difficulty of transcending or transforming reality in toto. Aksenov's narrator comments later on the eventual fragility of all media: "How much time could we buy in this way? A century, a thousand years? But [Cronus] always gets it back, be it in marble, on canvas, in words, in any medium. In the end he devours it all" (450; 378). Like Cronus, the violent regime of the bad fathers will foil this attempt, shutting down the show. Perhaps the Soviet authorities were not the only problem, however. The show was supposed to involve an eclectic array of "children of the twentieth century," including Stalin, Hitler, Brigitte Bardot, Valentina Tereshkova, Khrushchev, Neil Armstrong, and Solzhenitsyn, projected into the gaps of the eroded and broken Pergamum frieze. This idea of Khvastischev's remained unrealized "for some reason," as the narrator remarks. Because these visual images are juxtaposed in jarring ways, the reader is invited to reflect on the transformation of these figures into artistic signs stripped of historical weight. The random assemblage of these persons together appears patently ridiculous if not simply irresponsible. There is thus a limit to the power of art to transcend history—Aksenov assigns that power to Jesus Christ alone (450; 378). Sabler's suave friend Silvester proves to be a weak link in the artistic assault on specific time and circumstance: he caves in at a crucial moment, when police forces arrive to break up the show of "Gods and Giants." Silvester, like other close friends of protagonists whose names recall "silver" (Argentov, Serebrianikov, Serebro, Zilberantsev), has betrayed his friend, like Judas betrayed Christ. Protagonist Sabler decides, predictably, to drown his sorrows in liquor. Perhaps the whole enterprise, doomed from the start, merely perpetuated a repetitive narrative about the intelligentsia's sense of its own salvific role, betrayed.

CRITIQUE OF THE SOVIET INTELLIGENTSIA

Despite the drama of the betrayal of the protagonists' intentions with "The Battle of Gods and Giants," Aksenov's use of the epithet "The Victim" for the protagonist in book 3 seems highly ironic. It suggests a mythological narrative about trauma and sacrifice associated with the Russian author[63] and with the intelligentsia as a class. Isaiah Berlin described the Russian intelligentsia's understanding of itself as similar to "a secular priesthood, devoted to the spreading of a specific attitude to life, something like a gospel." Historian Sheila Fitzpatrick characterized the intelligentsia as "a classless group united by moral concern for the betterment of society, the capacity for 'critical thought' and, in particular, a critical, semi-oppositionist attitude toward the regime."[64] On the one hand, Aksenov did revive in *The Burn* the idea of spiritual values and social service these descriptions of the Russian intelligentsia reflect. However, he undercut the mythology of martyrdom and cast doubt on the moral purityof his peers, even as he called out the sins of their fathers.

Aksenov reflected directly on his critical treatment of the mythology of the Russian intelligentisa at the beginning of book 2. As Russians, his authorial narrator sardonically notes, "What we like is some heavy, masochistic problem . . . That is what we need, and it is not our fault." He goes on to comment skeptically on his own mouthing of such generalizations:

> Not our fault? Really? But who let the genie out of the bottle, who cut themselves off from the people, who groveled before the people, who grew fat on the backs of the people, who let the Tatars into the city, invited the Varangians to come and rule over them, licked the boots of Europe, isolated themselves from Europe, struggled madly against the government, submitted obediently to dim-witted dictators? We did all that—we, the Russian intelligentsia. (221; 189)

As we know from the climax of the Congo scenes, the protagonist himself seems in thrall to images of innocence, violation, heroism, and vengeance that he has assimilated and made his own. In light of this, the recurring images in book 3 of the Dinosaur with the face of a Ryazan peasant (467, 492, 518; 391, 411, 433)[65] and Cheptsov on the surveillance screen (474, 489, 505; 397, 409, 423), seem particularly significant. They appear to represent projections of the two entities between which members of the Russian intelligentsia typically see themselves: the dumb and submissive but massive people on the one hand, and the maliciously watchful eye of the regime on the other. The ubiquity of these figures in book 3, in which they turn up in the Parisian landscape and in the English countryside as well as in the Russian capital, speak to the persistence of mythologies and habits of thinking that continue to infect the mind of the *intelligent* even in emigration and during the freest flights of fancy. The presence of these figures in this mental landscape suggests that the protagonist, like others of his class, feels haunted by images of the people and the regime he has himself created or perpetuated.

Aksenov made explicit here the mythological complex associated with the character of the beloved. His protagonist muses, "My love, my sweetness—Russia, Alisa, Moscow! I leaned my back against the garbage can" (494; 413). On the one hand, the passage suggests that the spiritual meaning associated with the names "Russia, Alisa, Moscow" has been discarded like so much trash by a society that has not properly valued them. On the other hand, it implies that the protagonist and his peers need to separate reality from myth. This seems particularly tricky in book 3 of *The Burn*. The protagonist in this portion of the novel displays a disturbing tendency to plunge himself into "garbage," which based on earlier scenes might represent his trashy lifestyle or which could in these later sections refer to the cast-off remnants of his culture's mythologized beliefs. Tellingly, Alisa appears just before this to be a "Siren" to the protagonist's Odysseus (493–94; 412–13). However, neither the revelation of Alisa as nefarious temptress and deceiver, nor the open-hearted acceptance of her as his ideal love and inspiration, proves to be a viable solution. Both faces of the myth of the feminine obscure the real lover and person. The same point applies, mutatis mutandis, to the country Russia and the city Moscow.

Other myths portrayed in this final book seem relevant for a critique of successful Soviet writers and the Soviet intelligentsia more generally. The myth of the "heart of Russia, still untouched by corruption" brings to mind the popular trend of Village Prose in Soviet letters (468, 502; 392, 420). Ostensibly critical of the regime, yet dangerously close to chauvinistic ideas the regime promoted, Village Prose played on fixed ideas about a purer Russian past and provincial core.[66] Aksenov's narrator contemplates the "eternal pigs" wallowing in their "eternal puddle" and the "eternal chickens" scratching in the "eternal dust" (504; 422): such repetition is parodic rather than seriously incantatory. The protagonist's father Apollinary Bokov encourages the protagonist not to be "like Solzhenitsyn" and count every bullet, suggesting the resignation or resentment of criticism associated with the more conformist wing of Village Prose. These scenes connect loosely to an actual car trip Aksenov took with his father to the Ryazan district. Aksenov, like his protagonist, combined Russian peasant roots from his father's side of the family with the Jewish ethnicity of his mother, a heritage he foregrounded briefly in the book (294–97; 249–52). The theme of Jewish identity was taboo in official print, and the tension of a "native" Russian identity with no place for Jews formed part of the unspoken subtext of Village Prose.[67] Merely to raise these issues was to dissent from official Soviet discourse. Aksenov evoked the nostalgic dream of this type of Russian nativist myth:

> Dad, tell me how beautiful this church was when you were a boy. After all, what is there left of your childhood if not this church, which shone with its azure-blue dome, its gilded crosses and stars, when they brought you here as a little boy under the fresh young greenery to celebrate Pentecost? Tell me about the little shirt you wore, embroidered with rooster, and about the smell of your hair that your mother, Avdotya, had anointed with sunflower-seed oil. (512; 428).

As opposed to this mythical native Russian spirituality, Aksenov's protagonist finds that the peasants are just as likely as urban dwellers to pitch in together for a drink. Immoderate consumption of food and piles of consumer goods (*shirpotreb*) (514; 430) have replaced the purer spiritual values he sought.

The protagonist seeks and finds the "underground inhabitant of Holy Russia" (*podzemnyi zhitel' Rusi*), but that person refuses to come out into the world (508–9; 425–26). Later, the "ancient, righteous-looking old man" with "Homeric" eyes whom the narrator finds in the store fails to impart truth. Instead he spews a venomous mixture of official clichés:

> Greetings . . . We have had big successes on the root-crop front. Tell the St. Petersburg proletariat to hold on, and we won't let them die of hunger. Death to the enemies of the Revolution! . . . There have been a lot of cattle abortions in the past five-year plan, a direct result of the consequences of arrant Trotskyism. . . . I say to her, "No good saying boo-hoo; get your stuff together and hand it over or we'll drag you all out onto the village threshing floor, where our enemies are lying already like so many sheep with their throats cut." Comrade Shvernik decreed that I should personally be paid seventeen rubles a month for unmasking the cult of personality, and no matter how hard the enemy attacks, we won't retreat a single step from the commanding heights! (514–15; 430–31)

This old man, like Tolya's geometry teacher in Magadan (282; 240), regurgitates formulas of State propaganda, hard bits of ossified language redolent with suggestions of terrible violence and devoid of any further referential sense in his garbled repetition. This language dehumanizes the speaker like its previous use dehumanized the victims his speech obliquely recalls.

Aksenov's use of language proves key to his artistry and his dissident vision. Aksenov exposed people, their illusions and strategies for getting by through clichés and cultural references. At its worst, language is revealed to be an integral part of a system of violence and domination. Aksenov likewise showed that language can be the medium of humanizing exchange, of dialogue. In a rare quiet conversation between the protagonist and Pat, the characters compare their feelings for their respective countries, revealing more about their authentic selves through dialogically exposed differences than they do in all the scenes of shared action and adventure. The protagonist tries to pin Pat down: "But all joking aside, this protoplasm of yours consists of human beings, of individual personalities, and each one of them has an intellect, a soul, a longing for God." Pat replies with a friendly barb: "Personality? Listen, you miscarried offspring of Stalinism, the only person who can claim to have a personality is the guy who manages to escape. Once you merge with a political or an anti-political system, you become a producer or a consumer, a guardian or a destroyer . . ." The protagonist is confused and saddened to find that his friend lacks the spiritual belief toward which he aspires, but the scene reveals their precious capacity to speak honestly with one another (123–24; 107–8). Similarly, protagonist Malkolmov courts Masha during some quiet time in the Congo, and their conversation underscores differences among émigré Russians and Soviet Russians. Malkolmov manages to convince Masha that her family's conception of the Soviet "Reds" is not adequate. He demonstrates, with the recording of a song by Soviet bard Bulat Okudzhava that moves Masha to tears, that life and culture continue in the Soviet Union (65; 58). The scene models another type of eros based not on ideals, but on real human difference. These prosaic moments show the protagonists' ability to express their particular reality and begin to learn about their interlocutor's experience. They do not tend to symbolic unity or mystical fulfillment. Stripped of mythologized plots and clichéd roles, the dialogue of characters in these scenes exemplifies the possibility of individual subject positions that can grow and develop through unfettered and down-to-earth human communication.

Thus, this prosaic vision suggests the human and moral complement from a Bakhtinian perspective to the crazy carnivalized life people have been living.[68] Although Aksenov appealed to a Christian framework to articulate an ethical, rather than aesthetic vision of transcending violence through forgiveness (an idea that resonates with his mother's humanistic message), Aksenov kept the focus of representation on the earth. A flight into the stratosphere, contemplated at the end, only leads to another encounter with Cheptsov (524; 439). Even the "Third Model" can only be glimpsed obscurely in terms of what a human can know. After joking about an "old gray man with a big white beard and kind green eyes," the priest initiates the protagonist into the concept of the "third model." Everyone needs God, he insists, and "We always have before us two models for comparison: a thing or an idea as the first model, and then a thing or an idea for comparison with it. . . . But we only seek a third model; agonizingly, and so far without results, we try to create a third model and through it to see the face of God." The theological discussion of the "Third Model" between the protagonist and the priest occurs at almost the exact midpoint of the book (265–68; 227–29). This placement suggests a sacred and ineffable center around which the endless infernal grotesques whirl, as in an illuminated medieval manuscript with an unreadable central text. Aksenov did not articulate sacred theses in a dogmatic way: his language demonstrated the possibility of rising above the infernal representations, but in this book redemption occurs only at the level of prosaic human conversation.[69]

Thus, Aksenov's use of language in *The Burn* resists both the violent uses of it by the regime and the mythological and ideal pretensions that infect the self-image and expression of the Russian intelligentsia. Critics and scholars have long appreciated Aksenov's innovative use of popular and contemporary voices alongside references to consecrated literature.[70] Aksenov's artistic strength—and the difficulty of translating his works—comes from his keen ear for the heterogeneous voices of contemporary Soviet society. Not only does this literary sensibility range significantly outside the realm of elite cultural references, it shows Aksenov's acute sensitivity to his historical moment. Aksenov's vision is both wide-ranging and specific, stretching across a very broad late Soviet canvas, from Magadan to Moscow, encompassing people from varying walks of life, acknowledging the historical trauma that unites them as Soviet people in this era. It has been possible to articulate

Aksenov's achievement in general terms. Iurii Maltsev, for example, in one of the earliest published reviews, compared *The Burn* to the work of Turgenev and Chekhov: one reads them to know what Russia was like in the middle and end of the nineteenth century, and one reads *The Burn* for a similarly precise artistic portrayal of the spirit of the age.[71] American scholar D. Barton Johnson similarly evaluated *The Burn* as Aksenov's chef d'oeuvre, "certainly the most eloquent description and diagnosis of the ups, downs, and ultimate demise of the liberal hopes of his generation during the Brezhnev years."[72] However, the specificity of Aksenov's portrayal of Soviet society at this time, including popular and literary cultural references, have made the work difficult for readers for whom those references are not obvious. This includes the Western reader and indeed most Russian readers today. The network of literary references that *are* more broadly recognizable would theoretically make possible a literary reading that would synthesize the work into a translatable whole, as a late modern exemplar of the Gogolian line in Russian literature, a grotesque social satire.[73]

ON THE CUSP OF A NEW ERA? DILEMMAS OF THE SAMIZDAT NOVEL

The problem with attempting such a comprehensive literary interpretion of *The Burn* has to do with the immediacy of the political and moral urgency addressed in the novel and Aksenov's choice not to adopt any comfortable distance from it. Aksenov's novel represented a burning response to specific events and persons of his highly politicized time. That urgency seems at odds with the forward-looking temporality of the avant-garde as Pierre Bourdieu described it, where the avant-garde work comes out of the tensions of a highly restricted field of artistic production and can be understood and appreciated by a wider audience only after time had passed.[74] Aksenov was not in that sense an "avant-garde" writer: he wrote for a mass audience as an official writer, and there existed no coherent restricted field or audience from and for which he was working in *The Burn*. The samizdat field at the time he wrote it, in the early 1970s, did not yet have its own internal, restricted, artistic logic.[75]

The Burn proves to be a curious case for a socio-literary analysis in part because in it Aksenov exposes for critical scrutiny his own *habitus*, his position as writer established within the social order.[76] Aksenov laid bare in the novel those aspects of his life and experience that had previously in his work been discreetly covered over. Notably, he treated his early experience in Siberian Magadan with parents who were political prisoners. He also held up for consideration the wild bohemian lifestyle in which he and other elite creative intelligentsia indulged as escape and compensation for their position with the State. The exposure of his past and formation pleased many of his more intellectual readers. It corresponded well to established dissident narratives about the trauma of the experience of Stalin's regime. Dissident authorities Vladimir Maksimov, Eduard Kuznetsov and Natalia Gorbanevskaia invoked the near universal respect for Aksenov as a person, and expressed appreciation for the Magadan scenes in his book, which feelingly evoked a common human core. However, having singled out the Magadan scenes for praise, all expressed reservations about *The Burn* overall.[77] Literary scholar Anatolii Zverev similarly characterized Aksenov as exceedingly honest, and expressed his positive judgment of the episodes set in Magadan as perhaps the best of what he wrote.[78] Aksenov's exposure of the other side of things, of the corruption and complicity of elite creative intelligentsia, proved harder to swallow: Zverev decried the incessant immaturity of all these "Apollinarevichs" who never fail to take the regime's bait and show their Soviet mentality through their petty bohemianism and frustrated rage. One can imagine how both the experimental flourishes and the representationof such behavior might have proved difficult for Aksenov's readers more generally because of the alienating experimental representation of an elite lifestyle they did not enjoy. The huge readership that had invested in Aksenov as "their own," spokesperson of their generation, might well have felt betrayed.[79]

Aksenov's compulsion to expose the regime would be comprehensible to lots of readers. However, unlike Solzhenitsyn, he did not take up the mantle of unadulterated "truth"; rather, like Siniavskii, Aksenov felt himself to be a product and part of the system he critiqued. His book attempted an avant-garde deconstruction of that Soviet subjectivity through the montage of material that made up the contemporary Soviet popular and literary imagination: like Witold Gombrowicz, Aksenov exposed the uncomfortable and unattractive perpetual adolescence to which his country consigned him and others like him, but for which those infantilized intellectuals also bore responsibility.[80] We might think of this as a cracked-mirror reflection of the romantic "Youth" Aksenov earlier portrayed.

If Aksenov's character Dmitrii in *Ticket to the Stars* resembles Flaubert's Frédéric Moreau as a youthful character embarking on adult life who refuses the illusions of established social trajectories, then Aksenov by contrast seems rather old at the time he writes *The Burn*. Aksenov seems "old" in the social sense Bourdieu discusses, as a writer who has already achieved great success, and therefore his rejection of the *illusio* of Soviet society in favor of the purer artifice of innovative literature, seems incongruous.[81] In part because Aksenov makes his "age" on the field, his position as an established Soviet writer, the object of representation in his protagonists, a conflict arises between Aksenov's success and the expected social "age" of an avant-garde writer.

More than the critical way he portrayed his generation and the rough treatment he gives to myths of the intelligentsia, however, *The Burn* simply did not seem sufficiently literary, that is, adequately distanced from real contemporary events and people, and divorced from institutional life and what Bourdieu would call the field of large-scale cultural production.[82] Aksenov, cognizant of his established status, used his elevated social position in two conflicting ways in *The Burn*. On the one hand, he offered a critical portrait of elite intelligentsia as part of his reaction against the system and his bid for dissident legitimacy. On the other hand, he tried to leverage his position as a leader in the Soviet literary field to remake the literary field with his samizdat publications. The command of the literary field to which he aspired (a command he would have enjoyed in official Soviet letters if popularity with readers could have given him real clout in the system), corresponds, I would argue, to the grand perspective sweeping from Siberia to the Baltic Sea and across all social classes and categories in *The Burn*.[83]

Aksenov's attempt to reconfigure the field can be seen in his work as lead editor on another samizdat project that appeared just before *The Burn*, the *Metropol* anthology. The anthology combined officially published writers and those who wrote for samizdat. It brought an American writer, John Updike, into the mix with Soviet Russian authors. The anthology was not particularly well received or resonant.[84] Arguably, it lacked literary focus and motivation. Although the authors did not emphasize political issues (and indeed, according to Kevin Klose, the editors avoided including Lev Kopelev and other authors known for their dissident views), the aim was to force a confrontation with the authorities. The public and spectacular nature of the edition can be seen in the format of the eight samizdat copies they produced, large typesetters' sheets with four pages affixed to each side, used for display in the event launching the anthology, rather than for regular samizdat circulation. Aksenov worked with Ardis publishers in the United States after the public presentation of the Russian text on January 18, 1979, to launch a print edition in April of that year. The English edition, not coincidentally, features a bird's-eye view of Red Square with a crowd of people, and it describes the collection as the one that caused a "celebrated clash between artists and government."[85]

Thus, Aksenov did not really stop working with a view toward the field of large-scale cultural production even when he turned to samizdat: he hoped that the literary force of his work as author and editor would impact that broad field through the international market. Bourdieu's method can be helpful for showing the difference between this large-scale field of cultural production and the restricted field of cultural production on which others worked as the samizdat field developed. According to Bourdieu, the symbolic capital of art on the field of restricted cultural production comes from a negation of the forces of the larger field, which are predominantly economic. In the late Soviet case, they were mainly political. Although Aksenov and his fellow writers mounted a *literary* rather than a political challenge to Soviet censorship and cultural institutions, that literary challenge had obvious public resonance and could be framed easily in political terms. Aksenov probably did not expect any direct profit from the venture, but he did plan to get high-profile international publicity: he wrote to Carl Proffer at Ardis to offer them the rights to Russian and English editions, saying he expected Gallimard or L'Édition Stock to do a French edition. This letter shows also that the "negotiations" with Soviet authorities from which nothing was expected to come were part of the strategic game designed to highlight the intransigence of Soviet institutions.[86] The boldness of Aksenov's bid to reconfigure the field of Soviet letters with his samizdat work can be understood in the context of a revolutionary state, marked by the discontinuities of political revolution, Stalininst authoritarianism, and the dethroning of Stalin and partial dismantling of the Gulag system under Khrushchev. Aksenov dreamed of accomplishing that kind of dramatic restructuring of the consciousness—if not the official institutions, of his readers. In this way, his ambition seems classically avant-garde. One of the ways we might use Bourdieu's method is to juxtapose the "real" relation of author and work to the social field against the ideology of art represented in the work or its reception. The circumstances of production and circulation of the work can be evaluated alongside the ideology promoted within the work.

In the case of *The Burn*, Aksenov's portrayal of a broad community of heterogeneous voices spanning political boundaries proves to be somewhat at odds with Aksenov's approach to his real community of readers. For if Aksenov's novel suggests his characters may ideally become more authentic through dialogic interaction with one another, he might through the samizdat work have more flexibly supported such dialogue. Samizdat offered the potential for readers to weigh in on the work, by choosing to circulate it if they wished, adding their own hands and voices and endorsement to it. Aksenov relied even in the case of this uncensored work almost exclusively on an institutional model of diffusion, counting on the fact that Soviet print outlets could be replaced by foreign, especially American, ones.[87] As a result, *The Burn*, a grand and massive novel, made weighty demands on Soviet readers to both address burning issues now and to read his portrait of late Soviet society in the context of the great time of acknowledged classics like Bulgakov's *Master and Margarita*, Gogol's *Dead Souls*, and Dante's *Divine Comedy*. This confusion of temporalities underscores some dilemmas of samizdat cultural production.

Chapter Three

Bitov's *Pushkin House*: Deconstructing the Late Soviet Subject

It's time for you to know: I'm also a
contemporary.
—Osip Mandelshtam

ANDREI BITOV began his writing career in official Soviet letters as a celebrated author of Young Prose like fellow author Vasilii Aksenov. Bitov took his own dissident turn early when he began his uncensored novel, *Pushkin House* (*Pushkinskii dom*), a work he described as his literary rebellion.[1] Bitov treated the same major taboo themes as Aksenov: the Stalinist camps, excessive drinking in Soviet society, the sex people were engaging in promiscuously but not discussing in print, and the problem of antisemitism after Stalin. Bitov, like Aksenov, directed his critique at his generation and people around him in Soviet society at least as much as he indicted the regime. However, these two samizdat novels could hardly be more different. Bitov, a Leningrad writer, does not treat actual people and events associated with power in Moscow the way Aksenov does. Bitov's novel refracts, rather than reflects, the social mood and problems of its time. In short, *Pushkin House* seems much more "literary": Bitov's work resembles the more obviously novelistic patterns of the bildungsroman in its fictional representation of the life and education of a young man.[2] *Pushkin House* also features a more ironic tone with a narrator whose playful interventions into the plot make for an emotional tenor and message that are harder to grasp than the unmistakeable (and justifiable) pain and anger of Aksenov's traumatized protagonists. Bitov did not write his work for a wide audience.

Thus, although Bitov began *Pushkin House* (written 1964–71) several years before Aksenov began *The Burn*, Bitov's novel seems like a more developed example of dissident autonomy. We can correlate the more literary and obviously artificial character of Bitov's novel to autonomy as Bourdieu described it. However, capturing the specific character of this literary autonomy as a projection of the late Soviet field requires finer analysis. As we saw in the case of Aksenov's novel, we can perform Bourdieu's critical juxtaposition of belief and reality by considering the idea of autonomy represented in the work alongside the reality of the work's production and circulation. Although Bitov's novel presents itself as a more literary and "autonomous" work than Aksenov's, it also did not circulate exclusively in the "free" literary system of samizdat. Instead, Bitov approached the deployment of his novel as a sort of strategic game that helped cover his tracks with the authorities, and that made readers question the boundary between official and dissident literature and between literature and life. Bitov in his own way critiqued both official culture and the culture of his liberal and dissident peers with this novel. He challenged both sides in part by subverting expectations and requirements of both milieus, deploying the work in a variety of forms and formats, as we shall see.

Like Aksenov, Bitov refused the official *illusio* of Soviet unity and post-Stalin social reform, turning from that falsehood toward the acknowledged illusion of art. However, unlike Aksenov, Bitov did not establish the relationship of the art of his novel to current events and social debates so directly. Because Bitov expressed his resistance in a more strictly literary and apparently disengaged mode, his novel *Pushkin House* garnered appreciation among critics later as one of the first "postmodern" works in late Soviet literature.[3] "Postmodern" in the context of Russian critical discourse meant an ideological autonomy roughly analogous to the autonomy from economic concerns Bourdieu described in modern Western literature.[4] Many critics identified Bitov as one of the first authors to open up a new, restricted field of literary production associated with Leningrad samizdat.[5]

If Aksenov's *The Burn* can be situated in the Gogolian tradition of Russian literature as channeled through Andrei Belyi, then Bitov's *Pushkin House* exemplifies the free and playful spirit associated with Pushkin, in part as transmitted through Nabokov. Nevertheless, this autonomy, as Bourdieu demonstrated, and contrary to much postmodern discourse, can be related to moral and social questions particular to the post-Stalin era in the Soviet Union. Bitov took a step back from official literary forms and constraints in order to critique what was wrong with his generation.[6] With his intensive investigation of the nature of authorship and subjectivity in *Pushkin House*, Bitov worked on the foundations of society: his vision of individual self-realization in the novel depended on the relation of the individual to others around him, an image of self and other that Bitov worked out through engagement with the cultural tradition. Bitov's mentor Lidiia Ginzburg possessed a strong sense of the connection between literature and history. Literary art for her, as for Bitov, provided space to reflect on historical experience and develop—or recover—the image of the human being in the twentieth century.[7]

Aksenov's novel showed the discontinuity of the late Soviet cultural field implicitly, in part through the confused temporality of repressed trauma coming to the surface within the book. That theme resonates with the break in cultural continuity occasioned by Stalin's policies. This break called forth eclectic referents to repressed modernist works. Aksenov and Bitov in their uncensored novels both employed the kind of dense and eclectic intertextuality Laurent Jenny describe as symptomatic of a society undergoing crisis and renewal.[8] The samizdat field of cultural production, having emerged alongside the official one, supported signs of this cultural disjointedness as long-repressed works resurfaced and helped spark new uncensored literature reflecting the lost heritage. The conflict between Aksenov's established social position and his avant-garde aspirations in *The Burn* speaks to the difficulties of working with this discontinuity. Bitov, by contrast, took on the cultural break as a theme—treated variously in terms of "disorientation" and living "interruptedly"—and a strategy. This chapter will examine how Bitov set up a seeming whole in order to confront the reader with discontinuity on a variety of levels in his uncensored work *Pushkin House*.

Aksenov's novel exemplified his own type of avant-garde style and intention—according to him, the avant-garde had roots in folklore, and it was therefore a more popular form. Aksenov also aimed to use the avant-garde like Maiakovskii and the Futurists did, for a "slap in the face of public taste," a challenge to readers from the intelligentsia whose idea of themselves involved a gratifying myth about their role. Bitov, too, aimed to provoke his intellectual readers to separate seeming freedom and ersatz intellectual labor from real independence. His method can be described as avant-garde in its closeness to the Formalist emphasis on literary art as a process of "making strange" (*ostranenie*):[9] Bitov aimed to cultivate among readers a capacity for conceptual analysis that destroys conventionalized perception through a kind of Cubist discontinuity. Bitov expressed the theme of temporal discontinuity in part by formally constructing a disjointed portrait of his protagonist Lyova, whose pieces must be conceptually synthesized by the active reader in a process that cultivates his or her own critical and creative capacities.

In this chapter, I will look closely at how Bitov put together his portrait of Lyova, shattering the smug sense of self Lyova represents with a critical evaluation of what Bourdieu calls the *habitus*, that is, the social positon and acculturated habits, of the late Soviet intellectual. Bitov drew on his own background, but his portrayal proves to be more conceptual than Aksenov's autobiographical representation of self in the protagonists of *The Burn*. I analyze Bitov's method with reference to Tolstoy's representation of contradictions in the forces shaping a personality. Bitov updated Tolstoy's realist techniques for his own time with a neo-avant-garde Cubist construction that drew on Formalist and romantic sources in an intentionally eclectic way. Bitov's dismantling of a seeming whole into fragmented parts—in the character Lyova and in the text of the novel—echoes in the deployment of the novel into pieces that straddle the line between official and unofficial, samizdat and tamizdat, and Soviet and post-Soviet publications. I will consider the means and goals of Bitov's deconstruction of the physical whole of the work. Toward the end of the chapter I return to passages of the novel that illustrate the way discontinuity in the subject and in the work underpin a dissident conception of a post-totalitarian subjectivity and society.

SHATTERING THE UNITY OF THE SELF: LYOVA'S CONTRADICTIONS

Bitov wrote his uncensored novel from the position of a person formed by that society: in *Pushkin House*, Bitov satirized his own generation and even his own persona as liberal Soviet author. Bitov directed a critical gaze on his alter ego Lyova, a protagonist whose biographical details, including being born in 1937, correspond to Bitov's own.[10] The match is not exact, of course: Bitov's authorial narrator retains distance from this protagonist, often commenting ironically on Lyova's experiences and character. In addition, Bitov's narrator, like Pushkin's authorial narrator in *Eugene Onegin*, discusses and openly manipulates the construction of the artistic work in which the protagonist appears. Bitov's literary rebellion entailed a critical look at the construction of Soviet character through an analytic deconstruction of protagonist Lyova Odoevtsev.

Bitov treated the formation of the late Soviet subject in a highly unorthodox way. Lyova appears far from your run-of-the-mill positive Soviet hero. That official type of hero has been shaped by progressive history and his consciousness of that history's forward march. He or she aims to be an effective agent of action for the common good. We usually find the positive Soviet hero in a highly coherent and conventional realist narrative. By contrast, Bitov set up Lyova as a dubious figure, encouraging a critical perspective by means of obtrusive commentary by the narrator and artful construction of the narrative. As a result, we see Lyova broken down analytically, with the contradictions that animate him exposed. Bitov found in Leo Tolstoy's psychological realism surprisingly appropriate means for this purpose. In *Pushkin House*, Bitov used Tolstoy, an author central to the official Soviet realist canon, to subvert official Soviet culture from the inside.

Bitov alluded to the school canon of literature in the novel's section headings. He referred to a number of classic works and authors from the nineteenth century literary tradition in Russia. The title of section 1, "Fathers and Sons" ("Ottsy i deti"), evokes Ivan Turgenev's 1862 novel of the same name. Section 2, "A Hero of Our Time" ("Geroi nashego vremeni"), establishes a point of reference in Mikhail Lermontov's novel *A Hero of Our Time* from 1839–41. The title of section 3, "The Humble Horseman" ("Bednyi vsadnik"), conflates the title of Pushkin's famous poem *The Bronze Horseman* (*Mednyi vsadnik*, 1833) with that of Fyodor Dostoevsky's *Poor People* (*Bednye liudi*, 1846). Bitov did not accord any work by Tolstoy such prominence. Nevertheless, Tolstoy's work provides a crucial subtext for *Pushkin House*. Bitov introduced this subtext more subtly: the narrator mentions Tolstoy's trilogy *Childhood*, *Adolescence*, and *Youth* early on as a sort of template for telling Lyova's story (18–19; 26). The trilogy suggests a bildungsroman, although in the case of Lyova we witness not so much the organic growth and development of the hero as the analytic diagnosis and deconstruction of him as a subject.

The Tolstoyan subtext supports the idea that Bitov projected himself into the prose, in order to turn his critical gaze on the formation of character in his generation. Lyova's name, Lev Nikolaevich Odoevtsev, echoes Tolstoy's first name and patronymic, a fact the narrator remarks (57; 64). Lyova's aristocratic origins recall Tolstoy's. Like Tolstoy's protagonist Levin in *Anna Karenina*, Lyova appears to be a limited sort of projection of the author into the text. As noted, Bitov shares a birthdate with Lyova, and both author and protagonist were born in Leningrad and work in literature. Significantly, Lyova as we see him in the novel is not a creative writer: he is Bitov without the literary talent, as Levin is for Tolstoy. Bitov discusses the apparent closeness of the character and the author in the text: "It's merely an optical illusion that [the author] is bringing the hero close to him. The edges of the chasm come closer together, but the chasm itself grows deeper" (222; 227). That "chasm" will prove to be of cardinal importance because the disjunction makes possible a critical examination of Lyova's character and his own authorship.

Bitov's character analysis in *Pushkin House* resonates to a significant degree with the method his mentor Lidiia Ginzburg described as Tolstoy's psychological realism.[11] Ginzburg, who wrote about Tolstoy's literary art in detail, regarded it as the culmination of the tradition of psychological prose in the nineteenth century. She explained the dynamism of Tolstoyan characters in terms of the multiple causal conditions they carry within themselves, conditions that interact with concrete circumstances in the context of various events. Because the origins of causal conditions are multiple, their action in any given circumstance inevitably involves contradictions.[12] Such contradictions form the various disjointed facets of Lyova's portrait. Along with contradictions, other unforeseen elements—the contingent and the accidental—produce an unprecedented literary evocation of "life" in Tolstoy's prose.[13]

Ginzburg appears to be a particularly important figure for understanding Bitov's project. She created a living link back to the work of the Russian Formalists with whom she had studied. Ginzburg adhered in much of her writing to the concept of literary evolution famously elaborated by her teacher Iurii Tynianov. According to this understanding, writers invent new forms and adapt established genres in response to changing historical conditions. Ginzburg wrote about the contemporary historical conditions for prose as she saw them. The lack of conflict in literary characters signaled the near-extinction of the intellectual hero.[14] Ginzburg argued that literature could be reanimated by an author's "direct conversation about life."[15] She modeled such an approach in her own memoirs and stories, which illuminated the Soviet cultural life she knew from the 1920s and later.[16] Ginzburg regarded herself and her generation of Russian intelligentsia with critical penetration. She wrote about the complex interaction of fundamental laws of human behavior, emotional facts, and the context of the Stalinist 1930s in order to explain the social mechanisms determining the life of the Soviet intelligentsia at that time, summarizing the characteristics of that generation unsentimentally in terms of "accommodation, justification, and indifference." Ginzburg asserted unequivocally: "No one escaped unscathed."[17] Thus, according to Ginzburg, there existed a special imperative to work on the human visage of Soviet intelligentsia after Stalin. Bitov's chatty narrator affects a light and ironic tone reminiscent of Pushkin's authorial narrator in *Eugene Onegin*. However, seen in context, this "direct conversation" implies the moral seriousness of Tolstoy's prose translated for the needs of Bitov's late Soviet time: Bitov recognized the crucial imperative to rehumanize his age, to revitalize the relationship between the individual and his time, to make it a constructive and creative one.

Bitov made his mark initially as a writer of short stories with strong psychological interest, and thus he entered Tolstoy's domain.[18] Ginzburg's analysis of Tolstoy's technique provides useful clues for understanding what Bitov does with the figure of Lyova. "Tolstoy's psychological analysis," she noted, was "a dissection of the infinitely differentiated conditionality of behavior."[19] Tolstoy presented a complex dynamic of inner and external forces proceeding from the "most general historical and social definitions, including all that is derived from them, to the infinitesimally minute influences that govern [an individual's] behavior. These impulses come from both the individual's inner nature and his external material surroundings."[20] As we shall see, Bitov devoted a considerable amount of the narrator's commentary within the novel to an analysis of the various factors conditioning Lyova's behavior.

Tolstoy occupied a central place in the Socialist Realist canon, but Bitov's appropriation of Tolstoy's psychological techniques resisted the constraints of official realism. Bitov recovered aspects of Tolstoy's writing that had been elided or downplayed in the Soviet era. Vladimir Lavrov remarked upon Bitov's discussion of shame as a topic evocative of a Tolstoyan spiritual dialectic not seen in Socialist Realism.[21] Bitov's narrator treats "shame" specifically with reference to intellectual subjects: "It's like being on a bus when you've got a couple of fellows bouncing ideas off one another, carrying on a loud 'intelligent' conversation and throwing big words around as though the bus were empty. . . . Frightfully shameful and awkward" (223; 228). Bitov juxtaposed this consideration of shame to a discussion of Tolstoy as author. Shame represents no less than the fundamental sense of self possessed by the intellectual hero. The sense of shame may express the consciousness of life not coinciding with art, or more generally of life not coinciding with the impulse to shape life to higher ends. Lyova possesses this sense of himself not coinciding with his ideals. His ability to feel shame marks him as a self-conscious and potentially creative intellectual hero. "It's awkward having a loud 'intelligent' conversation on the bus," the narrator notes, adding "Lyova is just the kind to get carried away and blurt out something inappropriate. Although, to his credit, I can add that he blushes easily" (224; 228). This "Tolstoyan" ability to feel self-conscious shame shows that Lyova has moral potential and helps distinguish him as an intellectual hero.

Indeed, Bitov aimed to resuscitate the classics from a deadened tradition as he revived the intellectual hero. He described the tension at the heart of the novel in these terms: "*Pushkin House* was born in large measure out of the struggle between my passion for literature and the rot in the school curriculum."[22] A clever image representing the domestication of Russian literary giants within a totalitarian world can be found in Vladimir Nabokov's *Invitation to a Beheading*, in which the job of the protagonist Cincinnatus consists of crafting literary dolls for schoolchildren: a little hairy Pushkin, a rat-like Gogol, an old Tolstoy, and Dobroliubov in glasses.[23] Bitov in *Pushkin House* identified and resisted precisely the kind of infantilizing distortion of Russian literature in Soviet institutions that Nabokov parodied. Bitov referred indirectly in the text of the novel to his sympathy with Nabokov. Bitov opened his "Prologue," entitled "What Is to Be Done?" with an epigraph from the beginning of Nikolai Chernyshevskii's eponymous novel of 1863.[24] Chernyshevskii does not figure among the literary greats Bitov seeks to bring back to cultural life. However, Nabokov parodied Chernyshevskii's wooden, ideological literature in his novel *The Gift*: Bitov claimed to have read Nabokov's *The Gift* and *Invitation to a Beheading* only when *Pushkin House* was three quarters completed, and indeed the subtitle of the "Prologue," "A Chapter Written after the Rest," helps place the reference within this later time frame.[25] Given Bitov's obvious sympathy for his Nabokovian subtext, we expect Bitov to use Chernyshevsky's programmatic novel as a foil for his own more substantial artistic engagement with the question "What is to be done?" Like Nabokov, Bitov struggled to free literature from the service of ready-made political goals and easily assimilated messages.

Bitov does not object to the classic works of Pushkin, Lermontov, Turgenev, and Dostoevsky as such. He does, however, resist the way they have been packaged by Soviet education:

> In *Pushkin House* I wanted to go over not so much the history of Russian literature as simply the school curriculum of literature, which wore me out in my schooldays. And not just because they taught us literature badly, but also because they were all the time explaining real things in terms of some kind of unreal causes. It turned out that all of previous history arose and moved exactly to this point, and that, apparently, irritated even a child's consciousness.[26]

Bitov deplored the crude teleology of Soviet ideological explanations and the smug hubris of its presentist orientation. Such an ideology rewarded adherents with a sense of their own importance, a self-satisfaction that came at the expense of an ability to apprehend "reality." Bitov illustrated the disastrous consequences of this type of education in the character of Lyova.

Lyova is a figure both individual and representative, based on literary models and generational specificities.[27] Bitov's narrator explores the determination and freedom of such a figure through an ironic treatment of the canonical Socialist Realist notion of "type."[28] Bitov called Lyova a "typical" character. The narrator playfully compares Lyova to Chernyshevsky's hero Rakhmetov from *What Is to Be Done?* "Possibly, like Lyova," he muses,

> we were impressed by our high-school discussions on the "nature of the typical" in literature; specifically, that even the individual phenomena of life may become objects of typical representation, if the writer examines the phenomena behind them which are merely individual now but for which a future has been ordained (Rakhmetov). (91; 96)

Rakhmetov's name appears here dropped in parenthetically to remind the reader of the obvious example of the "typical" character in Soviet letters, who serves as a touchstone for the creative deformation of the notion of the typical Bitov accomplishes with his protagonist Lyova. Bitov introduced ambiguity to the term "type" through his tongue-in-cheek exposure of the teleological historical theorization necessary to evaluating phenomena as "typical." Ginzburg's explanation of Tolstoy's innovations in light of the realist tradition can again help illuminate what Bitov is doing. Ginzburg explained Turgenev's contribution to the portrayal of the individual personality in nineteenth-century realism in terms of the "type."[29] Turgenev's Rudin or Bazarov appear conditioned by their historical time in a way that Balzac's or Flaubert's characters do not. Thus, Bitov's treatment of the concept of "type" in the first section, entitled "Fathers and Sons" after Turgenev's best-known novel, does not seem surprising. By contrast, Tolstoy, according to Ginzburg, "liberated the depiction of the individual human being from the strict constraints of an ideal artistic model," including that of the historically conditioned "typical" character.[30] Bitov similarly tried to break Lyova out of a hardwired Marxist historical determinism that formed the Soviet literary background against which he sought to distinguish his own psychological approach. Bitov used a light touch to destabilize the monology of the official realistic "type": his narrator points out that in colloquial speech, "type" (*tip*) simply means "oddball," or eccentric. The hepcat (*stiliaga*) (20; 28) and Lyova's Uncle Mitya elsewhere in the novel exemplify this sense of the word. The narrator opines that the term applies to those who exhibit the effects of an excessively formative influence of their time. This historical influence renders such "types" eccentric, rather than broadly representative of a class or trend in its historical development, as Soviet ideology would have it.[31] The eccentricities of the hepcat stand out to the Soviet public and to readers. By calling Lyova a "type," Bitov invites us to explore whether Lyova and his peers exhibit their own deformities due to the influence of their time. If so, how fixed are those traits? Bitov's multifaceted treatment of words and characters makes them strange and introduces the space for critical analysis and creative play.

The character Lyova recalls predecessors from the Russian literary tradition that was, as Rufus W. Mathewson characterized it, "hero-centered, if not heroic."[32] Like Pushkin's Onegin and Lermontov's Pechorin, Lyova fails to realize himself in a positive way: he is a latter-day superfluous man. Such a "hero" obviously differs from the Soviet ideal and challenges Marxist-Leninist ideology, according to which the more just socialist society of the U.S.S.R. eliminated the contradictions that had produced such superfluous men.[33] Bitov presents his readers with a conundrum, however: if the superfluous man appeared to be a negative character because of his alienation from society, Lyova's negative traits proceed from his excessive integration with his society. Lyova's greatest failure is the "suppression of revolt" (*smirenie bunta*) (291; 292), occurring near the end, when Lyova repairs the items at the Museum of the Pushkin House Institute which he has destroyed. The narrator refers to that event as a "hinted death" (*namek na smert'*) (132; 137): it appears to be a moral or spiritual defeat. In this sense, Lyova's "superfluity" is measured against the judgment of the implied author or the reader who expects him to be a heroic intellectual by resisting his Soviet environment. Lyova does not satisfy this unofficial expectation either.

Lyova fails in other ways. Bitov exposed the conditioning causes that produce his weaknesses. A grandson of the great literary scholar Modest Platonovich Odoevtsev, Lyova represents a scion of the Russian intelligentsia.[34] He works as a literary scholar and possesses generally liberal views: he should be a cultural leader. However, although endowed withan excellent pedigree, Lyova cannot seem to make effective use of his heritage—he proves in most cases to be intellectually and morally weak.[35] In part this is because he has been trained by family and education to believe in his own natural superiority: Lyova learned from a very young age that he enjoys a historical advantage over even the greatest minds of the past, so that he considers his own time "to be better than Turgenev's in that one had to be so great, gray, and bearded back then, just to write what could be so well mastered in our day by a boy as little (though very gifted) as Lyova . . ." (13; 19). Lyova, who is about eleven years old at the time of Alexander Pushkin's 1949 sesquicentennial, has "read 'all' of Pushkin" for the occasion.[36] The quote marks in Bitov's text imply the narrator's critical distance from this artificially inflated claim. Little Lyova, however, simply marvels at his own impressive feat, naively waiting for success on the path opened up to him. "To endure this waiting one needed 'willpower' [*sila voli*]," the narrator observes. The quote marks again cast doubt on "willpower" as a standard-issue positive virtue inculcated by Soviet education. The narrator describes Lyova sunk into his armchair alone with a book, noting that the "willpower that Meresyev had plenty of in the absence of legs, Lyova had too little of in the presence of arms" (13; 21). The Soviet hero Aleksei Meresyev provides another ironic foil to Lyova.[37] The narrator's remarks about lacking willpower suggest that Lyova engages in figurative masturbation (here literalized) rather than real reading. The path opened up to Lyova by this type of education involves gratification that renders him impotent: it requires no real encounter with something outside Lyova himself in the literary work.

Lyova's capacity for moral and spiritual growth proves to be hindered also by a family that exhibits what the narrator calls a "marvelous psychological phenomenon" necessary for their survival: absolute "apoliticality" (14, 95). As Bitov's narrator explains it, the family members keep their ideals, variously described as "fortitude, patience, dignity," and "duty, honor, and dignity," almost entirely walled off from life (94–95; 100–101). Lyova learns that his father betrayed his grandfather, Modest Platonovich. Grandfather's powerful scholarly method had fallen out of favor, not unlike Formalism did in actual Soviet cultural politics. Grandfather had been arrested and sent to the Gulag for years. Lyova's father made his career at the cost of denouncing his father's method (39; 45–46). The family's inability or refusal to face up to this fundamental betrayal manifests in their apolitical stance and euphemistic language. The narrator, by contrast, draws attention to this use of language and the psychology of avoidance it implies: Lyova's parents speak of grandfather's arrest obliquely as his having been "taken" away "in time," which was "lucky," while they enjoyed the fortune of not having been "touched" (12; 20). Lyova imagines he breaks through this wall of denial when he confronts his father. The reader suspects it is not so simple. The narrator ironically describes the way the father's shadow gets cast under Lyova's feet as Lyova imagines he has "stepped over" his father: Bitov would not so crudely illustrate the symbolic importance of the event, although Lyova might see and rejoice in what he thinks is a sign of his triumph. The description of the scene tends to undermine the credibility of his protagonist's self-satisfied conviction (40; 46–47).

In fact, Lyova shows he has not transcended this Stalinist legacy of the family precisely at the moment when he tries to distance himself from it. Lyova attempts to ingratiate himself with his grandfather by discussing his father's betrayal. His grandfather is appalled. He recognizes a new kind of betrayal in Lyova: "In the seed! There's treachery already in the seed!" (80–81; 88). Lyova understands from this reaction that he has made a "mistake." Bitov highlights the word "mistake" with quote marks and the reader for this reason may perceive echoes of Khrushchev's speech about Stalin's "mistakes" at the Twentieth Party Congress in 1956.[38] Khrushchev did not manage to root out Stalin with that speech. Similarly, Lyova's inadedquate consciousness of his "mistake" has not overcome his father's Stalinist betrayals.

In that important conversation with Lyova, Grandfather also comments directly on Lyova's bad education. "The present-day system of education must be a more serious business than I thought," Grandfather tells him, "neither facts nor conditions nor reality exists for you, only concepts of them" (76; 82). Lyova seems not to know what his grandfather means. Modest Platonovich's diagnosis of the problems of Lyova and his generation confront Lyova with a conundrum Lyova cannot assimilate: "I seem to have been called a fool," Lyova thinks, stunned (77; 83). The overwhelming importance of the positive self-image inculcated in Lyova by his family and his schooling, combined with the actual fragility of that artificial image, makes it impossible for Lyova to see past the slight and understand Modest Platonovich's greater point. In this way, Lyova proves his grandfather's contention that he cannot perceive reality. Subsequently, Lyova's disorientation increases and takes on another reality thanks to his heavy drinking. The intoxication from alcohol underscores the more pernicious and ubiquitous poisoning Lyova and his generation have undergone.

Subsequent to this meeting, Lyova, overwhelmed by contradictions he cannot effectively analyze, turns to inauthentic work and buries his sullied triumph and the lesson his grandfather tried to impart. Lyova and his father together organize and popularize grandfather's legacy after his death. The narrator comments with obvious skepticism on the "important and noble, almost selfless" role they played: "It looked like work, it had objective reality, with this difference, that it had already been done, and moreover long ago, by another man already dead" (87; 93). Lyova's work with his father on Grandfather's legacy appears to be an instance of the liberal solution to the Stalinist heritage, which involved the rehabilitation of Stalinist convicts and the recovery of suppressed aspects of the cultural legacy. In their meeting, Grandfather had cast doubt on liberal hopes for escape and independence: "You will put the liberal mill to work unmasking false notions, allegedly for the sake of the 'true' ones that are now still forbidden but so much desired" (65; 72). There is no independence, Grandfather claims: "You're for, against, in between—but only in relation to the system. It's the only stake you're tethered to" (66; 73). Lyova has failed to confront and grapple with his implication in the system.

In section 2, we learn about the influence of Lyova's friends. Lyova at the beginning of this section comes under the erotic spell of Faina. Lyova will go on to break the heart of his potential partner Albina, whom the narrator endorses as a person who possesses something "good and pure" (172; 177). Faina, by contrast, appears hopelessly vulgar and often simply mean. The contrast of Lyova's submissiveness to Pechorin's autonomy constitutes a mark of Lyova's specifically Soviet modernity. Indeed, it seems plain that Faina's action on Lyova represents a displacement of Stalin's ability to compel adoration and subservience in the Soviet population by force. The story of Faina begins with Stalin's death, on March 5, 1953 (132; 137). In ensuing chapters, Faina and Mitishatyev, both negative characters in Lyova's life, exhibit a fascination with strength expressed in the way they act on Lyova. Faina tells Lyova, "You ought to let me feel your strength" (145–46; 151). Similarly, Mitishatyev's "peculiar influence" over his friend Lyova depends on a "power play," a crude show of strength Mitishatyev makes comically literal when he invites Lyova to fight physically: "Let's wrestle" (190; 196). Mitishatyev and Faina both compel Lyova thanks to an answering mechanism in Lyova himself. With them, Lyova allows himself to be drawn into a disgraceful game of "Who wins? [*kto—kogo*]."[39] Lyova fails to understand how his attempts to defeat his friends draw him more tightly into a vicious circle.

In addition, the liberal tendencies of the period of the "Thaw" after Stalin's death influence Lyova, interacting with other factors, including his family conditioning, and his university and work environments. "It was in this historic time," the narrator says,

> to which we have alluded by means of the narrow trousers, that Lyova successfully finished high school and entered the university under his father. No, he wasn't one of those, the desperate, he didn't go to ridiculous extremes—but he, too, profited by the fruits of their defeats, gradually narrowing his

> trousers at the lawful rate, though also to the utmost limit. Not ridiculously and not dangerously . . . we can't say with any confidence what educates us or when. At the university, in the era of *Youth* (the magazine), he was training himself to cope within maximum (optimum) but permissible (permitted) limits: to fill the available space. (22; 29–30)

The reference to the width of pants connects this discussion of Lyova to the foregoing passage about the hepcat (*stiliaga*) from the early 1950s, who risked much more at that time and thus more authentically represented the urge to rebel. Such hepcat "fighters" (*bortsy*) helped accustom the Soviet public to the "permissibility of the different." This was a grand struggle, the narrator suggests, but one that proved difficult to appreciate, especially in retrospect. After all, notes the narrator, they waged their battle in fashion:

> They endured persecutions, picketings, exclusions, and evictions so that two or three years later Moscow Garment and Leningrad Clothing would independently switch to twenty-four centimeters instead of forty-four. In a state the size of ours, that's a good many extra trousers.
>
> But we're beginning to sound mawkish [*No nas perekashivaet v deshevku*]. (19–20; 27)

The narrator's slippery tone highlights the implicit disconnect between a typical economic calculus and the more elusive human costs and gains. Of course, those hepcats were not aiming to change the specifications of factory clothing. Their more significant achievement consisted of opening up a space of individuality and nonconformity in Soviet society. Lyova can affect a look more individual and free as a result of the hepcats' struggle, without actually risking anything himself. For the knowing reader, the narrator's reference to the factory "Moscow Garment" (*Moskvoshvei*) recalls Mandelshtam's odd lines about coinciding with the time. Bitov quoted them in his commentary: "I am a man of the Moscow Garment epoch– / Look how I bristle in my suit! / Look how I walk and talk."[40] The date of this poem, not provided in the novel, is 1931. The line that precedes these is, "It's time for you to know: I'm also a contemporary."[41] Of course, Mandelshtam was not a contemporary in the usual positive Soviet sense. He was arrested for his poems and died in a forced-labor camp ten years after he wrote these lines. His own difficult struggle to express and critique his contemporary time puts Lyova's own choices to shame. The eccentricity of and risk taken by the hepcats and Mandelshtam contrast in an unflattering way Lyova's comfortable conformity as well as his failure to be what he presents himself to be.

Among the liberals at Pushkin House where he works, Lyova enjoys a reputation for honesty and moral "cleanliness" (*chistoplotnost'*) (105; 110).

The narrator turns this "reputation" into an object of analysis: how is it made, what does it consist of, what is its texture (*faktura*)? (104; 109). The narrator casts doubt on how well it corresponds to Lyova's actual characteristics. He analyzes Lyova's reputation as a set of qualities somehow absorbed by Lyova before he realized and took conscious control of them. Lyova tended not to occupy clearly staked out positions. Others charitably attribute this to a "certain sober clarity of thought." This interpretation helps others and Lyova avoid the fact that real moral courage would require taking clear positions and the risks they entail. Lyova understood that his vagueness protected him, or "maybe he didn't—because even to understand such a thing is much too candid and cynical, and Lyova can't fairly be accused of that" (105; 110). The narrator makes explicit the moral ambiguity that Lyova conveniently fails to perceive. While exculpating Lyova from personal cynicism, the narrator does not let him off the hook: he tells a story about how Lyova refused to help a friend in need when it would have really cost Lyova. This cowardice effectively guts Lyova's good reputation in the eyes of the reader. Perhaps most damning is the ease with which Lyova overcomes his discomfort when he meets the former friend later and receives the cold shoulder: "Lyova reacted almost calmly, discovering with surprise that perhaps they hadn't been such good friends as he thought, because he found in his heart no bothersome impulse" (106–7; 112–13). Lyova's coworkers prove willing to be mostly satisfied with a circumstantial explanation of Lyova's failure to be present to help. Given the narrator's framing of the incident, this reaction appears no more creditable to Lyova's coworkers than Lyova's behavior does to his own character. The narrator wryly remarks, "On the whole, now that it was less overblown, [Lyova's] reputation was even more convenient, placid and safe . . . People didn't count on Lyova too much; so far as they did count on him, he didn't let them down" (107). After this episode, we are told, Lyova tends to avoid close relationships. However, he becomes rich in the less obliging category of friendly acquaintances (*priiateli*) (108; 113). Once again, Lyova avoids facing up to his own failings.

One character perceives Lyova in a flattering light for his own idiosyncratic reasons. Readers meet Lyova's retired coworker Isaiah Borisovich Blank, a "noble old man," late in section 3. Blank possesses distinctive personal "neatness" (*opriatnost'*) (262; 266), a term that echoes but differs from Lyova's reputed cleanliness (*chistoplotnost'*). The narrator validates Blank's neatness as a sign of cultivation. Blank, a Jew, exemplifies moral and cultural nobility independent of ethnic aristocracy. Blank expects of Lyova similarly noble characteristics and tends to bring out the best in him. He sees in Lyova "a truth not yet manifested in his life," as the narrator puts it (262; 266). However, Lyova proves vulnerable to manipulation by his friend Mitishatyev, who delights in offending Blank and damaging Lyova's good credit with him through antisemitic remarks made while Lyova is too drunk to notice or care. Lyova has a premonition of this catastrophe. He knows beforehand that the meeting between Blank and Mitishatyev will result in the shameful exposure of his own duality: essentially a weak character, Lyova is one person with Blank and another with Mitishatyev (261; 264). This dramatic incident, occurring in 1967, brings Lyova up to the present time of the writing of the novel and nearly completes Bitov's portrait of him as a problematic "hero" of his late Soviet generation.

Read against the Tolstoyan subtext, the split in Lyova occasioned by the confrontation between Blank and Mitishatyev dramatizes Tolstoy's idea of inevitable contradictions. In Tolstoy's literary art, the forces acting on an individual depend on "different causes belonging to different spheres of life. Since they function simultaneously, they inevitably enter into conflict with one another."[42] Once Lyova sobers up, news of his offense to Blank horrifies him. Lyova insists to Mitishatyev that he would not be capable of insulting Blank. Mitishatyev recalls with malicious glee how he told Blank about things Lyova and Mitishatyev had discussed, stressing their antisemitic cast. As Mitishatyev recalls it, Lyova remained silent through that conversation, and then sported a smile "like . . . like porridge. You smiled and nodded" (300; 301). Once again, Lyova failed to perceive what is happening, remaining passive and vague. Lyova might want to excuse himself on the pretext of simple drunkenness, but the larger context provided by the narrator shows that Lyova's passivity—his refusal to take a stand, his lack of demonstrated character, and his willing submission to forces in his life that tend to intoxicate or blind him—amounts to a deformed character. Bitov gives shape to the opposing forces that act on Lyova in the characters of Blank and Mitishatyev. Lyova's knowledge of the contradiction they represent for him, and his inability during the confrontation with Mitishatyev to escape from the sense of a terrible duality within himself, signify the awakening of an analytic perspective in Lyova's own consciousness. Lyova's good reputation and his comfortable sense of self are shattered. While failure precipitates this awareness, Lyova's awareness of this failure potentially inaugurates more authentic self-knowledge and might lead to greater maturity and a stronger character. The duel and destruction of the literary museum at Pushkin House that follow this scene represent externally and fantastically the fragmentation and disorder Lyova has experienced within himself. The narrator's observation that Lyova comes to know the "full sorrow of crushed rebellion" when he puts the museum back in order (326; 327) possesses the same irony Bitov employs elsewhere. In one sense, of course, Lyova's anger at Mitishatyev signifies his rejection of the malicious forces he represents and his desire to annihilate them. In another sense, however, Mitishatyev is a phantasm, a fantastic projection of the conditioning Lyova carries within himself. Lyova cannot simply destroy all the things that have shaped him and his world his whole life—he can only try to pull them apart in order to know with more critical awareness what those pieces are and how he might creatively reconstruct himself.

LYOVA: A CUBIST PORTRAIT

When Bitov's narrator muses about Lyova's status as a type, he describes the basic conditions that determine him as such. They include separation from his ancestry: the fact that Grandfather has been gone in the camps creates a disjuncture in family life that is definitive for the environment of half-truths and separation from reality in which Lyova is reared. The lack of facts, the unrevealed lie, creates the environment in which a person learns "not to trust his own inherent, naturally precise sensations and emotions." That is, people become alienated from themselves and their own being in the world. They cease to be masters of their own deeds. The narrator suggests this "disorientation" (*dezorientatsiia*) cannot be limited to Lyova but is typical of people at this time. Moreover, this disorientation is, in some way "what the whole novel is about" (92; 98).

This passage follows Lyova's encounter with Modest Platonovich, where we see that reconnecting with his Grandfather does not rectify the situation. Similarly, Grandfather complains that the thirty years of his life lost to the camps cannot be undone by rehabilitation. Grandfather addresses the cultural counterpart to the rupture Stalin's purges effected in the lives of so many Soviet citizens and families. He tells Lyova, "Now, you think that '17 destroyed, devastated our previous culture. But it didn't; it canned and preserved it. What matters is the break, not the destruction" (64; 71). Simply digging up previous concepts and words, like "Russia, homeland, Pushkin . . . the word, the nation, the spirit," finding the repressed Tsvetaeva, or discovering an unofficial side of Pushkin will not rectify the sense of disorientation. Lyova and other liberal intellectuals like him still misperceive themselves and their reality. Those reared in Soviet culture, according to Grandfather, are not capable of an independent and creative relationship to this legacy: they can only consume it (65; 73). Bitov addresses the sense of historical and cultural disjuncture in his final note of the commentary where he parodies the ages of poetry: "People wrote after the Golden Age of Pushkin, Lermontov, and Gogol—worse, but they wrote. Both the silver and the bronze age have departed. But still to come are the copper, the tin, the wood, the clay, the potato, and finally the cardboard age—and all these will still be literature—before the synthetic age finally arrives, infinite as eternity . . . There is yet something to be done."[43] Bitov as author advocates coming to terms with the mixed-up age and with the break—if there is yet "something to be done," there remains also the possibility of getting in touch with one's reality and one's reactions to that reality sufficiently to be author again of one's own words and deeds.

Bitov explored the effects of this "break" in Lyova's personality, exposing his contradictions. He imitated the fractured texture of a broken world in the narrative construction of the novel, in order to facilitate the reader's active awareness of a world in need of creative authorship.

The confrontation between Mitishatyev and Blank and the exposure of Lyova's contradictions results in "the final break [*obryv*] in Lyova's fading reality" (316; 317). The shattering of Lyova's reality appears mirrored in the destruction of the Museum at the Pushkin House Institute occasioned by Lyova's duel with Mitishatyev. As a result, by the end, we see a fragmented protagonist in a setting that has been torn apart. If Lyova merely restores the institutional order of his environment, his failure in these final scenes begs the question: what would a creatively constructive relationship to the shattered elements be?

As we saw, Bitov used psychological analysis, drawing on the tradition of Tolstoy, to split apart Lyova's personality into discontinuous pieces that cannot be easily reconciled. Similarly, Bitov splits the narrative apart from a coherent whole into a story punctuated with digressions and insertions, alternative versions of episodes and metanarrative meditations on the writing of the novel itself. In part, perhaps, Bitov's method echoes Tolstoy's own digressions in *War and Peace*. However, the discontinuity and artificiality of *Pushkin House* exceeds the bounds of nineteenth-century realism. In fact, we might compare Bitov's novel to a Cubist painting: Lyova seems not entirely unlike the broken and faceted human figure in Pablo Picasso's *Portrait of Daniel-Henry Kahnweiler* (1910).

This comparison will not seem far-fetched if we recall that Shklovsky described Laurence Sterne's *Tristram Shandy* and Pushkin's *Eugene Onegin* as novels that resembled "a picture by Picasso."[44] Edward Brown called Sterne's and Pushkin's novels "key precursors" of *Pushkin House*.[45] We may easily perceive similarities among the garrulous narrators of all three novels, and thus Bitov's kinship with the romantic-ironic tradition preceding the realism of the nineteenth century.[46] In each of these three novels, the frequent digressions mimic the narrator's willful train of thought. Such digressive passages disrupt chronological and expected narrative logic, representing a human element that always resists being typecast according to rigid conventions or predetermined logic.

Shklovsky's comments underscore a similarity between that digressive literary technique and the Cubist approach to conceptual representation, which opposed conventional ways of rendering visual perception in painting.[47] Bitov's novel, like those of Sterne and Pushkin, challenges the reader to examine readerly expectations and question artistic conventions. All three writers reflected in their novels on how the human mind orders representation and resists confinement to an established order. These novels provoke readers to be critically aware of the distinction between real life and the representation of it.

Collage, like Cubism, creates contradictions.[48] Bitov introduced the idea of a collage at the beginning of the novel with the scrap of newspaper inserted into the "Prologue." The narrator vows, "We will try to write so that even a scrap of newspaper, if not used for its ultimate purpose, might be inserted at any point in the novel, serving as a natural continuation and in no way violating the narrative" (6–7; 14). The narrator's statement, as in many other instances, seems ambiguous: of course, the newspaper scrap graphically interrupts the text and makes us wonder about its relationship to the narrative, which is not obvious. By referring to the scrap's "ultimate purpose," the narrator points toward the original context of the article even as he disavows it in favor of the supposedly seamless narrative composition. The ambivalent significance of Bitov's scrap resembles the effect of newspaper collage elements in Picasso's *Still Life with Violin and Fruit* (1912). In that composition a scrap may be read as if it appeared in a newspaper, but it also functions as a representation of a bowl for the fruit arranged on top of it. The sign points in two directions, back to the original context and around itself to the artistic work.[49]

Bitov's use of a collage element introduces a similarly ambiguous semiotic valence. We will naturally read the text of the scrap and wonder about the world outside, about "what is happening now" as reflected in a real newspaper. However, we also seek to accommodate the scrap's meaning as part of a coherent narrative within the novel. The narrator's protestations notwithstanding, that coherence does not simply exist: it has to be created in the mind of the reader. Ellen Chances identified the source of the scrap to be a 1971 article, "The Connection between Times," from the official newspaper *Literaturnaia gazeta*.[50] The article talks about the debts non-European ethnic groups within the Soviet Union owe to Pushkin and Russian poetry, suggesting the use of Pushkin for the cultural politics of empire.[51] The scrap therefore evokes the significant sociohistorical ground outside of the novel: the novel acquires its coherence as a figure distinguished from that background of official cultural politics. The piece of newspaper stands out from the novel by highlighting what the novel is not, because Bitov's novel as an uncensored, alternative work does not aspire to the political power implicit in the state's hegemonic use of culture. Given this, we can appreciate how Bitov fashioned the scrap to make a point about official culture. Pushkin's name appears nowhere in full in the scrap (the English edition renders the whole name but it is not found in the original). The official cultural authorities represented by the article have not grasped Pushkin and cannot determine and control his meaning as a source of cultural creativity.[52]

However, the author of the article raises questions he does not answer, and this suggests a certain openness that Bitov echoes in his own way in his novel. The article's author employs leading questions, such as, "How did translation of *The Bronze Horseman* give rise to the splendid realism of the Avarians' latest poetry?" The author asserts that such questions and their answers would make the topic of a "great and useful book." Bitov does not share the Soviet state's agenda of canonizing Pushkin as a central figure for non-Russian peoples, but he does in another sense aim to write a "great and useful book" about the influence of Pushkin in another society, his own. Bitov's novel dramatizes real openness regarding how people might, in independent and creative ways, access and use their cultural heritage. In this way, Bitov displaces the idea of the newspaper article and uses it differently in his work. Bitov's deliberate fashioning and insertion of the text shifts the accent from the translation between national languages and cultures evoked in the article, to the problem of historical time foregrounded in the article's title, "The Connection between Times." Formulating a creative response to one's historical time and the cultural heritage constitutes a central problem of Bitov's *Pushkin House*. As distinct from the author of the article, Bitov thinks that the "connection" to Pushkin and his time can only be established in provisional and individual ways that never entirely span the distance between Pushkin and those who inherit his works.[53]

Bitov leaves other items in the text only partially assimilated, so that they exhibit the ambivalent significance of the collage element, pointing to an original context in historical reality as they fit inorganically into Bitov's text. Words such as the old-fashioned "ether" (*efir*) and "cruet" (*flakon*) (5–6; 14–15) are examples. The figure of the "hepcat" (*stiliaga*), although of more recent vintage, also already belongs to a past era and sounds rather quaint. Like the "gumdrop soldier" that will not melt on History's tongue (21; 29), these elements retain some unassimilated historical strangeness in Bitov's prose and carry a multifaceted significance that Bitov's text tends to illuminate.

Cubist and collage works illustrate visually the principle of parataxis—because there is no single defining perspective, there is no center of the work to which everything must tend. Bitov's frequent use of ellipses and digressions creates a similar fragmented feel at the level of the narrative and overall novelistic structure. Bitov referenced the related technique of montage. After Lyova's fateful encounter with Mitishatyev and Blank in section 3, memories appear as "flaring scenes, framed by the boundary of forgetfulness." The narrator compares the scenes Lyova recalls to a film, highlighting the discontinuity of memory: "The darker and deeper the gaps of forgotten episodes, the brighter the remembered frame between" (333; 334). Montage, like Cubism and collage, demands that the audience consider disjunctively juxtaposed scenes and creatively discern the intellectual relationship that bridges the discontinuity.

We can treat scenes in the novel according to this logic of montage. Lyova's restoration of the museum at the Pushkin House Institute after his duel with Mitishatyev apparently represents entropy, the suppression of the energy of self-awareness and rebellion in a process of reconstruction that merely reconstitutes the established order. However, another little-examined pair of scenes preceding the duel suggests, I will argue, the creative and ethical potential Lyova possesses and which might be realized in life. Bitov's text leaves open the possibilities for synthesizing Lyova's shattered self—he might collapse back into mindless conformity or he could become a more perceptive, ethical, and creative human being actively engaged with his real life.

These two episodes, placed at the end of section 2 before the final confrontation between Mitishatyev and Blank in section 3, suggest a potential in Lyova that remains largely unrealized in the text. In "Madame Bonacieux," we see Lyova alone in the Pushkin House Institute, looking out a window to see Faina walking with another man. In the "Appendix" that immediately follows, "The Hero's Profession," Lyova's article on Pushkin, Lermontov, and Tiutchev is discussed. In "Madame Bonacieux," the narrator describes Lyova's habitual way of regarding Faina. Lyova has in his mind a picture out of Alexandre Dumas's *The Three Musketeers*, in which Faina as Madame Bonacieux falls to her death while Lyova/D'Artagnan races in a tragically doomed attempt to save her (216; 221–22). The romantic drama depends on the heroine's death. By contrast, Lyova's prosaic revelation when looking out the window at Faina (he has assumed the position of Mme. Bonacieux from the picture) boils down to the awareness that she is not a player in his drama. She is real and independent: "The fact was Faina herself" (218; 223).

The episode described in "Madame Bonacieux" chronologically relates to the third section, since it occurs while Lyova is on duty at the Institute during the November holiday. This scene also provides us with evidence for the precise date of the holiday described: Lyova thinks it has been fourteen years since high school ended. He completed high school the spring Stalin died, in 1953, so this is 1967 (215; 220). The placement reflects a nonlinear principle of composition—coming at the end of section 2, it represents a real moment of maturation as opposed to the false threshold of Stalin's death and erotic awakening at the beginning of section 2. It also forms a unit with the apparently unrelated discussion of Lyova's article. Together, the scenes provide a positive focal point to balance the pessimistic aftermath of Lyova's duel. We find here an artful equipoise of narrative tensions that resists conventional linear progression and makes us work to understand not only the actual dates and chronology of events but also the point of their nonlinear arrangement in the novel.

The recognition of Faina's autonomous existence in "Madame Bonacieux" complements the successful expression of Lyova's own perspective in the article "Three Prophets." The narrator validates Lyova's impression that this work is "the real thing," saying Lyova expressed "a lot that was his own" (224; 229). The narrator does not minimize the eccentricity of Lyova's fixation on a special threshold age—27 years old—in the biographies of Pushkin, Lermontov, and Tiutchev. This age also resonates with Dante's age in *La vita nuova* and suggests a subtle and possibly ironic comparison between Dante's achievement of a new style and the aspirations of Bitov's novel. The narrator does not conceal the error and idiosyncracy of Lyova's argument about a "duel" among the authors he treats. The "duel" is a word he "rides," "long and beautifully, from sentence to sentence, stitching them together like the bobbin in a sewing machine" (231; 235). The idea seems fantastic partly because Tiutchev supposedly conducts a secret duel with Pushkin, carried on without Pushkin's knowledge. The scholarly exposition of the idea seems subject to reproach also because Lyova has not read Iurii Tynianov's article "Pushkin and Tiutchev" (236; 239).[54]

While the article is not perfect, Lyova finished it, and this is significant: Lyova managed to express himself, to commit himself to a form others could read (as opposed to the articles that remain in Lyova's head). He also shined a light, albeit from an eccentric position, on the authors and works in question.[55] In the context of the novel, Lyova's remarks in the article on historical jealousy and the romantic obsession with primacy relate to Lyova's jealousy of Faina. They pertain also to the narrator's comments on the historical advantage of Lermontov's *A Hero of Our Time* over Bitov's novel (129; 133), and to the author's thoughts about his hero in "Achilles and the Tortoise" (341; 342). In all cases, the desire to control or express one's own view and place in the world must be tempered by recognition of the irreducible otherness of fellow human beings and their expression, as well as the inability ever to realize oneself fully in a finished form. In the article, Lyova begins to grapple analytically with these central issues of creative self-expression.

Tiutchev in this article embodies Lyova's "recognition of himself, his impartial confrontation with his own experience," as the narrator tells us (241; 244). This writing of an image of himself represents creative potential for Lyova. Perhaps Bitov did not know of Mikhail Bakhtin's essay "Author and Hero," but the concept of authoring oneself that Bakhtin elaborated there seems close to what the narrator says about Lyova's achievement at this moment—he has expressed himself authentically.[56] Insofar as Lyova represents the author, this moment helps validate the creative potential of Bitov and the late Soviet writer he represents. This late Soviet writer must live belatedly, after the break, "interruptedly" (*preryvno*), like Tiutchev (226; 231). Having rejected Soviet progressive ideology, as Bitov did, the writer finds himself left out in the historical cold, as it were. Bitov realizes creatively his difficult position of being more or less disconnected from the continuous traditions of the Russian past and Western culture. The author's "function" (*naznachenie*), to pick up a term from the final pages (352–54; 353–55) is to realize himself wherever he is, and to forge new links in the chain of culture.[57] Like Modest Platonovich, Bitov resists the tragic narrative about what has been lost, and eschews the heroic romanticism of the dissident pose. Both find freedom where they stand.[58]

DECONSTRUCTING THE WHOLE OF THE WORK

Bitov deconstructed the seamless whole image of the late Soviet intellectual subject for his discontinuous portrait of Lyova, and he challenged readers' expectations regarding the integral unity of the artistic work. *Pushkin House* as a title encompasses a nonlinear assemblage of parts, comprising within the digressive three sections of the main text variations on plot segments, narrator's commentary, and inserted texts and epilogues. In newer editions, the novel comes with an extensive commentary. In the Limbakh edition, the corpus includes addenda to the commentary, a dossier on the novel, articles about the novel, a bibliography, and further materials for a bibliography. This capacious, heterogeneous assemblage of pieces written by Bitov and others challenges our notion of the single-authored text in a way that echoes Bitov's ideas about the life of cultural works and illustrates an innovative approach to the boundary between official print and samizdat.

Stanislav Savitskii traced the history of publication of *Pushkin House* in samizdat, tamizdat, and print. This history illustrates the mutual influence of official and unofficial spheres, as well as the possibilities for clever play on the border between the two.[59] Savitskii pointed out that Bitov pursued both censored and uncensored publication in a savvy and almost programmatic way. Having registered his intention to publish a novel with the official publishing house Sovetskii pisatel' (Soviet Writer) in 1968, Bitov secured an advance and laid the groundwork for unofficial circulation. The official publishers finally decided to reject the novel after receiving the full text in 1971. Having sent the manuscript to the offices of Sovetskii pisatel' and then in 1972 to the official publisher Sovremennik (The Contemporary), as well as the Soviet journal *Novyi mir* (*New World*), which obliged him with a third rejection in early 1976, Bitov could plausibly claim that the novel had gotten around without his knowledge or permission.[60] Thus, Iurii Karabchievskii's article with extensive quotes from the manuscript, published in the émigré journal *Grani* (*Facets*) in 1977, and finally the publication of the whole novel *Pushkinskii dom* by the U.S. publisher Ardis in 1978 (the same publisher that put out the first Russian edition of Aksenov's *Ozhog*), did not necessarily incriminate Bitov himself. It did, however, mean that he would not be published in Soviet print again until perestroika, in 1987. In an attempt to help his case, Bitov wrote a "Foreword" ostensibly from the publishers for the Ardis edition, in which they claimed to have published the novel without Bitov's knowledge. Bitov also asked publisher Carl Proffer of Ardis to write a letter to VAAP, the Soviet writers' union, explaining how he got wind of the novel, and exculpating Bitov. The letter asserted (humorously) that the manuscript of *Pushkinskii dom* had been found on the desk of Vladimir Nabokov shortly before his untimely demise.[61] The mystification had the practical goal of protecting Bitov from charges by the authorities. The fanciful grace note about Nabokov's desk (Carl's idea or Bitov's?) suggests the point may have consisted of playing the game for the sake of its amusing mystifications more than for the actual protection it could afford him, which was little.

Bitov's mystifications multiplied as he played on the boundaries between official and unofficial culture and between his own authorship and collaboration or dialogue with readers. Sections of the novel passed censorship and appeared in official Soviet journals in the 1970s. Chapters about Uncle Dickens (Uncle Mitya) without the explicit reference to the camps appeared in the journal *Zvezda* (*Star*) in 1973. Excerpts on Lyova's romance came out in the journal *Avrora* in 1975, while the story of Lyova's romance with Albina appeared in the journal *Druzhba narodov* (*Friendship of the Peoples*), also in 1975. Bitov published the appendix "Achilles and the Tortoise" as an article in the newspaper *Literaturnaia gazeta* (*The Literary Gazette*) in that same year with a letter by a made-up citizen who supposedly recognized Bitov's protagonist from *Aptekarskii Island* and wanted to know if the character was real. The piece provoked letters from actual readers and further publication.[62] Bitov published Lyova's article on "Three Prophets" in the scholarly journal *Voprosy literatury* (*Questions of Literature*) in 1976. Although he specified this was the hypothetical work of a protagonist in a novel, not all who debated the merits of the piece seemed to have entirely grasped the implications of that framing.[63]

Bitov thus orchestrated a growing body of writing around his novel as he also multiplied the forms that novel could take. The novel appeared published at last in the U.S.S.R. in the journal *Novyi mir* in 1987, the same year the English edition came out in a lovely translation by Susan Brownsberger with Farrar, Straus and Giroux in the United States. Bitov's commentary also appeared in *Novyi mir* in 1989, the year that the publisher Sovremennik finally put out the novel as a separate book.[64] In the meantime, a bibliography of publications from and about the novel appeared as "A Phantom Novel" ("Roman-prizrak") in the Vienna journal *Wiener Slawistischer Almanach* (1982), from E. Khappenenn, another of Bitov's mystifications (Bitov's pseudonym here sounds like "A Happening"). Truly, the novel was an event, a partially orchestrated, partially contingent "happening" that reflected the forces bearing on its existence, including the skepticism of Soviet authorities, the enthusiasm of some readers and the exasperation of others.[65]

Bourdieu's analysis prompts us to question the stakes and ground of the "game." As in Aksenov's case, Bitov's position in the official literary field mattered for how he saw and played his possibilities: Bitov could be sure his manuscript would be accepted and seriously considered in the editorial offices to which he sent the manuscript, and his name recognition made plausible the claim that the manuscript was "leaked" from those offices into samizdat. Unlike Aksenov, Bitov's game playing made the work seem more literary and autonomous from political issues—there was no obvious burning truth or angry exposure of specific officials, and thus the novel's publication in the West did not mean forced exile the way publication of *The Burn* did for Aksenov. At the same time, however, the Ardis publication negatively impacted Bitov's publishing prospects for almost a decade in the Soviet Union. Bitov would be willing to suffer this loss of his position on the playing field because of the possibilities for symbolic and real gains on the restricted field of samizdat cultural production. His publications in the United States probably did not mean significant remuneration—the publishers at Ardis undertook publications in Russian for the sake of the symbolic capital they garnered by helping to return Russian modernist works and develop the literary legacy that grew out of them.[66] Broadly speaking, the cachet of Russian literature in the context of the Cold War must have helped the status of both *The Burn* and *Pushkin House* with editor Jonathan Galassi, known for his more "avant-garde," that is, more complex and less immediately marketable literary acquisitions, first at Random House, and then at Farrar, Straus and Giroux.[67]

Bourdieu's theory about different types of capital helps us appreciate that the symbolic capital on the American and the Russian literary fields was real, not just some screen or cant covering up political or economic motives: his model also suggests that this symbolic capital involved a denial of its complex dependence on the political and economic context. Soviet Russia was the enemy: therefore, people cared about things Russian. They needed to challenge the simple black and white political picture. A number of intellectual readers were willing to work through big and complicated literary works because they believed that understanding Soviets as human beings and appreciating the expression of their experience mattered.

THE PARTIAL PERSPECTIVE: A TENTATIVE SUBJECTIVITY

Embedded within the solid timbers of section headings that advertise the novel's links to major Russian classics, implying the novel's accessibility for literate readers, we find curious, multifaceted nuggets highly specific to the cultural world of Bitov's generation. Scholar Omry Ronen singled out the "childish word Gastello" from the "Prologue" of the book.[68] Bitov deftly transposed Gastello, the name of the iconic World War II pilot who flew his damaged plane into a machine-gunner's nest, from the canon of Soviet propaganda into the subjective and lyrical lexicon of a person who was young during the war, for whom the name was part of the cultural landscape of childhood. Gastello in the novel names the wind Bitov used to open his novel. Bearing down on the empty city, this wind brings the perspective in cinematic fashion from a broad view from on high lower and closer, eventually entering through the broken window to survey up close the devastation of the museum at the Pushkin House Institute and the dead body of Lyova amongst the debris. This preliminary shot piques the reader's interest for the investigation that follows (3–5; 11–13). Toward the end we see the scene repeated, when we already know the whys and wherefores of Lyova, who he is and how he got to that point (312–14; 313–16).

As Bitov evoked it, the "childish word Gastello" implies the perspective of the historically located individual of Bitov's generation, as opposed to the relatively faceless addressee of Soviet propaganda. Most immediately, however, Gastello names the wind. This "flat wind the color of an airplane," is a wind *like* an airplane that has sucked up all the sky to slam into the city onto which it falls. The wind appears as a "thief with its cloak streaming." This phrase, repeated verbatim to close the passage when it appears again late in the novel, connects these scenes to Lyova's imagination of himself like d'Artagnan, riding to the rescue of Madame Bonacieux, "with his cloak streaming" (216; 221–22). The phrase is repeated, too, within this scene, emphasizing the fixed character of Lyova's romantic (and childish) imagination. Bitov thus drew an analogy between his authorial appropriation of a heroic cliché in Gastello and Lyova's assumption of the role of d'Artagnan in his imagination. There is a difference, however. Lyova does not at first reflect on his self-aggrandizement at the expense of another. Bitov's artful variation of the motif prompts critical scrutiny.

Lyova looks out of his high window like a "director and god" on Faina and her companion walking below. He feels the sharp wind and sees the sky, the "blue of torn-in-half space" cleared by "war vehicles," that is, by airplanes that have chased away the clouds for the November 7 celebrations taking place that day. Bitov in the "Commentary" discussed persistent rumors in the Soviet press that special airplanes were being used for the holiday, presumably to seed the clouds and clear the skies.[69]

Thus, the sky is associated with airplanes that symbolize, both as "war vehicles" and as airplanes that seed the clouds to control the weather, the hubris of a State that presumes to see and control everything from its godlike perspective. Bitov obviously rejects that kind of violence; somewhat more subtly, I think, he tempers the potential of the artist or intellectual to put himself in that place. In the next chapter, Lyova in an ecstasy over his articles thinks, "The vault, the dome!" (252; 256). The dome suggests Acmeist aesthetics and the related architectural metaphors for art favored by Bitov. In particular, the dome or cupola represents convergence achieved, perhaps even a moment of total unification.[70]

However, Lyova's lesson in the Madame Bonacieux episode consisted of learning *not* to see oneself as the godlike director. The gaps and absences provide glimpses of the free sky and air given to us, and which our efforts at best can only frame.[71] The clear hole in the sky Lyova sees when he looks out the window of the Institute resembles the glimpse of sky Modest Platonovich catches and comments upon at the end. He thinks, at that moment in 1921, "behind is the abyss, ahead is nonexistence, on the left and right they've got you by the elbows, . . . and yet the sky overhead is free!" (354; 354). This revelation, coming as it does with the knowledge that Modest Platonovich will be imprisoned shortly, might recall Dostoevsky's memoirs of time in prison camps and his glimpse of the sky "remote and free." This experience marked a turning point for Dostoevsky. Accepting suffering and being among the Russian people became key elements in a "freedom" embraced at the end of Dostoevsky's memoirs.[72] Subsequently, as we know, Dostoevsky would go on to stunning artistic productivity.[73] However, Modest Platonovich's skeptical statements in this section about "secret" freedom, evoked in Blok's poem from the event in 1921 marking the anniversary of Pushkin's death, suggest he does not endorse the vulgar fetishization of a struggle or hidden meaning (353; 354).[74] We saw this earlier in the novel in his conversation with Lyova, where he cautioned against mindless "mining" of words, works, and meanings previously forbidden, as they imagine it (65; 72).[75] Dostoevsky spoke about Pushkin who "died in the full flower of his creative development, and unquestionably . . . took some great secret with him to his grave. And so now we must puzzle out this secret without him."[76] This enigmatic end to an ecstatic speech shows Dostoevsky pronouncing prophetically in the context of a messianic national vision with more than a little chauvinism in it.

Although Bitov does not mention Dostoevsky's speech about Pushkin explicitly, the intertexts linking Pushkin, his death, and the secret would be obvious enough to most Russian readers. The more subtle Tolstoyan intertexts (Tolstoy being, as opposed to Dostoevsky, more "freely" available in the Soviet canon of literature) of *Pushkin House* provide an alternative resonance for the image of the sky and the theme of revelation. We can compare Lyova's revelations as depicted at the end of section 2 to Levin's revelation of the meaning of life at the end of Tolstoy's *Anna Karenina*. Levin senses an ontological goodness that cannot be explained by reason. His instinctive knowledge contrasts with his half-brother Koznyshev's intellectual arguments and with Anna's literary imagination of her life. Tolstoy treats Levin's revelation as a function of his imperfect human perspective: "Lying on his back, he was now looking at the high, cloudless sky. 'Don't I know that it is infinite space and not a round vault? But no matter how I squint and strain my sight, I cannot help seeing it as round and limited, and despite my knowledge of infinite space, I am undoubtedly right when I see a firm blue vault, more right than when I strain to see beyond it.'"[77] Despite the fact that Levin thinks everything will be different after his revelation, he still gets irritable and argues with his brother. Levin interprets his insight in a way that highlights its difference from the Slavophile and chauvinist arguments of his brother: he realizes that his revelation, grounded in the Christian faith he sucked in with his mother's milk, connects him to a universal good, but gives him no right to judge Buddhists, or people of the Muslim faith. He can only see what he can see. Although this connects him to everyone who shares the infinite sky, it does not give him the perspective of God.[78]

Bitov's author in the text renounces his godlike power to determine the ultimate fate of his characters when he "meets" his protagonist Lyova at the end. This impossible meeting after the reconstruction of the museum represents a "rupture" (*razryv*) in the artistic text, an opening out to life (350; 351). The author confesses he knows NOTHING (*NI-CHE-GO*) of Lyova (351; 351). Thus, the figure of Lyova, even in the midst of his apparent spiritual defeat, represents the freedom of human possibility.

Lyova thus stands ultimately for a post-totalitarian ideology of the subject in Bitov's work. The imperative for constructing a partial, humanized, and imperfect individual authority among other subject positions proceeds directly from the hubris of a society that sacrificed countless lives, and morally and intellectually incapacitated those not destroyed by the purges in the name of its utopian goal. Bitov honored the modernist genius represented by Modest Platonovich, but he acknowledged the historical experience intervening since the time of that flowering and deforming its expression in the present. In *Pushkin House*, the modernist idea of genius and creative invention stands in a complementary relation to the eccentric expression of individuality, represented by Uncle Dickens, who is no creative genius, but who represents the value of being oneself anyway, that is one who resists the pressure to conform and and the blandishments of a general truth.[79] Bitov's narrator in the book channels this eccentric spirit in his style, mitigating the imposing creative prowess of the novelistic author for whom he stands.

The ontological truth implied by the particular vision of freedom Bitov cultivated with the work can be seen alternatively through the Bourdieusian frame, which brings us back to the social reality. In the accretion of further sections of the book, and the orchestration of other people's interventions on the novel or sections of it, Bitov expressed this deliberate reduction of the author's status as sole creator of the work, particularly as it lives through its various publications. *Pushkin House* the book becomes a medium for conversations and exchanges, an open platform for role-playing, as modeled and instigated by Bitov. The book represents a forum people can join with letters to the editor or interventions in the journal conversation, or interviews for the dossier. These paratexts are not simply extra—Bitov includes them in the Limbakh edition (and in other forms elsewhere) because they are part of the organically expanding corpus of the work in its social life. More than this, the novel's documented reception, its critical consecration as a new "postmodern classic" in Russia, its entry into the stable of works handled by publishers abroad, including Ardis and Farrar, Straus, and Giroux, opens up the possibilities for literary analysis beyond the text of the work itself to the kinds of negotiation of institutional and personal identities that occur not only in the unified field of culture, but through the domestic and cross-cultural exchanges of literary works, particularly in the presence of somewhat inflated symbolic capital.[80]

We shall begin to attempt this kind of analysis in chapter 5. First, however, we shall see this imaginative implication of audience identities even more clearly in the case of Erofeev's Venichka. What Bitov's novel shows is that the avant-garde destruction of the illusory whole in samizdat need not only target the regime or the intelligentsia—it can break down the romantic modernist model of the author and the confining integrity of the work, in the interests of realizing a new sort of simultaneously individual and intersubjective authority for its late Soviet time. Bitov's consciousness of the extended temporality of the text encompasses the break, in the sense that it assumes its own dissolution and reconstitution into somewhat different forms, over time, with the active participation of readers. The image of the author is, then, as Bitov shows it to be, reduced to a more limited perspective that does not yield its primacy to readers, but acknowledges their role in validating the truth of his vision and the resonance of his voice.

Pushkin House helps clarify the distinctiveness of the late Soviet field as compared to Bourdieu's modeled contexts. Bitov's novel reinforces the point seen already in the case of *The Burn* about an international readership and market charged first by political forces and only secondarily by commercial potentials. It helps us appreciate the correlated symbolic capital of unofficial Soviet literary work in the West, where the interest differed from that of Soviet readers. Western readers had their own relation to the political context of the Cold War. Bitov's novel further suggests the discontinuity of the dissident cultural field. Although *The Burn* and *Pushkin House* came from authors who were roughly peers in the Soviet literary field (both being successful Young Prose writers), the works look very different from one another, each being a highly individual synthesis of eclectic sources and realization of dissident imperatives and freedoms. *Pushkin House* subsequently is found grouped together with other "postmodern" works from the field of unofficial literature. At the time these books were written in the late 1960s and early 1970s, however, the unofficial field seemed less marked by any such artistic trend and more host to a collection of individual attempts to say a new word united mostly by their refusal of official beliefs.

Dissident subjectivity in Bitov's novel appears more developed than it does in Aksenov's novel: Bitov's subject implies a consciously partial individual authority, as opposed to the all-seeing and all-powerful godlike author known from modernist works and echoed in Aksenov's novel. Bitov as author displayed the self-consciously eccentric artistic individuality of the early dissident field, before any perceptible trends or milieu of producers in the dissident field coalesced and before the means of evaluation and consecration were quite clear.[81] Bitov's subject Lyova possesses freedom at the end of the novel, but that is all—whether he would realize his individuality in a way that can be communicated and resonate with others remained beyond the scope of what the novel's author chose to represent.

Chapter Four

On the Knife's Edge: Venichka's Performance in *Moscow Stations*

"Actually, if I die sometime—and I'm going to die very soon, I know that—then I'll die without accepting this world."
—Venichka

VENEDIKT EROFEEV'S *Moscow Stations* (*Moskva–Petushki*, 1969),[1] differs from *Pushkin House* and *The Burn*—Erofeev's work is thinner, more spiritual and, one could say, much freer.[2] Erofeev debuted as a samizdat writer from outside the official Soviet system. He described his novel *Moscow Stations* as a work written for a small circle of friends, and his protagonist Venichka seems like an intimate portrait of himself.[3] In Bourdieu's terms, Erofeev did not possess the *habitus* of Aksenov and Bitov, who were already established writers in the Soviet literary field when they undertook their uncensored novels. Moreover, unlike those authors, Erofeev did not directly treat public debates or the character of his generation in his samizdat work. Nevertheless, for a number of Russian readers, Erofeev's novel exerted a "generation-shaping" influence, by some accounts surpassing that of even Solzhenitsyn's *Gulag Archipelago*,[4] a work more widely read, but also more reflective of specific issues. Erofeev's work strikes a universal note. Tom Courtenay, who played Venichka in the British stage adaptation of *Moscow Stations*, said, "Yerofeyev is just such a sympathetic character to me. Listening to him is like listening to that Mozart piece, the Divertimento, which seems to take in everything—the sadness, the heartbreak, the beauty, the fun in spite of it all."[5] This "universal" quality speaks to the work's artistic autonomy from the late Soviet field.

Looking at the situation through the lens of Bourdieu's critique, we can ask how this "universality" gets constructed and what it says about the social world from which it seems so free. We can also interrogate the portrayal of the hero and his engaging personality, wondering why the figure of Venichka resonates as strongly as it does.[6] Venichka's inimitable voice guides readers along his fantastic journey from an unknown stairwell in Moscow to Kursk Station and out of the city on the regional electric train with a lot of hard drinking and meandering musings, away from the capital and toward the people he loves in provincial Petushki. Venichka must be the only Muscovite who has never seen the Kremlin: "Everybody says: the Kremlin, the Kremlin. They all go on about it, but I've never seen it." This is one of the aspects of Venichka's character that is both patently artificial and yet so amusing as he presents it that we willingly suspend disbelief. Whenever Venichka is looking for the Kremlin he winds up at Kursk Station, he says (1; 139). The detail suggests his personal eccentricity, and the powerful centrifugal thrust of his character propelled away from symbols of political power. Venichka presents himself as a rare exception, a man sui generis. "I'm the soberest man in the world," says Venichka despite all he has drunk. He has at that point lost his way and ended up back in Moscow by the Kremlin walls, pursued by the gang of four who kill him at the end (123; 238). Venichka has a great truth to tell about his society from a position where drunkenness is sobriety, and madness is reason. No matter that lots of other people at this time drank—Venichka drinks for different reasons, performing some kind of purification and ritual service.[7] Clearly, there is much in this tale that yields to symbolic—if ambivalent or polysemous—interpretation. And humble, homeless Venichka, in his own way, traces the length and breadth, the height and depth of his world. His extraordinary observations, combined with personal idiosyncracies revealed in intimate asides, contribute to a contradictory and compelling vision of a human being, seemingly the last person standing in his world.

Venichka and his author appear to occupy a position entirely apart from the regular social world. Venichka says more than once in the text that he is an orphan from Siberia, describing himself this way to people in authority whose sympathy he seeks. "I'm from Siberia, you see, I'm an orphan" he says to the waiters before they throw him out of the Kursk Station Buffet (8; 145).[8] In life, too, Erofeev was fond of emphasizing his foreignness, prefacing remarks with the phrase, "From my otherworldly [*potustoronnei*] perspective . . ."[9] Erofeev imagined his distance from the institutions and familiar social world of his Moscow friends to be a remove from the world *tout court*. Precisely by affecting this perspective of otherness, Erofeev—as Venichka—more potently reflected the dynamics of his actual social environment. Because this is an autonomous artistic image, however, we will need some time to explain the significance of Venichka's spiritual and artistic character for an analysis of the social field.

VENICHKA—PERFORMING INCONSOLABLE GRIEF

One of the most compelling aspects of Venichka's personality is his melancholy.[10] Venichka's grief seems like evidence of an authentic interiority. In part this melancholy seems so authentic because it is so out of tune with the official atmosphere of optimism and celebration of the time. That atmosphere became heightened during the so-called Era of Anniversaries, which began with the celebration of fifty years since the Revolution in 1967 and continued through the celebration of one hundred years since the birth of Lenin in 1970.[11] Late in the book, Venichka sees a woman dressed all in black. He thinks she looks like the woman in a painting of 1884 by Ivan Kramskoi: "She's the spitting image of 'Inconsolable Grief,' just like you, Yerofeev, I thought straight away, and burst out laughing, inwardly" (113; 230). Venichka had compared himself to the figure in Kramskoi's painting early in the book, when he was describing himself as, "the saddest of all drunks" (30; 163).

Venichka laughs inwardly when he sees the figure to whom he had compared himself standing before him, although that laughter seems wholly out of tune with the attitude the woman represents. Such dissonance captures the principle of contradiction that is the crux of Venichka's complex personality. If melancholy is what people see, Venichka's incongruous laughter inside provides the foil to it. The suggested depth of interiority contrasts with the generally flat and over-determined character of Soviet rhetoric. More often, Venichka creates a contrast with the forced public merriment of the Soviet world by speaking of a grief he carries inside. His melancholy provides a contrast to official culture, which presents a seamless and unforgiving whole, like the stockings of the cruel waitress who refuses to serve Venichka sherry in the morning: "Watching the woman walk away, I felt some disgust. Especially at her white stockings, with no seams. Seams would've calmed me down, maybe, unburdened my soul and conscience" (7; 144). Venichka's melancholy later provides a foil to the unofficial carnivalesque merriment of informal drinking on the electric train.

Such grief has a literary pedigree, of course. Venichka rails against the "bastards" who have forced people to "hide their tears, and show off their laughter! Miserable bastards! They've left us nothing but grief and fear, and on top of that—on top of that, they've made laughter public, yes, and banned tears!" (113–14; 230). The line recalls Nikolai Gogol and his famous statement in *Dead Souls* about viewing life "through laughter seen by the world and tears unseen and unknown by it."[12] Erofeev's reference to Gogol helps us connect Venichka's comments to a tradition of satirical critique.

The connection of *Moscow Stations* to Gogol, signaled most obviously by the subtitle *"Poema"* (*An Epic Poem*), also suggests generic instability. Like Gogol's *Dead Souls*, Erofeev's novel straddles its status as prose work and the tradition of epic poetry it evokes.[13] Venichka highlights this generic instability in an ironic aside as he looks for who might have swiped his bottle of vodka on the train: "God only knows what genre I'll be in by the time we reach Petushki. Since Moscow it's been all philosophical essays and memoirs, poetry and prose, Turgenev-style . . . Now, it's a whodunit!" (52; 182).

The reference to Kramskoi's painting suggests a visual quality to the literary work that might be relevant when we think about the graphs and the lemma that present special stimulus for those readers who copy out the text for samizdat reproduction. Nevertheless, visual artistry as such does not seem to have been a particular interest of Erofeev's, who showed no special feeling for painting, although he was said to be passionately interested in music.[14] Another generic kinship we can examine to help elucidate Venichka's persona is the kinship between Erofeev's prose and theatrical works.

Erofeev wrote dramatic works after *Moscow Stations*, including *Walpurgis Night, or The Steps of the Commander* (*Val'purgieva noch', ili shagi komandora*, 1985), as well as the beginnings of a play called *Dissidents, or Fanny Kaplan* (*Dissidenty, ili Fanny Kaplan*), which remained unfinished. Moreover, *Moscow Stations* appears to have appealed strongly to readers as a work possessing its own dramatic potentials. Stephen Mulrine adapted the text of the novel for a BBC radio play. This version of *Moscow Stations* went to the stage at the Traverse Theatre in Edinburgh in 1993, then the Garrick Theatre in London, before it came to the New York Union Square Theatre in New York in 1995.[15] A number of successful stage adaptations of *Moskva–Petushki* for the Russian stage exist, including the Moscow Taganka theatre production directed by Valentin Ryzhii in 1996, with Aleksandr Tsurkan in the role of Venichka.[16] That production featured a saxophone player for extended stretches of musical interpretation and it highlighted the physicality of Tsurkan's acrobatic acting.

Readers of *Moscow Stations* will recall a striking early scene after Venichka has just gotten on the train and begun to drink. Perhaps someone saw him struggling to take those first drinks, he thinks. He imagines an alibi:

> I could've been rehearsing something. Yes, that's it—I could've been rehearsing that immortal tragedy *Othello, the Moor of Venice*, playing all the parts at once, say. Like, for instance, I could've been unfaithful to myself, betrayed my own convictions. Or rather, I've begun to suspect myself of infidelity, and I whisper some really frightful stuff into my own ear! And so there I am, I've fallen in love with myself on account of my suffering, as much as my own person, and I start to strangle myself. Yes, I take hold of my own throat, and start choking. Oh, who the hell cares what I was doing! (14; 150)

In fact, no one was watching. The "vacant, bulging eyes" of other passengers on the train seem unresponsive and barely human. The idea that Venichka might be a lone performer in a hostile world makes us think of another Shakespearean play, *Hamlet*.

The constitution of individual subjectivity in conditions of a hostile world is both a late Soviet problem and a modern issue, canonically embodied in Hamlet. This Shakespearean subtext—noted by many scholars and readers of Erofeev's text—suggests that the establishment of an authentic late Soviet identity depends on rejoining a conversation about world culture. Erofeev's "Hamletism" resonates within world culture and with past Russian and Soviet engagement with the figure of Hamlet.[17] Venichka refers to himself as a "thoughtful prince" (*prints-analitik*) (25; 159), a formulation that recalls Ivan Turgenev's characterization of Hamlet in his famous 1860 essay "Hamlet and Don Quixote."[18] Venichka exhibits the intellectual complexity and inwardness so characteristic of Hamlet as Harold Bloom explained him in his treatment of Shakespeare's "invention of the human."[19] "I have that within which passeth show," Hamlet declares. Venichka likewise tells us that "the things that really concern me, I never say a word about, not to anyone." Venichka reveals quite a bit, of course, about being fired, being laughed at by women and rejected by his girlfriend, about his love of and anxiety for his son. Nonetheless, there remains something mysterious in his "bellyful of grief" that is his own and inexpressible. That internal core is made up of "sorrow and fear for the most part, plus muteness [*nemota*]" (29; 162). The chiaroscuro of the dark depths hidden inside and its difference from the brilliant talker seen by the world creates our sense of Venichka's depth as a personality.

That contrast also defines the tension of *Moscow Stations* as an artistic work consisting entirely of Venichka's narration, that is, his performance. We can say the work balances between theatricality and absorption, a provocative mix for late twentieth-century avant-garde works. Michael Fried famously developed a contrast between absorption and theatricality as the basis for discriminating between good and mediocre abstract painting and sculpture of the 1960s. In Fried's opinion, the good works were "anti-theatrical, which is to say that they treated the beholder as if he were not there."[20] Fried valued absorption in painting and sculpture as opposed to what he considered to be mediocre theatricality. Marjorie Perloff, by contrast, emphasized the theatrical potentials of the poetic text as distinct and positive qualities of the experimental poetic works she analyzed.[21] We can use the terms of this debate to describe Erofeev's creation of a dynamic text in *Moscow Stations* based on the opposed forces of absorption and theatricality.

Venichka's foolishness functions in most cases as a visible exterior show whose deeper meaning depends on the private grief he feels. Early in the book, after the difficult moments of his hangover pass, Venichka helps stage a sort of carnival through his irreverent reference to canonical authors and sentiments. Even while still suffering, Venichka previews his witty demolition of piety associated with heroic Soviet rhetoric. While suffering from a hangover at the beginning of the book, Venichka declares he would be ready to live on earth for an eternity if only someone would, "show me a corner . . . where there's not always room for heroics [*podvigam*]" (7; 144). The statement brings to mind and distorts the canonical romantic revolutionary spirit expressed in Maksim Gorkii's story "The Old Woman Izergil": "In life there is always a place for heroic feats [*podvigam*]!"[22] Later, when Venichka tells his audience the recipes for cocktails, he advises them they had better write a recipe down: "Man is only given one life, and he has to live so as not to make mistakes with recipes" (*Zhizn' daetsia cheloveku odin raz, i prozhit' ee nado tak, chtoby ne oshibit'sia v retseptakh*) (48; 178). The line recalls the famous quotation from Nikolai Ostrovskii's Socialist Realist classic *How the Steel Was Tempered*: "The most valuable thing a man has is his life. He is given only one life, and he has to live so as not to feel tormenting pain at the thought of wasted years."[23] Venichka's cocktails feature names like "Spirit of Geneva" and "A Loveless Kiss," also known as the "Inessa Armand," referring to the object of Lenin's affections (49, 51; 179, 181). Venichka cleverly parodies the exalted sentiments and fixed forms of official rhetoric and the canon. Venichka sends up socialist principles and revolutionary mythology in the episode with the cocktails and later in the "Petushki Revolution" which takes up the three chapters beginning with "Orekhovo-Zuevo to Krutoe." That revolution is waged chiefly in order to make sure the stores are open to sell liquor as long as possible, and it is likewise narrated so as to deflate the elevated sentiments and canonical commonplaces of Soviet culture. Venichka's association of everything with drinking brings to mind Bakhtin's remarks about the carnivalesque debasement of exalted principles to the realm of matter and the body.[24]

Bakhtin wrote about the fool, the rogue, and the clown as types featured in literature of the Middle Ages. He stressed the theatrical and public character of these figures whose whole character was on the surface.[25] Similarly, the carnival does not tolerate any private or hidden world within the individual. As Bakhtin wrote, "There is in Rabelais' novel no world of interiority."[26] When Venichka finds himself in a Rabelaisian type of situation, his inner depth poses a problem. Venichka's roommates in Orekhovo-Zuevo enjoy a utopian sort of life described in terms that recall Rabelais's Abbaye de Thélème:

> When I moved in there were already four other blokes in this one room, so I was the fifth, and we were like soul-brothers, never a cross word between us. I mean, if one of us fancied some port, he'd get up and say, "Right, lads, I fancy a drop of port." And the others would say, "Great idea—we'll have a drop too." And if one of us fancied a beer, then we all had to have one. (15; 151)

This happy utopia goes bad, however, as the four roommates begin to resent Venichka's unwillingness to get up and go to the bathroom in front of them:

> I'd drunk some beer and got depressed, so I was just lying there, fed up. And I see the four of them quietly surrounding me . . . accusingly, with the sort of bitter look of people can't get access to some secret I'm harbouring.
>
> "Right then, get up and go."
>
> "Go where?"
>
> "Where do you think? You see? There you go again—we're fleabites, we're just garbage, and you're Cain and Manfred."

Venichka's Rabelaisian roommates turn against him precisely because of his physical modesty: they take his reticence, which proceeds from some inner, inexpressible feelings, to be a sign of his arrogance and disdain for them. The carnival, like the revolutionary society, has no tolerance for privacy or individuality. Thus, carnivalesque debasement offers a way to undermine the stifling force of an ossified and exalted culture, but as in the other novels of this period, it proves as Erofeev portrays it to be a false solution. In fact, the carnival arguably represents the reverse side of the coin of Soviet officialdom.[27]

Many Russian readers have recognized a subtext for Venichka's jocular show in the holy fool (*iurodivyi*) from Russian Orthodox tradition.[28] This identification explains much: the contradictions and paradoxes characterizing Venichka's speech can be found in the image of the holy fool, who debases himself in a foolish spectacle in order to arrest people's attention and turn it eventually to higher things. Like Venichka, the holy fool was an outsider in society and with respect to authoritative institutions: a popular religious figure who often did not meet with official approval of the religious establishment.[29] The holy fool, like Venichka, reproached society for spiritual flaws. Scholar A. M. Panchenko wrote that if in cynic culture the principle of shock reigns, the cardinal principle of the culture of the holy fool is reproach. The Russian Orthodox holy fool differs from European fools for whom laughter itself is the cure: the holy fool leads his audience through laughter to tears and the message of salvation.[30]

It seems that Venichka aims to reveal a divine truth, although he will not state it clearly. Contemplating the tears of the woman embodying "Inconsolable Grief," he thinks, "Oh, if I could only think of something to say, some word of mine that would incinerate all those bastards [*gadov*]!" (114; 231). Venichka does not specify who the "bastards" are, but it is clear that these are the ones who have mandated laughter and banned tears, that is, those who have flattened society and human life into the superficial unity he opposes. Venichka's word choice in this scene brings to mind Pushkin's programmatic poem "The Prophet" ("Prorok," 1826), in which the poet is struck down for his blasphemous tongue and raised up again by God who gives him a mission to sear the hearts of men with his word.[31] Venichka will not purport to possess such authority: his foolishness represents a perversion of true authority, played out in a corrupted version of the hagiographic plot. Venichka compares his unhappy career to a "Crucifixion" that takes place after his "Ascension" (24; 158). After Venichka passes out and dreams of a revolution, he dreams also of assuming the office of President of the new Republic, ironically declaring himself to be a person "standing above the Law and the Prophets," like Jesus. Shortly thereafter, he steps down, saying, "Citizen delegates, . . . if I ever have any children, I'm going to hang a portrait of the Governor of Judea, one Pontius Pilate, on their wall, to teach them cleanliness. Yes, Pontius Pilate washing his hands, that's what the portrait'll be. And that's exactly what I'm doing. I'm getting up and washing my hands" (98–99; 218–19). Instead of Jesus, Venichka seems to emulate Pilate.

Venichka's truth has to be sought in the structure of what he is saying: his perversion of the Christian motifs, a superficial corruption concealing that which he holds dear, mirrors the perversion of ideals he sees in the society around him. His dream of the Revolution calls into question Revolutionary ideals, which lack the depth of truth he himself possesses. Venichka and his friend Tikhonov discuss the goals and means of effecting revolution around Petushki. Vadim Tikhonov is the "beloved first born" of the novel's dedication, an epithet suggesting the relationship St. Francis had with his first disciple Bernard.[32] Venichka talks of doing revolutionary things by decree. For example: "'The hands of the clock shall be moved two hours forward, or an hour and a half back, which way being immaterial, as long as they are moved.' Or: 'The word "devil" shall henceforth be spelt "divel," and a letter of the alphabet is to be abolished, once it has been decided which'" (95; 216). Erofeev satirizes the grandness of revolutionary changes. The fact that time could be shifted backward or forward underscores the way revolution—including the Bolshevik Revolution and the French Revolution whose techniques it borrowed—does not so much change the world as introduce a violently arbitrary character into the relationship to the world by forcing a ruling clique's view onto society.

By the end, the realist grotesque of Bakhtin's carnival (and the materialist society of which it is one version) becomes the romantic grotesque. Carnivalesque laughter, which "demolishes fear and piety," leads in Bakhtin's account to a realistic apprehension of the world.[33] The realistic grotesque Bakhtin described gives way in Venichka's narrative to an alienating romantic grotesque.[34] Venichka awakens after his dream of revolution to a dark and confusing world. He does not know which way the train is going. It turns out that windows on both sides of the train have been written over with a rude word; as a consequence of the ubiquity of this "popular" writing, Venichka has trouble orienting himself (110–11; 228–29).[35] Satan and a Sphinx appear among other phantoms to torment him.

Ultimately, Venichka is killed. His four shadowy murderers recall by their number and hostile attitude the four roommates from Orekhovo-Zuevo. In one sense, of course, the end reveals the revolution to be a bloody mess, and the authorities to be no better than murderous thugs. However, the identity of these killers cannot be definitively established. They might indeed recall the four fathers of the Marxist-Leninist state, whose faces appeared together in many public places—Marx, Engels, Lenin, Stalin. They might also seem to be the Four Horsemen of the Apocalypse.[36] This fluid identity fits with the characteristic ambiguity of the romantic grotesque, as Kayser described it: "But who effects the estrangement of the world . . . ? These questions remain unanswered. Apocalyptic beasts emerge from the abyss; demons intrude upon us. If we were able to name these powers and relate them to the cosmic order, the grotesque would lose its essential quality."[37] The lack of specific agency in the scene of Venichka's murder relates to the absence of clearly defined targets of satire throughout the work. We might recall Siniavskii's distinction between artistic and judicial language: in the case of the former, the more capacious a literary figure, the more exact it is.[38] Erofeev's work is literary in this sense, and the breadth of his figures contributes to the sense that Erofeev eschews specific satire in order to evoke an existential condition. *Moscow Stations* effectively illustrates an autonomous literary position in that the world of the novel can be correlated to Erofeev's Soviet reality, but its significance is not confined to it.

"WORDS, WORDS, WORDS"

Venichka, like Hamlet, is a master of verbal manipulation. To Hamlet's "words, words, words" we can counterpose Venichka's "self-generating Logos" (*samovozrastaiushchii Logos*) (79; 203). Venichka's wit resembles Hamlet's wordplay, because both suggest the emptiness or inadequacy of words. As in Hamlet's verbal jousting with Polonius and then with Rosencrantz and Guildenstern, Venichka also uses the sharpness of his nimble wit to fend off those who would seek to pin him down and destroy him.[39] The web of words conceals an ineffable—but vulnerable—depth.

Insofar as this web of words covers over the essence of the protagonist's personality, it parodies the official rhetoric that has by this time become a total and hermetic veil of discourse cutting Soviet people off from reality. Alexei Yurchak called this the "hegemony of representation" in the late Soviet period. He convincingly demonstrated that the system of rhetoric and visual and verbal signifiers became more centrally coordinated and codified after Stalin. Yurchak described the "hegemony of representation" as "a system in which all official institutions, discourses, and practices are always-already produced [*sic*] and manipulated from the center as one unique discourse." He elaborated:

> In the case of late socialism the hegemony of representation can be visualized as a symbolic order of tightly interconnected signifiers that were exclusively state-controlled and permeated most aspects of everyday life in the official sphere. These were verbal formulas (structural elements of the politicized discourse of the official sphere, such as names of soviet institutions and public organizations and formulaic phraseology of official speeches), visual images (posters, pictures, placards, monuments), mass rituals (Party and Komsomol meetings, elections, and November and May parades), the topics in the media, literature, popular culture (all of which were controlled by centralized bodies and ministries), and tightly structured events of daily public life (the use of public transport, work at a Soviet enterprise where wages were centrally fixed, study in a Soviet school with centrally adopted curriculum, and shopping in a Soviet store with unified centrally controlled prices and choices).[40]

Not surprisingly, such ossification became the target of jokes. For example, a series of jokes about the Civil War hero Vasilii Chapaev, featured in Dmitrii Furmanov's novel and the Vasiliev brothers' entertaining 1934 film of the same name, emerged around the time of the celebration of the fiftieth anniversary of the October Revolution.[41] Erofeev's novel, subtitled in at least one edition "A novel-joke" ("Roman-anekdot"),[42] evokes this culture of popular humor. Erofeev parodies the popular reappropriation of ubiquitous elements of official culture when the men from Venichka's cable-laying crew use highly charged names of military figures from the Soviet press for their own bawdy purposes—"Well, how'd it go with that Nina in No. 13, did you *abba*?' And back he'd come with a smug grin, 'You bet—she was just *dayan* for it!'" (21; 155).[43] As the scene suggests, such jokes create a sense of informal imagined community with more life in it than the official version of Soviet unity.[44]

However, Erofeev's play on the names of Abba Eban and Moshe Dayan parodies such jokes no less than the official propaganda they target. In the novel, Venichka's crew represents a social collective of dubious substance, whose shared activities comprise mainly drinking and shirking work. This reality is hilariously incongruous with the Socialist pledges they send off once a month: "We would write, for example: 'To mark the occasion of V. I. Lenin's forthcoming centenary, we pledge ourselves to eliminate industrial injuries.' Or else, 'On the occasion of the glorious centenary, we shall strive to ensure that every sixth worker takes a correspondence course at an institute of higher education.' I mean, injuries and institutes, for Christ's sake, and we're tucked out of sight playing brag, and there's only five of us anyway!" Venichka observes (21; 155).

Venichka tries to awaken his men to more spiritual values with Aleksandr Blok's poetry. Blok's poem "The Nightingale Garden" has much that speaks to their experience, Venichka argues: "Right at the centre of the poem—that is, if you cast aside all those perfumed shoulders and impenetrable mists, the rosy towers in their smoky vestments, etc.—at the very heart of the poem is a tragic figure, dismissed from his job for drunkenness, whoring and absenteeism" (21; 156).[45] The men's response, however, is to throw aside their regular drinking habits and drink only the cologne Fraîcheur. This hardly represents a significant development of their moral and spiritual selves (22; 156).

Before Venichka can properly study their souls as he intends to do, he gets fired. Venichka calls this his "Crucifixion," alienating him from society: "And I solemnly swear to you now, that to the end of my days I shall embark upon nothing which might bring about a repetition of my unhappy experience of life at the top" (24–25; 158). His authority as brigade leader represented a modest social position. Venichka's renunciation of such a position parodies the kind of refusal of the social order and its illusions we saw in Flaubert's character Frédéric Moreau, in Aksenov's Dmitrii from his early novella *Colleagues*, and, with different implications, in Aksenov's own decision to forego his established place in official Soviet literature.[46] Aksenov registered the bitter anger felt at the end of the 1960s in light of the disconnection from official celebration and unity, so out of tune with the disillusionment and dread created by the invasion of Czechoslovakia. Erofeev, who did not refer to that event so specifically, conveyed the lonely sorrow and existential desperation attending that gesture, despite the comically inflated nature of Venichka's pronouncement.[47]

Venichka's rhetoric differs from official discourse in that it is personal and individualized, possessing emotional depth. It has, as Bakhtin would say, a "signature."[48] The issue of an author's name and the kind of subjectivity that gets constructed in literary work is related to this personalization. Part of the problem with the jocular response to official propaganda and other types of Soviet hegemonic representation is that, like the carnival whose spirit they convey, those jokes do not accommodate the expression of a committed or engaged individual subjectivity. The communal or folk nature of such witty interventions posed a kind of trap for writer Iuz Aleshkovskii. Aleshkovskii won warm appreciation from friends for his songs and oral improvisations among company at the table, but these appeared to lack the weight of authorial commitment. When Aleshkovskii wanted to make a literary name for himself, he turned to the genre of the novel.[49] Venichka's witty repartee functions as a literary representation of this kind of ephemeral improvisation, which Erofeev's novel suggests might destroy the subject because it lacks risk and an anchor in real life. As becomes clear later in the book, Venichka's carnivalesque relationship to words threatens to annihilate him. Venichka manipulates bits of reified official culture in the first part of his train journey as we have seen. By the end, however, the disembodied bits of discourse called forth by his jocular speech return as disorienting cues to something he has forgotten or cannot access. "Right, right—the most important question is . . . For some reason or other I can't get Chekhov out of my head. Yes, and Schiller, Schiller and Chekhov, I haven't the faintest idea why" (116; 232). These names come from the discussion of great cultural figures in the chapter "Yesino to Fryazevo" (58; 186), but Venichka's drunkenness, which corresponds in some respects to the intoxication of a revolutionary society, has made him forget what those names were supposed to signify. Venichka at this point in the journey has become trapped in a world of phantoms that turn increasingly hostile and violent. If we take this together with the silence of God and the angels in response to Venichka's pleas (e.g., Venichka asks, "Lord, why hast Thou forsaken me?" but "The Lord was silent" [130; 243]), the resulting impression is that all of culture, not just the official rhetoric and propaganda, has become a collection of mere images, phantoms without any substance the protagonist can access or engage.

This disjunction of words and culture from substance threatens Venichka. We can compare this situation to the threats to subjectivity in Aksenov's and Bitov's novels. In those novels, also, dense intertextuality serves as a literary representation of a society in crisis. While the three authors show this in different ways, all three highlight the divorce of cultural referents from their reality or sources, and the eroded boundaries of the subject that result. In Aksenov's *The Burn*, for example, when the protagonist and Pat head for the Crimea, they enthuse over the cultural resonance of their destination. Pat and the protagonist intone the beginning of Osip Mandelshtam's poem, "Sleeplessness, Homer, tight sails . . . ," although they cannot come up with more than the first two lines. Thus, even as they seem to be headed for the origins of culture, they reveal the tenuousness of their connection to it (165; 144).[50] Their companion Alik Neyarky, by jarring contrast, quotes Soviet classics: "A friend told me, you only get one life . . . and you have to live so as not to feel tormenting pain at the thought of wasted years" (168; 146). Neyarky seems unaware the line he cites from "a friend" comes from Ostrovskii's novel *How the Steel Was Tempered*. Imprecise knowledge of sources relates to the characters' moral confusion. Neyarky is casually and viciously violent, and the protagonists seem not to notice: "There's a lovely little town here waiting for us boys! Come on—let's slit open its belly and wrap its guts around our swords!" (169; 147), says Neyarky. The statement takes on more disquieting significance when the reader puts together

Neyarky's participation as one of the "mercenaries" in the Congo, whose trans-historical role is conveyed through references to the seventeenth-century European setting of Schiller's play *Wallenstein's Camp*, which features mercenaries, too. Aksenov relied on a web of intertexts to reveal the greater significance of characters, places or events. His protagonists ignore the specificity of those intertexts at their peril. Pat and the protagonist do not react to Neyarky's apparently unmotivated burst of aggression. Once in the Crimea, the protagonist assumes the role of a Don Juan character called "Stranger in the Night" (*Tainstvennyi v nochi*),[51] a persona suitable for the carnivalesque masquerade that ensues, another round of escapist carousing in the guise of a mysterious persona lacking real identity or responsibility.

Bitov in *Pushkin House* treated the issue somewhat differently. As we saw in chapter 3, Modest Platonovich argues to Lyova that the recovery of repressed sources, the mining of the word, concepts, or works is a worthless pursuit as engaged in by the liberals of Lyova's generation who want only to consume what they uncover. Such consumption can only distract from the development of a self-possessed and creative relationship to their historical moment. With Lyova's treatment of Tiutchev, Bitov advocated living "interruptedly," that is, coming to terms with the discontinuity of culture so as to develop one's own meaningful perspective and voice.

Bitov treated this cultural discontinuity in the "Commentary" in terms of a breakdown in the representation of history, where the Golden and Silver Ages give way to inferior ages and eventually a synthetic age beyond narrative logic. Erofeev echoed Bitov's theme of cultural discontinuity in a representation of the end of history in *Moscow Stations*. Venichka narrates this end for Semyonych the ticket controller. Earlier, Venichka evoked his own, highly eroticized personal paradise in Petushki where his girlfriend resides ("Oh, those long ginger eyelashes . . . Oh, sorcery and the wings of doves!" [35; 167]). In his encounter with the controller Venichka plays the feminine role of a Scheherezade to stoke Semyonych's dreams and desires. Semyonych is willing to collect the fare in drinks from passengers who lack tickets and money. He has already drunk quite a deal by the time he gets to Venichka. Venichka has no vodka to share with Semyonych, but Semyonych knows he can force a good story out of Venichka. Venichka has already fed Semyonych a scabrous version of most of world history. Only the end is left. Venichka's account of the end of history mixes together biblical imagery and Soviet propaganda, culminating with unbridled erotic fantasy: "And there will be goodness and beauty . . . the tormentor and his victim will merge in a kiss." Semyonych gets excited: "Merge in a what?" Venichka goes on to say, "And the woman of the East will cast off her veil! Yes, she will finally fling off her yashmak, that oppressed woman of the East! And they shall lie down" (88; 210). Too befuddled to distinguish fiction from reality, Semyonych starts to take off his clothes. We as readers know along with Venichka that this story woven out of bits of other narratives functions as a way of distracting a man by appealing to his desires. The scene comically exposes utopian fictions as Semyonych literally exposes himself. Following this humorous episode, however, things take a more serious turn. Venichka, who is also highly intoxicated, becomes disoriented and ends up going the wrong direction. His journey begins to collapse in on itself, realizing in the plot the lack of orientation and progress implied by the exhaustion of guiding historical narratives.

This collapse, a lack of depth implied by the end of history, has in fact been there all along, expressed by an eclectic mix of insubstantial cultural references. However, while Venichka was still guiding the conversation, we might have been fooled into thinking his substance as a character anchored the reality of his world. For example, Venichka models the human responsiveness that grounds culture in his conversation with Black Moustache (the name Venichka gives to a loquacious fellow passenger) and the other riders sitting with them on the train. Black Moustache has developed a whole theory about history and drinking that involves writers Kuprin and Gorkii, Schiller and Gogol, along with composers Mussorgskii and Rimskii-Korsakov, and Herzen and the Social Democrats, all of whom get dragged in to support the simple idea that all good men drink. The Decembrist (nickname of another of the passengers) objects that Johann von Goethe did not drink. Black Moustache is flummoxed. When Venichka sees that Black Moustache's theory, "his whole elegant system, constructed out of impassioned and brilliantly stretched points," has been "publicly demolished," Venichka thinks to himself, "Give him a hand, Yerofeev, . . . Spit out an allegory or something" (62; 189). Venichka comes up with the idea that Goethe projected his desire to drink onto his heroes. He does not intervene because he believes in the truth of Black Moustache's system. Rather, Venichka sees that the man is crestfallen, and he wants to help. After Venichka's explanation, good cheer is restored. There exists a human dimension to communication that exceeds the truth value of the propositions. Real responsiveness depends on seeing what is needed for the sake of humanity in a particular situation.

Vencihka saves Black Moustache's system, not for the sake of the system, but because he feels human fellowship with him. To be sure, Erofeev is not endorsing the Soviet system as something worth saving—far from it. However, he recognizes the impulse to make sense of the world with stories and systems as part of human nature. That impulse gets humanized in its eccentric expression, by a character far from power, whose idiosyncratic theory is obviously a fiction. In this way, we see again an endorsement of autonomous art in the fiction recognized as such, as opposed to the unacknowledged lie of the official (and supra-personal) system.

Shortly thereafter, Venichka incorporates that human feeling into his own witty commentary. He conjures up the friendly phantom of Maksim Gorkii to help make a point in the discussion about women:

> D'you know what Gorky said on Capri? He said, "The measure of any civilization is how it treats its women." So I turn up at a shop in Petushki . . . And [the woman attendant is] looking at me, thinking, will I give this shit his change? Meanwhile I'm looking at her, thinking, will this cow give me my change? Well, actually, no, I'm not looking at her at that precise instant. I'm looking through her and beyond. And what is it that presents itself to my unthinking gaze? The island of Capri, no less. Agaves and tamarind trees, and Gorky sitting underneath them, with his hairy legs poking out of his white ducks. And he's wagging his finger at me: "Don't take that change. Don't dare take that change!" And I wink at him. But I've got bugger all to eat, I say. "I mean, okay, great, I'll get something to drink, but what am I going to eat with it?"
>
> And he says: "It doesn't matter, Venya. You'll just have to put up with it. If you want to eat—don't drink." So I walk out and leave the change. Of course, I'm angry. "Huh, measure!" I think. "Civilisation!" "Oh, Maxim Gorky, some bloody Maxim you are, what made you come out with that stuff on Capri—was it stupidity or drink? It's all very well for you—you can sit chomping your agaves, but what've I got?"
>
> Everybody laughed. (67; 193–94)

The story is broadly comic because of the familiar treatment of a canonical figure. That comedy gives new life to a serious sentiment about treating people well that Venichka derives from Gorkii's tired cliché and reinvigorates with his bracingly realistic story of the encounter with the woman at the shop. Thus, we might conclude that even if words like "civilization" have been cut off from their referents, they might be given new force by an individual's creative application of the values they represent in contemporary reality.

As an antidote to the violence of repeated propaganda clichés or deluding myths, Aksenov's novel suggests dialogue, the kind of unforced and un-predetermined conversation in which people recognize their identity and respond to that of their interlocutor, as do the protagonist and Masha in one scene and the protagonist and Pat in another rare moment of ordinary human conversation in *The Burn*. Bitov in *Pushkin House* demonstrated Lyova's positive potential for self-knowledge and recognition of others in Lyova's clear-eyed perception of Faina at the end of section 2. Erofeev combined the social character of Aksenov's dialogue with the individual emphasis of Bitov's psychological account. By doing so, Erofeev evoked the possibility of a social field with real depth, combining the authentic individual and the need for interpersonal response. Erofeev convincingly developed an image of interior subjectivity in Venichka. He went further than Aksenov or Bitov in showing how vulnerable such individual subjectivity remains without the response that would validate it.

Erofeev evoked the existential threat attending the issues he treated. This threat manifests in the suspicion that there may be no other human beings in Venichka's world. Erofeev called into doubt the possibility of a human response, because ultimately we are not sure about Black Moustache or any of the other characters Venichka encounters: are they human?

The drinkers Venichka spies after returning from his first drinks seem more like caricatures than characters. One wears a bodywarmer and looks really thick ("*tupoi-tupoi*"). The other in a heavy overcoat looks really intelligent ("*umnyi-umnyi*") (14–15; 150). While we might take this to be Venichka's half-drunk assessment of them, later companions seem entirely grotesque. In particular, the body of the grandson on the train is somehow backwards with "a neck that doesn't grow into his torso, it grows out of it," while his eyes are "gaping" and his mouth "squinting." His grandfather Mitrich has eyes leaking like two drowning victims, and his bald head looks "dead" (54; 183). These characters' traits seem strangely isolated. Overall the characters seem defective, only partially developed. Taken as a group, Venichka's interlocutors seem in fact like projections of his own consciousness. Black Moustache, for example, represents Venichka's rhetorical prowess. Grandfather Mitrich represents Venichka's compassion. The woman with no front teeth ironically evokes Venichka's search to define his personal identity. We can interpret all of the people he meets in terms of various expressions of Venichka's own psyche.[52] Indeed, more than one scholar has concluded that the entire journey, including the episodes on the train, takes place entirely inside Venichka's own head. He begins and ends in an unknown entranceway—perhaps there was no physical journey at all.[53]

Such solipsism threatens to undo Venichka's performance—there is no one to appreciate him, to respond with depth and feeling to the expression of Venichka's soul. At the end, back in Moscow, Venichka solicits people to recognize the trouble he is in, to show him mercy and give him shelter. Venichka, pursued, cold and scared, knocks, observing plaintively, "Surely it can't be that difficult to open the door, and let a person get warm for a couple of minutes? I don't understand it" (124; 239). Nearer the end, he addresses us, readers outside the text: "You people out there, humanity, I don't know you too well . . . I'd like to know where your soul is these days, to know for sure if the Star of Bethlehem's going to shine out again, or even just flicker. That's the main thing, because all the other stars have just about had it, and even if they are shining, they're not worth two spits [*dvukh plevkov*]" (125; 239). Guiding values have to be reconstructed by the collective as well as the individual. So far, there is no real communication or response in Venichka's world in the book to make that possible.

Venichka projects such human communication—necessary for his identity but impossible to find in his existing world—into the future. One of the ways he does this is through the theme of children. Venichka's son, his boy living somewhere beyond Petushki, represents hope for the future, for the kind of human connection, recognition, and love Venichka craves. For the time being, the toddler can only repeat back to his father what he hears. Worried about the boy's illness, Venichka tells him not to die, having learned only the letter "Iu" (Ю): "You surely understand that, that it's stupid," Venichka says, and the boy replies, "I understand, Father" (32; 165). That letter Ю will be the last thing Venichka sees, a reminder of his boy that is simultaneously a graphic symbol for the piercing of his throat that has just taken place (131; 204). Again, however, this boy may be another projection of Venichka's own personality, specifically, his concern for his own ability to survive.

Venichka tends to infantilize himself. The name Venichka, the form that appears most often when the protagonist refers to himself, represents a childish diminutive, spelled phonetically as a child might, rather than the orthographically correct "Venechka."[54] Venichka addresses himself in soothing and encouraging tones, speaking to himself as one would to a child: "It doesn't matter," or "Never mind," he repeats to himself when hung over in the morning or scared at night. Venichka channels his anxiety through imagined interlocutors, thinking that he seems to them vulnerable as a helpless child. "What are they thinking?" Venichka wonders about the Angels and their embarrassed silence. Do they think, "Somebody'll strangle me like a kid? Or knife me like a little girl?" (25; 161)

Erofeev associates children with death or the threat of death throughout the text. A calculation of how much alcohol can be bought with change from empty bottles is sealed with the contention, "Any child knows that. They might not know how Pushkin died, but they know that much" (66; 193). Later, the threatening Sphinx presents Venichka with a math riddle, glossing over the price of sherry, because "every child knows the price of sherry" (108; 227). A bit later, Venichka uses the more mature-sounding last name, perhaps to affect a more adult posture and thereby give himself courage: "Never mind, Yerofeev, never mind . . . '*Talitha cumi*', as your Empress said when you were stretched out in your coffin . . . The further you go, the easier it'll get. After all, you yourself told that little boy when he was ill: 'One, two, buckle my shoe, get out of bed, sleepyhead . . .' Keep away from the tracks, that's the main thing" (122; 237). Venichka here recalls the words from the story of Jairus's daughter, raised from the dead, to whom he has compared himself. Venichka remembers his little boy's illness from the Friday before last. He fears his boy will come to harm and prays, "Oh, merciful God, don't let anything happen to him, not now, not ever!" Venichka imagines specific ways the boy might hurt himself by falling from a roof or the stove, with a knife or a razor, or by burning himself (32; 164).

We could interpret this in a specifically authorial way according to the lights of Bourdieu's field of restricted productions: Venichka's tendency to get sidetracked in the promise of erotic fulfillment associated with his girlfriend in Petushki represents the aspect of authorial desire for immediate recognition and praise among the audience. Not for nothing is she a "ballad in A flat major" (*ballada lia bemol' mazhor*, a loose anagram for *bliad'*, or prostitute) (34; 166). She suggests at some level the author's desire to get something for his pleasing rhetorical performance. The little boy represents a more serious hope for the real human results of the connection made at the site of the text, fruit of the union of author and reader that must, like the boy, grow into maturity and independence. Bourdieu's model suggests that consecration, and the cultural capital associated with it, can come to the eccentric or avant-garde work only over time. Erofeev's novel is not excessively formally experimental—it does not seem avant-garde in that sense. However, Erofeev did avoid the features that would have made the work a sure-fire dissident seller. "He revealed no body counts, exposed no officials, and engaged in no ideological debates," Remnick wrote.[55] Moreover, as the samizdat work of an unknown writer, *Moscow Stations* had no certain future. Erofeev expressed that uncertainty in part through the figure of the sick young son.

At the end, of course, it is Venichka who dies. I propose that the existential threat under which Venichka labors and to which he seems to succumb at the end obliquely conveys the human or social condition of the late Soviet world as Erofeev sees it, as well as the particular vulnerability of the dissident author. Venichka finds himself in a world with no other human beings to answer him. The dissident author, particularly one with no established position on the Soviet literary field, cannot be sure anyone will respond to his work. The two sides of this dilemma might be understood in a way that resonates with Venichka's performance in the text if we take up the construction of subjectivity as discussed by Eve Kosofsky Sedgwick. Sedgwick proposed an alternative model for constructing subjective identity through performative utterances, that is, statements that impact the social situation. J. L. Austin had previously described performative utterances as the complement to constative utterances. If constative utterances represent a preexisting reality, the performative utterance brings about a reality. Austin provided the example of the phrase "I do," in a marriage ceremony: that statement *effects* the state of marriage, rather than conveying it as an already existing fact.[56] In this way, performatives are oriented to the future, and they depend on the social context in which a person is recognized, within the proper circumstances, as having the power to create such a reality. Sedgwick offered an alternative paradigm for the performative and the kind of subjectivity it implied. While the dependence on social context and audience of the formulation "I do" might be concealed by the grammar emphasizing first-person agency, Sedgwick's alternative performative example, "Shame on you," captures the complexities of social and interpersonal dynamics as they impact the constitution of the individual "I." In the phrase, "Shame on you," the "I" is effaced, and the social attitude projected tends to negate the subjectivity of the "you" to whom it is directed, producing (when the reproach is felt) a longing on the part of that object of the utterance to reestablish a social connection that has been broken.[57]

Various shades of shame color the three samizdat novels examined in this study. As we saw, Aksenov revealed in *The Burn* the disgrace (*pozor*) felt by his alter ego as a teenager distraught by his mother's arrest and conscious of the social outcast it made him. This disgrace echoed in adult situations with officials who publicly shamed the protagonist or forced him into uncomfortable compromises and closeness with the regime. Bitov's novel *Pushkin House*, subtitled in the French edition "A Novel of Infinite Humiliation,"[58] illustrates the situations in which Lyova is forced to confront his failings, shortcomings his education has tended to cover over with the smug ideology of progress. Shame is offered as a potentially constructive feeling, a sign of the re-emergence of the intellectual hero. Erofeev's Venichka talks a great deal about his modesty and shame.[59] He tries to protest to his roommates in Orekhovo-Zuevo: "I mean, it's not that easy, just to get up and go . . . 'Cause there's a kind of shame, sort of a holy precept, ever since the days of Ivan Turgenev—and then later, the oath on Sparrow Hills."[60] The roommates remain unimpressed. They tell Venichka that with such shameful views (*c takimi pozornymi vzgliadami*) he will always be alone and unhappy (17–18; 152–53). This modesty (*tselomudrie*) becomes the reason for Venichka's embarrassment when friends introduce him to ladies as the person who never passes gas. His confused explanations do not help his standing—"He does it out loud, and he says what he's doing isn't *bad*. He says it's actually *good*!" (19; 153–54) In this situation, too, Venichka proves incapable of communicating his meaning in a way that people around him will understand.

In all these novels, the feeling of shame signals a broken social connection. We can relate this to the dissident decision to refuse the general illusion and take up a stand apart, making oneself an object of ostracism, misunderstanding, censure, and ridicule. Aksenov's emphasis on the shame of the awkward teenage years is intriguing: he suggests that dissident shame only exposes the kind of humiliation inflicted on Soviet people in the violent process of destroying and remaking a revolutionary society through purges. Bitov's novel suggests that dissident shame can be a productive feeling, implying recognition of the rift between what one wants to be and what one is, a difficult but necessary confrontation of the breakdown in communication creating the possibility of reconstructing oneself in a more authentic way. Erofeev, once again, goes to the essence of the matter: his focus on children and death highlight this shame as an existential issue.

Sedgwick talked about the initial experience of the infant whose caretaker turns away as a moment precipitating the breakdown of communication and the feeling of basic threat to life that broken communication represents for the helpless child. Although later experiences of shame and humiliation do not usually seem so dire, a shadow of that original experience of broken communication as existential threat lingers in the adult psyche, and such a breakdown could indeed be physically threatening for the marginalized person.[61] Venichka bares the fundamental emotional character of that breakdown in communication. He also demonstrates what Sedgwick contended—that signs of shame paradoxically function as a sort of communication. Sedgwick pointed out that "blazons of shame, the 'fallen face' with eyes down and head averted—and to a lesser extent, the blush—are semaphors of trouble and at the same time of a desire to reconstitute the interpersonal bridge." Sedgwick went on to suggest that shame is the affect "that most defines the space wherein a sense of self will develop."[62] Venichka, and Erofeev in life, depicted often as modest, shy, unsure of themselves, perform the dissident shame that at once signals the breakdown of false social unity and communication of the urgent desire for new bonds of communication to grow. The dissident subjectivity Venichka represents is tentative, vulnerable, and in need of social response—his performance of shame proves to be perhaps more compelling than his ready wit and the popular laughter it elicits.

The performative aspect of Venichka's performance in *Moscow Stations* means that the kind of witty banter and fellowship in which Venichka engages are not representations of a social collective that exists but a perverted projection of the real human relationships for which Erofeev aims. Erofeev exposed a world full of phantoms, bereft of human contact and real possibilities for engagement. Venichka's words demonstrate the emptiness of the world he sees: they also point more subtly toward the kind of human communication he desires.

AIMING FOR THE FUTURE

Moscow Stations can be viewed as a poetic work structured on the basis of taut oppositions, but its status gets complicated by the systematic perversion or contradiction of those relationships. Venichka's characteristic stylistic shifts from the high register to the low and back up to the high again illustrates this structural principle, dubbed "counter-irony" by commentators.[63] An intriguing example can be found in Venichka's discussion of hiccups in the chapter "Kilometre 33 to Elektrougli": Venichka sets up a comic juxtaposition of high and low with the philosophical terms *an sich* and *fur sich*, applied to the study of hiccups. "Naturally, you'll try to establish some sort of periodicity . . . But life will topple all your half-arsed constructions," Venichka tells his listeners. He uses the unpredictability of hiccups to demonstrate the intractability of physical reality to any theory: "You know, the leaders of the world proletariat, Karl Marx and Friedrich Engels, are supposed to have made an in-depth study of changes in social structures, and on that basis they were able to predict a whole heap of stuff. But they'd have been completely foxed by this one." The humorous lowering of ideal categories and models by means of an unruly physiological function then unexpectedly returns us to (more proper) contemplation of the heights: the hiccups end, and in the silence that ensues, having gained knowledge of the fate that rules us beyond our schemes, we learn that "[God] is inscrutable, and in consequence—He is. Therefore be perfect as your Father in Heaven is perfect," Venichka admonishes us (45–46; 175–76). The energy produced by the comic lowering of ideal cognitive schemes gets channeled into a thrust upward that is also, I would argue, a push out into the future, beyond the text that represents a world still enthralled by false schemes and the hubris of a regime based on theory.

The tensions of the text push forward toward the emotional impact of the end and Venichka's murder. If his mixed-up references to the Gospels make us want to believe some kind of future and fulfillment will be possible for Venichka after his brutal end, his last words challenge that wish: "Since then, I've never regained consciousness. And I never shall," he says (131; 244). Moreover, this statement casts doubt back on the entire text and the place from which the narrative voice speaks. We can take the text in the time we read it as a narration in the present (like a performance). Indeed, the text seems to foreclose the possibility that events could be narrated from any retrospective angle after the murder. Venichka's speech does not fully conform to this condition, however: for example, when Venichka describes himself standing in the middle of Kursk Station Square "like a statue," for "precisely one minute," he seems to occupy two enunciative positions at once, corresponding to two distinct time zones. Venichka simultaneously fulfills the roles of subject (I-now) and object of narration (I-then).[64] At that moment he speculates that the people looking at him are wondering whether he should be sculpted "for the edification of the peoples of antiquity" (9; 145–46). The record of Venichka's speech is this sort of "edifying" monument,[65] perhaps, although it is not clear why this should be for the peoples of antiquity. Narrative time, like the historical time implied by the reified and eclectic cultural references, has no rational progression or logic.

From this paradoxical position, Venichka transforms his late Soviet reality, appealing to Russian readers and an international audience. Vladimir Muravev, a friend of Erofeev, talked about his work in terms of ritual, sacraments and transfiguration (*preobrazhenie*). Erofeev's *Moscow Stations* is an epic poem about Soviet everyday life brought face to face with world culture, he said.[66] Certainly, references to the Gospels function as a key method for transforming the image of the late Soviet world and a person in it, adding depth and grandeur to what Erofeev portrays as a soulless reality. However, imposing narrative coherence on the work through a systematic application of the Gospels would destroy the network of tensions that give *Moscow Stations* its transformative potentials. The mixed-up culture and chronology represented in the text combined with the text's resistance to any dogmatic reading mean that the significance of Venichka's figure and his performance range more widely. The laughter followed by death in Venichka's story recall older patterns of ritual: Venichka seems like a carnival king who is killed at the end in a kind of ritual cleansing. For example, the execution of a mock king formed part of Saturnalia and of the Babylonian festival of Sacaea. Such rituals were reprised in the Christian tradition. The practice of burning a Straw Man at the end of the Carnival on Ash Wednesday is a Christian enactment of the renewal associated with the scapegoat.[67] These archetypal patterns resonate also in the story of Christ, crowned King of the Jews before Crucifixion. This incarnation of the story does appear to have special significance in the text, although its presentation does not warrant a crude imposition of Erofeev's Christian belief onto the work. The trans-historical character of patterns associated with ritual and transformation help the work appeal to readers as material for more varied and less dogmatic interpretations.

Erofeev's *Moscow Stations* as a novel of ritual represents an alternative to the codified official novels of Socialist Realism.[68] Eccentric as Erofeev's idiosyncratic, genre-bending interpretation of the Soviet novel is, he shares with official works their orientation to the future and an edifying function, though not, I would argue, a specifically Christian message. He resists the dogma of Socialist Realism through a more open evocation of subjective identity and human response. The spectacle of Venichka's journey, his life and his death, develop an image of the human, individual and irreplaceable, whose voice can only be substantiated on the basis of the many different voices that respond to him. Moreover, we can see here pretty clearly the function of the restricted field of cultural production as Bourdieu described it: Venichka as lyrical persona represents a negation of the Soviet positive hero. Erofeev's notebooks show how consciously and deliberately he constructed such a literary persona for himself.[69] By the same token, the ritual of *Moscow Stations* both invokes and opposes the ritual of Socialist Realist novels according to the denegation of the larger social forces that Bourdieu defined as the engine of autonomous art.

The scene of Venichka's death forms the crux of this edifying function. In a Christian reading, it might confirm Venichka's status as a sort of late Soviet prophet, purifying with his death the world he represents, and giving to his voice a special type of authority. However, Venichka's death makes him more like Hamlet and less like the traditional holy fool, whose death typically is not seen.[70] The Christian reading seems not so certain. In the New Testament, the Greek word *kairos* means the "fateful and decisive point," the moment of opportunity given by God. The believer must recognize God's design,[71] and in imitation of Jesus, he must subordinate his own will and perception to the revelation of that design. Jesus did not know the divine *kairos* of his life in advance—he saw it only when it came, and ultimately he was ready to die.[72] *Kairos* was revealed at the Crucifixion, and it will be revealed at the last judgment. Although Venichka evokes both of those events in his description of the action unfolding in his life and at the end, he himself does not recognize the time of his death as *kairos*. In ancient Greek, the word *kairos* in the context of archery signifies the long, tunnel-like aperture through which the arrow has to pass, implying that the arrow must be fired accurately and with enough power to penetrate. In the context of weaving, *kairos* indicates the "critical time" when the weaver must draw the yarn through a gap that momentarily opens in the warp of the cloth being woven.[73] Taken in these senses, Venichka's text exemplifies the skill and art of ancient *kairos*: Venichka weaves his material together in such a way to deliver effective hits of humor and pity. The fact that the end throws us back onto the tensions of the text and Venichka's living voice suggests this older meaning of *kairos*. Moreover, the contradictory twisting, or "perversion" of categories enacted in many ways throughout Venichka's performance implies that if Venichka's voice is the arrow that must penetrate our minds and hearts to move us, it aims also to be the receptacle for our interventions: *we* must recognize the *kairos*. The text represents a "critical time" we must perceive to be a meaningful ritual or transformation if it is to be realized as such. Venichka's text opens up with the hole ripped into it by his violent annihilation, creating the long tunnel of *kairos* that we must enter with our own voices in response.

MOSKVA–PETUSHKI IN SAMIZDAT AND BEYOND

With its performative potentials, Erofeev's work responded more specifically to the conditions of the unofficial field of culture than either Aksenov's or Bitov's samizdat novels. The production and deployment of both *The Burn* and *Pushkin House* reflected those authors' position in the official Soviet literary establishment, including their orientation to the possibilities for print publication that their positions created. Erofeev, not being part of the establishment, showed in *Moscow Stations* that he was more specifically attuned to the dependence of the samizdat text on individual audience response. Samizdat readers needed to support the life of this work, talking about it to friends, copying and passing it along: otherwise, it would simply disappear. Erofeev expressed this fact artistically through the potentials of Venichka's text as "performance." Shakespeare provides a valuable point of reference, because his work has been used to illustrate the modern literary ideology of the romantic genius author, an ideology associated with the practice of silent reading of an ideal text that perfectly conforms to the author's conception.[74] However, as plays, Shakespeare's works also appear performed and adapted for the needs of the historical and social context; that is, the realization of the text varies and depends on the audience.[75]

While it alludes to and echoes to some degree Shakespeare's classic dramas, *Moscow Stations* also illustrates a relatively specific neo-avant-garde performative aspect. This performativity implies the juxtaposition and twisting of accustomed oppositions, including, as we have seen, the conjunction of theatricality and absorption that links Venichka to the figure of Hamlet but also expresses the frustration with an artificial public culture in the Soviet Union after Stalin. The mixture of high seriousness and carnivalesque materiality driving Venichka's characteristic "counter-irony" relates to this same disillusionment and longing for renewed values. Another performative "twist" occurs with the conflicting cues about whether *Moscow Staitons* is written or oral: Venichka emphasizes the "oral" aspect of his narration when he bids his audience to "write down" the cocktail recipes (48–50; 178–80). The cues are contradictory, because as readers we see the recipes on the page in front of us. However, that very artifice helps us appreciate the concept of an informal story told, as it were, about friends and for friends.[76] In other instances, Venichka draws our attention to his graphs of the brigade crew's alcohol consumption and to Black Moustache's lemma, which are drawn on the pages of the text we read (23, 64; 157, 191). These parts of the text require more obviously active participation by the reader who copies them. Thus the performative orientation to the co-creative function of the audience comes to the fore at the moment when the fact of the written text is emphasized—that materiality of the text twists accustomed modern categories.

The oral character of Venichka's performance likewise reflects artistically the relatively unfixed and spontaneous character of the samizdat text. It is as though Venichka speaks to friends, then those friends relay to other friends what Venichka said. Zorin talked about the way phrases from Erofeev's work got fixed in the imagination of samizdat readers, becoming new aphorisms that expressed unofficial resistance of the spirit to progressive ideology and a sense of the absurdity of life in the late Soviet era.[77] Venichka's hung-over evaluation early on the day of his journey provides one good example: "Everything on earth ought to happen slowly and out of joint, so we don't get above ourselves, so we remain sad and lost" (2; 140).[78] That statement conveys also to the foreign reader some of the flavor of the late Soviet moment as seen through Venichka's special lens. Another favorite, "Udder, yes: sherry, no" (*Vymia est', a kheresu net*) (6; 143), depends more on the Soviet experience of deficit goods. The practice of quoting from beloved texts seems to be both characteristically Russian and generational. The novels of the satiric duo Ilia Ilf and Evgenii Petrov and Bulgakov's *Master and Margarita* served as sources for such popular quoting before *Moscow Stations*. Thus, the practice may well have influenced the style of Erofeev's work, as Iurii Levin contended.[79] In the reception of *Moscow Stations*, the initial group of readers would have been smaller than for the other two published books, so that quotation from this samizdat source would foster a sense of solidarity and kinship among that relatively small audience who knew and appreciated Venichka's wry outlook on things before the work's publication in the late perestroika era.

This aspect of Erofeev's style has roots in a tradition of literary representation of oral speech (*skaz*) in Russian letters.[80] Usually, however, the oral speech is perceived as such by contrast to the literary norm associated with the author. Erofeev became much more closely identified with his character Venichka. This identification, the closeness of which seems nearly unprecedented in modern Russian prose, also underscores his lack of an established social position (and public profile) on the larger literary field. As a result, the author "Venichka" seems more accessible to everyday life and readers—he strikes one as a potentially intimate and informal companion. This type of authorial persona stands in striking contrast to the priestly or masterful poses assumed by modernist creators, from the Symbolists like Blok to Constructivist El Lissitzky.[81] Thus, the particular orality of Erofeev's text links it to a more general neo-avant-garde trend that seeks to recover openness to the moment in part through imitating the rhythms of normal speech.[82]

The "avant-garde" in Bourdieu's usage cannot be limited to the most radical forms of art described by Bürger or any other theoretician: Bourdieu's avant-garde refers more broadly to the temporality of the restricted field of cultural production, where such works appear least likely to receive immediate wide renown. The avant-garde aims to purify the symbolic capital of the restricted field and achieve future consecration. Erofeev had no ready audience—he was the "youngest" of the three authors considered here in terms of social position (born in 1938, he was biologically only six years younger than Aksenov and about the same age as Bitov). If *The Burn* garnered relatively strong initial response, *Moscow Stations* took time to be appreciated, but it achieved more sure consecration as a work that depended less on specific political and social debates, a work that expressed the existential experience of the late Soviet person who had become alienated from his world.

Following its early circulation in samizdat, Erofeev's novel first appeared in foreign publication in the Russian-language Israeli journal *Ami* (no. 3, 1973). A French edition came out from Albin Michel in 1976, *Moscou-Pétouchki*.[83] The YMCA Press, noted for its publication of Solzhenitsyn and other dissident works in Russian, published *Moskva–Petushki* in 1977. A German translation, *Die Reise nach Petuschki*, appeared in 1978 (Munich: Piper). Anglophone readers produced no fewer than three translations into English—the first, by H. William Tjalsma, *Moscow to the End of the Line* (New York: Taplinger), appeared in 1980 and was republished in 1992 (by Northwestern University Press). J. R. Dorrell (Jana Howlett) published her excellent translation, *Moscow Circles* (London: Writers and Readers Pub. Cooperative), in 1981. Subsequently, Mulrine took up the book for dramatic adaptation. When the theatrical production in English reached New York, David Remnick wrote, "Unlike Solzhenitsyn or Sinyavsky, or any number of other samizdat writers, [Erofeev] didn't seem to be saying anything of great importance." Moreover, "he does not cater to the American taste in Soviet writers: he does not preach."[84] Erofeev's voice seemed genuinely fresh. More than in the case of the other two novels, that voice stimulated readers and publishers to create their own versions, to make Venichka's wit and wisdom resound through a variety of different frameworks and media.

By 1991, following Erofeev's untimely demise, he was an "acknowledged classic of Russian literature."[85] We see abundant evidence of this consecration in the perestroika era, when print publications of *Moscow Stations* began to appear in the Soviet Union, along with an evening in spring, 1988, featuring "The Two Erofeevs," Venedikt and Viktor (Viktor being one of the young writers excluded from the Writers' Union after the 1979 publication of the almanac *Metropole*).[86] Many interviews with Venedikt Erofeev appeared, highlighting his colorful biography and views.[87] The statues of Venichka and his beloved mounted ten years after the author's death show his consecration in durable bronze. Scholarship at home in Russia and abroad highlights the importance of Erofeev's voice in recent Russian letters, particularly his *Moskva–Petushki*.[88]

On the one hand, Erofeev's novel demonstrates convincingly that by 1969 there existed a viable and creative unofficial field capable of generating new cultural activity. Erofeev's work cannot be imagined without that developed samizdat outlet to stimulate it. His novel shows how important that new field of culture was becoming. Response to the work over time, including its delayed consecration, confirms Erofeev's role in helping to define a new field of unofficial letters.

Erofeev's consecration raises interesting questions about the real effects of such autonomous art in impacting the social order, however. Personally, Erofeev's fame abroad was not enough to convince authorities to let him out for treatment of the throat cancer that killed him by 1991.[89] As in the case of Erofeev's illness, so it was for various aspects of the social order contested by dissidents—the hopes for real amelioration depended on foreign responses and interventions. This was true in the case of uncensored literature and art, which was validated (and often made available) by international publication and reception. It held true also for political pressure, brought to bear by democratic dissidents through their supporters in the West. At the same time, Soviet authorities firmly controlled institutions and borders: Erofeev died in the Soviet Union, not having lived to get out beyond its borders or to see the end of the Soviet era.

Bourdieu's critical approach reinforces the idea that autonomous activity more often perpetuates the status quo and existing structures of power in a society. His model does not have much to say, however, about the relationships existing across the boundaries of political states and economic systems. Erofeev's refraction of the late Soviet condition into *Moscow Stations* resonates because of its independence; that is, its lack of dogma and openness to appropriations by a heterogeneous readership including Soviet, former Soviet, and foreign readers. The relationships among Soviet dissidents and their friends in the West will form the subject of the next chapter.

Chapter Five

Samizdat and the Extra-Gutenberg Condition

This history begins from the voice . . .
—Viktor Krivulin

LEV RUBINSHTEIN—librarian, poet, essayist, and innovative verbal artist associated with Moscow Conceptualism—talked about how he understood the character of his avant-garde art.[1] He said: "For myself, avant-gardism always meant the extremely conscious unofficial status of my (and my friends') situation and existence in local culture. Moreover, I mean unofficial status conceived as aesthetics and poetics."[2] Rubinshtein's conception of what the avant-garde meant in his context resonates with what Aksenov said about the avant-garde as a tradition outside of the official Soviet mainstream. For Rubinshtein, reflecting on these topics during perestroika, the avant-garde also entailed awareness of a specifically unofficial, or dissident, position in late Soviet culture. As we know, many unofficial literary authors and artists objected to the term "dissident," which suggests the political interpretation of independent activity often imposed by Western observers. According to Bourdieu's model the symbolic capital associated with autonomous activity cannot be automatically converted into either economic or political terms.[3] In that spirit my usage of "dissident" emphasizes the common move of these Soviet citizens to take up a position apart, however they might choose to present this space apart. Rubinshtein's description of the avant-garde sensibility as consciousness of the unofficial situation of cultural activity suggests the kind of critical reflection on the social structures of dissidence we have been pursuing in this study.

Bourdieu's description of the cultural avant-garde also makes the occupation of a "place apart" an object of critical reflection. Bourdieu critiqued the belief in a space of freedom from the larger social field with its political and economic forces that his avant-garde implies. His critique exposed the ideology of freedom and change as something that masks the essential continuity of the social field and its structures of domination. Bourdieu's critique is oriented to the modern capitalist society in France where hopes for revolution had faded. The Soviet context differed, but a basic analogy might be drawn: the emergence and development of dissidence accompanied the loss of hope for real political change occurring in the late 1960s. The era that came to be known as Brezhnev's stagnation produced the search for cultural freedom and independent values we see in dissidence. Taking a cue from Bourdieu's skepticism, we might ask whether the ferment of dissident activity produced any real change in the structure of Soviet society.

If the ideology of dissidence was freedom, the view of society from that space apart varied depending on where one stood. One common feature, however, was the dissident perception of discontinuity. In the late phase of socialist society in the U.S.S.R., dissidents resisted the superficial unity of all areas of society and cultural production by bringing out the discontinuities and cracks that official façade concealed in the name of maintaining the status quo. As we have seen, Siniavskii described his personal experience in terms of encountering a "stumbling block." Stressing the aesthetic dimension of his dissidence, he located his stumbling block in the experience of seeing modernist culture rooted out under Stalin—such cultural repression signified the more profound social intolerance resurging after World War II.[4] The uncensored novels we have seen likewise illustrate a dissident sense of alienation and discontinuity. In *The Burn*, Aksenov revealed the rupture in the social fabric caused by Stalin's camps, and the mass, unmotivated arrests of Soviet citizens that populated them. The youth Tolya suffered from those events, and the adults of a later era labored under the effects of suppressed trauma. Aksenov's use of a mixed-up and chaotic narrative chronology, along with his own avant-garde prose style, artistically evoked the fractured Soviet society that succeeded the Stalinist experience. In *Pushkin House* Bitov explored the effects of interrupted cultural, social, and generational ties through the education and psychology of his protagonist Lyova. Both novels show how the moral and spiritual fabric of Soviet society had been torn apart. In *Moscow Stations*, while not in the main addressing specific traumatic events of Soviet history, Erofeev showed their disruptive effects in the loss of connection between words, concepts, cultural figures, and the real world and meanings they used to convey.

Unofficial literary works like these illustrate the discontinuities of the late Soviet world as seen from a dissident perspective in part because the view of these authors had been formed through the uncensored texts of samizdat, which brought back repressed works and revealed those facets of Western and world culture that had been excluded by the relatively hermetic world of official Soviet print. Samizdat provided an alternative forum for excluded culture of the past and the present. Rubinshtein described his own unofficial poetic texts, which resembled a card catalog, this way: the text, he said "is an object, an expanse [*ob"em*], a Not-Book, a child of the 'extra-Gutenberg' existence of literary culture."[5] Rubinshtein's characterization of the mode of the text as "extra-Gutenberg" recalls the better-known formulation by Anna Akhmatova, who spoke of the "pre-Gutenberg" culture of the Soviet period, in which people resorted to memory and oral transmission, handwriting and typewriters for works not allowed into Soviet print.[6] Dissident texts, that is, samizdat, made available works and discussion of experiences repressed from official culture. Samizdat made such exclusion visible. It also created the possibility of new types of engagement.

In this chapter I consider the social structures and temporal modes attending dissident modes of the text, or samizdat. Samizdat as a textual culture challenged the dominant print paradigm from within, creating a space apart for alternative cultural production and communication. Samizdat realized dissidence in a material sense. As an "extra-Gutenberg" textual culture, samizdat made possible a dissidence that challenged the hegemony of the Soviet regime precisely in its artificial unity as a modern, centrally administered social structure: samizdat created a much more discontinuous field of cultural production and circulation than that associated with the modern print paradigm. This discontinuity engendered an eclectic mix of social behaviors. It makes us confront the networks of varying social fields and economic systems, thereby ultimately also challenging the unity of Bourdieu's social field. This challenge suggests that the possibilities for converting symbolic capital might be greater than his model allows.

A BRIEF REVIEW OF THE HISTORY OF SAMIZDAT

The best-known dissident works have been historical exposés like Solzhenitsyn's *Gulag Archipelago*, or documents about human rights from members of the democratic movement. Unofficial literary and artistic works lacked the public urgency of such works, being oriented, like the works Bourdieu ascribes to the cultural avant-garde, to reception over the longer term. While they provided less immediately usable information, these literary and artistic works possess additionalinterest today as texts that reflect on the dissident space of freedom and new possibilities for realizing the self and social relations. Erofeev, one of the most apparently "free" of dissident literary authors by virtue of his outsider status, engaged most specifically the samizdat mode of the text in his novel *Moscow Stations*. That work pointed toward the creation of more authentic, direct and co-creative bonds among authors and readers.

Samizdat represented a structural change in the field of cultural production in the Soviet Union after Stalin. This was not a recapitulation of the prerevolutionary underground or the émigré liberal press, in part because Soviet citizens used their personal typewriters and photographic cameras to create samizdat texts.[7] The practice of typing and passing uncensored texts did not become widespread or systematic until after Stalin.[8] Indeed, we are hard pressed to find much in the way of informal production and circulation prior to Khrushchev's Secret Speech at the XXth Party Congress in 1956, in which he denounced Stalin's cult of personality.[9] People attribute the neologism "samizdat" to Moscow poet Nikolai Glazkov, who typed his poetry at home into notebooks and gave them his own imprint "Samsebiaizdat," beginning in the 1940s.[10] Glazkov worked various jobs, including acting the role of the peasant Efim who invents a flying machine in the prelude segment of Andrei Tarkovskii's film *Andrei Rublev* (1966). Perhaps Glazkov's choice was not entirely fortuitous: for him and others samizdat served as a contemporary form of innovative popular creation. The term "samizdat" began to be used among relatively elite intellectual circles in Moscow in the late 1950s or early 1960s and it did not enter wider usage until the late 1960s.[11] At that time, Soviet officials began referring to "samizdat" in the official press.[12] Soviet authorities were trying to come to grips with new challenges. In 1966 new laws came on the books, including Article 190–1 for slander against the Soviet system, and Article 190–3 for public meetings that disturb the peace. These new laws aimed to deal more effectively with challenges from an increasingly restive Soviet public. In 1967, the KGB established the Fifth Directorate to deal with dissidents. By 1970, KGB officials talked about samizdat as a threat: Iurii Andropov, then head of the KGB, wrote in a memo in 1970 that "so-called samizdat has undergone a qualitative change in recent years. If five years ago it was ideologically defective artistic works that mainly passed from hand to hand, documents of a programmatic political character are now acquiring even greater dissemination."[13]

In the West, academics and people in government took note of the burgeoning unofficial system. A concerted effort to disseminate samizdat took shape on the basis of an earlier commitment to broadcast émigré literature for Soviet listeners who lacked access to it in Soviet print. Gene Sosin wrote about a discussion on the topic that took place in the fall of 1965 at New York University regarding the mission of Radio Liberty. The Radio could provide a valuable service for Soviet listeners by broadcasting works of Russian émigré literature, such as the stories of Ivan Bunin, which they could get from the pages of the New York émigré journal, *New Journal* (*Novyi zhurnal*). Sosin and others saw their role in facilitating an alternative flow of culture. He said, "While Soviet Russian has degenerated into 'newspeak,'" émigré works represent "the continuity of the humanitarian Russian tradition, the humanistic values, the literary values, which some day are going to be replenished at home in some kind of new variant that inevitably has to take into consideration fifty-odd years of Soviet history."[14] Shortly thereafter, the staff at Radio Liberty would seize that new variant directly from samizdat. Albert Boiter described the formation of the Samizdat Research Unit at Radio Liberty in Munich for collecting and analyzing samizdat. By the early

1970s, Radio Liberty began broadcasting and making available to interested researchers these uncensored materials.[15] Other Western press began paying attention, too: the *Index on Censorship* from 1972 covered samizdat news and dissident activities. The Western audience and publishing opportunities did not create Soviet dissidence or uncensored texts, but they did prove to be crucial in supporting the development of that alternative culture.

One of the samizdat editions that helped foster this importantWestern interest, after Aleksandr Ginzburg's uncensored *White Book* on the trial of Siniavskii and Daniel', was the Moscow samizdat bulletin *Chronicle of Current Events* (*Khronika tekushchikh sobytii*, 1968–83). The first issue of the *Chronicle* reported on the trial of Ginzburg and his fellows involved in preparing the *White Book*, and the *Chronicle* marked a new self-awareness of dissidence and samizdat as such. Founding editor Natalia Gorbanevskaia wrote in an anonymous survey from the final issue of the bulletin's first year:

> During the last few years *samizdat* has evolved from a predominant concern with poetry and fiction towards an ever greater emphasis on journalistic and documentary writing. . . . Readers of *samizdat* (they are also its volunteer publishers) have received during the year a regular flow of documents, open letters, speeches, commentaries, articles, news items etc. In other words, samizdat, in addition to its role as a supplier of books has begun to fulfill the functions of a newspaper.[16]

A narrative about a continuous and coherent development of dissidence from "Cultural Opposition" to "Political Opposition" enjoyed currency among democratic dissidents, including those involved with the *Chronicle*.[17] Gorbanevskaia's account of the more social function samizdat had grown to fulfill reflects the same narrative arc. A broader view of the variety of works produced and circulating in samizdat in the 1970s and into the 1980s suggests this narrative is tendentious. It served a purpose in the late 1960s for defining the identity and social purpose of democratic dissidents. Likewise, the KGB's interpretation of the "qualitative change" of samizdat into a political threat helped justify the existence of its new institutional body and initiatives devoted to monitoring and controlling dissident activity.

Gorbanevskaia's comments in the *Chronicle* speak to the central role of samizdat in supporting the establishment of new identities for groups and even institutions like those rights activists whose organ it was.[18] The samizdat system and the uncensored text produced and circulated within that system provided a site for people to perform new identities defined in relation to the discontinuities made visible by samizdat (even if that dissident activity did not necessarily mean relinquishing one's position in the official social field). In addition, the mechanics of circulation and reproduction for further circulation of samizdat typescript copies implied a new and historically specific relationship of cooperation among readers and authors and publishers—readers took an active role by choosing to accept a samizdat text that might be risky, and they became volunteer publishers by copying the text (which was time-consuming) and passing it on to others. Readers in the Soviet Union and in the West who passed on a text endorsed it as true or valuable. In the case of samizdat this process took on special significance, because there was no preexisting institutional guarantee of the worth of any given samizdat text.

SAMIZDAT AND PRINT CULTURE

It may surprise us now to realize how suspicious dissident reports, essays, and literary works seemed to Western readers when they first began to arrive in the 1960s. Even Solzhenitsyn—one of the most consecrated dissident figures now—struck many readers initially as dubious. Martin Dewhirst, who worked at Radio Liberty, said "in America there were people who, for years, said that Solzhenitsyn did not exist, and that it was probably the KGB that concocted those pieces and sent them to the West to confuse Western public opinion."[19] French Communists accused Solzhenitsyn of being a Nazi sympathizer when his *Gulag Archipelago* appeared in France.[20] Back in the Soviet Union, Solzhenitsyn's credibility came under fire from hard-line nationalists, who viewed his second marriage as evidence of a Jewish-Masonic plot. Mikhail Kheifets, who was imprisoned with Vladimir Osipov, editor of the nationalist samizdat journal *Popular Assembly* (*Veche*, 1971–74), claimed that the split over Solzhenitsyn's divorce and remarriage broke that journal.[21] Kheifets related the version of events he had heard from Osipov, who claimed that his co-editor Svetlana Melnikova had begun working for the KGB. Melnikova, for her part, claimed that the problems of the editorial collective proceeded from Osipov's lackluster performance and his covert receipt of funds from the émigré NTS organization.[22]

We take it for granted now that Solzhenitsyn's works represent some of the most important documents of the Stalinist prison camp experience as well as literary achievements of high rank. Solzhenitsyn himself asserted the importance of literary artists, and the weight of the truth they could reveal:

> ONE WORD OF TRUTH OUTWEIGHS THE WHOLE WORLD.
>
> (*ODNO SLOVO PRAVDY VES' MIR PERETIANET*).[23]

Solzhenitsyn's truth as revealed in the *Gulag Archipelago* might seem today as solid and reliable as the hard, dry land emerging out of a shifting sea of lies and obfuscation in his eponymous metaphor. In his memoirs about working at Radio Liberty, Gene Sosin colorfully conveyed the idea of such a "sea" of Soviet lies in the second edition of the *Big Soviet Encyclopedia* (*Bol'shaia Sovetskaia Entsiklopedia*, 1949–58). After the arrest of Lavrentii Beria, chief of the NKVD in 1953, subscribers to the encyclopedia, already in receipt of volume 5 with a long article about Beria, were mailed a substitute entry on the Bering Sea and instructions to cut out "Beria" and replace it with information about the sea.[24] In fact, however, the validity of Solzhenitsyn's truth, like that of other texts arriving through samizdat channels, had to be established.

Samizdat, as an extra-Gutenberg culture, destabilized the modern paradigm of print. Print culture as we have come to know it involves *standardization*, *dissemination*, and *fixity* of the text.[25] Dissemination means the broad distribution of copies of a text; standardization refers to the fact that these copies are identical, and fixity refers to the preservation of texts in print. Together, these features help knowledge be shared and built across geographic distance and over time. Elizabeth Eisenstein linked this print culture to the Scientific Revolution, the Renaissance, and the Reformation.[26] Along with this revolution in knowledge production, the new, modern sense of self in the West got constructed as more markedly individual. It was associated with private reading of the sacred word and the possibility of making a name through scientific and artistic innovation.

Adrian Johns argued that our assumptions about print culture, including the characteristics Eisenstein outlines, were in fact socially constructed rather than natural qualities flowing from the advent of print technologies: "What we often regard as essential elements and necessary concomitants of print are in fact rather more contingent than generally acknowledged. Veracity in particular is . . . extrinsic to the press itself, and has had to be grafted onto it."[27] Johns pointed out that the modern print paradigm Eisenstein described has been so taken for granted by most of us that we have forgotten the instability of early print culture: "early modern printing was not joined by any obvious or necessary bond to enhanced fidelity, reliability, and truth. That bond had to be forged," Johns insisted. He elaborated:

> If an early modern reader picked up a printed book—*De Natura Libri*, perhaps—then he or she could not be immediately certain that it was what it claimed to be, and its proper use might not be so self-evident. Piracy was one reason. . . . More broadly, ideas about the correct ways to make and use books varied markedly from place to place and time to time. But whatever the cause, it is not easy for us to imagine such a realm, in which printed records were not necessarily authorized or faithful. What could one know in such a realm, and how could one know it? We ourselves routinely rely on stable

> communications in our making and maintenance of knowledge, whether of the people around us or of the world in which we live. That stability helps to underpin the confidence we feel in our impressions and beliefs. . . . Instability in records would equally rapidly translate into uncertainty of judgment. The most immediate implication, then, would be epistemic.[28]

Samizdat helped reveal the epistemic instability that had been lurking around the edges of print since its beginning. In this way while samizdat exposed the Soviet regime's abuse of facts and tendentious framing of discussion in the pages of the main official newspaper *Pravda* (*Truth*), it can also remind us of the epistemic uncertainty of all our communications and the function of social protocols that structure their value and function. Samizdat texts exhibited the unstandardized, spontaneously disseminated, and unfixed character of oral culture.[29] As Venichka's speech in *Moscow Stations* suggests, this oral quality served in the late Soviet era to tie communication again to the body and the individual, the intimate community and informal relations, suggesting authenticity. Osip Mandelshtam had declared, "I alone work from the voice," in his defiant and uncensored *Fourth Prose* (*Chetvertaia proza*), which was written in 1930 and circulated unofficially decades later. Late Soviet poet Viktor Krivulin and others took that statement as inspiration for their own samizdat activity.[30]

Eisenstein discussed the standardization of multiple copies of a text, which made possible the availability of verified texts to a whole community of interested readers, as in the standard scholarly editions we know today. Samizdat implied the loss of standardization. A samizdat version and the printed text to which it referred could differ significantly one from the other.[31] Natalia Trauberg translated a number of G. K. Chesterton's essays and two of his books, *St. Thomas Aquinas* and *St. Francis of Assisi*, for samizdat in the 1960s. The translation into samizdat involved more than the difference between English and Russian words. As Trauberg said:

> The fate of manuscripts in samizdat is perfectly medieval: they were not under our control, we did not direct them, unknown people made their own additions. . . . Moreover, translation for samizdat produced its own particularities. Many allusions, which would not be understood without extended commentary, I had to excise—for example, references to untranslated books of Huxley and Faulkner, and even to translated works, because they were not after all well known to Russian readers. Sometimes I myself shortened, for example, passages that seemed to me to be repetition, because I was in a great hurry. In a word, this was in no way an academic preparation of a manuscript.[32]

Nor were samizdat copies of particular items necessarily equivalent to one another: Leon Uris's *Exodus*—which was hugely influential in the unofficial Jewish national revival in the Soviet Union—circulated in various Russian samizdat translations. In one version, the translators cut out large portions of the 600-plus-page novel for the sake of brevity, and on principle: they deemed the romance Uris had created between Ari Ben-Canaan and the Christian woman Kitty inappropriate for Zionist reading. The resulting text was approximately 150 pages. Another, even shorter, translation resulted from the retelling of the story by one prisoner in camp who had read the book in English before incarceration. An inmate who heard the story was so impressed that he wrote it down from memory after being released. The resulting typescript was just 70 to 80 pages. That version itself was altered in further reproductions.[33]

The samizdat text would not necessarily be widely disseminated the way printed texts generally could be assumed to be.[34] It was too difficult to type large numbers of identical texts—with thin paper and carbons and strong fingers one might get up to seven or eight copies, but the final copy would hardly be legible.[35] Photographing typescripts made it possible to produce significantly more copies, although photograph paper was relatively expensive and resulted in a bulky text—such paper was thick and tended to curl.[36] Moreover, the KGB might seize copies. Copies might also be lost—as in the case of samizdat translations of Jorge Luis Borges and Eugène Ionesco from 1959 or Venedikt Erofeev's legendary lost novel *Dmitrii Shostakovich*.[37]

Conversely, copies might proliferate out of control: Petro Grigorenko, a Red Army general who became a dissident, described the fate of a letter he wrote in response to a scathing ideological review of Aleksandr Nekrich's book *1941. 22 June* that appeared in issue 9 (1967) of the Soviet journal *Voprosy istorii KPSS* (*Questions in History of the CPSU*). Grigorenko offered his own analysis, which largely coincided with Nekrich's, of why the beginning of World War II resulted in such disaster for Soviet troops. Although Grigorenko's analysis was critical of Soviet leaders, it was not outrageously so—he left out points in hopes of passing censorship.[38] Grigorenko's acquaintance Sergei Pisarev saw the typescript of the unpublished letter and asked for a copy to read. Grigorenko asked Pisarev not to give it to anyone else, as it was meant for regular journal publication, not samizdat. A few days later, returning the text, Pisarev could hardly contain his enthusiasm. He praised the work and said the high opinion was not only his: "I gave it for one night to my acquaintance, a Doctor of Economics, and when he brought it back, he said he did not sleep the whole night. He read it and understood he had to have such a work in his own library. He got a typewriter, put ten pieces of paper and copied it in one night. He brought me one copy as a present."[39] Whether the doctor was able to do all ten copies at one time, or whether he did it in two sessions, samizdat texts had a tendency to multiply uncontrollably. When Grigorenko reminded Pisarev that he did not want the text in samizdat, Pisarev dutifully returned to the doctor and promised Grigorenko that they had collected all copies. One way or another, however, the letter ended up in samizdat, and the official journal turned down Grigorenko's request for publication because it was already in samizdat: "I've received already four 'samizdat' copies of your letter. So we will not publish it. We are not popularizers of 'samizdat,'" the journal editor informed him.[40]

In his memoirs, Grigorenko expressed wonder at the "marvel of popular creation" that was samizdat. The means of entry into the system of distribution were multiple and the methods of multiplication obscure.[41] Once released into unofficial circulation, the text assumed a life of its own, but this life was spontaneous and unpredictable, and it was not fixed in official Soviet print.

The fixity of the text, more or less assured by print culture as Eisenstein described it, made possible the preservation of knowledge and the progress of scholarship, both humanistic and scientific.[42] In the case of samizdat, a text might or might not be picked up and established as part of the corpus of known, available texts. Grigorenko claimed not to know why certain texts enjoyed heavy circulation in samizdat networks, while others, which he might have judged to be equally worthy, in effect died for lack of circulation.[43] Samizdat could mean new life for texts that might otherwise disappear, but it did not necessarily mean the text would be fixed. The long trajectories of certain texts that passed through samizdat and the feats of labor and skill required to support them are legendary: Nadezhda Mandelshtam, widow of the poet Osip Mandelshtam, memorized her husband's texts, many of which were not safe to preserve even in typescript at home. Soviet publication was uncertain and could not cover the politically sensitive pieces, like the epigram on Stalin: "We live without sensing the country beneath us" (composed in 1933). Thus it fell to publication in the West, in "tamizdat," or publication "over there," which became possible in the late 1960s, to fix Osip Mandelshtam's *Collected Works* as well as Nadezhda Mandelshtam's memoirs.[44] Similarly, Joseph Brodsky's poetry, well known through private readings and samizdat circulation, had to be published abroad. Vladimir Maramzin devoted himself to the significant task of collecting Brodsky's works, a task that cost him his liberty and Soviet citizenship.[45] On a much broader scale, Konstantin Kuzminskii, with the help of his blind friend Grigorii Kovalev, recorded the ephemeral creations of Soviet nonconformist poets and got them published in America in the massive and curious *Blue Lagoon Anthology*.[46]

Fixing a samizdat text—and this of course happened only to a portion of such texts—meant in most cases that the text traveled out of Soviet samizdat and was published in a printed Western edition. However, with the advent of samizdat, the trajectory of texts from unfixed existence to print was not unidirectional in some ideal modern sense: as we already saw in the cases of texts authored by Chesterton and Uris, printed editions could make their way from the West into samizdat and be reproduced there in much less stable variants. Mikhail Bulgakov's novel *The Master and Margarita* (*Master i Margarita*) is also curious in this regard: the text was rescued from obscurity and fixed in a Soviet print publication (in the journal *Moskva*, 1966–67), which subsequently circulated in a samizdat version with excised portions typed and taped into the journal version (thereby calling into question the authenticity of the official Soviet version). There were also many texts of Leningrad samizdat that did not achieve Western publication. The reasons could be practical or principled: it was not easy for everyone to claim a Western publisher's attention, and in the opinion of some, especially Leningraders, publication of a samizdat text abroad attested to a political or commercial interest at odds with the purity of an autonomous culture.[47]

The Bourdieusian critique of dissident autonomy, which the dissident aesthetes tried to purify, might point out the dependence on Western audiences and Western print, even in the case of those who chose to forego the pursuit of immediate fame in Western publication. The fact of Western attention made the whole field of dissident culture possible. If samizdat helped expose the discontinuities of Soviet culture, it also facilitated the crossing of boundaries that promised to knit them together again, reestablishing the connections to "world culture"[48] and which seemed to many late Soviet writers like the ideal reality to which their works aspired.

EPISTEMIC INSTABILITY AND THE VALIDATION OF SAMIZDAT TEXTS

The viability of samizdat texts not guaranteed by institutional existence depended on the interest and belief of readers, including readers in the West. The material instability of a samizdat text not fixed in print comes with the epistemic instability of a work whose truth value or other merits cannot be taken for granted. The trustworthiness of the samizdat text had to be established through social protocols. Like the production and circulation of samizdat, these protocols had a specific character at this historical moment: they absolutely depended on the investment by Western readers.

Adrian Johns talked about the issues dogging early modern texts. In that case, piracy played a key role. Johns devoted considerable attention to the phenomenon of piracy, by which he meant any violation of copy ownership or propriety.[49] In samizdat culture, one of the important analogues to piracy can be found in the possibility of KGB infiltration. However, if piracy constituted a relatively marginal phenomenon in print culture (though it appeared to be much less marginal in Johns's account of the early history of the book), the specter of KGB provocation was ubiquitous in samizdat. Conspiracy theories simply obsessed many who participated in samizdat culture, and they created doubts abroad too. Journalist and author Michael Johnson said that in the 1960s, there was skepticism about dissidence and samizdat among Western observers: "It took a while for us journalists in Moscow to understand what was going on."[50] At that time there were doubts about the authenticity of Grigorenko's dissidence, and issues of the *Chronicle of Current Events* were "treated with some disdain by the foreign press" for about six months after they first became known in the West. Then, said Johnson, in January 1968 it all changed: Amnesty International sent in an observer team, and they verified that the dissident activity was real.[51] Amnesty subsequently extended its imprimatur to the *Chronicle* by assuming its republication.

Editors of samizdat periodical publications worked on protocols to receive information and feedback securely: the *Chronicle of Current Events* instructed its readers to pass along any information they wished to communicate to the *Chronicle* editors (whose names and addresses were not published on the edition) through the person who gave them a copy of the *Chronicle*. That person would pass the information to the one from whom the copy was received and so on through the chain. There was a caveat: "Do not try to trace back the whole chain of communication yourself, or else you will be taken for a police informer" (*Khronika*, no. 5, December 31, 1968).[52] Revolt Pimenov, editor of an early samizdat information leaflet, *Informatsiia* (Moscow, 1956–57), found out during his trial that, despite his precautions, some items of information he received and circulated were wrong. Most could be traced to a single acquaintance whom, following the revelation of wrong information, he suspected of working for the KGB. However, a couple of other false items came, as Pimenov learned later, from foreign radio transmissions. Pimenov had been on guard against information from the broadcasts of the BBC, Deutsche Welle, or Voice of America. He regarded them to be unreliable and would not have included the information had he known the source.[53] Doubt could, then, extend beyond potential KGB interference.

But KGB provocations did exist. Grigorenko acknowledged that some samizdat texts, which looked no different from others, were KGB falsifications of samizdat. They were immediately sniffed out as such by the samizdat public; he claimed that "there never was in my memory an instance of a KGB document getting any circulation."[54] The task of recognition would have been more difficult for foreigners and those living abroad: the anti-Soviet émigré organization, the Popular Workers' Union (Narodno-Trudovoi Soiuz, NTS), assembled a collection of samizdat documents (many of which it published in its Russian-language journals *Posev* and *Grani*). A number of item descriptions for the archived collection were marked "KGB falsification."[55] However widespread the incidence of KGB infiltration and textual falsification may actually have been, the paranoia about KGB provocation is highly characteristic of samizdat culture, and it testifies to the epistemic instability of these texts.

This instability raises the question, how did people dealing with samizdat texts determine what was reliable information? By what method were facts, people, and discrete texts judged to be what they purported to be? In practice, the veracity of samizdat information was established in the Soviet Union through trials for "libel" (Article 190.1 of the Soviet Russian Criminal Code). Pimenov said that only fewer than ten of more than one hundred items in his materials were judged false.[56] The trial of Sergei Kovalev, primarily for his work with the *Chronicle of Current Events*, helped demonstrate the credibility of that samizdat publication as an unofficial source of news: of 694 discrete items in the relevant materials, only 7 were finally entered into the case by Soviet authorities as libelous, and only 2 details of items from the *Chronicle* were factually dubious.[57]

Western organizations publicizing samizdat information acknowledged the need to establish reliability and credibility. Radio Liberty broadcast hundreds of samizdat documents back to the Soviet Union, and it reproduced thousands of samizdat pages for circulation in the West in its print collections: the *Materials of Samizdat* (*Materialy samizdata*), a series of documents initially prepared for internal circulation at Radio Liberty between 1971 and 1991, and the *Collection of Samizdat Documents* (*Sobranie dokumentov samizdata*, 1972–78).[58] In a statement from 1973 on the back cover of the *Register of Documents* for the Samizdat Archive, Radio Liberty claimed: "The *Arkhiv Samizdata* is a systematized collection of copies of samizdat documents written in the Soviet Union and sent abroad. Each such document received is carefully examined for authenticity, and only then registered and stored in the archive."[59] While the statement does not specify how this was done, the abundant Radio Liberty research files at the Open Society Archive testify to the amount of work that went into the process of assembling information about names, organizations, and events. Galina Salova, who worked as research editor to prepare editions for broadcasts on Radio Liberty and for publication in the series *Materials of Samizdat* from 1977 to 1994, said that two independent verifications were required for each fact—a person's release from prison, for example.[60] Reverend Michael Bourdeaux, who founded Keston College in 1969, spoke about the widespread distrust of samizdat in the 1960s. Keston monitored the oppression of religious groups in the U.S.S.R. At the Center for the Research and Study of Religious Institutions (Centre des recherches et des études des institutions réligieuses, Geneva), for which Bourdeaux worked in 1966–69 reviewing the Soviet press, Bourdeaux's superiors objected to his proposal to use information obtained from samizdat sources. After founding Keston College, Bourdeaux and his staff were scrupulous about establishing the reliability of information that they circulated (to Radio Liberty, among others). They carefully checked the authenticity of names and facts against the official Soviet press: thus when the official paper *Soviet Latvia* (*Sovetskaia Latviia*) referred to the imprisonment of Baptist dissident Iosif Bondarenko, the reference provided some basis for trusting Bondarenko as a samizdat source. The existence of the unofficial Baptist church and of its samizdat publications, the *Herald of Salvation* (*Vestnik spaseniia*) and *Brotherly Leaflet* (*Bratskii listok*), was confirmed by a 1966 Soviet book on the Baptist religion, part of the official series the Library of Contemporary Religions.[61] Around the same time, the Soviet press attacked Michael Bourdeaux for his book on religion in the Soviet Union (*Opium of the People*, 1965), identifying Bourdeaux (incorrectly) as a friend of the unofficial Baptist Initiative Group (Initsiativniki) and its head Georgii Vins. This negative official reference brought Bourdeaux's existence as a reliable Western channel to the attention of Vins, who subsequently contacted Bourdeaux to provide information and texts.[62]

Thus, the cross-referencing of printed and nonprinted texts, of Soviet official sources and dissident sources, functioned epistemically to constitute reliable knowledge. There were other, softer methods used, however: the credibility of institutions like the Radio Liberty Samizdat Research Department and the Keston Institute built up over time, as did their research files and reliable Soviet contacts. Other softer methods included evaluating the "internal consistency" of documents received,[63] and a sort of instinct developed over time for reliable vs. provocative information on both sides of the Iron Curtain. Pimenov said that if an item reported to him seemed scandalous, it was usually not true.[64] Important in this regard was the tone in which information was delivered: the *Chronicle of Current Events* was famous for its dry professionalism,[65] observed also in discussion of dissident information in the West. A contrast to that style can be found in the emotional and scandalous testimony of Richard Wurmbrand, a Romanian priest persecuted for his faith.[66] The newsletter *Catacombes* (*Messager supraconfessionnel de l'église du silence*, Courbevoie, France, 1971–92), proved itself similarly prone to emotional and provocative reporting on the persecution of religion in Communist lands, and its presentation of facts might be suspected to be insufficiently precise.[67]

Personal contacts and networks of trust and reliability mattered tremendously. Sosin described the reception of Andrei Amalrik's essay "Will the Soviet Union Survive until 1984?" (1980). Now a famous document of the Soviet dissident movement, the essay caused a scandal upon its arrival at Radio Liberty in 1968. Amalrik was then unknown to the general public. Part of the staff regarded the content as Russophobic and potentially problematic for the station's public relations. Was it a provocation? Professor Karel van het Reve, a former Dutch correspondent in Moscow who became secretary of the Alexander Herzen Foundation in Amsterdam, vouched for the authenticity of the document on the basis of his personal knowledge of Amalrik. Consequently, the station broadcast the text in six installments, with caveats and disclaimers, in the series "Documents from the USSR."[68]

Beyond the truth or falsehood of particular facts and the authenticity of a document or a name, some more subtle questions arise in the epistemically unstable textual system. What constitutes a valuable text? The twin to the threat of "KGB falsification" that haunted samizdat is "graphomania," the uncontrolled sickness of writing. Writers of uncensored texts may be particularly prone to it, since the mere fact of being unpublished (i.e., repressed) can contribute to an exaggerated sense of the worth of what one writes.[69] Ardis Publishers, begun in Ann Arbor, Michigan, by Carl and Ellendea Proffer in 1971, specialized in publishing samizdat texts, mainly of the literary and cultural variety, and their role in supporting unofficial late Soviet literature can hardly be overstated. How did they choose what to publish? Writer and editor Igor Efimov, who worked for Ardis, claimed that Carl Proffer's literary taste was inscrutable.[70] Actually, the Ardis endeavor seems to illustrate well the power of the belief in autonomy arising from the late Soviet field. In the preface to the first issue of the Ardis journal *Russian Literature Triquarterly* (1971), the editors asserted: "We will not publish articles on literary politics or similar cold-war criticism of either the American or Soviet variety. This is a literary journal, not a political one. . . . The contents reflect the tastes of the editors, the needs of English-speaking readers, and chance." Priscilla Meyer's programmatic article in that same issue complained along the same lines about a politically motivated American neglect of Soviet literature: "The usual reason given for this neglect is that the literature is not worth analyzing on its aesthetic merits, and it is true that the post-Stalin period is less interesting to aestheticians than others. But why, then, has the richer period of the 1920s suffered a similar fate? While the circumstances of the suppression of Mayakovsky, Olesha, Pilnyak, Babel, Zamyatin, and Zoshchenko are frequently related, there are remarkably few stylistic examinations of their work. The American perception of Soviet literature is distorted by political bias and should be examined."[71] The Proffers got copies of the modernist works they published from sources in the Soviet Union as well as from Western antiquarian bookstores, relying to a large extent on the suggestions of Russian friends about what was interesting and needed to be recovered. Among these, Nadezhda Mandelshtam and Vladimir Nabokov were particularly authoritative sources.[72] On the basis of these older works and Nabokov's Russian works, Ardis gained a reputation for interesting publications. They subsequently used that symbolic capital to back some new uncensored Soviet works, too, including Russian editions of Aksenov's *Ozhog* (*The Burn*) and Bitov's *Pushkinskii dom* (*Pushkin House*) (they tried to get Erofeev's *Moskva–Petushki*). The presentation and promotion of one of their biggest publications of contemporary uncensored Soviet literature is indicative of the way symbolic capital gets extended to new writers: Sasha Sokolov's *Shkola dlia durakov* (*School for Fools*, 1976), which they published in Russian, won Nabokov's praise as "an enchanting, tragic and touching book" ("*obaiatel'naia, tragicheskaia i trogatel'neishaia kniga*"). Nabokov's words were printed on the cover and appeared in most reviews of the book. That extension of symbolic credit to the new avant-garde work by the consecrated author is not unique, obviously (think of Derzhavin's recognition of the young Pushkin and Akhmatova's patronage of Brodsky), but the cross-border dynamics of the Soviet–émigré-American lines of exchange seem characteristic of the dissident literary situation.

Broadly speaking, the questions surrounding the epistemically unstable text have to do with what may be considered valuable or significant and what is true or usable information: the evaluation may involve a complex mixture of judgments and needs. In the case of the samizdat historical collection *Memory* (*Pamiat'*, nos. 1–5, 1976–81), new types of materials were presented for the historical record. These included items from personal archives, letters, memoirs, and unpublished historical investigations. Reviewing the collection after its appearance in the West, historian Mikhail Geller referred to Maksim Gorkii's assertion that, "we need to know everything about the past, not as it is already told, but as it is illuminated by the teaching of Marx-Engels-Lenin-Stalin."[73] Geller's point was that the system itself deforms history. Worse, as pointed out in the editorial preface to the first issue of *Memory*, historical documents were kept hidden and perhaps even destroyed: "The archives of the VChK-GPU-NKVD—organizations with their hand on the pulse of Soviet history—went up in smoke through the chimneys of the Lubianka in October 1941, and the archives of the MGB-MVD, as some believe, were also burned in 1953."[74] In the light of this historical situation, the authority vested in institutions of record and of publication for historical truth could give way to the testimony kept by those millions of citizens whose lives this history touched.

Thus, *Memory* asserted the worth of otherwise unvalidated forms of historical testimony. Yet this posed a problem acknowledged by the editors:

> Our collection cannot, unfortunately, become a really scientific publication. A scientific editing process would necessarily demand verification of the trustworthiness of the sources of information that appears on the pages of *Mem-*

> *ory*. But since *Memory* is compiled by us from materials that . . . cannot make it into censored print, most of the sources required for verifying them are for the most part located in special sections of the libraries and archives [sections closed to the public]. To a great extent this will depend on the reader. We believe that the beginning we have made will have a real chance of success only if readers furnish us with new materials, make our publications more precise, add to our publications.[75]

However, this dialogue was in practice limited to the circle of intelligentsia in Moscow and Leningrad who knew the editors and their work.[76] The names and contact information of editors residing in the U.S.S.R. did not appear on the publication: Natalia Gorbanevskaia's address in France was given instead. The issues, at 600 to 800 typescript pages, would have posed a real problem for clandestine circulation. The feedback loop was not realized on a large scale.

In the model of using unpublished documents as historical record, as proposed by the editors of *Memory*, then, verifiability depends on community involvement. However, what kind of community could that have been? Broad public participation was extremely difficult to realize. The problem concerns the perusal as well as the distribution of 800-page typescript volumes: what readers would be motivated to spend their time reading such extensive materials? In the case of the Soviet Union at that time, the risk incurred by such an endeavor would also have been prohibitive for most, though attractive for some. In terms of subject matter, the theme of volume 1 of *Memory*—the Stalinist camps—proved compelling in Solzhenitsyn's treatment. However, other accounts of the camps before and after failed to spark wide interest and debate. The *Memory* collections appear to have been done for specialists and for establishing an alternative historical record rather than engaging a broad, active public debate at that time in the U.S.S.R. In fact, *Memory* was published abroad, and its mission of presenting unpublished historical documents from personal archives and libraries was continued and extended by the Western periodical series *Past* (*Minuvshee*). This demonstrates again that fixing the samizdat text for public consideration happened most often through tamizdat and was not a purely internal Soviet affair.

In the case of specific national, ethnic, or faith-based issues, moreover, broad public interest could be quite difficult to generate. The case of Jewish emigration is paradigmatic in this regard, illustrating the strategies of discursive and media amplification required to make a broad impact. Early Jewish samizdat publications devoted to the struggle to emigrate show the efforts to link the Jewish issue to the broader principles of human rights. The samizdat journal *Exodus* (*Iskhod*, 1970–72) featured two epigraphs on the cover of each issue: one, about Jerusalem, from Psalms 136:5–6; the other, concerning the right of every person to leave a country and to return to it, from Article 13, part 2, of the Universal Declaration of Human Rights.[77] The linkage was successful. Human rights at that time had tremendous power as a discourse.[78]

By contrast, the movement on behalf of Soviet Germans found it much more difficult to attract attention. In a review of the Soviet German samizdat journal *RePatria* (1974), Igor Ratmirov spoke with respect of a German campaign for emigration that had at last become a public issue with wide resonance. However, just a few months previously, the German cause seemed insignificant to most, as he explained:

> I remember a conversation in spring of 1974 with one of the most famous Soviet dissidents. We were speaking about the trial of V. Klink and F. Shnarra and the publication of the collection *RePatria*. In answer to my request to speak out in defense of V. Klink and F. Shnarr, he tried to convince me it was pointless, like the whole German national movement, because no one needs these Germans and they cannot interest even the government of Willi Brandt (in this, it would seem, lies their difference from the Jews). It is good to see that recently among Russian dissidence there has been a growing revaluation of this negative attitude.[79]

Ratmirov argued that the German national cause should matter also to other national movements. However, the comment of the "famous" dissident suggests there had been a lack of a successful public relations campaign to activate public opinion and political interest abroad. That response outside of the Soviet Union made a tremendous difference, and samizdat politics needed it.

Cultural samizdat also gained significance by being picked up abroad. Zoia Krakhmalnikova's collections of Christian materials, which appeared under the title *Hope* (*Nadezhda*, 1977–82), were republished by the NTS publishing house Posev (Possev) in Frankfurt beginning in 1978. From the messy copies of the typescript preserved in the NTS collection, it is obvious that *Hope* was designed to be sent abroad for publication, after which it would be recirculated for its Soviet audience. Posev issued advertisements to people in the West to support the edition so that copies of it could be smuggled back into the Soviet Union.[80] Krakhmalnikova reflected on the various forms of the collection and their meaning for different readers:

> Texts and witnesses to Christ, about the life of the Church and about the reality of this life become appreciably more valuable from an apologetic viewpoint if they appear in printed form, for publication shows the reader that the

> text is acknowledged as having real worth by someone other than the writer. Publication is in itself of spiritual benefit. I can also tell for instance to whom I should give a printed copy of *Hope* and who would benefit more from a typed one.[81]

The final comment is rather obscure. What type of person would appreciate the typed copy more than the printed one? It is clear from Krakhmalnikova's comment about the different sorts of copies that form has meaning, however. Krakhmalnikova's statement also highlights the fact that different readers might be reading the text with various senses of its value—the printed copy might represent validation by a larger community of believers, while the typed copy could represent the authentic expression of Soviet believers. This observation can be extended to the tamizdat version. The publication of *Hope* by the anti-Soviet émigré organization NTS had a potential political subtext,[82] even though this was disavowed in the foreword to the Frankfurt edition: "The publication of *Hope* by whoever has undertaken it cannot pursue any goals of a commercial or political character."[83] The statement may indeed reflect the views of many who supported the edition and who read it in the Soviet Union. The worth of the printed edition of which Krakhmalnikova spoke was not necessarily political, but it was not less powerfully compelling to supporters who believed rather in its spiritual value.

Curiously, after Krakhmalnikova's arrest in 1982, issues 11 and 12 of *Hope* appeared from Posev as the product of an anonymous group in the Soviet Union who carried on Krakhmalnikova's work. However, no typescript copies for these issues are preserved in the archive, and one wonders if it was in fact a samizdat edition. Perhaps the support from people and organizations in the West, or the propaganda value of the ecumenical Christian editions, was great enough to motivate Posev to try to keep it up as a pseudo-samizdat publication.

The samizdat text—epistemically unstable, unfixed—is a text that must travel and which changes form as it is realized in succeeding contexts. These forms have significance for the degree and type of reliability and worth perceived to be invested in the text. Samizdat materializes the types of exchanges among Soviet readership and, crucially, with an audience abroad that made dissident cultural freedom possible.

SAMIZDAT TEXTS AS GIVEN OBJECTS

Avant-garde reflection on the unofficial situation can provide helpful clues to the construction of dissident "freedom." This freedom depended more on the new networks of textual exchange than on the modern idea of the individual genius writer. Before there was Moscow Conceptualism, there was the group publishing *Art of the Commune* (*Iskusstvo kommuny*, Moscow, 1962–63), a samizdat journal continuing, as it were, the avant-garde edition of the same name published in Petrograd in 1918–19 (the double numeration on issue 6 of 1963, which is also issue 33, refers back to the abruptly discontinued Futurist edition, which stopped at number 19).[84] Experimentation with the form of texts in *Art of the Commune* of the 1960s looks in retrospect like a forerunner of Moscow Conceptualist attention to the text, as reflected in the comments of Lev Rubinshtein quoted above. Indeed, the social group in which *Art of the Commune* was born included future Sots-artist Aleksandr Melamid.[85] Issue no. 6 (33) of *Art of the Commune* features the text of a speech by the chairman of the Ideological Commission, L. F. Ilichev, which has been simply cut out of an official Soviet paper and pasted into its own pages. The section title "Questions of Degeneration" ("Voprosy marazma") under which Ilichev's speech appears humorously frames his remarks as long-winded and empty sententious official pronouncements on the responsibility of art and the artist.[86] The point we can take from this is that the transposition of content from one form of the text into another radically alters its significance.

The samizdat form possessed its own aura or force field, which helped attract readers and motivated them to reproduce the text. There has long been acknowledgment of the aura of the samizdat textual object—the mythologized dog-eared text—but little analytic attention has been given to it. The samizdat typescript really did exert a powerful sense of promise and peril, for the simple reason that it could be quite dangerous. Martin Dewhirst, who smuggled texts in and out of the Soviet Union for NTS during frequent trips between 1959 and 1964[87] and who worked for Radio Liberty beginning in the late 1960s, spoke of a great sense of responsibility to the people who gave texts to be smuggled out. During his visit to Prague in August 1968, he received a typescript of Vladimir Voinovich's classic comic novel *The Life and Extraordinary Adventures of Private Ivan Chonkin*, among a whole suitcase of samizdat texts: "It was an incredible experience for me to sit in my cheap hotel room with a Soviet tank right in front of the hotel on the street, at the end of August 1968, reading Voynovich's novel about this Soviet soldier during the Second World War."[88] He took the typescripts out, and Voinovich's novel was subsequently published: "As a result, the wife of the author was interrogated. So were her parents, who were both given a real grilling. They both died a few days later. So one was very conscious of the moral responsibility one had in such a situation."[89] Voinovich's satirical novel did not reveal military secrets, nor was it straightforwardly "anti-Soviet." Moreover, Dewhirst's motivation for beginning his samizdat work with NTS cannot be described as anti-Soviet fervor: on the contrary, he felt an interest in helping Soviet society move forward along the promising path of liberal reform begun in 1956 with Khrushchev's "Thaw." At that time, the end of the 1950s and beginning of the 1960s, if one believed people should be able to read what they want to read, NTS was "the only game in town" for helping the cause.[90]

Later, there was Radio Liberty. Dewhirst described the care they took there with copies of original samizdat typescripts:

> If somebody said that he wanted to send some samizdat to the West but he didn't want it to be published, then that was fair enough. It was put in the huge safe of the Samizdat Section of Radio Liberty in Munich and was not even retyped. Everything else, incidentally, was re-typed because in those days it was still felt, rightly or wrongly, that every typewriter in the Soviet Union had been checked and that one could have key prints, like voice prints, and furthermore that one could tell from a carbon copy, as well as from the original, on which typewriter such-and-such a work had been produced.[91]

Dewhirst's reflections highlight the human element of these textual transactions. Dewhirst also spoke about the way these exchanges transcended economic and political calculations and even made such considerations seem improper:

> In my own personal experience. . . . I had never come across a single Soviet citizen who actually made money out of re-typing samizdat and selling it to friends and colleagues. . . . So here was the dilemma. I was sitting there and getting paid by, first of all, the CIA for a year or so after I first arrived, and then by the US Congress. I was paid in Deutschmarks, and the income supplemented my basic university salary to no small extent. I think all the people who worked in this very small Samizdat Section in Radio Liberty worked extremely hard. Possibly we were over-compensating for our guilt complex at having a cushy job, handling works which had been sent out through various channels at considerable personal risk.[92]

Dewhirst's comments need not be taken as a cue to sentimentalize or mythologize the character of the samizdat text or the people involved in its production and circulation. We should always be alert to the possible financial and political implications of particular instances of textual transmission and reproduction. In particular, the role of the CIA and Western intelligence agencies in supporting the networks of tamizdat remains an area in need of thorough research and sober analysis.[93]

At the same time, we cannot simply reduce those transactions to a simple political or economic logic. Following Bourdieu's concept of the diverse types of capital, both material and non-material,[94] we can propose that the samizdat text as an object of exchange reflects the mix of interests we would expect from its cross-border peregrinations. On the one hand, when the samizdat text gets converted to tamizdat publication, it may entail a more or less open conversion of dissident autonomy into political significance or economic gain. On the other hand, as we know from Bourdieu, symbolic capital resists conversion into other types.[95] In fact, we might find that the samizdat text can become the object of a more traditional kind of exchange as it creates new social ties among individuals and groups from different cultures. Marcel Mauss's analysis of exchanges in traditional societies captures the way such objects can carry and confer identity among the participants. Mauss gave special attention to the terms in which participants themselves spoke about exchange, an analytic imperative Johns has expressed in his call for a new history of the book.[96] Mauss explored the *hau*, the spirit of things given among Maori people. The *hau* proceeds from the giver (and the act of giving), and it has the power to compel the recipient to further exchange. A Maori informant, Tamati Ranaipiri, described it this way:

> I will speak to you about the *hau* . . . . The *hau* is not the wind that blows—not at all. Let us suppose that you possess a certain article (*taonga*) and that you give me this article. You give it me without setting a price on it. We strike no bargain about it. Now, I give this article to a third person who, after a certain lapse of time, decides to give me something as payment in return (*utu*). He makes a present to me of something (*taonga*). Now, this *taonga* that he gives me is the spirit (*hau*) of the *taonga* that I had received from you and that I had given to him. The *taonga* that I received for these *taonga* (which came from you) must be returned to you. It would not be fair (*tika*) on my part to keep these *taonga* for myself, whether they were desirable (*rawe*) or undesirable (*kino*). I must give them to you because they are a *hau* of the *taonga* that you gave me. If I kept this other *taonga* for myself, serious harm might befall me, even death. This is the nature of the *hau*, the *hau* of personal property, the *hau* of the *taonga*, the *hau* of the forest.[97]

Mauss stressed the fact that in this Maori understanding it was the object itself (the *taonga*) that compelled anyone into whose possession it came to further exchange: the thing received is not inactive. Even when abandoned by the giver, it still possesses something of that person.[98]

In samizdat textual exchange, too, the textual object given possesses the spirit (the identity) of its owner or owners—this may encompass the author and/or typist or reader who passes it on—and that spirit confers responsibility on the recipient for proper further exchange, as people like Dewhirst understood it. The reproduction is not the same as the original: it is a new textual object but one that, like its predecessors, bears the traces of the person or group passing it on. In Mauss's account, the items of ritual exchange (called the *kula* exchange in the Trobriand Islands of Melanesia) also represent more than simple objects. Mauss explained that the *vaygu'a*, the "essential objects in these exchange-gifts," are "not unimportant things, mere pieces of money. Each one, at least the dearest and most sought after— . . . has its name, a personality, a history and even a tale attached to it. So much is this so that certain individuals can even take their own name from them."[99] Such items must be treated with respect and caution—they carry the spirit of the giver, and they confer identity on the recipient. These gift items support social relations and serve to bind communities. This might be a useful model for thinking about these samizdat texts socially, as the basis of identity and community, as well as items representing cultural capital and political weight. Samizdat forged alternative publics within the U.S.S.R., and it supported significant informal social links across international borders.

The evolving interest in Mauss's studies of traditional societies follows the changing fortunes of first structuralist and then post-structuralist idioms, rather like the changing approach to the study of print.[100] Structuralists Claude Lévi-Strauss and Claude Lefort, who were among the first commentators of Mauss's work, found his reliance on indigenous concepts to be an analytic weakness.[101] Subsequently, however, exactly those things regarded as weaknesses from the structuralist point of view seemed to the next generation of ethnographers to be most innovative, supporting a new interest in objects, in material culture, in reconstruction of indigenous explanations, and in personal relations. Florence Weber discussed this changing attitude to Mauss's work. She cited as proof of the productivity of Mauss's methods, previously dismissed or disparaged, the ethnographic work of the 1980s–2000s by Arjun Appadurai, Michel Callon, Pierre Lascoumes, Yannick Barthe, Luc Boltanski, Laurent Thévenot, Florence Weber, and Jacques Godbout.[102] In addition, Jacques Derrida critiqued Lévi-Strauss's apprehension of Mauss from Derrida's own post-structuralist perspective. Lévi-Strauss eliminated the affective and the magical from the theory of gift, and he privileged the logic of exchange and relation "in order to eliminate the question of the thing." For Derrida, "to reduce the latter to exchange is quite simply to annul the very possibility of the gift."[103]

For critical purposes, the turn to the real material aspect of "the thing" provides a way of objectifying patterns of thought and belief in order to analyze them. For Derrida, the "question of the thing" functions for him, like the written trace in writing, as a means for breaking the charm of rational thought so enamored of its assumed clarity it can lead to the greatest mystifications. In the case of dissident freedom, the turn to the material reality of the production and exchange of samizdat texts has more than one purpose. Most obviously, it allows us to consider the social context, the economic and, especially, political forces dominating the field in which Soviet dissidence emerges proclaiming to be free of those forces. Bourdieu's critique of the autonomy of literature and art suggests this type of demystification: ideologies of culture tend to conceal the social realities that help reproduce hierarchy and structures of domination precisely where they are most vigorously denied. We can look at who is publishing tamizdat and ask what political interests might be overtly or covertly involved. We can question whether the autonomous literature and art of samizdat circulates widely enough among Soviet citizens and has enough obvious value to them to impact social attitudes on a broad scale. The ideology of avant-garde literature and the material and social difficulties associated with samizdat production and circulation suggest how unlikely such broad social impact is, at least in the short term.

A complicating factor arises with the fact that in the case of dissidence we are not talking about a single society or system. We should make this explicit, too. Bourdieu shows that the beliefs associated with autonomy are not natural—they are constructed, contingent.[104] They are, therefore, specific to the social system in which they arise. The exchange of samizdat between Soviet authors and Western readers and publishers entails not only a conversion of symbolic capital into material gain or political significance: it also manifests as a conversion of one type of symbolic capital into another. The Western supporters of dissidence—academics, publishers, philanthropists, area specialists, and community activists—had their own autonomous beliefs in the values of these works and of the labor required to help disseminate, standardize, and fix them. The quest for identity and new types of social relations through samizdat exchange appeared on both sides of the Iron Curtain. Samizdat facilitated a shared quest to make that Curtain fall.

While such efforts did not precipitate the regime change that finally occurred, they did preview the kind of extra-Gutenberg digital and global age we inhabit now. There is no uniformity among systems and no more single modern narrative from which the truth and value of texts can derive. Instead, the effect of social networks, and the impact of real material circumstances—including political conditions and technical platforms for actually circulating texts—makes it imperative that we pay attention to whom is being heard, how and why.

Conclusion

Soviet Dissidence and Critical Subjectivity in an Extra-Gutenberg Age

> The dissident movement is, in my opinion, primarily an intellectual movement; it is a process of independent and unintimidated thinking. At the same time these intellectual or spiritual aspirations are correlated to a feeling of moral responsibility, which is bestowed upon a man and forces him to think, speak, and write independently without regard for the norms and prescriptions of the state.
> —Andrei Siniavskii

IN HIS ESSAY on dissent written for a Western audience, Andrei Siniavskii suggested that the dissident was an admirable figure—someone who takes risks to act and speak according to the dictates of conscience.[1] Elsewhere in that essay, Siniavskii portrayed dissidents as rather more complex figures, and we have seen that complexity in his writing practice and the practice of fellow uncensored authors. As we noted, Siniavskii's writing straddles the line between the Soviet cultural establishment and the dissident field, making him an impure figure. Moreover, Siniavskii's alter ego Abram Terts hardly embodies moral rectitude—he provokes readers, not just the State, and he enacts a kind of stylistic dissidence that does not directly illustrate the spiritual aspirations and moral responsibility of which Siniavskii speaks. Similarly, the projections of Vasilii Aksenov, Andrei Bitov, and Venedikt Erofeev found in their uncensored writing hardly fit the heroic mold of the dissident writer. Rather, they illustrate the moment of critical self-reflection that proves to be key to the construction of dissident subjectivity and imagination of a different future toward which that subjectivity is oriented. This process necessarily precedes and underpins the heroic poster-ready image of the freedom fighter. If that figure no longer represents political or economic force, we might look at it again with the experience of samizdat novels as a "gumdrop" lingering on the tongue of history, with substance through which we can still work.[2]

The dissident might yet prove to be useful as one of the already estranged hypostases of the quest for freedom. As the major imaginative works of Soviet dissidence make plain and the production and circulation of samizdat illustrates more broadly, the dissident's task was not only or not even to challenge the Soviet state directly. Instead, the dissident aimed for something more basic: he or she sought to model the kind of active and critical relationship to self and context that readers are asked to adopt when they take up the dissident text.

Samizdat underscores the fact that this active and self-conscious subjectivity of the dissident was necessarily a shared phenomenon. Pierre Bourdieu's model of the cultural field provides one useful tool for describing the ways people derived and inspired activity from those around them as they positioned themselves relative to other players and established rules of the game to invent new ways of acting. Bourdieu's model discourages idealization of the freedom and heroism of players on the autonomous field. It does suggest, however, that dissidence entailed a powerful belief in freedom shared among Soviet dissidents and their readers and supporters abroad. While Bourdieu's critical method helps us evaluate the construction and effects of that belief, it would be reductive to dismiss dissident freedom as a cynical illusion. The symbolic value of dissident autonomy was real, and it generated considerable cultural and social activity in the late Soviet era. Moreover, while dissident activity did not topple the Soviet Union, it did illustrate new ways of being and behaving for an extra-Gutenberg age. In these concluding remarks, I will consider some of the implications of Bourdieu's models for critical analysis of Soviet dissidence and the samizdat mode of the text as a condition that pushes the boundaries of Bourdieu's analysis. I will also take a look at some implications of Soviet dissident culture for analyzing critical subjectivity in a global, digital age.

BOURDIEU AND AUTONOMY IN THE CONTEXT OF SOVIET DISSIDENCE

Bourdieu's model of the cultural field features people observing rules of the game together and occasionally challenging or changing those rules. In chapter 1 we saw evidence of the transformation of the Soviet cultural field in the mid-1960s when people including Andrei Siniavskii and Aleksandr Esenin-Volpin effectively challenged the rules of official Soviet society, opening up a new "space of possibles" where we would see what people came to recognize as Soviet dissidence.[3] Siniavskii's literary independence and Volpin's legalism manifested a tense relationship to one another—both implied a struggle against determination from above, by State authorities, but each in addition pushed off from the other to establish a distinct claim to autonomy. This relationship demonstrates the kind of competition on the field Bourdieu analyzed and it sets up the dynamic of intra-field tensions that plays out throughout the development of the field of Soviet dissidence, from its emergence around this time until its repression by Soviet authorities in the early 1980s,[4] and its eventual dissolution in the ferment of a completely different social situation beginning in 1987 with glasnost and perestroika.[5]

Bourdieu talked about different autonomous fields embedded in the same larger socio-economic context, juxtaposing the fields of politics, philosophy, and religion.[6] In the case of the U.S.S.R. in the late Soviet period, we see that autonomous spheres relate to one another. In light of the all-encompassing ambitions of the State to regulate all aspects of life, these various groups and types of autonomous activity appear to be part of one dissident field. They can all be seen as departures from one unified and centrally controlled official Soviet system that in general refused to recognize any type of independent activity as legitimate.[7] Another factor justifying the gathering together of democratic, literary, religious, national, music fan, and other types of independent groups is their use of samizdat for unofficial production and circulation of texts.[8]

The chief reason for grouping various independent communities and trends together as part of one large dissident field is to appreciate the dynamics of how these groups relate to one another in collaborative and competitive ways. Examples of collaboration include the national and religious groups that partnered with the democratic dissidents to publicize their causes using the mutually beneficial discourse of "human rights," which had enormous power among Western audiences at this time.[9] The collaboration helped the democrats, who were thus able to expand their reach beyond the intelligentsia of the capitals, who tended to fill their ranks.[10]

Competition arose in the attempt to take up positions in what Bourdieu called a "limited field of cultural production" within the dissident field, that is, a place removed from the channels for converting the symbolic capital of dissidence into political influence or material gain. We see this most clearly among the Leningrad dissident literati, and particularly in the ethos articulated by Viktor Krivulin.[11] In his history of autonomous literature of this period, Krivulin recalled the exaggerated aestheticism of the 1966 uncensored almanac *Fioretti* (Leningrad) as a significant forerunner of the "separation [*rassloenie*] of the once unified artistic-political space of uncensored literature." After August 1968 the center of literary samizdat moved to Leningrad, he contended. Meanwhile, "Muscovite non-political samizdat becomes gradually commercialized. Something like an underground literary market opens up, where an increasingly large role is played by editions published abroad and clandestinely brought across the cordon. In the end, tamizdat proves more viable in a market sense than samizdat."[12] As part of the attempt to establish and maintain a restricted cultural position, Krivulin and other editors of the samizdat journal *37* (1976–81) objected to the characterization in one American newspaper article of their journal as part of the "underground." They complained that the American journalist confused politics and aesthetics. The journalist missed the point that Leningrad unofficial culture does not simply oppose official Socialist Realism—it expresses its own positive aims.[13] These aims included the purification of a restricted cultural position. Subsequently, younger members of Leningrad unofficial culture complained about the social and political engagement of their elders, Krivulin and his coeditor Goricheva. These and other dissident writers likewise contested the position of poet Joseph Brodsky.[14] This might seem contradictory, given how fully Brodsky seemed to embody poetic autonomy.[15] The contradiction disappears when we consider the development of the field over time with the help of Bourdieu's model: Krivulin, Elena Shvarts and like-minded poets eventually achieved their own level of consecration. That unofficial establishment, like the resounding consecration of Brodsky as a canonical figure meant that the younger "avant-garde" had to contest the legitimacy of their elders as part of their own bid to establish a new, and avowedly more purely autonomous, position.

To be sure, there are limits to our ability to emulate Bourdieu's sociological and economic analysis. We have difficulty establishing with certainty the numbers of copies of any samizdat text and the scope of the audience.[16] We know a little about the way materials for producing texts were procured and how they were produced. Occasionally readers did pay and this practice, meant to cover costs, seems to be insignificant for some claims of autonomy, although occasionally groups boasted about their purely non-economic model.[17] Groups employed typists, usually women, who often worked for a modest fee. Beyond the domestic market, a systematic study of the foreign contracts, print runs, and profit from foreign print editions of samizdat texts remains to be done. Bourdieu's model presumed a unified and isolated French field. The late Soviet case cannot be cut off from the international market and multiple means of publishing and circulating texts in different countries over time. Present evidence remains scattered and anecdotal.[18]

Conceptually, however, the usefulness of Bourdieu's model lies, perhaps even more than the skepticism with which it encourages us to treat dissident claims to autonomy and freedom, in the way it facilitates an appreciation of the relationship of various claims to autonomy to one another. This concerns individual dissidents and dissident groups in the field. Bourdieu's model also pushes us to examine the effects of external forces. In the case of

Soviet dissidence, we find that in addition to pressures exerted by the Soviet government, the impact of forces from abroad was great.

For example, we know the unofficial Jewish national movement collaborated early on with members of the democratic movement.[19] The further development of these movements meant a strategic distancing of the Jewish "cultural movement" in the U.S.S.R. from the democrats beginning in the early 1970s. Individuals and organizers of the Jewish movement found this necessary, for various reasons. Aleksandr Voronel, who began the samizdat journal *Jews in the USSR* (*Evrei v SSSR*, 1972–79) in that period, felt he could do more by focusing on the problems of his own community, highlighted in that journal. Organizers and their supporters in Israel and abroad also felt it would be strategically sensible to focus on education and Hebrew learning and step back from any public involvement in the struggle with Soviet authorities over rights.[20] In part, the reorientation reflected a strategic move to protect Soviet Jews from charges of anti-Soviet activity. Some high-profile individuals like Anatoly (Natan) Shcharansky continued to work with democratic dissidents, and the issue of Jewish emigration as a human rights concern made its way, thanks in part to the endorsement of Andrei Sakharov, to the U.S. Senate.[21] The role of external forces in influencing what kind of dissident cultural production should occur and how it might be converted varied from group to group and could be significant. At the same time, individual preferences and actions could play a leading role.

Samizdat always implied tamizdat, even if for the most autonomous literary groups such print publication and wide recognition were deferred. All of this Soviet dissident activity depended from the beginning on foreign audiences and participation. Thus, when we consider the amassing of symbolic capital on the dissident field, we should ask what possibilities for conversion existed for various types of dissidence into cultural, economic, or political capital over time. We should also be alert to the exchanges of symbolic capital that imply changes from one form of symbolic capital to another: in chapter 5 we saw that "gift" exchanges, that is, exchanges not predominantly determined by economic or political calculations, implied new constructions of subjectivity for the people involved, on both sides. Individuals in the West who supported dissidents and dissident activity often did so for the sake of their own values and ideals. This was a major phenomenon of the Cold War, in which individuals outside the Soviet Union devoted years of labor to assisting Soviet dissidents with no commensurate economic rewards to justify the effort. Such people included Martin Dewhirst at Radio Liberty, Edward Kline of Chekhov Publishing, Carl and Ellendea Proffer of Ardis Publishers, and many others.[22]

The global networks of samizdat and tamizdat distinguish Soviet dissidence from the original model Bourdieu developed of a modern cultural field embedded within one coherent national socio-economic context. If we can take the model of a unified field of autonomy out of the totalitarian context and project it into a global context of networked claims for autonomy, we might produce a critically dynamic picture of autonomy. Arguably this is what Bourdieu did by acknowledging the different forms a critical *intention of autonomy* could take in various local contexts—here secular, there religious.[23] The belief in autonomy benefits from this kind of plurality and contingent varieties of expression. Bourdieu summarized his aim at the end of *The Rules of Art* to re-create the image of culture and "freedom" by stripping it of its specific modern bourgeois mythologies. For him, the field of culture still grounded the intellectual's critique of power. And although expressions of autonomy differ, there was common cause to be made in the name of that goal.[24] Bourdieu resisted the label "theoretician," and reflected on the biases of his own perspective[25] there could be many. Bourdieu took up the critique of a reified concept of autonomy in his own French context not to demystify autonomy once and for all. Rather, he aimed to rethink the quest for autonomy as part of a historically embedded, living process of intellectual engagement. In this view, then, autonomy as an ideal should be appreciated as the sum of its many historically and socially grounded expressions. Soviet dissident "autonomy"—materialized in samizdat and related through it to sister forms of belief—helps detach the quest for autonomy from exclusive realization in the context of the capitalist West, pluralizing the ways in which that quest might be pursued.

THE DISSIDENT SUBJECT AND AUTONOMY BEYOND THE USSR

One of the bourgeois mythologies that seem unviable in the context of Soviet dissident culture of samizdat is the myth of the individual author. The imposing figure of the dissident suggests, however, that this challenge to the exclusive hegemony of the author does not quite line up with the post-structural insistence that the birth of the reader must come at the price of the death of the author.[26] Both the author and the reader participate in the publication of samizdat, their roles blurred in their function as informal publishers of the text. Both invest themselves in this activity and take a measure of risk. In fact, robust subjectivity associated with their different positions on the samizdat field is required to support the life of the unauthorized text. This therefore looks like a dialogic model of subjectivity, depending as it does on multiple authentic subjects.[27] Working from a Bourdieusian perspective on the various positions in the field and networked relations between fields, we can note that the subjectivities involved exist in a relationship of temporal discontinuity inasmuch as one prior imagination of the text (the author's) necessarily precedes that of the reader's and may imply a wholly different understanding of the text's potential. As distinct from a dialectical model, there is no necessary progressive trajectory from one position to the other. For example, when critics asserted the "postmodern" character of Bitov's *Pushkin House* at a time when "postmodern" meant good or interesting, they commodified it in terms of cultural and indeed economic value. However, the author Bitov or a subsequent reader might prefer to defer such a conversion of the work's aesthetic capital by, for example, connecting the novel back to the literary art of Tolstoi and Pushkin and Sterne. Oriented (perhaps by the author, and maybe by the reader), to that "great time" of culture, the work possesses potentials for meaning and value that unfold in unpredictable ways and cannot be known in advance.[28]

The temporal discontinuities of the field of autonomy[29] and its pluralized and networked variants suggest also a different way of approaching the "end of history" supposed to be characteristic of the postmodern era. Edith Clowes referred to this postmodern end of history and proposed that in its wake, attention to space became more pointed in post-Soviet writing.[30] Notably, this spatial turn applies as Clowes analyzed it to recent imaginations of national identity.[31] Modernism, of course, featured its own version of spatial imagination as detailed by Joseph Frank, and we can see echoes of that modernist spatialization in the samizdat novels examined here, particularly in Aksenov's sweeping view that aims to bring everything all "swirled together."[32] Nevertheless, these samizdat novelists' difference from that modernist model, their refusal to commit to a static image or pronouncement of a theological word, along with their orientation to audience reaction and the life of the text beyond its initial authorship and form, imply a commitment to the future history of the text, to an alternative imagined (and not preprogrammed) future rooted in a genuinely collaborative creation of meaning. The independent creation of alternative chronologies characterizes dissident communities, who departed in their irregular samizdat publications from the unified, homogeneous time of official print.[33] In this way, multiple, alternative chronologies replace the unified History of the state and monologic ideology. Critical subjectivity in the extra-Gutenberg era remains oriented to history, but the public potential of that critical intervention will depend on the creation of a meaningful relationship among established historical narratives and their alternatives.

In light of contemporary debates about activism in the extra-Gutenberg conditions of a globalized, digitally networked present, samizdat and Soviet dissidence can provide a usefully low-tech point of comparison. We recognize today that new social media platforms like Facebook and Twitter do not by themselves generate revolutions.[34] The human element is crucial. Media historian Lisa Gitelman stressed the dual character of media, which is part technology and part social protocol built up around that technology: media are "socially realized structures of communication."[35] The attention of samizdat authors like Krivulin and Bitov to Osip Mandelshtam's emphasis on the role of the voice helps underscore the need for critical and individualized voices that communicate meaningfully in the context of a more fluid, "oral" type of extra-Gutenberg environment. Media scholar Henry Jenkins likewise resisted the isolation and idealization of new media in his accounts of contemporary culture and civic engagement. He emphasized the interaction of new and old forms of media, as well as the rise of new forms of social affiliation and knowledge creation that exploit these evolving clusters of mediated interconnection.[36] The collective knowledge of fan communities discussed by Jenkins might be likened to the work of citizen-journalists or citizen-scientists, which complements—but does not replace—institutionalized forms of knowledge creation and dissemination. In the context of Soviet dissidence, the phenomenon of what we might today call the "citizen-historian" became quite important. Alekseeva is only the most obvious example of a person who out of conviction and identification with the cause of democratic dissidents made the effort to tell the history of her movement, since that need would not or could not be served by existing authorities and institutions.[37] People who "dropped out" of official institutions in the 1970s or were forced out because of visa refusal or other sanctions often turned to humanitarian types of activity that entailed this more informal and voluntary type of knowledge-building as part of their bid to reimagine themselves and their alternative communities.

I would argue that Soviet dissident culture and the kind of "participatory culture" Jenkins analyzed in light of new media vary in degree, not in kind.[38] Their juxtaposition, however, might be instructive. Writing fan fiction or remixing parts of popular songs foregrounds the way audience members may assume the function of author relative to texts that move them, while the freer circulation of content in new media facilitates the publication of such works in a way that reminds us of samizdat. For its part, samizdat and dissidence underscore the fragility of free culture and civic engagement.[39] This vulnerability may manifest in new globally networked ways today. Ethan Zuckerman wrote about what he called "intermediate censorship," that is, the implementation of government directives to block connections for selected web addresses by Internet Service Providers (ISPs) and Online Service Providers (OSPs) that host social networking sites and blogs. These nodes of mediation, built into the infrastructure of digital communication, can support or stifle the transmission of real human voices. Zuckerman found in analyses of cases involving Chinese blogging hosts and U.S.-based OSPs that the problem had to do with the need of OSPs to interpret government regulations and to generate operating profit: it could be time-consuming and expensive to try to accommodate dissident communications. Therefore, scholars and activists have a role to play—an often prosaic role, that might remind us of the months and years of data collection and fact-checking by editors of the Moscow *Chronicle*—in clarifying regulations and helping companies keep their channels open to those types of communications.[40] It seems most likely that those scholars and activists who engage in this kind of supporting role will do so out of their own principled interests and values, whether or not they see direct political impact from their work.

One of the objections to the notion that Facebook or Twitter can facilitate revolution is that virtual participation lacks the kind of personal investment and risk associated with American civil rights demonstrations in the 1960s,[41] or, we might add, Soviet dissidence. Such a comparison reiterates a romanticized view of 1960s engagement and suggests the kind of revolutionary collapse of the distance between culture and politics (and between leaders and their publics) that goes along with it. In the West, people became disillusioned with the power of street demonstrations and carnivalesque behavior, but a belief in the revolution that never arrived lingered. In the Soviet Union, people saw that collapsing the distinction between the people and their leaders in the revolutionary society resulted in an intractably corrupt and dysfunctional system: reform for "Socialism with a human face" proved to be impossible in those conditions. The kind of participatory culture Jenkins and his group research among today's youth in America reflects a willingness to engage in alternative forms of self-construction and community building *whether or not* they see an immediate outlet for political demands, and in this way it reminds us of Soviet dissidence. Moreover, it is interesting to note that the basis for the kind of participatory culture Jenkins described is found in fictional works and music. While J. K. Rowling's *Harry Potter* series is commercially viable popular literature, the appropriation of characters and plot lines by fans is not economically motivated. The autonomy of that cultural activity differs fundamentally from ad campaigns that spin off from movies and from the use of social engagement campaigns by companies to secure the loyalty of target demographics.[42] And while the translation of the skills and values honed in participatory culture into the civic engagement of the Harry Potter Alliance[43] shows (some amount of) political potential, the legitimacy of that potential depends on the initially autonomous status of the grassroots culture from which it springs.

Autonomous culture—whether we locate that autonomy in some act of creation imagined to be original or in the critically engaged circulation and alteration of texts—provides the possibility for critical reflection, analysis, and imagination. These are activities in which critical subjectivity is formed by the individual in tandem with a social community or communities. The ways construction of a critical subjectivity may play out will differ, but, still today, to paraphrase Mandelshtam, these histories begin from the voice.

Notes

INTRODUCTION

1. Venedikt Yerofeev, *Moscow Stations: A Poem*, trans. Stephen Mulrine (London: Faber and Faber, 1997), 79; and Venedikt Erofeev, *Moskva–Petushki*, in *Zapiski psikhopata* (Moscow: Vagrius, 2000), 203.

2. Erofeev received an invitation to travel to France for an operation to treat his throat cancer in 1986. Soviet authorities would not grant Erofeev an exit visa because of gaps in his work record, as discussed in Igor Bolychev's interview with Erofeev, "Umru, no nikogda ne poimu . . . ," *Moskovskie novosti* (December 10, 1989), 13.

3. "I alone in Russia work from the voice," Mandelshtam wrote angrily in his uncensored *Fourth Prose* (*Chetvertaia proza*, 1930), in Osip Mandelstam, *The Noise of Time*, ed. and trans. Edward Brown (New York: Penguin, 1986), 181.

4. A brief biographical sketch appears in Mulrine's "Foreword" to *Moscow Stations*. Erofeev's biography has seemed particularly susceptible to mythologization thanks in part to Erofeev's own lively accounts for journalists and scholars who paid him intense attention in the late 1980s and 1990s. See Elena Ignatova, "Venedikt," *Neva* 1 (1993): 220–21. Facts about Erofeev's early life, including time spent in an orphanage after his father's arrest, can be found in Tamara Gushchina, "Venedikt Erofeev, Pis'ma k sestre," *Teatr* 9 (1992): 122–44.

5. Erofeev, *Moscow Stations*, 7; Yerofeev, *Moskva–Petushki*, 22.

6. Andrei Zorin, "Opoznavatel'nyi znak," *Teatr* 9 (1991): 122.

7. Tom Courtenay, who played Venichka in a theatrical adaptation of the novel, made this statement, as quoted by David Remnick, "The Lush Life of a Muscovite," *The New Yorker* 71, no. 33 (October 23, 1995): 37.

8. Pierre Bourdieu's ideas about the autonomy of art and the field of cultural production can be found in his book *Les règles de l'art: Genèse et structure du champ littéraire* (Paris: Éditions du Seuil, 1998 [1992]), appearing in English as *The Rules of Art: Genesis and Structure of the Literary Field*, trans. Susan Emanuel (Stanford, Calif.: Stanford University Press, 1992). A related collection with helpful orienting introduction to Bourdieu's concepts is Pierre Bour-

dieu, *The Field of Cultural Production: Essays on Art and Literature*, ed. Randal Johnson (Oxford: Polity, 1993). Craig Calhoun also sketched out Bourdieu's key concepts, including his notion of different types of capital and the mechanisms of conversion between them. See the chapter "Habitus, Field, and Capital," in Craig Calhoun, *Critical Social Theory: Culture, History, and the Challenge of Difference* (Oxford: Blackwell, 1995).

9. Bourdieu explained the autonomous field of cultural production as an "anti-economy" resistant to economic and political forces where people try to amass a symbolic capital whose value stands in inverse proportion to economic or political value. Thus, Bourdieu said, "the literary and artistic world is so ordered that those who enter it have an interest in disinterestedness" (*The Field*, 40).

10. In this way my approach differs from other well-known and provocative studies of this culture, including Boris Groys's analysis of the avant-garde's will to power in *Gesamtkunstwerk Stalin* (Munich: Carl Hanser Verlag, 1988, translated as *The Total Art of Stalinism*, trans. Charles Rougle [Princeton, N.J.: Princeton University Press, 1992]); and Mikhail Berg's *Literaturokratiia* (Moscow: Novoe literaturnoe obozrenie, 2000), which draws on Bourdieu to set up the relationship of literature to cultural and economic power.

11. I take up this argument in the conclusion.

12. See in particular Hal Foster's "What's Neo about the Neo-Avant-Garde?" in *The Duchamp Effect*, ed. Martha Buskirk and Mignon Nixon (Cambridge, Mass.: MIT Press, 1996).

13. Jean-Jacques Rousseau, *The Confessions of Jean Jacques Rousseau* (London: J.M. Dent & Sons, 1933), vol. 1, 1.

14. Jochen Hellbeck, *Revolution on My Mind* (Cambridge, Mass.: Harvard University Press, 2006), 3.

15. See Donna Tussing Orwin, *Consequences of Consciousness. Turgenev, Dostoevsky, and Tolstoy* (Stanford, Calif.: Stanford University Press, 2007), 112.

16. Hellbeck, *Revolution*, 9–10. Hellbeck explored the roots of Stalin-era ideology in the specific adoption of German idealistic philosophy such as Hegel's laws of history (ibid., 351).

17. Benjamin Nathans, "Thawed Selves: A Commentary on the Soviet First Person," *Kritika* 13, no. 1 (2012): 181–82

18. See the accounts in Sidney Bloch and Peter Reddaway, *Soviet Psychiatric Abuse: The Shadow over World Psychiatry* (London: Gollancz, 1984).

19. For example, Iurii Andropov spoke while still head of the KGB about the scourge of dissidents as agents of foreign propaganda. See "Doklad tovarishcha Iu.V. Andropova," *Izvestiia* 213, no. 18668 (September 10, 1977): 2.

20. Kharkhordin referred to Michel Foucault's elaboration of the "panopticon" type of prison as a metaphor for Western subjectivity. He described Russian Orthodox religious practices to help illuminate the difference of traditional Russian approaches to the constitution of the responsible self. See Oleg Kharkhor-

din, *The Collective and the Individual in Russia: A Study of Practices* (Berkeley: University of California Press, 1999).

21. Kharkhordin, *The Collective*, 270. Bolshevik attacks on the "cult of the individual" referred to German Romanticism and its translation of the Stoic idea of cultivation of the soul (ibid., 193).

22. Kharkhordin, *The Collective*, 270.

23. See their article "Soviet Russia," in *Dissent and Opposition in Communist Eastern Europe: Origins of Civil Society and Democratic Transition*, ed. Detlef Pollack and Jan Wielgohs (Burlington, Vt.: Ashgate, 2004), 113.

24. The name of Petro Grigorenko's memoirs summarizes the attitude of the democratic movement: *In the Underground You Meet Only Rats* (*V podpol'e vstretit' mozhno tol'ko krys* (New York: Izdatel'stvo Detinets, 1981).

25. See Vladimir Bukovsky, *To Build a Castle: My Life as a Dissenter*, trans. Michael Scammell (London: André Deutsch, 1978), 97.

26. See Andrei Siniavskii, "Dissidentstvo kak lichnyi opyt," *Sintaksis* 15 (1986): 131–47, which appeared in English as Andrei Sinyavsky, "Dissent as a Personal Experience," *Dissent* 31, no. 2 (1984): 152–61. Siniavskii wrote about dissidence as a personal experience and an artistic practice. He emphasized the generational specificity of Soviet dissidents formed within the Soviet context ("Dissent," 154). One might compare this description of the generation of dissidents outlined by Siniavskii to Zygmunt Bauman's account of "Second-Generation Socialism," in *Political Opposition in One-Party States*, ed. Leonard Schapiro (London: Macmillan, 1972).

27. See Jerome McGann, *The Textual Condition* (Princeton, N.J.: Princeton University Press, 1991), 10–11.

28. Bourdieu compared the field to "a prism which *refracts* every external determination" (*The Field*, 164). Randal Johnson elaborated on these prismatic effects, noting that the degree of autonomy of a given field can be gauged by its ability to refract external demands into its own logic (*The Field*, 14).

29. Bourdieu wrote of *Sentimental Education*, "A true example of the absolute masterpiece, the novel contains an anlysis of the social space in which the author was himself located and thus gives us the instruments we need for an analysis of him." See Bourdieu, "Is the Structure of *Sentimental Education* an Instance of Social Self-Analysis?" (*The Field*, 145).

30. See Liudmila Alekseeva, *Istoriia inakomysliia v SSSR: Noveishii period* (Vilnius-Moscow: Vest', 1992), 203. This important account of the period appeared in English as Ludmilla Alexeyeva, *Soviet Dissent: Contemporary Movements for National, Religious, and Human Rights*, trans. Carol Pearce and John Glad (Middletown, Conn.: Wesleyan University Press, 1985), 276–77.

31. For more on the Moscow *Chronicle*, see Chapter 5.

32. Brodsky was arrested in 1964 and charged with "parasitism" (*tuneiadstvo*) for not having an officially registered job. The transcript of the trial by

Frida Vigdorova showed a young man asserting that his right to call himself a poet came "from God." That transcript circulated in samizdat and was published abroad, helping to make Brodsky's case one of the most celebrated trials of the mid-1960s and drawing attention to the repression of independent literary efforts in the Soviet Union. See Alexeyeva, *Soviet Dissent*, 297, 327; and Alyssa Dinega Gillespie, "Joseph Brodsky," in *Russian Writers Since 1980*, ed. Marina Balina and Mark Lipovetsky (Detroit, Mich.: Gale, 2004), 17–32.

33. Lev Loseff quoted these lines in *Joseph Brodsky: A Literary Life*, trans. Jane Ann Miller (New Haven, Conn.: Yale University Press, 2011), 219. Loseff contextualized the lines in terms of the dead end of carnality and the limitless space of Eros. Konstantin Rogov put the lines in a more social frame as a sort of "manifesto of timelessness," of stagnation begun at the end of the 1960s, in his introduction to the special issue of *Rossiia/Russia*, Issue 1 [9] *Semidesiatye kak predmet istorii russkoi kul'tury*, ed. K. Iu. Rogov (Moscow: O.G.I., 1998), 9.

34. Petr Vail and Aleksandr Genis called the 1968 occupation of Czechoslovkia the "final blow to all hopes," in *60-e: Mir sovetskogo cheloveka* (Moscow: Novoe literaturnoe obozrenie, 1996), 5. Rogov called the invasion of Czechoslovakia the "key cultural myth" of the era. See his and other similar evaluations of the significance of 1968 (*Semidesiatye*, 9 and passim). Arlen Blium echoed the common characterization of 1968 as a watershed, marked by a sharp division created at that time between official, censored culture and the culture appearing in samizdat and tamizdat. See A.V. Blium, *Kak eto delalos' v Leningrade: Tsenzura v gody ottepeli, zastoia i perestroika, 1953–1991* (St. Petersburg: Akademicheskii proekt, 2005), 18.

35. Alexeyeva, *Soviet Dissent*, 323–24.

36. The song "Pokolenie dvornikov" appeared on the album by Grebenshchikov's band Akvarium (Aquarium) called *Equinox* (*Ravnodenstvie*, 1987). Grebenshchikov either picked up or coined a common formulation for a phenomenon recognized as characteristic of the era. Bukovskii noted that the dropouts of the 1970s were preceded in the 1960s by a trend of young people who failed to finish their degrees because they were unable or unwilling to accede to ideological demands placed on their work. See Bukovskii, *To Build*, 124–25. Andrei Amalrik called these early dropouts the "generation of 1956," in *Notes of a Revolutionary*, trans. Guy Daniels (London: Weidenfeld and Nicolson, 1982), 21.

37. Aksenov wrote enthusiastically about Western hippies following trips abroad to London and California in one published essay. He compared the hippies of London and San Francisco to Russian Futurists, underscoring their common opposition to bourgeois society in "Kruglye sutki non-stop" ("Around the Clock Non-Stop"), *Novyi mir* 8 (1976): 84–87. In his uncensored novel *The Burn* (*Ozhog*), Aksenov produced a nuance critique of the confused and superficial attitude of Western student demonstrators, and the lack of freedom of Soviet citizens to organize any spontaneous demonstration, even an ideologically cor-

rect, anti-Vietnam demonstration. See Vassily Aksyonov, *The Burn: A Novel in Three Books (Late Sixties–Early Seventies)*, trans. Michael Glenny (New York: Random House, 1984), 252–53, 417.

38. See Bourdieu's section entitled "Art and Money," with a schematic drawing of the field of cultural production situated inside the field of power and social space. The special symbolic capital of the restricted field of culture, constructed on the basis of a belief in autonomy, represents the opposite of regular exchange value in the larger economy (*The Rules*, 124).

39. Philip Boobbyer wrote: "The Soviet dissidents are not easy to define. The Soviet regime itself happily labelled its opponents 'dissidents' because the words had anti-social and extremist connotations. Partly for this reason, oppositionists generally did not like the term 'dissident.' The dissidents sometimes preferred to describe themselves as '*inakomyslyashchie*', literally, 'people who think differently,' because it was a less loaded term." See Boobbyer, *Conscience, Dissent and Reform in Soviet Russia* (London: Routledge, 2005), 75.

40. Jonathan Bolton, drawing on observations by Czech dissident Vaclav Havel, wrote about the fact that dissidents' activity aimed most of all for an international audience, whose selective and idealizing perception of the dissidents obscured the heterogeneous views and often messy local conditions in which they acted. Jonathan Bolton, *Worlds of Dissent: Charter 77, The Plastic People of the Universe and Czech Culture under Communism* (Cambridge, Mass.: Harvard University Press, 2012), 2.

41. While feminist scholar Nancy Fraser regarded Jurgen Habermas's original notion of a unified critical public too abstract and reductive, she defended it as a necessary conceptual bulwark against the long-standing "failure" in dominant circles of Marxist thought to appreciate the need to distinguish arenas of public discourse and association from the apparatuses of the State. See Fraser's "Rethinking the Public Sphere: A Contribution to the Critique of Actually Existing Democracy," in *Habermas and the Public Sphere*, ed. Craig Calhoun (Cambridge, Mass.: MIT Press, 1992), 109–10.

42. I propose this to be possible and necessary despite the influential argument of Alexei Yurchak in *Everything Was Forever Until It Was No More: The Last Soviet Generation* (Princeton, N.J.: Princeton University Press, 2006). Yurchak rather uncritically followed the opinions of his sample set of Leningraders who absolutely disavowed associations with commonly recognized "dissidence" or any direct political implications of their informal cultural activity.

43. Groys, *Gesamtkunstwerk Stalin*.

44. One can cite Iurii Karabchievskii, who wrote the unflattering *Voskresenie Maiakovskogo* (Moscow: Sovetskii pisatel', 1990) as evidence of this tendency.

45. Of this official Soviet Maiakovskii, Boris Pasternak said: "I do not comprehend the later Maiakovsky . . . I remain indifferent to those clumsily rhymed sermons, that cultivated insipidity, those commonplaces and platitudes . . . And

the remarkable thing about it is that this worthless, nonexistent Maiakovsky has come to be accepted as revolutionary . . . Maiakovsky was beginning to be propagated compulsorily like potatoes in the reign of Catherine the Great. That was his second death. For that he is not to blame." Bowlt and Konecny quoted Pasternak in their introduction to *A Legacy Regained: Nikolai Khardzhiev and the Russian Avant-Garde*, ed. John E. Bowlt and Mark Konecny (St. Petersburg: Palace Editions, 2002), 13.

46. Mandelshtam said, "I divide all the works of world literature into those written with and without permission. The first are trash, the second—stolen air" (*Fourth Prose*, 181).

47. Akhmatova's interactions with young poets are discussed in some detail in *Anna Akhmatova: Poslednie gody: Rasskazyvaiut Viktor Krivulin, Vladimir Murav'ev, Tomas Ventslova* (St. Petersburg: Nevskii dialekt, 2001).

48. Nadezhda Mandelshtam wrote in her memoirs: "To the question: 'What is Acmeism?' M. once replied: 'Nostalgia [*toska*] for world culture.'" See chapter 53, "Italy," of her *Hope Against Hope*, trans. Max Hayward (New York: Atheneum, 1970), 246.

49. On the mythology of the Silver Age, see Robert P. Hughes, "Pushkin in Petrograd, February 1921," in *Cultural Mythologies of Russian Modernism: From the Golden Age to the Silver Age*, ed. Boris Gasparov, Robert P. Hughes, and Irina Paperno (Berkeley: University of California Press, 1992), 204–13; and Dmitrii Segal, in "O vozmozhnoi tipologii 'serebrianykh vekov,'" in *L'Âge d'argent dans la culture russe*, ed. Jean-Claude Lanne (Lyon: Centre d'Études Slaves André Irondelle, 2007), 3–18.

50. This seminar represented the "last refuge of twentieth century poetry, which increasingly fell under pogroms and prohibitions [*zaprety*]," Siniavskii recalled. "They swarmed as best they could [*khudo li bedno li koposhilis'*] to the cover of Maikovskii, his artistic fellows . . . Malevich, Tatlin . . . Whitman-Verhaern-Rimbaud . . . "The One-and-a-Half-Eyed Archer of Benedikt Lifshits? . . . But isn't he an enemy of the people? . . . But he's a friend of Maiakovskii!" wrote Siniavskii in his colorful style. From the last chapter of Siniavskii's memoirs *Spokoinoi nochi*, in Abram Terts, *Sobranie sochinenii v dvukh tomakh*, vol. 2 (Moscow: SP 'Start,' 1992), 579–80, translation mine.

51. See Lev Losev, "Tulupy my," *Novoe literaturnoe obozrenie* 14 (1995): 209–16, 209.

52. Siniavskii collected materials of the Brigade, housed presently in the Siniavskii Collection, Box 104, F. 14, 16, Hoover Institution. Siniavskii's wife Mariia Rozanova attended meetings of the Brigade (interview July 8, 2003).

53. Recollections of these meetings can be found in Aleksandr Daniel' and Arsenii Roginskii, eds., *Piatoe dekabria 1965 goda v vospominaniiakh uchastnikov sobytii, materialakh Samizdata, dokumentakhpartiinykh i komsomol'skikh organizatsii i v zapiskakh Komiteta gosudarstvennoi bezopasnosti v TsK KPSS*

(Moscow: Zven'ia, 2005), 6; and among memoirs collected by Liudmila Polikovskaia, *My predchuvstvie . . . predtecha . . . Ploshchad' Maiakovskogo, 1958–1965* (Moscow: Zven'ia, 1997).

54. Gennadii Aigi described about ten exhibits organized by Nikolai Khardzhiev at the Maiakovskii Museum in the 1960s, which included works by El Lissitzky, Kazimir Malevich, Vladimir Tatlin, Pavel Filonov, Velimir Khlebnikov, Mikhail Larionov, Natal'ia Goncharova, and others. Aigi wrote that Khardzhiev "came up with a simple, but very clever, move. He called his series of exhibitions 'Illustrators of the Works of V. V. Maiakovsky.' Neither the official censors nor the Museum administration could object." See Gennady Aigi, "Nikolai Khardzhiev and the Maiakovsky Museum, Moscow," in Bowlt and Konecny, *A Legacy Regained*, 43–44. Mounting the shows proved not to be simple: see "The Future Is Now! Excerpts from an Interview with Ira Vrubel-Golubkina" (*Legacy Regained*, 30, 364, footnote 49).

55. This trend crystallized by the late 1970s–1980s among the Moscow Conceptualists. Their practice was distinctive for the use of apparently unusable contemporary Soviet material, according to Andrei Zorin, "'Al'manakh'—Vzgliad iz zala," *Lichnoe delo No.* __ (Moscow: V/O "Soiuzteatr," 1991), 247–48.

56. Bourdieu wrote about the development of "a more autonomous sector—or, if you will, an avant-garde" at the heart of each genre (*The Rules*, 120). The avant-garde corresponds to a "research" sector as opposed to a commercial sector. He noted that "the occupants of avant-garde positions who are not yet consecrated . . . have an interest . . . in making the success or recognition that certain avant-garde writers may obtain in the long term appear as the effect of a repudiation or a compromise with the bourgeois order" (ibid., 123).

57. See Margarita Tupitsyn's description of the dual thrust of Moscow Conceptualist critique of official forms and dissident modernism in *"About Early Soviet Conceptualism": Global Conceptualism: Points of Origin 1950s–1980s* (Queens Museum of Art, 1999), 99–107, 99. Conceptual artist Ilia Kabakov explicitly articulated his negative response to dissident modernism as a formative impulse. He felt impatience with his contemporaries' reverence for Andrei Tarkovskii's films and Anna Akhmatova's poetry as works expressing transcendent values. Kabakov wanted to know what made art "art," and how art could be made in the conditions of late Soviet culture, where official institutions dominated materials and venues. See Matthew Jesse Jackson, *The Experimental Group: Ilya Kabakov, Moscow Conceptualism, Soviet Avant-Gardes* (Chicago: University of Chicago Press, 2010), 75.

58. Bourdieu, *The Rules*, 157–59.

59. Peter Bürger, *Theory of the Avant-Garde*, trans. Michael Shaw (Minneapolis: University of Minnesota Press, 1984), 109n4.

60. See Foster's critique of Bürger, "What's Neo," 10–16.

61. Soviet author Veniamin Kataev coined the term "mauvism." Richard

Borden explored writing that can be covered by that label in *The Art of Writing Badly: V. Kataev's Mauvism and the Rebirth of Russian Modernism* (Evanston, Ill.: Northwestern University Press, 1999).

62. Soviet press coverage of the conference on the novel included I. Anisimov's "Leningradskii dialog o sovremennom romane," *Inostrannaia literatura* 11 (1963): 246–52.

63. See Vasilii Aksenov, "Mne dorogi sud'by romana," *Literaturnaia gazeta* 103 (August 27, 1963): 3. A decade later, in 1973, speaking to an American scholar, Aksenov cited Andrei Belyi, the prose of the 1920s, and the tradition of the avant-garde. See Priscilla Meyer, "Interview with Vasily Pavlovich Aksenov," *Russian Literature Triquarterly* 5–6 (1973): 570–71.

64. Significant events included the publication of Ilia Erenburg's memoirs *People, Years, Life* (*Liudi, gody, zhizn'*) in the important thick journal *New World* (*Novyi mir*) between 1960 and 1965, which opened up a world of modernist art and literature and international cultural ties between Russia and the West. Also significantly, top prize at the Third International Film Festival in Moscow in 1963 went to Federico Fellini's *8½*. The film aroused controversy: Iurii Zhukov wrote a scathing review, "Vosem' s polovinoi krugov kinematograficheskogo ada," *Literaturnaia gazeta* 87 (July 20, 1963): 3. Such official Soviet disapproval and international success helped make Fellini an important Western influence on Aksenov and Bitov.

65. Katerina Clark analyzed the codified nature of Soviet novels in terms of the "master plot" and variations in her classic study *The Soviet Novel: History as Ritual* (Chicago: University of Chicago Press, 1981). The novel provided the key forum for developing the ideologically important category of the Soviet positive hero. Rufus W. Mathewson wrote, "The solemn Russian novel of character with its rudimentary plot structure was peculiarly well designed to focus attention on the moral responsibilities of individuals." Later, he noted that four novels completed between the overthrow of RAPP (1932) and the beginning of World War II show "the full range of possibility in Soviet literature." The novel form dominated the canon of prerevolutionary literature in official Soviet literary history and in Soviet art. See Mathewson, *The Positive Hero in Russian Literature* (Evanston, Ill.: Northwestern University Press, 1975), 14, 233.

66. Bukovsky, *To Build*, 114.

67. For a postcolonial critique of the broadly held belief that prose corresponds to a more sophisticated stage than poetry in the development of a people's culture, see Ranajit Guha, "Historicality and the Prose of the World," in *History at the Limit of World History* (New York: Columbia University Press, 2002), 13–15.

68. See also Andrei Siniavskii, "Prostranstvo prozy," *Sintaksis* 21 (1988): 25–31, on the privileged place of prose in the literary process.

69. Bakhtin reconceived Goethe's opposition of epic and drama, where

drama represented the present, as opposed to the past of the epic. For Bakhtin, the novel opposed the epic past with a dynamic novelistic present that showed the present becoming the future. See Galin Tihanov, *The Master and the Slave: Lukacs, Bakhtin, and the Ideas of Their Time* (Oxford: Clarendon, 2000), 52–55. For an analysis of Bakhtin's description and evaluation of the novel, including his tendency to treat the novel as a "hero" in certain periods of his work, see Gary Saul Morson and Caryl Emerson, *Mikhail Bakhtin: Creation of a Prosaics* (Stanford, Calif.: Stanford University Press, 1990), 301, 307–8.

70. Bakhtin's book *Problemy tvorchestva Dostoevskogo* appeared in Leningrad in 1929, but did not receive much attention. The revised second edition, *Problemy poetiki Dostoevskogo*, appeared first in Moscow in 1963. A third edition in Moscow in 1972, and a fourth edition in Moscow in 1979 help underscore the popularity of Bakhtin's work beginning in the 1960s. For an overview of the issues involved in publishing Bakhtin, see the introduction to *Rethinking Bakhtin. Extensions and Challenges*, ed. Gary Saul Morson and Caryl Emerson (Evanston, Ill.: Northwestern University Press, 1989), 1–60.

71. Bakhtin's book appeared in 1965 as *Tvorchestvo Fransua Rable i narodnaia kul'tura srednevekov'ia i Renessansa*. Helene Iwolsky translated it as *Rabelais and His World* (Cambridge, Mass.: MIT Press, 1968).

72. Joseph Frank quoted Kaganskaia in "The Voices of Mikhail Bakhtin," in *Through the Russian Prism: Essays on Russian Literature and Culture* (Princeton N.J.: Princeton University Press, 1990), 32. The original appeared in Siniavskii's journal in emigration: see Maia Kaganskaia, "Shutovskoi khorovod," *Sintaksis* 12 (1984): 152.

73. Aksenov commented on his preference for the avant-garde and the grotesque as modes with roots in folk art in several places, including Meyer, "Interview with Vasily Pavlovich Aksenov," 570–71; Vassili Axionov, "Comment on devient un 'produit d'exportation' en Union soviétique," *Le Monde* (April 14, 1978); and in the 1982 "Interview with V.P. Aksenov," in *Vasiliy Pavlovich Aksenov: A Writer in Quest of Himself*, ed. Edward Mozejko, Boris Briker and Per Dalgard (Columbus, Ohio: Slavica, 1984), 24. More discussion of Aksenov's development of an avant-garde style appears in chapter 2.

74. While for many older intellectuals, the Thaw era was a "catastrophe," an "excruciating process of self re-evaluation," for Aksenov's generation it was "the start of a great carnival. Down with Stalin! Up with jazz!" See Vassily Aksyonov, "A Soviet Émigré Takes the A-Train," *New York Times* (May 3, 1987): SM 60.

75. Petr Vail' and Aleksandr Genis called "Jews" and "sex" two of the most taboo topics in the U.S.S.R. in the 1960s (*60-e*, 298). When I asked Bitov about what made *Pushkin House* uncensored, he referred to four taboos (*zaprety*) he broke there: the camps (*gulag*), promiscuity (*bliadstvo*), excessive drinking (*p'ianstvo*), and the Jewish question (*evreiskaia tema*). The last three topics proved to be de facto off limits in much dissident writing (Interview with Bitov,

May 17, 2000). Aksenov agreed that the impulse to break the silence on important topics motivated him as well, and he concurred with Bitov's list of primary taboo themes (Interview with Aksenov, April 12, 2003). The two writers recalled comparing notes around 1971 on the growing size of their respective uncensored novels—in addition to the genre, length mattered!

76. William Taubman wrote about the "endless official condemnations" of the Anti-Party conspirators, all using this precise formulation for Shepilov in *Khrushchev: The Man and his Era* (New York: W.W. Norton, 2003), 313.

77. From Siniavskii's 1975 review of Georgii Vladimov's novel *Faithful Ruslan*, entitled "Liudi i zveri," *Kontinent* 5 (1975): 367–404. An abridged English translation of the review appeared as "Beasts and Men," trans. William E. Harkins, *New York Review of Books* 26, no. 21–22 (1980): 22–24.

78. Aksyonov, *The Burn*, 138. As the train arrives, an announcement requesting passengers to leave the cars and register *"nach Auschwitz,"* increases the sense of deadly threat. The scene also recalls Mikhail Bulgakov's *Master and Margarita*, with its madcap chase scenes, fires, and musical motifs. The crunching melons might recall Berlioz's head, which was severed by a streetcar.

79. The rigidity of formulations in official print became worse in the post-Stalin era. See Yurchak's analysis in chapter 2, in which he described the normalization of all authoritative forms in that period (*Everything Was Forever*, 37).

80. Aleshkovskii's imitation of popular labor camp songs, including the well-loved "Comrade Stalin, You're a Real Big Scholar" ("Pesnia o Staline: Tovarishch Stalin, Vy bol'shoi uchenyi," 1959) and "Cigarette Butt" ("Okurochek," 1963), reportedly became famous as supposedly anonymous folk creations. His novellas *Nikolai Nikolaevich* (1970) and *Kangaroo* (1974–75) showcased his masterful *skaz* (marked oral) style, featuring creative use of profanity and Soviet clichés. Bitov discussed them in "Pamiatnik literatury kak zhanr," in *Piatoe izmerenie: Na granitse vremeni i prostranstva* (Moscow: Izdatel'stvo Nezavisimaia gazeta, 2002), 224–50.

81. For example, the "short" and "long" tirades of profanity by Peter the Great are part of folk and literary lore. See Iurii Annenkov's account of poet Sergei Esenin's recitation of the short (37 words) and long (260 words) tirades in Annenkov's *Dnevnik moikh vstrech: Tsikl tragedii* (Moscow: Khudozhestvennaia literatura, 1990), 267–68.

82. Bitov insisted that Aleshkovskii's Soviet words were untranslatable like profanity, but he attempted to explain the elided referents of a few of the terms, including "Comrade Rasstrelli" and "Pasha Angelina" in "Pamiatnik," 248.

83. Bitov, "Pamiatnik," 239.

84. Ibid., 241–42.

85. Venedikt Erofeev, "Proza iz zhurnala *Veche*," in *Zapiski psikhopata* (Moscow: Vagrius, 2000), 259–60. The essay appeared as "Through the Eyes of an Eccentric," in *The Penguin Book of New Russian Writing: Russia's Fleurs du*

Mal, ed. Victor Erofeyev and Andrew Reynolds (London: Penguin, 1995), 126–45, esp. 140.

86. Aksyonov, *The Burn*, 80.

87. Andrei Bitov, *Pushkin House*, trans. Susan Brownsberger (Normal, Ill.: Dalkey Archive, 1998), 35.

88. On the "rings" of humiliation and betrayal rooted in the Stalin era and binding characters in *Pushkin House*, see Ellen Chances, *Andrei Bitov: The Ecology of Inspiration* (Cambridge, Eng.: Cambridge University Press, 1993), 202–45.

89. See also the narrator's discussion of quotations in titles found in newspapers, on books and films in the "Italics Mine" segment opening section 2 (*Pushkin House*, 129–31).

90. I discuss in chapter 4 in particular the light-hearted conversation about Chekhov, Schiller, and Goethe between Black Moustache and Venichka. Those names come up again at a dark time during Venichka's journey (*Moscow Stations*, 116).

91. Yerofeev, *Moscow Stations*, 123.

92. Bürger, *Theory*, 72.

93. Bürger claimed that montage differed from techniques of composition developed since the Renaissance because the insertion of material not fashioned by the artist meant the destruction of the unity of the painting as a whole, all of whose parts have been fashioned by the subjectivity of its creator. He contrasted inorganic montage to the "man-made organic work of art that pretends to be like nature," projecting "an image of the reconciliation of man and nature" (*Theory* 77, 78).

94. See Hays, "Photomontage and Its Audience; El Lissitzky Meets Berlin Dada," in *The Avant-Garde Frontier: Russia Meets the West, 1910–1930*, ed. Gail Harrison Roman and Virginia Hagelstein Marquardt (Gainesville: University Press of Florida, 1992), 180.

95. In addition to Calhoun ("Habitus, Field, and Capital"), see Randal Johnson's lucid introduction (Bourdieu, *The Field*, 1–25), and articles in *Pierre Bourdieu: Key Concepts*, ed. Michael Grenfell (London: Acumen, 2008).

CHAPTER ONE

1. In English, Amalrik's memoirs bear the title *Notes of a Revolutionary* although *Notes of a Dissident* (the original title is *Zapiski dissidenta*) would have been a more exact translation. Perhaps the title "Revolutionary" seemed more marketable. See Andrei Amalrik, *Notes of a Revolutionary*, trans. Guy Daniels (London: Weidenfeld and Nicolson, 1982).

2. Amalrik, *Notes*, 5.

3. Liudmila Alekseeva acknowledged Amalrik's priority in this important

area: "The first regular contacts with the West were established by Andrey Amalrik" (Alexeyeva, *Soviet Dissent*, 284). Amalrik first became acquainted with foreigners in the early 1960s through his involvement with nonconformist art and he later served as a link, a "liaison officer," between dissidents and foreign correspondents. See Andrei Amalrik, *Notes*, iii, 7, 9, 20, 24, 39 and passim.

4. Amalrik, *Notes*, 26.

5. Amalrik's activity and acquaintances spanned groups of nonconformist artists and democratic dissidents. He began to serve as liaison with foreign journalists at the time of the trial of writers Andrei Siniavskii and Iulii Daniel and was an intermediary trusted by both sides (Amalrik, *Notes*, 3, 20).

6. Andropov proposed the establishment of the Fifth Directorate in 1967 to deal with political dissidents. After talking in his speech about unity, he mentioned the dissidents, whose cause he claimed had been inflated by bourgeois propaganda. Dissidents resembled thieves, bribe-takers, speculators, and other criminals who deserve punishment: "And let them not demand in such instances humaneness. We consider it humane to defend the interests of society," declared Andropov. This speech, delivered, on the hundredth anniversary of Feliks Dzerzhinskii's death, appeared in print as "Doklad tovarishcha Iu.V. Andropova," *Izvestiia* 213 (September 10, 1977): 2 (translation mine).

7. See Marcus Levitt, *Russian Literary Politics and the Pushkin Celebration of 1880* (Ithaca, N.Y.: Cornell University Press, 1989).

8. Stephanie Sandler's discussion of Aleksandr Pushkin's poem "Exegi Monumentum" (1836) explains nicely the powerful precedent in Russian culture for this type of separate poetic authority (*Commemorating Pushkin: Russia's Myth of a National Poet* [Stanford, Calif.: Stanford University Press, 2004], 21–25).

9. Bourdieu summarized the paradoxical character of intellectuals who depended on the autonomy of culture, yet whose public identity meant crossing back over to comment on political issues: intellectuals of this type emerged with commentary on the Dreyfus affair (*The Rules*, 340).

10. Bourdieu defined a field thus: "As I use the term, a field is a separate social universe having its own laws of functioning independent of those of politics and the economy" (*The Field*, 162–63). The field entails specific forms of capital and a relationship among players on the field, whose moves are conditioned by a feel for the game (*habitus*) on that field. On the interdependence of *field*, *capital* and *habitus*, see Patricia Thomson, "Field," in *Pierre Bourdieu: Key Concepts*, ed. Michael Grenfell (Stocksfield, U.K.: Acumen, 2008), 69.

11. A fuller treatment of Volpin's strategy and its origins can be found in Benjamin Nathans's article "The Dictatorship of Reason: Aleksandr Vol'pin and the Idea of Rights Under 'Developed Socialism,'" *Slavic Review* 66, no. 4 (2007): 630–63.

12. Bourdieu used the term "agents" in his early work *Outline of a Theory of Practice*, trans. R. Nice (Cambridge, Eng.: Cambridge University Press, 1977),

and it serves as a general term for the subject in many discussions of his method. The agent does not exist in isolation but is related to the field through *habitus*. The field represents a structure of probabilities, of rewards, gains, profits, or sanctions, with some measure of indeterminacy: the agent uses the *habitus*, or feel for the game, developed from experience on the field to bend the rules of the game. On this ability to bend the rules, see Pierre Bourdieu and Loïc J. D. Wacquant, *An Invitation to Reflexive Sociology* (Chicago: University of Chicago Press, 1992), 18–19.

13. Sinyavsky, "Dissent as a Personal Experience," 152.

14. This correspondence was published as "Perepiska Andreia Siniavskogo s redkollegiei serii 'Biblioteki poeta': Izmenenie sovetskogo literaturnogo polia," with an introduction and commentary by Ann Komaromi, *Novoe literaturnoe obozrenie* 71 (2005): 175–99. The volume in question appeared as Boris Pasternak, *Stikhotvoreniia i poemy*, with an introductory article by A. D. Siniavskii; technical editor L. A. Ozerov; general editor V. N. Orlov (Moscow: Biblioteka poeta, 1965).

15. Sinyavsky, "Dissent," 154.

16. Ibid., 154.

17. Catharine Theimer Nepomnyashchy, "Andrei Siniavsky (Abram Tertz) (1925–1997)," in *Dictionary of Literary Biography*, vol. 302, *Russian Prose Writers after World War II*, ed. Christine Rydel (Farmington Hills, Mich., 2004), 296–316. Siniavskii's roots in the study of an avant-garde modernist tradition can be seen in the study by Menshutin and Siniavskii, *Poeziia pervykh let revoliutsii: 1917–1920* (Moscow: Nauka, 1964).

18. Vladimir Pomerantsev, "Ob iskrennosti v literature," *Novyi mir* 12 (1953): 18–45.

19. The term "Socialist Realism" appeared in the Soviet press beginning in 1932 and was promulgated in this formula at the First Writers' Congress in 1934.

20. Andrei Siniavskii, "Poeziia i proza Ol'gi Berggol'ts," *Novyi mir* 5 (1960): 225–36.

21. A. Men'shutin and A. Siniavskii first wrote about the new poetry in "Za poeticheskuiu aktivnost' (Zametki o poezii molodykh)," *Novyi mir* 1 (1961): 224–41. For their response to critics, see "Davaite govorit' professional'no," *Novyi mir* 8 (1961): 248–52.

22. Siniavskii declared Pasternak to be against stereotypes and clichés in the broad sense of the word, though the phrases of common speech were an antidote to literary cliché. See Siniavskii, "Poeziia Pasternaka," in Pasternak, *Stikhotvoreniia i poemy*, 24, 28.

23. Andrei Siniavskii, "Odin den' s Pasternakom," *Sintaksis* 6 (1980): 135.

24. Craig Calhoun examined Bourdieu's analysis in terms of a theory of the reproduction of fields of relations. Even imagining revolutionary struggle draws on categories of perception and thought from the past, which may be a revolu-

tionary past, as in the late Soviet case. Bourdieu observed that real structural change, like the rupture in traditional practices and the shift from direct relations to indirect and mediated ones, occurred most often as the result of exogenous influences from outside the field—such as influences exerted by the dissidents' foreign audiences. See Craig Calhoun's discussion of "Habitus, Field, and Capital," in *Critical Social Theory* (Oxford: Blackwell, 1995), 142–43, 146.

25. See A. Siniavskii, "Poeticheskii sbornik B. Pasternaka" (review of Boris Pasternak, *Stikhotvoreniia i poemy*, ed. N. Kriuchkova [Moscow, 1961]), *Novyi mir* 3 (1962): 261–63.

26. A typescript of the transcript of the meeting at which Moscow writers voted unanimously to request Pasternak's exile did somehow circulate (a typescript copy was preserved among Siniavskii's papers). Hoover Institution, Siniavskii Collection, Box 58, F. 3, "Stenogramma obshchemoskovskogo sobraniia pisatelei, 31 oktiabria 1958 goda." Although published in the New York émigré journal *Novyi zhurnal* 83 (1966), the transcript was not widely publicized or discussed in the late 1950s.

By contrast, at the end of the 1950s and beginning of the 1960s, Pasternak's poems from *Doctor Zhivago* reportedly became some of the most widely circulated typescript texts, representing a transition between the private sharing of poems and the more developed network of unofficial circulation that would be called "samizdat" by the mid-1960s.

27. A detailed account of these events can be found in Priscilla Johnson and Leopold Labedz, *Khrushchev and the Arts: The Politics of Soviet Culture, 1962–1964* (Cambridge, Mass.: MIT Press, 1965), 101–9.

28. Siniavskii received an official invitation from editor in chief Vladimir Orlov in June 1962. Siniavskii subsequently received communications from the editorial director, A. Ninov, and from editor G. M. Tsurikova. "Perepiska," 186–87.

29. From Orlov's commentary addressed to Siniavskii, conveyed with a letter from Tsurikova, September 11, 1963 ("Perepiska," 188–91). On the use of the term *prorabatyvat'*, see Efim Etkind's linguistic digression in his *Zapiski nezagovorshchika: Barselonskaia proza* (St. Petersburg: Akademicheskii proekt, 2001), 132–39.

30. In one summary statement, Bourdieu said of authors: "By entering the game, they tacitly accept the constraints and the possibilities inherent in that game (which are presented not in the form of rules, but rather as possible winning strategies)" (*The Field*, 184). Orlov described constraints in terms of winning strategies for dealing with them.

31. The handwritten note in which Siniavskii said this is not signed and has no date in the preserved documents ("Perepiska," 191).

32. Bourdieu defined the field of restricted production as one that reproduced the rupture with the economic order inside the cultural field. In the dis-

sident case, the rupture with the ideological or political order was reproduced by those dissidents who disavowed the political interest of their writing (*The Rules*, 121).

33. See Siniavskii's comparison of Pasternak's lyrical "I" with those of other poets ("Poeziia Pasternaka," 18–19).

34. Siniavskii, "Poeziia Pasternaka," 36.

35. Compare Bourdieu's similar attempt to negotiate the concept of the subject as "agent," a description that eschewed the Scylla of romantic individualism and the Charybdis of vulgar Marxist determinism. Johnson, in Bourdieu, *The Field*, 2–5.

36. Orlov's criticism of Siniavskii's commentary on the Gospel poems appears in point 5 in his letter of February 15, 1964. In September 1963, it seemed the poems would be included and commented on in the article. But Tsurikova's letter of October 23, 1963 indicated the verses would most likely be excised. Although Orlov's letter of February 15, 1964 again suggested the poems would be included, they were cut from the published edition—only 16 of the 25 poems, coyly titled "Verses from a Novel," appeared ("Perepiska," 195, 189–90, 193). The large series (bol'shaia seriia) of publications from Library of the Poet aimed to be definitive, complete editions. Therefore, publication of the Gospel-themed poem "Avgust" in *Iunost'* 8 (1965), almost immediately after the edition appeared, must have been irksome to editors.

37. Siniavskii, "Poeziia Pasternaka," 40.

38. Ibid., 41.

39. *Vse nyneshnei vesnoi osoboe. / Zhivee vorob'ev shumikha. / Ia dazhe vyrazit' ne probuiu, / Kak na dushe svetlo i tikho. / Inache dumaetsia, pishetsia, / I gromkoiu oktavoi v khore / Zemnoi moguchii golos slyshitsia / Osvobozhdennykh territorii.*) The "I" (*ia*) of line three yields expressive potential to the impersonal constructions of the other lines, Siniavskii noted, "Poeziia Pasternaka," 48.

40. From Tsurikova's letter of October 12, 1963, and Orlov's letter, February 15, 1964, "Perepiska," 191–92, 194–96.

41. Siniavskii, "Poeziia Pasternaka," 10. Information about Siniavskii's conversations with Elena and Evgenii Pasternak based on personal correspondence with them (e-mail correspondence, November 20, 2003).

42. Tsurikova's letter of October 23, 1963, and Orlov's letter, February 15, 1964 ("Perepiska," 192–93, 194–96).

43. The foreword (*predislovie*) is signed by the editorial board (*redaktsionnaia kollegiia*) of the Library of the Poet (Biblioteka poeta) publishing house. Pasternak, *Stikhotvoreniia i poemy*, 5–6.

44. Marietta Chudakova explored the author's identification with Christ in Pasternak's *Doctor Zhivago* and Mikhail Bulgakov's *Master and Margarita*. She considered these figures emblematic of the limits of that (modernist) literary

epoch, beyond which literature could no longer proceed. Chudakova speculated that the popular and collective heroes of Solzhenitsyn's works represented the next cycle. See Chudakova, "Pasternak i Bulgakov: Rubezh dvukh literaturnykh tsiklov," *Literaturnoe obozrenie* 5 (1991): 11–17. Siniavskii's creations, including both heroes of his stories and Terts as alter ego, suggest a new, less highly serious alternative in the late Soviet age, challenging readers to rethink the role of the author and the boundaries of the artistic work.

45. In his book *Strolls with Pushkin* (*Progulki s Pushkinym*), Siniavskii's irreverent treatment of Pushkin offended the sensibilities of a broad Russian readership. On this and other provocations by Siniavskii-Terts, see the introduction of Catharine Theimer Nepomnyashchy's book *Abram Tertz and the Poetics of Crime* (New Haven, Conn.: Yale University Press, 1995).

46. Bourdieu wrote about the "avant-garde" as one of the poles or sectors within a space of cultural production, defined by its antagonistic relationship to a sector that facilitates the conversion of symbolic capital, for example, a "commercial" sector (*The Rules*, 120).

47. Ginzburg asked Andrei Amalrik to help facilitate contacts between dissidents and foreign journalists (Amalrik, *Notes*, 3–4).

48. "Poslednee slovo Andreia Siniavskogo," in *Belaia kniga o dele Siniavskogo i Danielia* (Frankfurt am Main: Posev, 1967), 305–6.

49. Alexeyeva, *Soviet Dissent*, 280.

50. "Iz vospominanii Vladimira Bukovskogo" and "Rasskazyvaet Dmitrii Zubarev," in *Piatoe dekabria 1965 goda v vospominaniiakh uchastnikov sobytii, materialakh Samizdata, publikatsiiakh zarubezhnoi pressy i v dokumentakh partiinykh i komsomol'skikh organizatsii i v zapiskakh Komiteta gosudarstvennoi bezopasnosti v TsK KPSS*, ed. A. Daniel' and A. Roginskii (Moscow: Zven'ia, 2005), 22–23, 29.

51. "Iz vospominanii Evgeniia Kusheva," in *Piatoe dekabria*, 24–25.

52. Art critic Igor Golomshtok "to this day recalls how everyone was asking whether Daniel and Siniavskii were good or bad people. Only Volpin was interested in the judicial details of the case." "Rasskazyvaet Iuliia Vishnevskaia," in *Piatoe dekabria*, 21.

53. "Rasskazyvaet Aleksandr Volpin," in *Piatoe dekabria*, 43.

54. I am indebted to Benjamin Nathans for sharing his manuscript work on the development of Esenin-Volpin's thought.

55. See Iurii Lotman's analysis of the particularly strong tendency in Russian culture to transfer principles of hagiography to secular writers in the post-Petrine period. Iu. M. Lotman, "Russkaia literatura poslepetrovskoi epokhi i khristianskaia traditsiia," in *Iu. M. Lotman i tartusko-moskovskaia semioticheskaia shkola* (Moscow: Gnozis, 1994), 364–79.

56. "Rasskazyvaet Liudmila Alekseeva," in *Piatoe dekabria*, 34–35.

57. On the mutual distrust between the older generation of liberals and the

younger rebels who came together for the demonstration Volpin organized, see the editors' comments before and after personal memoirs (*Piatoe dekabria*).

58. See the text of the "Grazhdanskoe obrashchenie" and discussion of variants, *Piatoe dekabria*, 18.

59. The 1880 Pushkin Celebration was seen as a "public validation of Russian intellectual life." Marcus Levitt wrote, "For many at the time, the Pushkin Celebration promised that the Russian intelligentsia had finally come into its own. Newspapers referred to the Pushkin Celebration as 'Holiday of the Intelligentsia' and 'Celebration of Russian Public Opinion,' an event that signaled the intelligentsia's legitimacy and its readiness to serve as a 'middle' class, intermediary between state and a nation" (Levitt, *Russian Literary Politics*, 17). Of course, there were differences between the Westernizer Turgenev and the Slavophile Dostoevsky that found dramatic expression during the course of the celebration (Levitt, ibid.).

60. Volpin nevertheless conceded Stroeva's point, fixed the meeting next to the poet in the "Appeal." He afterward referred to her involvement by calling this a coauthored text. The text was not signed (*Piatoe dekabria*, 43).

61. Bourdieu explained the situation of Flaubert's Frédéric Moreau, a young man in Flaubert's novel *Sentimental Education* who is "entering into life," that is, about to undertake one or another of the possible social games that will establish his position, but who finds himself unable to take any of the established games seriously (*The Rules*, 13). It seems no coincidence that the Meeting, like many protest actions, was full of young people eager to express themselves in new ways.

62. Calhoun described Bourdieu's "key original insights" as his delineation of immaterial forms of capital—cultural, symbolic, and social—as well as material or economic capital, with varying levels of difficulty in converting the former to the latter. Bourdieu takes care to emphasize that symbolic capital, the interest of "disinterest" is not trans-historical or universal—it arises out of the conditions of the particular field (*Critical Theory*, 140–42). The field of restricted cultural production, which serves as the analogy for the dissident field of cultural production, is characterized by the distinctive symbolic capital players compete to dominate (See Bourdieu's "The Market for Symbolic Goods," in *The Rules*, 141–73).

CHAPTER TWO

1. Aksenov said that two KGB officers came to him in 1977, and said they had seen his novel in manuscript. The officer named Chentsov had risen in the ranks and was incensed at his portrayal as Cheptsov in Aksenov's novel (my interview with Aksenov, 2003). The officers warned Aksenov that if he published the book, he would have to emigrate.

2. Phone transcripts show that in October 1979, Iurii Trifonov took the opportunity afforded by being abroad to tell Carl and Ellendea Proffer at Ardis Press that Aksenov wanted to wait to publish *The Burn*. In a subsequent letter of December 11, 1979, Trifonov told them Aksenov had definitely decided to emigrate, and therefore they could go ahead with the publication of *The Burn* in Russian (Ardis Press Archive, University of Michigan Hatcher Library, Box 21). First published in Italian by Mondadori under the title *L'ustione*, the Russian version of Aksenov's novel appeared as *Ozhog: Roman v trekh knigakh: Pozdnie Shestidesiatye, Rannie Semidesiatye* (Ann Arbor, Mich.: Ardis, 1980). The English edition came out a few years later as Vassily Aksyonov, *The Burn: A Novel in Three Books (Late Sixties–Early Seventies)*, trans. Michael Glenny (New York: Random House, Boston: Houghton Mifflin, 1984).

3. Aksenov talked about having just four copies of the manuscript initially and sharing them with only a few friends (my interview with Aksenov, 2003). According to another interview, perhaps 40 or 50 people saw it in Moscow before publication. From Don Swaim's interview with Aksenov, November 1983, http://www.wiredforbooks.org/vassilyaksyonov/.

4. "In *The Burn*, I wanted to obtain everything, to whirl it around in all possible ways: format, philosophical, historical, political . . ." See the "Interview with V. P. Aksenov," by Inger Lauridsen and Per Dalgard, Washington, D.C., December, 1982, in *Vasiliy Pavlovich Aksenov: A Writer in Quest of Himself*, ed. Edward Mozejko, Boris Briker and Per Dalgard (Columbus, Ohio: Slavica, 1984), 24.

5. Evgeniia Ginzburg's memoirs, entitled *Krutoi marshrut*, circulated widely in samizdat, in perhaps as many as 5,000 typescript copies, making it one of the most popular works in samizdat, according to Olga M. Cooke and Rimma Volynska, "Interview with Vasilii Aksenov," *Canadian American Slavic Studies* 39, no. 1 (2005): 9–36, 22. Ludmilla Alexeyeva also listed Ginzburg's memoirs as a top choice in samizdat at that time (*Soviet Dissent*, 327). Published in English as *Into the Whirlwind*, trans. Paul Stevenson and Max Hayward (New York: Harcourt, Brace, Jovanovich, 1967), the second volume appeared as *Within the Whirlwind*, trans. Ian Bolan (New York: Harcourt Brace Jovanovich, 1981).

6. Aksenov's stepfather Anton Walter practiced medicine in the camps. Aksenov reflected ironically on how this unfolded for him: "I did become a doctor. But, of course, I soon dropped it and decided on literature. I chose to poison people rather than cure them." See David Remnick, "What's a Vassily Aksyonov?" *Washington Post* (February 15, 1987): w20.

7. On Aksenov's involvement with "Young Prose," also called "New Wave" writing, see J. J. Johnson, "V.P. Aksenov: A Literary Biography" (in Mozejko, Briker, and Dalgard, *Vasiliy Pavlovich Aksenov*, 32–52, 34). Critic Stanislav Rassadin championed the new young writers. He identified Aksenov as a leader of the "Sixtiers" in his article "Shestidesiatniki," *Iunost'* 12 (1960): 58–62.

8. Priscilla Meyer discussed objections to Aksenov's prose by some Soviet critics in "Aksenov and Soviet Literature of the 1960s," *Russian Literature Triquarterly* 5–6 (1973): 450. Deming Brown noted that the "joking, mocking, sceptical, off-beat language" of Aksenov's narrator in works of the early 1960s seemed shot through with "a startling emotional authenticity," and that the use of jargon by his characters expresses profound dissatisfaction with the "stale, hypocritical, hollow vocabulary" plaguing Soviet public life. See Brown's "Vasili Aksenov at 33," *Russian Literature Triquarterly* 2 (1964): 78, 79. Soviet critics seemed less impressed. G. Iu. Karpenko cited objections in the Soviet press to Aksenov's vulgarization of literary language, in "Literaturnaia kritika 1960-kh godov o tvorchestve Vasiliia Aksenova," in *Vasilii Aksenov: Literaturnaia sud'ba*, ed. V. P. Skobolev and L. A. Fink (Samara: Izdatel'stvo Samarskii universitet, 1994), 21.

9. Quoted and discussed by Oleg Kharkhordin, *The Collective and the Individual*, 350.

10. Kharkhordin wrote of the feeling of the time: "Words weren't to be trusted after 1956" (*The Collective and the Individual*, 346). He showed Dmitrii's implicit choice of deeds over words (ibid., 351–52).

11. Bourdieu, *The Rules*, 13.

12. Fellow writer Anatolii Gladilin described the reading of the novella for a crowd at the Moscow Writers' Union and reactions to it, in "Stal'naia Ptitsa," *Kontinent* 14 (1977): 358. Although intended for Soviet print, the novella appeared ultimately without official Soviet authorization in the United States in 1977. Plastinkin's interpretation of Samson Sabler's jazz playing in *The Burn* as a "struggle against petty-bourgeois mentality" seems to parody this kind of standard spin on challenging works for the Soviet censors (49; 41). Page numbers here and throughout the chapter refer to the English edition, e.g., Aksyonov, *The Burn*, 49; followed by the Russian edition, Aksenov, *Ozhog*, 41.

13. Some Soviet propagandists suggested that Americans intentionally introduced the Colorado potato beetle as part of a plot against Soviet agriculture. Mochenkin embodies this suspicious tone, looking always for invaders and enemies in ordinary situations. See the note in Vassily Aksyonov, *Surplussed Barrelware*, ed. and trans. Joel Wilkinson and Slava Yastremski (Ann Arbor, Mich.: Ardis, 1985), 92, note 12. Volodia quotes Esenin ("Do not be grieved or of sorrowful countenance," and "May this evening's unutterable light stream over your little hut") in a letter to his girlfriend Sima (ibid., 96, notes 56 and 57, and passim).

14. A. Vishevsky and T. Pogacar discussed Aksenov's skillful mix of registers and careful rendering of oral speech for humorous effects, "The Function of Conventional Language Patterns in the Prose of Vasiliy Aksenov" (in Mozejko, Briker, and Dalgard, *Vasiliy Pavlovich Aksenov*, 132–33).

15. Lauridsen and Dalgard ("Interview with V.P. Aksenov," 20). Aksenov mentioned Hemingway's *The Sun Also Rises* as a prototype for the carnival.

16. See the introduction on Mikhail Bakhtin's works, the warm reception they received in the 1960s and the subsequent disillusionment with ideas derived from them. In *The Burn*, Aksenov glossed his young character Tolya's bright-eyed hopefulness in terms associated with this Soviet spirit of the 1960s: "Oh, youth, youth, golden carnivals!" (225; 192)

17. Evgenii Evtushenko, "Fekhtovanie s navoznoi kuchei," *Literaturnaia gazeta* 4, no. 5330 (January 30, 1990): 7, 13.

18. See Lermontov's poem "The Poet's Death" ("Smert' poeta," 1837), in which he called out the "greedy, hungry pack standing around the throne" as "murderers of Freedom, Genius, and Glory," in Mikhail Lermontov, *Major Poetical Works*, trans. Anatoly Liberman (Minneapolis: University of Minnesota Press, 1983), 108–9. Translation slightly altered for sense. Aksenov evoked this romantic pose in the last scene of *The Burn* with the small and quixotic statue of Lermontov, the "Russian Scotsman," dwarfed by the large buildings surrounding a busy Moscow intersection (527; 441).

19. Aksenov's novella *Rendezvous* (written in 1968, published in the Soviet journal *Avrora*, 1971) featured a fantastically multifaceted protagonist, Leva Malakhitov, who is a poet, chess player, hockey player, musician, engineer, and children's theatre director, and can be seen as a precursor to the five adult protagonists as opposed to the five in *The Burn*. See Konstantin Kustanovich, *The Artist and the Tyrant: Vassily Aksenov's Works in the Brezhnev Era* (Columbus, Ohio: Slavica, 1992), 89.

20. I compared the works in greater detail in "Vasilii Aksenov and Evgeniia Ginzburg in Magadan: Re-conceiving Authorship Through the Gulag Experience," *Gulag Studies* 5–6 (2012–2013).

21. See Ginzburg's chapters 7–10 in volume 2 of her memoirs (*Within the Whirlwind*, 254–304).

22. See Natasha Kolchevska, "The Art of Memory: Cultural Reverence as Political Critique in Evgeniia Ginzburg's Writing of the Gulag," in *The Russian Memoir: History and Literature*, ed. Beth Holmgren (Evanston, Ill.: Northwestern University Press, 2003), 148–49.

23. Ibid., 152.

24. Priscilla Meyer discussed the moral values of Aksenov's novel with reference to Evgeniia Ginzburg's memoirs and Mikhail Bulgakov's novel *Master and Margarita*, in "Aksenov and Stalinism: Political, Moral, and Literary Power," *Slavic and East European Journal* 30, no. 4 (1986): 519–20. Nina Efimova explained Aksenov's morality in terms of Nikolai Berdiaev's Russian orthodox philosophy. See N. A. Efimova, *Intertekst v religioznykh i demonicheskikh motivakh V. P. Aksenova* (Moscow: Izdatel'stvo MGU, 1993).

25. Marianne Hirsch, "The Generation of Postmemory," *Poetics Today* 29, no. 1 (2008): 103–28. Varlam Shalamov drew the analogy between the Holocaust and the Stalinist camps in the context of a literary art that had to justify its means

and aims in new ways after those massive traumas: "It seems to me that the person of the second half of the twentieth century, the person who has survived war, revolution, the fires of Hiroshima, the atom bomb, treachery, and—crowning all this—the shame of Kolyma and the ovens of Auschwitz—this person who has survived the scientific revolution simply cannot fail to approach questions of art differently than before." From Shalamov's letter to I. P. Sirotinskaia, 1971, in Varlam Shalamov, *Novaia kniga: Vospominaniia, Zapisnye knizhki, Perepiska, Sledstvennye dela*, ed. I.P. Sirotinskaia, (Moscow: Eksmo, 2004), 839–40. Translation mine.

26. Cynthia Simmons drew the line connecting Aksenov's turn from realism in 1963 toward "phantasmagoric" art to Siniavskii's advocacy of that kind of art in his essay "On Socialist Realism." See Simmons, *Their Fathers' Voice: Vassily Aksyonov, Venedikt Erofeev, Eduard Limonov, and Sasha Sokolov* (New York: Peter Lang, 1993), 28.

Aksenov said, "Without the grotesque, I just can't work." He identified the source of the grotesque as folklore and connected it to the artistic avant-garde. The grotesque and avant-garde experimentation come from deep in folk art, according to Aksenov, as opposed to rootless realism, a nineteenth-century creation associated with "cheap superficial positivism" (Lauridsen and Dalgard, "Interview with V.P. Aksenov," 24). Aksenov made similar comments regarding the avant-garde in his interview with Priscilla Meyer ("Interview," 570–71); and in Vassili Axionov, "Comment on devient un 'produit d'exportation' en Union soviétique," *Le Monde* (April 14, 1978).

27. Aksenov also recalled Khrushchev's violent reaction to abstract art at the Manège exhibit in December 1962, and his intemperate response to Aksenov, Voznesenskii, and others at the meeting in March 1963, as events that facilitated his turn to a more "avant-garde" style, which he explored first in plays. From *Conversations in Exile: Russian Writers Abroad*, ed. John Glad, trans. Richard and Joanna Robin (Durham, N.C.: Duke University Press, 1993), 72. See Aksenov's plays, including *Always on Sale* (1963), *Kiss, Orchestra, Fish, Sausage (PORK*, 1964), *The Four Temperaments* (1967, the text appeared in the *Metropol* almanac), and *Aristophaniana with Frogs* (1967–68), in the collection *Aristofaniana s liagushkami: Sobranie p'es* (Ann Arbor, Mich.: Hermitage, 1981).

28. Priscilla Johnson and Leopold Labedz described the event in *Khrushchev and the Arts: The Politics of Soviet Culture, 1962–1964* (Cambridge, Mass: MIT Press, 1965), 36–37. Johnson and Labedz called the "fathers and sons" problem "perhaps the most delicate issue in Soviet life" at that time. The problem turned on responsibility for the purges, and the loss of fathers or sense of alienation from them (ibid., 26).

29. Aksenov described the incident in "Zima trevogi nashei, ili kak marksist Nikita uchil pisatelei partiinoi pravde," *Strelets* 1, no. 65 (1991): 182–202. William Taubman provided a detailed account of Khrushchev's immoderate lan-

guage and confused ranting at this event, in *Khrushchev: The Man and his Era*, 594–96.

30. Aksenov spoke about colleagues at the journal *Youth* (*Iunost'*) asking him to publish his statement of loyalty and save their journal (*Conversations in Exile*, 77).

31. Bürger (*Theory*, 77–78). See the introduction of this study for more on the avant-garde assault on integral images of subjectivity in the nonorganic work.

32. Efimova, *Intertekst*, 16, 6.

33. Meyer noted the "La Dolce Vita aspect" of Sanya, "Aksenov and Stalinism," 519–20.

34. The song is "Migrant Birds Are Flying" ("Letiat pereletnye ptitsy," 1948), music by M. Blanter, words by M. Isakovskii (http://classic-online.ru/ru/production/25729).

35. Kharkhordin quoted official critic Felix Kuznetsov, who identified Aksenov as a particular offender in the creation of what was censured as surrogate emancipation (*The Collective and the Individual*, 343).

36. Stanislav Rassadin, "Budem chitat' Plutarkha?" *Oktiabr'* 1 (1991): 205.

37. Svetlana Boym discussed the love of Western goods found among the broad mass of Soviet citizens in the Seventies. These hard-to-obtain items signified in specific ways unfamiliar to consumers in the West. See Boym's *Common Places. Mythologies of Everyday Life in Russia* (Cambridge: Harvard University Press, 1994), 65.

38. In *The Burn* Aksenov drew the character Blazer from his acquaintance Andron Mikhalkov-Konchalovskii, filmmaker (Interview with Aksenov, April 2003). In the novel, Blazer's father enjoyed the official honors and status accorded the author of the "Hymn of Our Native Fields," just as Sergei Mikhal'kov, father of Andron and Nikita Mikhal'kov, did for his composition of the Soviet anthem (290; 246).

39. On the love of Western things among children of the Soviet elite, see Aksenov's memoirs, *In Search of Melancholy Baby* (New York: Random House, 1987). Soviet people more broadly felt a sense of kinship for Americans after World War II, he explained. See Vassily Aksyonov, "A Soviet Émigré Takes the A-Train," *New York Times* (May 3, 1987): SM 60. Yurchak also discussed the Soviet "Imaginary West" (*Everything Was Forever*, 158–206).

40. Willis Conover produced and announced a jazz program on Voice of America that was very important to Soviet listeners. See Vassily Aksyonov (*In Search*, 18); and Yurchak (*Everything Was Forever*, 180–81).

41. English phrases and indeed all renderings of foreign language in *The Burn* appear highly idiosyncratic. Glenny smoothed out many of them in the English translation. I believe their erratic form has significance. Aksenov played with a hybrid style in his later works, including *The New Sweet Style*, a novel about a Soviet émigré in America, where Anglicisms abound in the Russian text.

As in *The Burn*, sometimes these English phrases appear spelled correctly in Latin characters, sometimes they appear in Cyrillic, occasionally with dubious grammar or usage, conveying how they might sound or be recorded and adapted by Soviet ears. See *Novyi sladostnyi stil'* (Moscow: Izdatel'stvo "Izograf", 1997); translated as *The New Sweet Style: A Novel*, trans. Christopher Morris (New York: Random House, 1999). In *The Burn*, Aksenov evoked the difficulty of translation with these defective renderings. He used them also to convey the imaginative character of Soviet engagement with the West in the context of a still relatively closed society.

42. See also the narrative passage in *The Burn* treating the "den [*berloga*] of the Moscow intellectual" and the signifying power of things and behavior associated with it in the late 1950s–early 1960s. Among characteristic items of special interest were tape recordings, new books, abstract paintings, political jokes, guitars, icons, and "manuscripts written on tissue paper," that is, texts that would later be called samizdat (390–91; 329).

43. Aksenov compared the Russian Futurists and the American Beat poets, the artistic impulse of the former defeated by ideology, and the latter by commerce in "Krylatoe vymiraiushchee" *Literaturnaia gazeta* 47, no. 5373 (November 27, 1991): 2. Aksenov treated this theme throughout his works—compare the remark in chapter 5 of *A Ticket to the Stars*, "Of course those are hack verses. Who doesn't write hack verses? Even Maiakovskii humbled himself, standing on the throat of his own song." See Aksenov, "Zvezdnyi billet," *Iunost'* 6–7 (1961): 22.

44. From an unpublished interview with Vasilii Aksenov by D. Barton Johnson, May 20, 1990, in Fairfax, Virginia.

45. Lauridsen and Dalgard, "Interview with V.P. Aksenov," 16–17.

46. On the monument and the activity around it, see chapter 1.

47. Discussion of the mythology of Silver Age modernism as foil to the avant-garde and Maiakovskii appears in the introduction.

48. Per Dalgard situated Aksenov's stylistic innovations in line with the Gogol-Belyi trend of Russian letters, characterized by musical prose effects and the use of the fantastic and grotesque ("Some Literary Roots," in Mozejko, Briker, and Dalgard, *Vasiliy Pavlovich Aksenov*, 69). In addition to Belyi's writing on Gogol and ornamental prose, Vasilii Gippius's study of Gogol illustrates the romantic and fantastic aspects, the demonology and creative narrative freedom elided in orthodox Soviet reading of Gogol's work as a socially conscious writer: see his *Gogol'* (1924, reprinted by Brown University Press, Providence R.I., 1963). Iu. B. Orlitskii likewise traced the use of poetic effects in prose by Aksenov and other writers of his era to the Silver Age and Andrei Belyi as an important point of reference.See Orlitskii, "Stikhovoe nachalo v proze Vasiliia Aksenova," in *Vasilii Aksenov: Literaturnaia sud'ba*, ed. V. P. Skobolev and L. A. Fink (Samara: Izdatel'stvo Samarskii universitet, 1994), 44–45.

49. Konstantin Kustanovich noted Aksenov's use of Symbolist models to help construct his own feminine Muse, which is philosophical and earthy. As elsewhere, Aksenov neither simply installed nor parodied the literary precedent. He took it over for his own artistic system. See Kustanovich, *The Artist and the Tyrant*, 157–58.

50. Symbolists including V. Ivanov and Belyi followed Vladimir Solov'ev in an understanding of realism based on the Platonic theory of universals as opposed to nominalism. See Irina Paperno, "The Meaning of Art: Symbolist Theories," in *Creating Life: The Aesthetic Utopia of Russian Modernism*, ed. Irina Paperno and Joan Delaney Grossman (Stanford, Calif.: Stanford University Press, 1994), 23, and 236–37, note 36.

51. See discussion by John Elsworth, "Andrei Bely's Theory of Symbolism," *Forum for Modern Language Studies* 11 (1975): 16. Elsworth acknowledged the complexity of Belyi's concept of reality: rather than rejecting objective reality, Belyi sought a more holistic attitude toward it, Elsworth argued (ibid., 318–19).

52. Feminine hypostases of the bird motif (densely enumerated in one passage, 26–27; 24) in *The Burn* appear symbolic of ideals, like Maurice Maeterlinck's Blue Bird, and capable of crossing borders, from Russia to Europe, like Aksenov's Heron, an updated version of Chekhov's Seagull. Characters in *The Burn* discuss mounting a play entitled *The Heron*, a project associated with the pure inspiration of the protagonists' youth. Aksenov's play *The Heron* (*Tsaplia*, 1979) premiered in Paris in 1984, and was staged in Belgrade and New York, according to D. Barton Johnson, "Vasilij Aksionov's Aviary: The Heron and The Steel Bird," *Scando-Slavica* 33 (1987): 45. In the play, the heron is simultaneously a bird and a Polish garment factory girl who speaks pidgin Polish, reminiscent of Alisa in *The Burn*. Like the novel, the play exhibits stylistic experimentation, with phantasmagoric elements and rhymed passages. Johnson surveyed the ambivalent potentials of the motif, associated in other aspects with betrayal or danger, like the Steel Bird.

In one digression, the narrative voice of *The Burn* comments on Cheptsov's hanging chin: "Please do not compare this dewlap [*zob*] with the pouch under a pelican's bill, in which the absurd bird stores its wretched but essential supply of fish for food. This dewlap, spotted and flabby, is intended for collecting our Komsomol badges!" (191; 165). Khrushchev himself, in a wild rhetorical flourish reported by Aksenov, mangled the seagull metaphor. In a speech to the creative intelligentsia, Khrushchev said, "After all, we Bolsheviks . . . we are like . . . we are like, we are like seagulls, comrades, yes, like seagulls! Of course, if a fox sneaks up to a fledgling, let's say . . . the fox, the fox sneaks up to the fledgling of the seagull. What the fox is doing at sea is not important, the main thing is the danger . . . all the seagulls rise up noisily, they raise an alarm and drive out the treacherous fox! That is the way we Bolsheviks raise an alarm when the imperialists sneak up to our artistic intelligentsia!" (Aksenov, "Zima," 197)

53. Sometimes red-haired, sometimes golden-haired, Alisa Fokusova, whose last name suggests she is a "trickster," is referred to also as the "vixen Alisa" (*lisa Alisa*) (254; 217), the tricky fox in Aleksei Tolstoi's Soviet version of the Pinocchio tale, the adventures of Buratino, *Zolotoi kliuchik, ili, Prikliucheniia Buratino* (Moscow: Eksmo, 2002).

54. Zhdanov's denunciation accompanied a resolution by the Party's Central Committee regarding the "ideologically harmful" works of the journals *Star* (*Zvezda*) and *Leningrad*. Zhdanov took up Formalist critic Boris Eikhenbaum's description of the "dual . . . nature of the lyric heroine's image—half a 'harlot' with stormy passion, half a 'beggar nun' able to pray to God for forgiveness," which had been part of Eikhenbaum's much more nuanced and appreciative analysis of Akhmatova's poetry.

55. The narrator is not specific about the year, but clearly has in mind real events: the Congolese civil war began when Belgium withdrew from its colony (formerly Zaire) on June 30, 1960. Leader of the independent Congo Patrice Lumumba wanted to keep Katanga, the richest section of the Congo, with copper mines and other mineral deposits, from seceding. The struggle over secession took place 1960–1962.

56. The original reads: "*Kak dolgo ty soobrazhaesh', kak dolgo rabotaet tvoe divnoe voobrazhenie!*" Glenny translated this as, "How long it takes for you to make up your mind, how long it takes for your divine imagination to function!" I believe the implication is not primarily that the protagonist is trying to make up his mind, but rather that he recognizes he is somehow indulging himself masochistically with the painful visualization of the scene.

57. The cinematic style of heroism will be shown in book 2 to have roots in Tolya's love for the American film *Stagecoach* (*The Journey Will Be Dangerous*). Tolya's stepfather Martin, doctor and priest, models an altogether different type of masculinity.

58. The Congo scenes roughly suggest such disparate prototypes as Friedrich Schiller's *Wallenstein* plays and contemporary Italian "shocksploitation" films, including *Africa Addio* (1966), released in a shorter version as *Africa, Blood and Guts* (1970) from the "Mondo Cane" series by Gualtiero Jacopetti and Franco E. Prosperi. Aksenov recalled seeing this film and following the scandal over the directors' non-intervention in scenes of mercenaries killing civilians (Interview with Aksenov, 2003). Aksenov initially wanted to cut the scene in Africa, as indicated on proofs (Ardis Archives, University of Michigan, Hatcher Graduate Library, B. 5, f. 12h, proofs of *Ozhog*, page 55). Friends persuaded him to retain the scene, because it was strong (*krutaia*) (Interview with Aksenov, 2003).

59. See Hyam Maccaby's analysis of this plot, "The Delectable Daughter," *Midstream* 16, no. 9 (1970): 50–60.

60. Aksenov saw pieces of the Pergamum frieze in East Berlin in 1971 and felt compelled by them (Interview with Aksenov, 2003). Aksenov mentioned the

frieze also in his officially published travelogue *Kruglye sutki non-stop*, where he alluded to the themes and images of his uncensored novel, creating what Lisa Wakamiya called a "complicit" or "tacit" relationship with the reader who would recognize the watermark of the officially nonexistent work *The Burn*. See Wakamiya's *Locating Exiled Writers in Contemporary Russian Literature* (New York: Palgrave Macmillan, 2009), 42–43.

61. The Phlegrean fields (Campi Flegrei) are an area of historic volcanic activity west of Naples, Italy. While much of it is underwater, the land above ground is not marshy. Calling it the "marshes" suggests an imaginative conflation of this area with the Baltic marshes on the edge of Europe, which Akșenov describes as the home of the Heron, one of his symbolic bird figures.

62. In Hesiod's *Theogony*, Cronus (also known as Saturn, a name whose phonetic kinship with the French phrase "*ça tourne*" Belyi exploited near the end of chapter 5 of *Petersburg* to describe circles of time and return) was the son of Uranus and Gaia, who rose up to castrate his father. After being told one of his children would overthrow him, Cronus feared his children and regularly ate them. Gaia gave Cronus a swaddled stone in place of baby Zeus, who eventually fulfilled the prophecy and took power. Cronus is sometimes depicted as "Chronos" (Time), a phonetic link Aksenov played with here.

63. The martyrdom of writers has been a constant and powerful trope of modern Russian literature since the time of Aleksandr Pushkin. See, for example, Paul Debreczeny, "'*Zhitie Aleksandra Boldinskogo*': Pushkin's Elevation to Sainthood in Soviet Culture," in *Late Soviet Culture: From Perestroika to Novostroika*, ed. Thomas Lahusen and Gene Kuperman (Durham, N.C.: Duke University Press, 1993), 46–68.

64. Jane Gary Harris quoted Berlin and Fitzpatrick in the context of her discussion of the imagination of the Russian intelligentsia in the middle and late Soviet eras. See Harris's "Lidiia Ginzburg: Images of the Intelligentsia," in *The Russian Memoir: History and Literature*, ed. Beth Holmgren (Evanston, Ill.: Northwestern University Press, 2003), 11.

65. The dinosaur, like most of Aksenov's figures, has multiple semantic potentials. In addition to being Khvastishchev's sculpture, the dinosaur bears connection to the discussion of Darwinism and prehistoric animals from Malkolmov's education, where the headless dinosaur that continues to walk and reproduce itself might suggest the Soviet regime after Stalin (67–68; 59–60).

66. Kathleen F. Parthé traced the emergence of Village Prose out of the "Ovechkin-style" essay in the late 1950s–early 1960s. By the mid-1960s, the term "*derevenskaia proza*" was in use. The movement declined by the late 1970s. See Parthé's *Russian Village Prose: The Radiant Past* (Princeton, N.J.: Princeton University Press, 1992), 81–83.

67. Aksenov criticized Village Prose (Derevenskaia proza) authors for be-

coming part of the Soviet establishment. He pointed out that a number of them were clearly antisemitic (*Conversations in Exile*, 81).

68. Dalgard discussed Bakhtin's influence on Aksenov's idea of carnival and the grotesque, in *The Function of the Grotesque in Vasilij Aksenov*, trans. Robert Porter (Aarhus, Denmark: Arkona, 1982), 140–41. Gary Saul Morson and Caryl Emerson discussed Bakhtin's concepts and an ethics and aesthetics of prosaic in *Mikhail Bakhtin: Creation of a Prosaics* (Stanford, Calif.: Stanford University Press, 1990). Bakhtin's own work offered dialogic alternatives to the radical unification of the carnival. See discussion, for example, in Tihanov, *The Master*, 273.

69. While evoking a surrealist swirl taking off into the heights, he intended always to keep the emphasis on the earth, Aksenov explained (Lauridsen and Dalgard, "Interview with V. P. Aksenov," 24).

70. A good analysis appears in Vishevsky and Pogacar ("The Function"). Efimova pointed out that Aksenov's evocation of myth often reflects the needs and tastes of the average Soviet reader (*Intertekst*, 19).

71. See Mal'tsev's review in the émigré journal *Kontinent* 29 (1981): 403–6.

72. Johnson, "Vasilij Aksionov's Aviary," 45.

73. Such a reading was, however, suggested by Anatole Shub, who compared *The Burn* to classic Russian novels, including Nikolai Gogol's *Dead Souls*, Andrei Belyi's *Petersburg*, and Mikhail Bulgakov's *Master and Margarita*. Shub contended *The Burn* was a "supremely ambitious work worthy of a great tradition." Indeed, he found that Aksenov's novel "makes Boris Pasternak's *Doctor Zhivago* seem sentimental and much of Solzhenitsyn's fiction seem wooden in comparison." Anatole Shub, "The Intelligentsia in the Fires of Stalinism," *New York Times*, November 25, 1984. *Dead Souls* and *Master and Margarita* seem more purely literary in that they incorporate little of the kind of specific references to contemporary events and people that mark Aksenov's novel. Aksenov's use of real historical and political material might be compared to Dante's *Divine Comedy*. The *Inferno*, in particular, was a key source for Gogol and arguably for *The Burn*. Aksenov referred to Dante in this novel and elsewhere.

74. Bourdieu, *The Rules*, 154–59.

75. It developed that restricted artistic portion later, most notably in Leningrad in the mid-1970s. See the conclusion on development of the field.

76. For Bourdieu, *habitus* is a central concept mediating between the agent and the social field on which he acts.

77. "A Conversation in the Editorial Office of *Kontinent*," in Mozejko, Briker, and Dalgard, *Vasiliy Pavlovich Aksenov*, 26–31.

78. Aleksei Zverev, "Bliuzy chetvertogo pokoleniia," *Literaturnoe obozrenie* 11/12 (1992): 9–17, 12.

79. Indicative of this adulation, fellow writer Sergei Dovlatov writes of Aksenov and Anatolii Gladilin that they were "idols of our youth," they were "our

own, personal writers." See Dovlatov, "Literatura prodolzhaetsia: Posle konferentsii v Los-Andzhelese," *Sintaksis* 10 (1982): 142.

80. Witold Gombrowicz's *Memoirs from the Time of Immaturity* (1933) highlights the theme of immaturity, which he shares with Aksenov. While I have found no specific references by Aksenov to Gombrowicz, it might be useful to compare what Aksenov does in *The Burn* to Gombrowicz's literary evocation of nonculture, underdevelopment, and the trash as described by Ewa Plonowska Ziarek. Gombrowicz in this way asks what the social function of literature will be, if not to develop the spirit of reconciliation promised by national culture. See Ziarek, "The Scar of the Foreigner and the Fold of the Baroque: National Affiliations and Homosexuality in Gombrowicz's *Trans-Atlantyk*," in *Gombrowicz's Grimaces: Modernism, Gender, Nationality*, ed. Ewa Plonowska Ziarek (Albany: SUNY Press, 1998): 223–24. Aksenov employed similar tactics to prompt an examination of the function of literature and the character of the collective, given the failure of the artificial unity promised by the Soviet state.

81. Bourdieu described "two modes of aging," referring to biological age and accumulated status on the field. He also described Flaubert's Frédéric in terms of his youth and his choice not to embark on a career that would entangle him in the official illusions of the social field (*The Rules*, 146–54, 12–13). I compared Aksenov's character Dmitrii to Frédéric early in this chapter.

82. When Farrar, Straus and Giroux decided not to publish *The Burn* after initially expressing interest, Joseph Brodsky's negative opinion of the novel was said to be to blame. See discussion of the dispute over Brodsky's influence and role in "Iz arkhiva Vasiliia Aksenova," ed. and intro. Viktor Esipov, *Voprosy literatury* 5 (2011): 12–13.

83. At the same time, it must be admitted that Aksenov's narrative point of view in *The Burn* hardly seems securely in control. In *Surplussed Barrelware*, the narrator retains an authorial perspective above the characters represented until the final section, when he validates their achievement of significant unity by joining them, so that "they" becomes "we" (86–90). By contrast, in *The Burn* the narrative point of view slides between identification with the protagonists' perspectives and a third-person transcendent point of view with no comfortable or consistent distinction.

84. Rassadin commented negatively on it in retrospect, noting that most others passed it over in silence (Rassadin, "Budem," 202).

85. Vasilii Aksenov et al., eds., *Metropol'. Literaturnyi al'manakh* (Ann Arbor, Mich.: Ardis, 1979). The work later appeared in English as *Metropol: Literary Almanac*, ed. Vasily Aksyonov, et al. (New York: W. W. Norton, 1982), with a foreword by Kevin Klose, who was Moscow bureau chief for the *Washington Post*, 1977–81. Aksenov described the work on the anthology and the consequences for some writers involved in his novel *Skazhi izium* (Ann Arbor, Mich.: Ardis, 1985).

86. Aksenov's letter to Carl Proffer, August 23, 1978. Ardis Press Papers, University of Michigan, Hatcher Library, Box 1, Folder V.A[ksenov] Correspondence, October 1977–January 1978. In another letter, Carl Proffer detailed for Aksenov what advance money Norton could offer to authors, saying, "I realize this is probably not very important, but just want to make it clear." What seems more significant is that the Norton editor showed "enthusiasm" about doing the publication, when others did not (letter dated March 6, 1979, Ardis Press Papers, Folder V.A. Correspondence, September 1978–December 1978).

87. Aksenov said that Random House sold more than 30,000 copies of *The Burn*. *The Burn*, although more complicated than his later works, sold more copies than they did in English. "Amerikanskim pisatelem ia tak i ne stal," *Inostrannaia literature* 1 (2003), http://magazines.russ.ru/inostran/2003/1/aksen.html#_ftnref2. Probably the talk of confrontation and literary scandal attracted the attention of the public in the United States at that time and made a difference in sales. By the late 1980s, Aksenov lamented what he saw as a failure of the American literary market to accommodate truly avant-garde art like his. He found in his new home a sort of commercial hegemony he likened to the ideological hegemony from which he had come. See Vassily Aksyonov's remarks in "An Exile in Literary America," *New York Times*, April 14, 1985, A52.

CHAPTER THREE

The epigraph for this chapter is from Mandelshtam's poem beginning "Midnight in Moscow" ("Polnoch' v Moskve. Roskoshno buddiiskoe leto . . . ," 1931), in Osip Mandel'shtam, *Sochineniia v dvukh tomakh* (Moscow: Khudozhestvennaia literatura, 1990), vol. 1, 177. The English translation appears in Ellen Chances, "The Energy of Honesty, or Brussels Lace, Mandel'shtam, 'Stolen Air,' and Inner Freedom," *Russian Literature* 51, no. 4 (2007): 503–29, esp. 510.

1. Andrei Bitov felt a need to rebel after seeing Osip Mandel'shtam's *Fourth Prose* in samizdat in 1963. This spirit, as Bitov told it, transformed his writing: "On the back of Mandel'shtam's *Fourth Prose* my second prose began." Andrei Bitov, "Posleslovie: Razgovor s knigoizdatelem," in *Dachnaia mestnost' (Dubl')* (St. Petersburg: Fond russkoi poezii, 1999), 94.

2. Karen Stepanian called *Pushkin House* the "grand 'novel of education' of our time" in "Chelovek prosveshchennyi," *Literaturnaia gazeta* 48, no. 5322 (November 28, 1990): 5.

3. Sven Spieker took up the postmodern designation to treat Bitov's work in *Figures of Memory and Forgetting in Andrej Bitov's Prose: Postmodernism and the Quest for History* (Frankfurt am Main: Peter Lang, 1996). Mark Lipovetsky and O. V. Bogdanova both singled out *Pushkin House* and Erofeev's *Moscow Stations* as exemplary works of Russian postmodernism: See Lipovetsky, *Russian Postmodernist Fiction; Dialogue with Chaos*, ed. Eliot Borenstein (Armonk,

N.Y.: M.E. Sharpe, 1999), 5–6; and Bogdanova, *Roman A. Bitova "Pushkinskii dom" ('Versiia i variant' russkogo postmoderna)* (St. Petersburg: Filologicheskii fakul'tet SPGU, 2002), 3.

4. Thus, for example, Boris Groys contrasted the Western Pop Art parody of commercial art to the Soviet Sots-Art parody of pedagogical mass art in order to set up his analysis of postmodern trends in Russia: see his "Text as a Ready-Made Object," in *Endquote: Sots-Art Literature and Soviet Grand Style*, ed. Marina Balina, Nancy Condee, and Evgeny Dobrenko (Evanston, Ill.: Northwestern University Press, 2000), 32–44, esp. 32–33. Lipovetsky claimed that one of the distinguishing features of Russian postmodernism is that it is "elitist to the core" (*Russian Postmodernist Fiction*, 3), a claim that invites Bourdieusian analysis as a belief constituting a field of restricted cultural production.

5. See, for example, Stanislav Savitskii's treatment of Bitov's place in Leningrad unofficial culture, *Andegraund: Istoriia i mify leningradskoi neofitsial'noi literatury* (Moscow: NLO, 2002).

6. Critics who insisted on the specific moral and social message of Bitov's novel include Iurii Karabchievskii, "Tochka boli: O romane Andreia Bitova 'Pushkinskii dom,'" *Grani* 106 (1977); and Chances, "The Energy of Honesty."

7. On the importance of Ginzburg as mentor for Bitov, see Chances (*Andrei Bitov*, 8–9). Lidiia Ginzburg, a pupil of Formalist Iurii Tynianov, was known in part as a scholar of psychological prose. She was also an independent thinker and writer of uncensored prose. In notebooks, she argued apropos of the tasks and discussions of literature in its historical moment that "precisely in the twentieth century the conversation started long ago about the vanity of life ended and another conversation began, about how to survive and live without losing a human visage." See Ginzburg, *Zapisnye knizhki: Vospominaniia. Esse* (St. Petersburg: "Iskusstvo-SPB," 2002), 198.

8. Laurent Jenny surveyed the variety of functions of intertextuality, including the exposure of ossified discourse and the incorporation of material that needs to be assimilated to be surpassed. He wrote, "Whatever its avowed ideological underpinnings, the intertextual use of discourses always has a critical, playful, and exploratory function. This makes it the most fitting instrument of expression in times of cultural breakdown and renaissance." See Jenny's 1976 essay "The Strategy of Form" in *French Literary Theory Today: A Reader*, ed. Tsvetan Todorov (Cambridge, Eng.: Cambridge University Press, 1982) 61.

9. *Ostranenie*, also translated as "defamiliarization," is Viktor Shklovsky's term for what literary language does, and it remains one of the most broadly recognized legacy concepts from Russian Formalist theory. Volf Shmid picked up Iurii Trifonov's description of Bitov's technique, recalling this concept as "sharp seeing" (*ostrovidenie*). For Shmid's analysis and Bitov's somewhat tongue-in-cheek comments about his update of this Formalist idea, see Shmid, "Andrei

Bitov—Master 'ostrovideniia,'" in *Imperiia v chetyrekh izmereniiakh*, 4 vols. (Moscow: TKO AST, 1996) vol. 1: 373–82, esp. 376.

10. The calculation of the "fateful" year in which Lyova was born can be made based on Lyova's age, which is sixteen in 1953. Andrei Bitov, *Pushkin House*, trans. Susan Brownsberger (Normal, Ill.: Dalkey Archive, 1998), 132–33; and Andrei Bitov, *Pushkinskii dom* (St. Petersburg: Izdatel'stvo Ivana Limbakha, 1999), 138. Subsequent page references to these editions will be given in parentheses, thus: (English edition; Russian edition).

11. Ginzburg singled out Bitov as the most outstanding prose writer of the group of young writers in Leningrad. She also identified Bitov's coeval Aleksandr Kushner as an exceptional poet in "Pole napriazheniia," *Literaturnaia gazeta* (January 15, 1986).

12. Lydia Ginzburg, *On Psychological Prose*, trans. Judson Rosengrant (Princeton: Princeton University Press, 1991), 246–56. The Russian original was published in 1971.

13. Ginzburg analyzed Tolstoy's representation of "life" in *On Psychological Prose*, 243. The evocation of "life" seems particularly important to Bitov. The epilogue of the novel concludes: "The novel is ended—life continues," (318; 319). Chances described Bitov's "ecological" prose in these terms: "He addresses the relationship of life to art, of life to our preconceived notions about life, of present life to past life" (Chances, *Andrei Bitov*, 10–11).

14. Ginzburg, *Zapisnye knizhki*, 199.

15. Ginzburg, *Zapisnye knizhki*, 209. Ginzburg also discussed the idea in an interview in the late 1980s. See Jane Gary Harris, "Lidiia Ginzburg: Images of the Intelligentsia," in *The Russian Memoir: History and Literature*, ed. Beth Holmgren (Evanston, Ill.: Northwestern University Press, 2003), 5.

16. Ginzburg's uncensored writing, both memoiristic and fictional, came out at the end of perestroika and later. See Ginzburg, *Zapisnye knizhki*; and Ginzburg, *Prokhodiashchie kharaktery: Proza voennykh let: Zapiski blokadnogo cheloveka* (Moscow, 2011).

17. Harris, "Lidiia Ginzburg," 24.

18. Ellen Chances surveyed Bitov's early and middle career, including his psychological prose (*Andrei Bitov*). Olga Hassanoff Bakich provided a close analysis of some of Bitov's method and themes in "A New Type of Character in the Soviet Literature of the 1960s: The Early Works of Andrei Bitov," *Canadian Slavonic Papers* 23, no. 2 (1981): 125–33.

19. Ginzburg, *On Psychological Prose*, 256.

20. Ibid., 257.

21. See Vladimir Lavrov, "Tri romana Andreia Bitova, ili vospominaniia o sovremennike," *Neva* 5 (1997): 186–87.

22. Bitov interview with Evgenii Shklovskii, "V poiskakh real'nosti," *Liter-*

aturnoe obozrenie 5 (1988): 33. Here and elsewhere, unless otherwise noted, the translation is mine.

23. See the description of Cincinnatus's state-assigned employment in Nabokov, *Invitation to a Beheading*, trans. Dmitri Nabokov (New York, 1959), chap. 2.

24. Marina von Hirsch examined these intertexts in "The Presence of Nabokov in Bitov's Fiction and Nonfiction: Bitov and Nabokov, Bitov on Nabokov, Nabokov in Bitov," *Nabokov Studies* 6 (2000/2001): 57–74.

25. Bitov, *Pushkin House*, 3; *Pushkinskii dom*, 11. See also Andrei Bitov, "Commentary," in his *Pushkin House*, trans. Susan Brownsberger (Ann Arbor: Ardis, 1990), 413; and "Kommentarii," in *Pushkinskii dom*, 398.

26. Bitov, "V poiskakh real'nosti," 33.

27. Iurii Karabchievskii treated Lyova as a representative of the generation to which he and Bitov belong. Lyova, Karabchievskii claimed, displayed the characteristics of their generation, born around the time of Stalin's purges (1936–38). This generation regarded weakness and indecision as less morally suspect than the positive heroic values associated with the recent bloody history of the Soviet Union. Lyova's unsympathetic portrayal forced readers of this generation to look at themselves and reexamine their assumptions, he argued. See Karabchievskii, "Tochka boli," 152–53.

28. Critic Vissarion Belinskii in the 1840s talked about "types" in literary works as indicators of social trends, and the term became central to critical realism up through Socialist Realism: Marxist critic Gyorgy Lúkacs described the "type" as the cornerstone of realism. See Lúkacs, *Studies in European Realism* (New York, 1964), 8–9.

29. Ginzburg wrote, "History as something capable of governing that experience and of structuring the personality from within defined a new type of psychological novel, the one created by Turgenev in response to the conditions of Russian social life." While Turgenev shared with Herzen an "all-pervasive historicism," Herzen did not strive for ideal typifications, "typifications of the sort that Turgenev in fact required" (*On Psychological Prose*, 239–40).

30. Ginzburg, *On Psychological Prose*, 243.

31. Bitov, *Pushkin House*, 92; *Pushkinskii dom*, 97–98. See also Bitov's remarks on Rakhmetov and Socialist Realism in his "Commentary," 390–91; "Kommentarii," 376.

32. The formulation can be found in Mathewson's *The Positive Hero in Russian Literature* (Evanston, Ill.: Northwestern University Press, 1975), 14.

33. The term "superfluous man" came from Turgenev's short story "The Diary of a Superfluous Man" (1852). Mathewson contrasted the alienation of the superfluous man in all his guises as a foil to the revolutionary hero as an "integrated man," in *Positive Hero*, 5–16.

34. Bitov based the figure Modest Platonovich on Russian theorist Mikhail Bakhtin and other prototypes ("Commentary," 387; "Kommentarii," 372).

35. In his interview with Ewa Bérard Zarzycka, Bitov described Lyova's problem in these terms: "Not to walk in lockstep with History, but to remain true to oneself." See *La quinzaine littéraire* (February 1–15, 1989): 7. See also Bitov, "V poiskakh real'nosti," 37.

36. Marcus Levitt noted that "the jubilee of 1949 reflected the emphasis on the patriotism and greatness of the Russian people which had been promoted since the war," and that "by this time the process of 'Sovietizing' Pushkin and asserting a monolithic socialist culture under his aegis may [be] said to have reached its saturation point." See Levitt, *Russian Literary Politics*, 166.

37. The story of Aleksei Meres'ev (Maresyev), a World War II hero whose legs were amputated, was well known from Boris Polevoi's novella *Povest' o nastoiashchem cheloveke* (1946), which Sergei Prokofiev made into an opera—his last—in 1947–48. The opera premiered only after the composer's death at the Bolshoi Theater in Moscow in 1960. See Simon Alexander Morrison, *The People's Artist: Prokofiev's Soviet Years* (Oxford: Oxford UP, 2009), 315, 329.

38. Khrushchev, for example, announced, "In order not to repeat the errors of the past, the Central Committee has declared itself resolutely against the cult of the individual." The full text of the speech appeared in Bertram D. Wolfe, *Khrushchev and Stalin's Ghost* (Westport, Conn.: Greenwood Press, 1957), 244. By assigning all the blame to Stalin and the "cult of the individual," Khrushchev avoided implicating himself and did not address the problem of how others could have failed to intervene or speak out about the purges and other tragedies.

39. Bitov, *Pushkin House*, 197; *Pushkinskii dom*, 203. Kurt Shaw wrote about the Alexandre Dumas subtext in Bitov's novel and the villainy of "strength." See Shaw, "French Connections: The Three Musketeers Motif in Andrei Bitov's *Pushkinskii dom*," *Canadian Slavonic Papers* 37 (March–June 1995): 194–98. Chances treated the theme of "strength" and traced the rings of violence and betrayal rooted in Stalin and played out with Faina, in "The Energy of Honesty," 515, 518.

40. Bitov, "Commentary," 378; "Kommentarii" 362.

41. Chances underscored the importance of Mandelshtamian subtexts including this one, in "The Energy of Honesty," 510.

42. Ginzburg, *On Psychological Prose*, 259.

43. Bitov, "Commentary," 414; "Kommentarii," 400. Slight differences between these two versions of the commentaries exist, and in neither case is this quite the end of the notes.

44. See Viktor Shklovsky, "Sterne's *Tristram Shandy*: Stylistic Commentary," in *The Novel: An Anthology of Criticism and Theory 1900–2000*, ed. Dorothy J. Hale (Malden, Mass., 2006), 32; and V. Shklovskii, "'Evgenii Onegin' (Pushkin

i Stern)," in *Ocherki po poetike Pushkina* (1923; reprint ed. The Hague, 1969), 211. On Shklovsky reading Sterne, see Emily Finer, *Turning into Sterne: Viktor Shklovskii and Literary Reception* (London: Legenda, 2010).

45. Edward Brown said this in his review of *Pushkin House* in *The Nation* (March 12, 1988): 346. In addition, Andrei Ar'iev considered *Pushkin House* to be written "just as freely as *Tristram Shandy*" (*Pushkinskii dom*, 460).

46. Wolf Schmid discussed Bitov's variation on the sentimental journey ("Andrei Bitov–Master 'ostrovideniia,'" in *Imperiia v chetyrekh izmereniiakh*, 4 vols. [Moscow: TKO AST 1996], vol. 1: 376).

47. In his popular survey of the history of Cubism, Douglas Cooper outlined Cubism's emphasis on a "conceptual" as opposed to "perceptual" way of rendering things. See Cooper, *The Cubist Epoch* (New York, 1971), 22.

48. E. H. Gombrich argued that the Cubists aimed to destroy mimetic illusion by creating contradictions: "If illusion is due to the interaction of clues and the absence of contradictory evidence, the only way to fight its transforming influence is to make the clues contradict each other." Cubism opposes illusion with "the introduction of contrary clues which will resist all attempts to apply the test of consistency." See Gombrich, *Art and Illusion: a Study in the Psychology of Pictorial Representation* (New York, 1960), 281–82.

49. Marjorie Perloff discussed the multiple signifying capacities of the scraps in Picasso's *Still Life* in *The Futurist Moment: Avant-Garde, Avant Guerre, and the Language of Rupture* (Chicago: University of Chicago Press, 1986), 49. See also the semiotic analysis of collage composition by Rosalind Krauss, *The Originality of the Avant-Garde and Other Modernist Myths* (Cambridge, Mass.: MIT Press, 1991), 34.

50. Chances identified the article as Nikolai Ushakov, "Sviaz' vremen," *Literaturnaia gazeta* (June 10, 1970), in *Andrei Bitov*, 211.

51. Levitt pointed out that Pushkin's works became in the late nineteenth century a tool for acculturating non-Russian groups within the empire, a use that continued under the Soviets (*Russian Literary Politics*, 157, 164).

52. Stephanie Sandler wrote that "the fear that someone has created a false image of Pushkin has kept alive a passion for the 'real' Pushkin." See her *Commemorating Pushkin*, 6.

53. Comparing the scrap to the article from which it is "torn" reveals that words like "all-embracing" (*vseob/"emliushchii*), "entirely" (*v ts/elom*), "one" (*od/noi*), and "word" (*slov/o*) have been significantly cut off at the lines indicated. Sandler noted that Bitov, perhaps uniquely in Russian culture, evokes a respectful distance from Pushkin (*Commemorating Pushkin*, 267).

54. Karabchievskii compared Tynianov's objective analysis of "Pushkin and Tiutchev" to Lyova's highly subjective article ("Tochka boli," 182–84).

55. At the same time, and according to Bitov's characteristically ambivalent logic, Lyova's eccentric idea "fails," and thus evokes the "living life" of authors

and works that Lyova has not and could not fully master. See Bitov's comments about the idea that fails and expresses the "break" (*lomka*) of the mind (or system) too enamored of its own reason, thus evoking "living life" (*zhivaia zhizn'*) in "Pokhval'noe slovo chudakam . . . ," *Literaturnaia gazeta* (September 7, 1983).

56. See discussion of Bakhtin's "Avtor i geroi" (published 1979) in Morson and Emerson, *Mikhail Bakhtin*, 186–89.

57. Bitov wrote that "literature is a continuous and uninterrupted process. If some link is hidden, or omitted, or seems to have fallen out, this doesn't mean that the link doesn't exist, that the chain is broken—for without that link there can be no continuation. It means that we are standing right where the link is missing" ("Commentary," 413; "Kommentarii," 399). Thus, Modest Platonovich's awareness of "the break" signifies consciousness of his own creative potential. Lyova's sense of fragmentation may be similar.

58. In essays from this period Bitov decried the tendency to lionize the "geniuses" of the past. He exhorted people to use words to express meanings that are most of all contemporary, without thinking them worse or more debased than in times past. See Bitov, "Ekologiia slova" and "Molchanie slova," in his *Piatoe izmerenie: Na granitse vremeni i prostranstva* (Moscow: Izdatel'stvo Nezavisimaia gazeta, 2002), 375, 398–99.

59. Savitskii, *Andegraund*, 66.

60. See Savitskii's dossier featuring facsimiles of correspondence with publishers and commentary in *Pushkinskii dom* (1999), 441, 451.

61. From Bitov's account, *Pushkinskii dom*, 455. Bitov had conveyed the manuscript to the Proffers through Vasilii Aksenov with the expectation that it would be published there, if not in the U.S.S.R. (ibid., 452).

62. Bitov, *Pushkinskii dom*, 445–46.

63. Discussion of "Tri proroka" appeared in a subsequent issue, "Nuzhny li v literaturovedenii gipotezy?" *Voprosy literatury* 2 (1977): 82–112. Sandler discussed the essay as an early rehearsal of Bitov's "ventriloquism" (*Commemorating Pushkin*, 268).

64. Bitov, *Pushkinskii dom*, 474–75.

65. Tatiana Gerasimova recalled stormy unofficial debates around *Pushkin House*: "These people were romantics, and therefore the novel troubled them. It seemed to them constructivist, not written in a single breath (*Pushkinskii dom*, 456–57).

66. I wrote about Ardis editors Carl and Ellendea Proffer, and their relationships with Osip Mandelshtam's widow Nadezhda, the Nabokovs, and Brodsky in "Ardis Facsimile and Reprint Editions: Giving Back Russian Literature," in *From Samizdat to Tamizdat: Transnational Media During and After Socialism*, ed. Friederike Kind-Kovács and Jessie Labov (New York: Berghahn Books, 2013), 27–50.

67. Galassi worked as an editor at Random House from 1981 to 1986, dur-

ing which time he edited Aksyonov's *The Burn*. In 1986 he moved to Farrar, Straus and Giroux, described as the smallest and most "literary" of the big eight publishing firms in New York. See Craig Lambert's profile of Galassi, "High Type Culture," *Harvard Magazine* (November 1997), accessed July 9, 2013, http://harvardmagazine.com/1997/11/books.html. Galassi's criteria as editor and the reputation of a house like Farrar, Straus and Giroux, in particular, correspond to the long-term calculation of cultural businesses as described by Bourdieu, those trading in the short term profits of the best-seller in favour of the prestige and long-run profits of the literary work that awaits consecration (*The Rules*, 153–54; *The Field*, 97–101).

68. Omry Ronen recalled the name Gastello from his childhood, already in Bitov's terms, as "the childish word Gastello," near the end of his "Otstuplenie," *Zvezda* 5 (2002), http://magazines.russ.ru/zvezda/2002/5/ron.html.

69. Bitov commented on the clearing of the sky for the November holidays and juxtaposed that fact to remarks about the weather, whose persistent intractability exposes and resists human attempts to harness and control her ("Commentary," 373–75; "Kommentarii," 358–59, and also 401).

70. Chances noted that in his story "Life in Windy Weather," Bitov's narrator uses the cupola of the sky to describe a moment of symmetry when things come together ("The Energy of Honesty," 507).

71. Chances again found the source of this idea for Bitov in Mandelshtam's statements about holes keeping together the design, as in Brussels lace in "The Energy of Honesty," 515.

72. Fedor Dostoevsky, *Memoirs from the House of the Dead*, trans. Jessie Coulson, ed. Ronald Hingley (Oxford: Oxford University Press, 1983), 7.

73. Bitov in his essay on *Memoirs from the House of the Dead* remarked Dostoevsky's desire "to amaze and shake" (*porazit' i potriasti*) people in all his work, from *Poor People*, to *Notes from the House of the Dead*, to his Pushkin speech (*Piatoe izmerenie*, 20).

74. References to the "function" (*naznachenie*) of the poet and the word refer to the essay by Aleksandr Blok, "On the Poet's Calling" ("O naznachenii poeta"), which he read at his last public appearance for the celebration marking 84 years since Pushkin's death at the Pushkin House, on February 19, 1921, an occasion distinguished by its gloomy focus on the twilight of Russian culture. See Boris Gasparov, "The 'Golden Age' and Its Role in the Cultural Mythology of Russian Modernism," trans. Eric Naiman, and Robert P. Hughes, "Pushkin in Petrograd, February 1921," in *Cultural Mythologies of Russian Modernism. From the Golden Age to the Silver Age*, ed. Boris Gasparov, Robert P. Hughes, and Irina Paperno (Berkeley: University of California Press, 1992), 14, 204–13.

75. Stanislav Rassadin similarly recognized the challenge of reading or hearing bard Aleksandr Galich as something other than a "forbidden" artist: "We—so far—are not readers," he said, reviewing the problem of "freedom," "secret

freedom," what it has meant for Russian poets in the past, including Pushkin and Blok, and what it could mean in the era of perestroika and glasnost, when almost everything was available in print again. Rassadin, ". . . svobody chernaia rabota," *Aprel'* 1 (1989): 239–47, esp. 241.

76. Fyodor Dostoevsky, "Pushkin (A Sketch)," in *A Writer's Diary*, vol. 2, trans. Kenneth Lantz (Evanston Ill.: Northwestern University Press, 1994), 1281–95, esp. 1295.

77. Leo Tolstoy, *Anna Karenina*, trans. Richard Pevear and Larissa Volokhonsky (London: Penguin Books, 2006), part 8, chap. 13, p. 800.

78. "And just as the conclusions of astronomers that were not based on observations of the visible sky in relation to the same meridian and the same horizon would be idle and lame, so my conclusions would be idle and lame if they were not based on that understanding of the good which always has been and will be the same for everyone, and which is revealed to me by Christianity and can always be verified in my soul. And I don't have the right or possibility of resolving the question of other beliefs and their attitude to the Deity" (Tolstoy, *Anna Karenina*, part 13, chap. 19, p. 816).

79. Bitov, "Pokhval'noe slovo chudakam . . ."

80. The Dalkey Archive Press reprinted *Pushkin House* in English in 1998, an equivocal sign that the novel retained its status in the post-Soviet era. That publication by a press at Illinois State University received support from the National Endowment for the Arts and the Illinois Arts Council, suggesting recognition of its cultural value, despite the fact that Bitov's work has not attained the level of consecration, and hence, commercial viability, of, say, Nabokov.

81. Literary and cultural historians could dispute this statement by pointing to the para-institutional literary society (LITO) with which Bitov and other authors were associated in the 1960s. It might be debated whether an unofficial literary consciousness in Leningrad took shape by the end of the 1960s or the middle of the 1970s (Savitskii, *Andegraund* 57, 59): what seems clear is that *Pushkin House* did not come out of a specific group dynamic.

CHAPTER FOUR

1. The chapter epigraph and references throughout the chapter are to Venedikt Yerofeev, *Moscow Stations: A Poem*, trans. Stephen Mulrine (London: Faber and Faber, 1997), 123; and Venedikt Erofeev, *Moskva–Petushki*, in *Zapiski psikhopata* (Moscow: Vagrius, 2000), 238. Occasional adaptations of the translated text have been made for clarity or style.

2. Erofeev gave the autumn of 1969 as the date of composition at the end of the text. He provided a different date for writing the manuscript in a letter to Svetlana Gaiser-Shnitman. See her *Venedikt Erofeev: "Moskva–Petushki" ili "The Rest Is Silence"* (Bern: Peter Lang, 1989), 21. Commentators have remarked that

Erofeev could be loose with the facts of his biography. Olga Sedakova, a friend of Erofeev's, insisted that she saw the manuscript of *Moskva–Petushki* in late 1969; therefore, that is the date I present (Interview, March 2001).

3. Erofeev said of the novel, "I wrote it for a small circle of friends, in order to cheer them up and to sadden them a little, too. Eighty pages to cheer them up and ten to make them forget all cheerfulness." From a BBC2 documentary directed by Pawel Pawlikowski, "From Moscow to Pietushki with Benny Yerofeev" (aired April 1990), http://www.youtube.com/watch?v=xxeeKDsN5Hc&feature=related. Compare to Pushkin's description of the novel *Eugene Onegin* as a "pied collection . . . spun from threads both sad and humoristic," written for friends (*Eugene Onegin*, trans. Charles Johnston [New York: Penguin Books, 1977]), 33.

4. Andrei Zorin, "Opoznavatel'nyi znak," *Teatr* 9 (1991): 119.

5. Courtenay is quoted by David Remnick in his review of the production of the theatrical adaptation in New York, "The Lush Life of a Muscovite," *The New Yorker* 71, no. 33 (October 23, 1995): 37.

6. Mikhail Epstein writes about the compelling "myth" of Venichka, and the tendency to conflate the author Erofeev with his most popular lyrical hero. See Epstein, "Posle karnavala, ili vechnyi Venichka," in *Vera i obraz* (Tenafly, N.J.: Ermitazh, 1994), 171.

7. People believed that Erofeev's drinking meant something. Friend Igor Avdiev asserted, "To drink is also an ascetic feat," one for which you abandon those you love, give up on your career and on other things. He quoted Erofeev saying, "Our drinking should be stripped . . . of the elements of farce and debauchery [*zabubennost'*]," in Nina Frolova et al., "Neskol'ko monologov o Venedikte Erofeeve," *Teatr* 9 (1991): 109. Sedakova said, "One felt that his way of life was not trivial drunkenness, but some kind of holy service" (ibid., 98). Epstein wrote about the "myth of [Erofeev's] non-drunkenness" ("Posle karnavala," 179), which judging by memoirs took root despite his in fact considerable drinking.

8. Venichka later claims to have tried the line on professors at the Sorbonne, again without success. Erofeev, born 1938 in the small town of Kandalaksha Station in the Murmansk administrative region, lived in a children's home in Kirovsk from 1947 to 1953. He and his brother Boris went there after his father was imprisoned and his mother departed for Moscow looking for work. Information about the family can be found in the publication by Erofeev's sister, Tamara Gushchina, "Venedikt Erofeev, Pis'ma k sestre," *Teatr* 9 (1992): 122–44.

9. Olga Sedakova remarked on his frequent use of this phrase ("Neskol'ko monologov," 98).

10. Karen Ryan-Hayes is one of several scholars to comment on this feature of Erofeev's work. She treated Erofeev's "curiously intense grief" and the theme of spiritual alienation in "Erofeev's Grief: Inconsolable and Otherwise," in *Venedikt Erofeev's Moscow-Petushki: Critical Perspectives*, ed. Karen L. Ryan-Hayes

(New York: Peter Lang, 1997), 101–21. Sedakova claimed of Erofeev the author, "Venia's real passion was grief. He suggested the word be written with a capital letter, like in Tsevtaeva: Grief [*Gore*]." She called it "The New Russian Grief" in a soulless, relentlessly materialist society: "The nightmare of the communist epoch was the Grief which he suffered from every day" ("Neskol'ko monologov," 100, 102).

11. Aksenov called the latter part of the 1960s the "Era of Anniversaries" (*epokha iubileev*) (*The Burn*, 391; 330). Siniavskii also cited the celebrations and the clichéd rhetoric associated with them as the context for the development of Soviet joke folklore. See Abram Terts (Andrei Siniavskii), "Anekdot v Anekdote," *Sintaksis* 1 (1978): 77–95, esp. 89.

12. Gogol's statement on the subject appears in part 1, chapter 7 of *Dead Souls*, trans. David Magarshack (London: Penguin Books, 1961), 143. Many have commented on the importance of Gogol as subtext, including Tatiana Tolstaia, quoted by Stephen Mulrine in his article "*Moscow Stations*: From Novel to Play," *Modern Drama* 41 (1998): 49. David Remnick remarked the connection ("The Lush Life," 36). E. A. Smirnova's article explored the links between Erofeev's work and Gogol's: "Venedikt Erofeev glazami gogoleveda," *Russkaia literatura* 3 (1990): 58–66.

13. Mark Al'tshuller wrote about the epic elements in "*Moskva–Petushki*' Venedikta Erofeeva i traditsii klassicheskoi poemy," *Novyi zhurnal* 146 (1982): 75–85.

14. Aleksandr Leontovich testified to Erofeev's reaction to and knowledge of classical music ("Neskol'ko monologov," 96–97). Erofeev professed to hate dissidents (in the common parlance this meant democratic dissidents): "I can't stand dissidents. They are to a person anti-musical. And therefore they are wrong about everything" (*Zapiski psikhopata*, 394). As the least representative of art forms, music represented a purity of autonomous art to which Symbolist poets aspired. Erofeev's association of anti-musicality with dissidents therefore can indicate his own desire to realize an art free from socio-political topicality.

15. See details of the British dramatic productions in the front matter of *Moscow Stations* (London: Faber and Faber, 1997).

16. This stage version traveled subsequently to Israel, the United States, and to provincial Russian cities. Aleksandr Tsurkan spoke in an interview about decisions to reduce the cast to practically one person, and to express the linguistic flexibility of the text physically through acrobatics ("*Moskva–Petushki*—Spektakl' ne o p'ianstve" from the newspaper *Nash Belgorod*, August 11, 2000. A copy of the article can be found at http://www.arctic.org.ru/2005a/aug2000.htm.

17. The resonances with Hamlet also signify Venichka's difference from the revolutionary actor and the positive Soviet hero. See Hellbeck on the negative Soviet evaluation of "Hamletism," that is, brooding thought as opposed to conscious action (*Revolution*, 8).

18. Svetlana Gaiser-Shnittman detailed references in Erofeev's novel to Hamlet and other Shakespearean texts (*Venedikt Erofeev*, 97–98, and passim).

19. See Harold Bloom on the importance of "inwardness" and "interiority" in Shakespeare's work and Hamlet particularly, in *Shakespeare: The Invention of the Human* (New York: Riverhead Books, 1998), 6, 409.

20. See Michael Fried, *Absorption and Theatricality. Painting and Beholder in the Age of Diderot* (Chicago: University of Chicago Press, 1980), 5. One of the essays in which Fried originally elaborated his understanding of this distinction was "Art and Objecthood," *Artforum* 5, no. 10 (1967): 12–23.

21. Perloff spoke about the spectacle created in the poetic work as *opsis*, citing Aristotle's six constituent parts of tragedy, from chap. 6 of the *Poetics*: *mythos* (plot), *ethos* (character), *dianoia* (thought), *lexis* (diction), *melopoeia* (rhythm and song), and *opsis* (spectacle). She critiqued the way both romantic and modernist theory privileged *lexis* and *melopoeia*, and asserted that *dianoia* was creeping in "through the back door" in the new performance poetry invigorated by *opsis*. See Perloff, *The Poetics of Indeterminacy: Rimbaud to Cage* (Princeton, N.J.: Princeton University Press, 1981), 288–89.

22. Eduard Vlasov cited the statement from Gorkii's work as a cliché of Soviet propaganda in his commentary "Bessmertnaia poema Venedikta Erofeeva 'Moskva–Petushki,'" in Venedikt Erofeev, *Moskva–Petushki* (Moscow: Vagrius, 2000), 162–63. Even this jolly barb conceals ironic pathos, however, in its allusion to Dostoevsky's *Crime and Punishment*, in which Marmeladov insists that a man must have at least one place to go. Paperno and Gasparov first noted the dual thrust of Erofeev's parody ("Vstan' i idi," *Slavica Hierosolymitana* 5–6 [1981]: 391).

23. The line "*Samoe dorogoe u cheloveka—eto zhizn'. Ona daetsia emu odin raz, i prozhit' ee nado tak, chtoby ne bylo muchitel'no bol'no za bestselno prozhitye gody*," from part 2, chapter 3 of Nikolai Ostrovskii, *Kak zakalialas' stal'*, in *Sochineniia v trekh tomakh* (Moscow: Izdatel'stvo TsK VLKSM "Molodaia gvardiia," 1967), vol. 1, 242 (translation mine).

24. Bakhtin treated the "material bodily principle" in Rabelais's work, including images of the human body with its food, drink, defecation, and sexual life, as a constituent feature of "grotesque realism." Grotesque realism works chiefly through "degradation" (*snizhenie*), lowering high, spiritual, ideal and abstract things to the level of matter and the body. Mikhail Bakhtin, *Rabelais and His World*, trans. Helene Iswolsky (Cambridge, Mass.: MIT Press, 1965), 18–19.

First circulated after Bakhtin's book on Rabelais and the carnival had become popular among Soviet intelligentsia, Erofeev's book certainly bears comparison to Bakhtin's exposition of the carnival, but it probably reflects more diffuse influences, as well. Erofeev was playing with notions of high and low already in notebooks from February 1957: "I ecstatically hail any deviation from the normal human order [*ot normal'no chelovecheskogo*]! But I cannot understand why preference is given to elevation [*'vozvysheniiu'*], if 'high' and 'low' are the same type of deviation from the general human order!" (*Zapiski psikhopata*, 58).

Bakhtin is said to have much appreciated Erofeev's novel, apart from the end. See Zorin ("Opoznavatel'nyi znak," 121).

25. See M. M. Bakhtin, "Forms of Time and Chronotope in the Novel," in *The Dialogic Imagination: Four Essays*, trans. Caryl Emerson and Michael Holquist (Austin: University of Texas Press, 1981), 158–59.

26. From Bakhtin's "Forms of Time and Chronotope" (*Dialogic Imagination*, 239). Compare also Bakhtin's contentions about the all-encompassing nature of the carnival, which cannot be seen as spectacle, because there are no "footlights": "Carnival is not a spectacle seen by the people; they live in it. . . . While carnival lasts, there is no other life outside it" (*Rabelais*, 7).

27. Epstein called carnival the "apotheosis [*zavershenie*] of the theory of revolution": during the carnival all must live according to its rules. Venichka resisted this carnival and Soviet, revolutionary culture by being delicate and shy ("Posle karnavala," 189–90).

28. Among those who have treated Venichka in light of the Holy Fool, see Epstein, "Posle karnavala," 174; Gaiser-Shnitman, *Venedikt Erofeev*, 116–21; and Mark Lipovetskii, "S potustoronnei tochki zreniia: Postmodernistskaia versiia dialogizma," in *Venedikt Erofeev's "Moscow-Petushki."* Parodies of church services from old Russian literature help demonstrate the moral purpose of apparently immoral behavior. Ziva Bencic compared *Moskva–Petushki* to works of the late seventeenth century, including "Sluzhba kabaku," "Prazdnik kabatskikh iaryzhek," and "Povest' o brazhnike," in "Obraz Venichki Erofeeva," *Russian Literature* 51 (2002): 243–60.

29. G. P. Fedotov, "The Holy Fools," in *The Russian Religious Mind* (Cambridge, Mass.: Harvard University Press, 1966), vol. 2: 316.

30. See the comparison of Russian holy fools and European fools in A. M. Panchenko, "Smekh kak zrelishche," in *Smekh v drevnei Rusi*, ed. D. S. Likhachev, A. M. Panchenko, and N. V. Ponyrko (Leningrad: Nauka, 1984), 80. The holy fool tries to make people cry over that which causes laughter ("*Rydat' nad smeshnym—vot blagoi effekt, k kotoomu stremitsia iurodivyi*") (ibid., 81). Panchenko also discussed the holy fool cursing the world out of concern for the moral health of society (ibid., 86).

31. Vlasov, "Bessmertnaia," 520.

32. Erofeev converted to Catholicism late in his life, a conversion witnessed and discussed by Natal'ia Shmel'kova, "Ni tsenzor, ni den'gi, ni golod: O Venedikte Erofeeve (1938–1990)," in *Vo chreve machekhi, ili Zhizn'-diktatura krasnogo* (St. Petersburg: Limbus, 1999), 9–114, esp. 44. Vladimir Bondarenko was indignantly unable to fit this fact into his Russian Orthodox reading of Venichka's life. See Bondarenko's "Podlinnyi Venichka: Razrushenie mifa," *Nash sovremennik* 7 (1999): 177–85. Erofeev's "holy foolish" qualities can be read against the

background of the Catholic Saint Francis of Assisi, a saint whose life he reportedly knew and loved in G. K. Chesterton's telling of it. Chesterton described Francis as having made a great fool of himself in the eyes of the world. Sedakova asserted that "Christian civilization was represented for [Erofeev] in Dante, in Pascal, in Aquinas, in Chesterton, and not here. How many times he said: 'I will never understand what they see in that "Trinity" of Rublev!'" ("Neskol'ko monologov," 101). If the evidence suggests that in life Erofeev possessed a sincere Christian faith, it also shows that he felt compelled to seek fresh and unauthoritarian ways of expressing that faith].

33. Bakhtin, "Epic and Novel," in *Dialogic Imagination*, 23.

34. Bakhtin concentrated on the comic and fearless realistic grotesque (*Rabelais*) and so did Soviet literary specialist Iurii Mann, who treated it as a feature of Nikolai Gogol's works in *O groteske v literature* (Moscow: Sovetskii pisatel', 1966). On the romantic grotesque and its inheritors, see Wolfgang Kayser's *The Grotesque in Art and Literature*, trans. Ulrich Weisstein (Bloomington: Indiana University Press, 1963).

35. Vlasov identified the short word most commonly written as graffiti: "prick" (*khui*) ("Bessmertnaia poema" 514). Modest ellipses appear in most printed editions, but the word "*khui*" was written out in the samizdat copy in the archive of the Sakharov Center (consulted spring 1997). Compare this rude graffiti to Tikhonov's two "clear and succinct" words chalked up on the fence at the beginning of the Petushki Revolution, a parody of Luther's 95 theses and Lenin's April theses (*Moscow Stations* 92; *Moskva–Petushki* 89).

36. Irina Paperno and Boris Gasparov read the four killers as the four iconic faces of communism in the Soviet Union—Marx, Engels, Lenin, and Stalin ("Vstan' i idi," 390). Indeed, a representation of those faces, with Stalin's rubbed out, remained above the stairwell in RGGU in Moscow in 1997 (author's observation, 1997). David Bethea suggested that the four killers recall the Four Horsemen of the Apocalypse from Revelation 6, in *The Shape of Apocalypse in Modern Russian Fiction* (Princeton, N.J.: Princeton University Press, 1989), 275.

37. Kayser, *The Grotesque*, 184.

38. See chapter 1 of this study on Siniavskii's defense of artistic language.

39. Hamlet, for example, jokingly calls Polonius a fishmonger and teases Rosencrantz and Guildenstern about being Fortune's "privates" (act 2, scene 2). All three, of course, are trying to find out Hamlet's true thoughts for the King.

40. Alexei Yurchak, "The Cynical Reason of Late Socialism: Power, Pretense, and the Anekdot," *Public Culture* 9, no. 2 (1997): 161–88, esp. 166–67. See also Yurchak's analysis of ossified Soviet language after Stalin, with examples (*Everything Was Forever*, 47–76).

41. Terts, "Anekdot," 88–89.

42. Siniavskii cites Erofeev's novel among examples of the culture of Soviet

jokes making its way into literature ("Anekdot," 91). The edition that foregrounds this aspect is Venedikt Erofeev, *Moskva–Petushki: Roman-anekdot* (Petrozavodsk: A/O 'KAREKO', 1995). "Roman-anekdot" appears on the cover, perhaps the publisher's ploy to stress the popular appeal of the work in this inexpensive paperback edition. *Moskva–Petushki i pr.* appears on the title page inside, and the more usual *Moskva–Petushki: Poema* appears on the back page with printing information.

43. The men here use the last names of Moshe Dayan and Abba Eban, Israeli military and diplomatic figures demonized in the Soviet press around the time of the Six-Day War. Those names phonetically evoke profane and slang language about sex, completely unrelated, of course, to the significance of the names in official propaganda.

44. Yurchak discussed this "imagined community" with reference to Benedict Anderson's analysis of the phenomenon ("The Cynical Reason," 167–68). Siniavskii talked about the fact that Russians, Jews, Czech, Polish, and so on all knew the same jokes, forming an informal community bound by folklore across national and State lines. He asserted that "we live in the epoch of popular oral art, of the prosperity of a huge folkloric genre ("Anekdot," 77).

45. On Blokian subtexts in Erofeev's novel, see N. A. Bogomolov, "Blokovskii plast v 'Moskve-Petushkakh,'" *Novoe literaturnoe obozrenie* 44 (2000): 126–35.

46. See the conclusion of chapter 1 for a comparison of Aksenov's actions with those of Flaubert's hero as described by Bourdieu.

47. The year 1956 meant more to Erofeev, it seems. Sedakova described the way the brutal suppression of the Hungarian uprising triggered an epiphany of despair for Erofeev: he bought a quarter-liter of vodka and a pack of Belomors, and became an alcoholic. Erofeev had seen what drinking did to his alcoholic father and brother, both of whom died in 1956. Although these losses provided a more personal reason for Erofeev's sense of loss, Sedakova submitted that in the most general sense, his drinking meant a renunciation of the Soviet system and of his life in it (Interview with Sedakova, March 2001).

Erofeev was also expelled from Moscow State University in 1956. In his notebooks, he listed the terrible events of 1955–57, noting they all fell on Friday (*Zapiski psikhopata*, 70–71). Friday, the day of Christ's Crucifixion, is also the day Venichka travels to Petushki—and the journey he narrates takes place on the thirteenth Friday in a row (39; 170).

48. On the concept of "signing" in Bakhtin, see Morson and Emerson, *Mikhail Bakhtin*, 69–71.

49. On Aleshkovskii's exemplification of a creative pseudo-folk approach to Soviet language as analyzed by Bitov, see the introduction. On the problem of genre and authorship in Aleshkovskii's work, see Bitov, "Pamiatnik," 226, 240–41.

50. Like modernist poets including James Joyce and T. S. Eliot, Mandel-

shtam referred to classical predecessors as part of a creative connection to the great cultural tradition they imagined as background for their work. The Crimea brought to mind associations with classical culture because of Ovid's exile there and by proximity to nearby Hylaea, a name evoking classical culture adopted by Russian Futurists. Bourdieu wrote about the "return to sources" as a typical strategy of the avant-garde (*The Field*, 84).

51. The name of the character refers to the title of the Frank Sinatra song and album (1966), a casual and not very exact connection to popular Western culture substituted for the return to classical roots.

52. Cynthia Simmons called these companions "doubles" of Venichka. See Simmons, *Their Fathers' Voice: Vassily Aksyonov, Venedikt Erofeev, Eduard Limonov, and Sasha Sokolov* (New York: Peter Lang, 1993), 76.

53. See Al'tshuller, "Moskva–Petushki," 84–85; Paperno and Gasparov, "Vstan' i idi," 399; and Cynthia Simmons, "An Alcoholic Narrative as 'Time Out' and the Double in *Moskva–Petushki*," *Canadian-American Slavic Studies* 24 (1990): 167.

54. The protagonist prefers "Venichka" to Venia or other more neutral and expected forms of his name, addressing himself as "Venichka" 21 out of 31 times in the text. See Natalia Vesselova, "Venichka, Venia, Venedikt Erofeev: The Paradigm of the Narrator's Name in *Moskva–Petushki*," *Essais sur le Discours de l'Europe Eclatée* 19 (2003): 33–39.

55. Remnick, "The Lush Life," 36–37.

56. Andrew Parker and Eve Kosofsky Sedgwick wrote about categories of constative and performative, the introversion and extroversion of the signifier, and the "mutual perversion" of those opposed categories in their introduction to *Performativity and Performance*, ed. Parker and Sedgwick (New York: Routledge, 1995), 3.

57. Eve Kosofsky Sedgwick, "Queer Performativity: Henry James's The Art of thc Novel," in *The Novel: An Anthology of Criticism and Theory, 1900–2000*, ed. Dorothy J. Hale (Malden, Mass.: Blackwell, 2006), 609.

58. Andreï Bitov, *La Maison Pouchkine: Roman de l'humiliation infinie*, trans. Philippe Mennecier (Paris: A. Michel, 1988).

59. Erofeev wrote in notebooks that "shame is the best of all 'noble feelings.' One can envy the dead many things, but not that they do not feel shame [*srama ne imut*]." The wording refers to the early chronicles that record what Prince Sviatoslav I supposedly said to his troops in 970 before fighting the Byzantines.

60. Venichka provides the first and last name of Turgenev, although there is hardly another, while he does not specify the names of Herzen and Ogarev, who took the oath as young teens together on Sparrow Hills. The formulations subtly suggest the canonical forms in which both have become part of Soviet culture: Venichka's linkage of them on the basis of shyness or modesty is his own.

See Vlasov's commentary for relevant points to which Venichka alludes (Vlasov, "Bessmertnaia," 200).

61. Sedgwick, "Queer Performativity," 609–10.

62. Ibid., 610.

63. Mikhail Epstein used the term "counter-irony" (*protivoironiia*), coined by Erofeev's friend Vladimir Muravev, to describe the particular tonal figure characteristic of Erofeev's style in "Posle karnavala," 171. Mark Lipovetskii visualized counter-irony as a downward- turned (*niskhodiashchiaia*) parabola in his article "S potustoronnei," 81.

64. Vladimir Tumanov explored the paradoxical effects of Venichka's contamination of I-now and I-then, with reference to Emile Benveniste's narratological categories. See Tumanov, "The End in V. Erofeev's 'Moskva–Petuski,'" *Russian Literature* 39 (1996): 8–9.

65. An actual monument was mounted ten years after Erofeev's death: two bronze statues of Venichka and his beloved, done by Iurii Kuznetsov and Sergei Mantselev, were unveiled in May 2000. The figure of lonely, hung-over Venichka trying to make his way to the train struck a popular chord. In fact, so many people expressed solidarity by drinking near the mock-up of the Venichka statue at the Kursk Station in Moscow that authorities demanded the removal of the monument from its original location. The two statues of Venichka and his beloved were removed from their original locations at the Kursk and Petushki train stations, respectively, and placed together on the Square of Struggle at the end of Dostoevsky Street in northwest Moscow. See the account by Anna Khrustaleva, "Otkryt pamiatnik Erofeevu," *Nezavisimaia gazeta* 86, no. 2148 (May 13, 2000): 2.

66. Vladimir Murav'ev, "Vysokikh zrelishch zritel'," in *Zapiski psikhopata*, 5–12, 9, 11.

67. See James Frazer, *The Golden Bough. A Study in Magic and Religion*, 3rd ed. (New York: Macmillan, 1935), vol. 2: 310–11, vol. 4: 113–14, and vol. 4: 232.

68. See the introduction for a discussion of novels in the Soviet context as the genre of the future, and, in the Socialist Realist variant, as codified ritual for Soviet education.

69. Much of what Erofeev wrote seemed like the opposite of the straightforward and positive character of the Soviet hero. Erofeev wrote in notebooks, "To the questions about 'one's identity' [*o 'sobstvennom ia'*] and so forth. I am the most wretched person to converse with for myself, but at any rate I know what I am about. I speak without mockery and without raising my voice." He also parodied the search for self and self transformation: "Overcoming one's identity [*svoe 'ia'*], finding one's identity and again losing it, pursuing oneself, acquiring oneself, again and finally overcoming one's identity, but then accidentally finding

it" (*Zapiski psikhopata*, 349, 350). More and more of Erofeev's notebooks have appeared since perestroika in Russian editions. The most complete seems to be Venedikt Erofeev, *Zapisnye knizhki* (Moscow: Zakharov, 2005).

70. Panchenko points out that one typically does not know when or where the holy fool dies ("Smekh," 84).

71. Jerusalem did not recognize the *kairos* of Jesus's coming to save it, and there can be no second chance (Luke 19:44), as described in the *Theological Dictionary of the New Testament*, ed. Gerhard Kittel, trans. Geoffrey W. Bromiley (Grand Rapids, Mich.: Wm. B. Eerdmans, 1965), vol. 3: 459.

72. See discussion of the relevant passages in *Theological Dictionary*, 3: 460.

73. Eric Charles White, *Kaironomia: On the Will-to-Invent* (Ithaca, N.Y.: Cornell University Press, 1987), 13.

74. The written text became, according to the romantic understanding, a transparent window into the mind of the author and/or protagonist. This romantic internalization of Shakespeare meant that *Hamlet* got taken over from a dramatic text into a text for silent reading. See Jonathan Bate, *The Genius of Shakespeare* (New York: Oxford University Press, 2008), 261.

75. The particular realization of the text depends also on the specificity of its printed version—versions vary. See Margreta De Grazia and Peter Stallybrass, "The Materiality of the Shakespearean Text," *Shakespeare Quarterly* 44, no. 3 (1993): 256–57. See also the Arden edition of *Hamlet* for discussion of variation.

76. Zorin repeated Erofeev's assertion about how the work was created, affirming this was "absolutely unofficial literature" ("Opoznavatel'nyi," 119).

77. Zorin, "Opoznavatel'nyi," 120. On the relation of unofficial Soviet literature to the absurd, see Savitskii (*Andegraund*, 141–64). Savitskii highlighted the work of Sergei Dovlatov, one of the few to appropriate successfully aspects of Venichka's persona.

78. Here and elsewhere I modify the very good Mulrine translation which captures the oral feel of the text particularly well. It seems one cannot resist trying to capture Erofeev's spirit in one's own voice.

79. Iurii Levin argued that Erofeev's particular style could be traced to the relatively widespread practice of ironic citation by members of the Soviet generation to which both Levin and Erofeev belonged. See Levin, "Semiosfera Venichki Erofeeva," in *Sbornik statei k 70-letiiu professora Iu.M. Lotmana*, ed. A. Mal'ts (Tartu: Tartuskii universitet, 1991), 498–99.

80. E. I. Orlova, "Posle skaza (Mikhail Zoshchenko—Venedikt Erofeev—Abram Terts," *Filologicheskie nauki* 6 (1996): 13–22.

81. Erofeev cited Blok and staged a humorous attempt to bring his Symbolist poetry close to regular people as represented by the Brigade crew. I mention El Lissitzky as a paradigmatic Constructivist creator in my discussion of the avant-garde in the introduction. Boris Groys stressed the reaction against that

kind of total mastery by artists of the historical avant-garde in what he calls "post-utopian" art. I treat that here as neo-avant-garde art, although Groys rejects the term, because in his opinion, "unofficial art . . . can by no means be considered a continuation of the avant-gardist impulse" (Groys, *The Total Art*, 78).

82. Marjorie Perloff drew on the description in Northrop Frye's *The Well-Tempered Critic* (Bloomington: Indiana University Press, 1963) of the "associative rhythm" of speech, which differs from the established rhythms of prose or verse. As Frye said, the unit of the associative rhythm is the "short phrase that contains the central word or idea aimed at, but is largely innocent of syntax. It is much more repetitive than prose, as it is in the process of working out an idea, and the repetitions are largely rhythmical filler." Erofeev's prose could be compared along these lines to what Frye called the "free prose" works by Robert Burton and Laurence Sterne, but it might also be considered alongside Erofeev's near-contemporaries among the neo-avant-garde poets analyzed by Perloff, including John Cage, Jackson Mac Low, Jerome Rothenberg, and David Antin. Perloff quoted Frye for this analysis in *The Poetics*, 39–40.

83. Translators of the French edition were Annie Sabatier and Antoine Pingaud. Their translation appeared subsequently as *Moscou-sur-vodka*, in 1990.

84. Remnick, "The Lush Life," 36–37.

85. Zorin, "Opoznavatel'nyi," 119.

86. Perestroika publications of *Moskva–Petushki* include the first, laughably inappropriate, serial publication in *Trezvost' i kul'tura* (*Sobriety and Culture*) 1–3 (1988), and publication in the almanac edited by Veniamin Kaverin, *Vest': Proza, Poeziia, Dramaturgiia* (Moscow: Knizhnaia palata, 1989, 418–506). The book appeared as a separate edition from the publisher Prometei (Moscow, 1989). By the 2000s, the publishing house Zakharov began to dominate publication of Erofeev's works in Russian. On the evening of the "Two Erofeevs," and Venedikt Erofeev's fame generally in this period, see Shmel'kova, "Ni tsenzor," 80, and passim).

87. Those presenting Erofeev in print beginning in perestroika include Igor' Bolychev, "Umru, no nikogda ne poimu . . ." (interview), *Moskovskie novosti* (December 10, 1989): 13. Irina Tosunian published "Ot Moskvy do samykh Petushkov" (interview), *Literaturnaia gazeta* (January 3, 1990): 5; she presented selections from his notebooks, "'. . . ia debelogvardeets'" (from notebooks), *Literaturnaia gazeta* (November 17, 1993): 6; "Dve bol'shikh, chetyre malen'kikh" (supposed excerpt from the "lost" novel *Dmitrii Shostakovich*) *Literaturnaia gazeta* (October 25, 1995): 6. Leonid Prudovskii published an interview with Erofeev that appeared in *Kontinent*—"Sumasshedshim mozhno byt' v liuboe vremia," 65 (1990): 411–30; and in the U.S.S.R. in *Aprel'*—"Zhit' v Rossii s umom i talantom . . ." 4 (1991): 236–50, before being republished in *Zapiski psikhopata*, 425–43.

88. As opposed to Aksenov, whose whole body of work receives attention, the majority of academic approaches to Erofeev overwhelmingly focus on *Moskva–Petushki*.

89. On Erofeev's invitations to France for an operation and the authorities' refusal to overlook gaps in his work record in order to grant him a visa, see the introduction.

CHAPTER FIVE

1. The chapter epigraph is from Viktor Krivulin, "Zolotoi vek samizdata," in *Samizdat veka*, ed. Anatolii Strelianyi et al. (Moscow: Polifakt, 1999), 342–54, esp. 343.

2. From Rubinshtein's paper for the 1988 conference "Chaos and Texts," entitled "Chto tut mozhno skazat' . . ." published in *Indeks (po materialom rukopisnykh zhurnalov)*, ed. Mikhail Romm and E. Bogatykh (Moscow: "Efa," 1990), 345–46. An English version appeared as "What Can One Say?" trans. Gerald J. Janecek, in *Re-Entering the Sign: Articulating New Russian Culture*, ed. Ellen E. Berry and Anesa Miller-Pogacar (Ann Arbor: University of Michigan Press, 1995), 214.

3. Bourdieu argued that in the case of the autonomous field of cultural production, "the economy of practices is based . . . on a systematic inversion of the fundamental principles of all ordinary economies." Thus, such production does not guarantee any correspondence between investments and monetary gains and it does not seek any immediate forms of honor or cultural authority from the existing establishment (*The Field*, 39).

4. Andrei Sinyavsky, "Dissent as a Personal Experience," *Dissent* 31, no. 2 (1984): 152–61, esp. 154. Siniavskii's dissidence is discussed more fully in the introduction and chapter 1.

5. Rubinshtein, "Chto," 345–46; and "What," 214.

6. "In a sense," said Nadezhda Mandelshtam, "we really do live in a pre-Gutenberg [*dopechatnaia*] era" (*Hope*, 380). The phrase "pre-Gutenberg" is relatively widely invoked for late Soviet culture and commonly attributed to Akhmatova. Viacheslav Ivanov wrote of visiting Akhmatova and seeing one of Brodsky's poems in her room. He knew the poem must have been written just days before in prison and expressed amazement at the speed with which items circulated. Akhmatova commented, "We live according to the slogan 'Down with Gutenberg!'" Ivanov also recalled that "she [Akhmatova] often repeated the contention that people read verses because they are not printed." From Ivanov, "Besedy s Annoi Akhmatovoi," www.akhmatova.org/articles/ivanov.htm.

7. Some scholars have emphasized the connections with earlier periods, including the persecution of writers in the immediate postrevolutionary and early Soviet years, and even back to religious dissent centuries before, as did Dmitri

Pospielovsky, "From Gosizdat to Samizdat and Tamizdat," *Canadian Slavonic Papers* 20, no. 1 (1978): 44–62, esp. 46.

8. The technological means for producing uncensored works in this period differed among Eastern European countries, but Soviet samizdat served as a basic model and impetus. For a comparative view, see Gordon Skilling, *Samizdat and an Independent Society in Central and Eastern Europe* (Columbus: Ohio State University Press, 1989); and *From Samizdat to Tamizdat: Transnational Media during and after Socialism*, ed. Friederike Kind-Kovács and Jessie Labov (New York: Berghahn Books, 2013).

9. Khrushchev's denunciation of Stalin unleashed a flood of personal accounts and responses to what had happened, but the Party's efforts following the speech to clamp down on dissent and discussion of Stalin tended to force discussion out of the official public sphere just at the time when people began vigorously to question the past and Soviet authority. See Polly Jones, "From the Secret Speech to the burial of Stalin: real and ideal responses to de-Stalinization," in *The Dilemmas of De-Stalinization*, ed. Polly Jones (London and New York: Routledge, 2006), 47, 54–55.

The staff of Radio Liberty spoke of the text of Khrushchev's Secret Speech, which was leaked beyond Party members and out to the *New York Times*, as the "first samizdat," although the term "samizdat" was not in use at that time. From the "Archival History of Samizdat Archives at the Open Society Archives," http://www.osa.ceu.hu/db/fa/300–85.htm.

10. Glazkov's often deliberately clumsy verse includes a poem called "Samsebiaizdat": "Samsebiaizdat is to me as dear, As tomorrow's roads are clear . . ." (*Samsebiaizdat mne tak zhe dorog, / Kak nachalo zavtrashnikh dorog* . . .). The typescript of "Samsebiaizdat," beginning "I'm sick of the sins of my youth . . ." ("*Nadoeli iunosti grekhi* . . ."), undated, but probably from the mid-1950s, can be found in the Historical Archives of the Research Center for East European Studies, University of Bremen, Germany, F. 105 (Albert B. Rusanov). Thanks to archivist Gabriel Superfin for bringing it to my attention.

11. On limited use of the term "samizdat" in some groups of Moscow intelligentsia at the end of the 1950s, see Aleksandr Daniel', "Istoki i smysl sovetskogo samizdata," in *Antologiia samizdata: Nepodtsenzurnaia literatura v SSSR, 1950-e–1980-e*, 3 vols., ed. V. V. Igrunov and M. S. Barbakadze (Moscow: Mezhdunarodnyi institut gumanitarno-politicheskikh issledovanii, 2005), 18. Nina Voronel had friends among those who would be in the Moscow democratic movement. In 1961, she said, there was none of what they would later call "samizdat": only a few daring souls would pass unpublished verses of Pasternak, Mandelshtam, and Tsvetaeva. See Nina Voronel', *Bez prikras: Vospominaniia* (Moscow: Zakharov, 2003), 137.

12. Julius Telesin, "Inside 'Samizdat,'" *Encounter* (February 1973): 25–33, esp. 25.

13. From "Zapiska KGB pri Sovete Ministrov SSSR ot 21 dekabria 1970 g., No. 3461-A," a document in the Bukovskii archive. The document included estimates on the growing geographic range of samizdat. Alexander Gribanov discussed this document, the earliest known discussion of samizdat as such in KGB papers: "Samizdat According to Andropov," trans. Masha Kowell, *Poetics Today* 30, no. 1 (2009): 89–106.

14. Gene Sosin, *Sparks of Liberty: An Insider's Memoir of Radio Liberty* (University Park: Pennsylvania State University Press, 1999), 114–15.

15. On March 16, 1971, Albert Boiter wrote from Munich to Richard Pipes at Harvard regarding his impression that "the samizdat phenomenon is on the verge of more systematic and even large-scale exploitation by many European research institutions." A London seminar in April of that year led to plans for publishing samizdat, drawn up by Peter Reddaway and circulated to a number of academic specialists including Bohdan Bociurkiw, Albert Boiter, Michael Bourdeaux, Abraham Brumberg, Ellen de Kadt, Peter Dornan, Max Hayward, Ed Kline, Leopold Labedz, Richard Pipes, Michael Scammell, Leonard Schapiro, Jack Stewart, Julius Telesin, Boris Tsukerman, and Karel van het Reve (Radio Liberty Corporate Files, Box 17, File 294.7, Hoover Institution). Boiter's published account appeared as "Samizdat: Primary Source Material in the Study of Current Affairs," *Russian Review* 31, no. 3 (1972): 282–85. A fuller retrospective look can be found in Olga Zaslavskaya, "From Dispersed to Distributed Archives: The Past and the Present of Samizdat Material," *Poetics Today* 29, no. 4 (Winter 2008): 685–87.

16. From the "Survey of Samizdat for 1968," quoted by Peter Reddaway in his introduction to *Uncensored Russia: The Human Rights Movement in the Soviet Union: The Annotated Text of the Unofficial Moscow Journal "A Chronicle of Current Events" (Nos. 1–11)*, trans. and ed. Peter Reddaway (London: Jonathan Cape, 1972), 35. For the Russian texts of *Khronika*, see www.memo.ru/history/diss/chr/index.htm.

17. Andrei Amalrik described the development of "opposition" in these terms in *Will the Soviet Union Survive Until 1984?* (New York: Harper and Row, 1970), 7–9. Michael Meerson-Aksenov repeated the formulation, stipulating that in fact the activity had spiritual sources, and that the repressive government made it "political": "In general, culture does not touch on politics. It is only totalitarian government that transforms culture into a political means and thus makes the independent artist its enemy." From "The Dissident Movement and Samizdat," in *The Political, Social and Religious Thought of Russian 'Samizdat'—An Anthology*, ed. Michael Meerson-Aksenov and Boris Shragin, trans. Nickolas Lupinin (Belmont, Mass., 1977), 19–49, esp. 29–30. Aleksandr Daniel' also characterized opposition as "literaturocentric" prior to the end of the 1960s. See Daniel', "Istoki," 26.

18. The *Chronicle* became its own sort of institution as the most established

and central of the Soviet samizdat editions. Amnesty International published the English translation, beginning with issue 17, as *A Chronicle of Current Events* (London, 1971–83). The British publication *Index on Censorship*, which began in 1972, regularly announced the appearance of issues of the *Chronicle* and featured news items taken from them (see the section "Index Index"). The *Chronicle*, almost exclusively among samizdat editions, achieved the status of a primary source of information because of its acknowledged reliability. Liudmila Alekseeva used the *Chronicle* as the source of material for her history of dissidence (Alexeyeva, *Soviet Dissent*).

19. Dennis O'Keeffe, Helen Szamuely, et al., *Samizdat, Based on a Discussion at the CRCE Led by Dennis O'Keeffe and Helen Szamuely* (London: Centre for Research into Post-Communist Economies, 2004), 26.

20. "L'Affaire Solzhenitsyn," in *La Fabrique de l'histoire*, a program with Emmanuel Laurentin on the radio station France Culture, Paris (December 11, 2007).

21. Mikhail Kheifets, "Russkii patriot Vladimir Osipov: Chast' 2," *Kontinent* 28 (1981): 158.

22. See Nikolai Mitrokhin's analysis of competing accounts in *Russkaia partiia. Dvizhenie russkikh natsionalistov v SSSR. 1953–1985* (Moscow: Novoe literaturnoe obozrenie, 2003): 476–77.

23. From Solzhenitsyn's *Nobel Lecture*, trans. F. D. Reeve (New York: Farrar, Straus, and Giroux, 1972), 69. The quoted statement appears in this bilingual edition in all-caps.

24. Sosin, *Sparks of Liberty*, 7.

25. Elizabeth Eisenstein, *The Printing Press as an Agent of Change: Communication and Cultural Transformations in Early-Modern Europe* (Cambridge, Eng.: Cambridge University Press, 1979).

26. Eisenstein discussed dissemination (*The Printing Press*, 71–80), standardization (ibid., 80–88), and fixity (ibid., 113–26), linking this print culture to the Scientific Revolution and the Reformation.

27. Adrian Johns, *The Nature of the Book: Print and Knowledge in the Making* (Chicago: University of Chicago Press, 1998), 2.

28. Ibid., 5.

29. In this way, samizdat can be related to the recovery of a more materially sensitive and contingent history. Paula McDowell, for example, finds that in Daniel Defoe's writing "an orality that is in fact coexistent with and inseparable from print is ideologically relegated to the past. The identity of both print and orality has had to be made." Paula McDowell, "Defoe and the Contagion of the Oral: Modeling Media Shift in *A Journal of the Plague Year*," *PMLA* 121, no. 1 (2006): 87–106, esp. 92.

30. Viktor Krivulin, poet and organizer of Leningrad unofficial culture, resembled Andrei Bitov (see chapter 3) in taking a cue for his uncensored writ-

ing from Mandelshtam. Krivulin described his milieu and the "Golden Age" of samizdat: "This history begins from the voice and not from the manuscript" (Krivulin, "Zolotoi vek," 343). Krivulin's role is also discussed in the conclusion.

31. Although it was not discussed officially in the Soviet Union, such variation from the text occurred of course in Soviet print publishing. See, for example, Maurice Friedberg's analysis *Russian Classics in Soviet Jackets* (New York: Columbia University Press, 1962). Friedberg displayed a keen nose for the biases of Soviet print culture. For example, he discussed the taming of Ernest Hemingway's language in this line: "No matter how, a man alone ain't got no bloody fucking chance." See Hemingway, *To Have and Have Not* (New York: Scribner, 1937), 225. In Russian translation the line read, "Still, a man alone can't do a damn thing [*ne mozhet ni cherta*]." From Kheminguei, *Sobranie sochinenii v chetyrekh tomakh* (Moscow: Goslitizdat, 1968), 631–32. In what Friedberg described as a "generally serious" Soviet study of Hemingway, the commentator treated the translation as the norm and the original as the departure, asserting, "In the original, Harry's last sentence is lexically sharply strengthened." Friedberg referred to Iu. Ia. Lidskii, *Tvorchestvo E. Khemingueia* (Kiev: Naukova dumka, 1973), 290. By contrast, in Friedberg's opinion, because of the lack of censorship, samizdat implied pure transmission. Friedberg referred to "an illegal samizdat translation of *For Whom the Bell Tolls* (presumably, faithful to the original) [that] circulated in the USSR some years prior to the appearance of the censored printed version in 1968." See Friedberg, *A Decade of Euphoria: Western Literature in Post-Stalin Russia, 1954–64* (Bloomington: Indiana University Press, 1977), 30–31.

32. Natal'ia Trauberg, "Vsegda li pobezhdaet pobezhdennyi? Natal'ia Trauberg o khristianskom samizdate," *Literaturnaia gazeta* (April 27–May 2, 2000): 11.

33. Viktor Fedoseev, a novelist, journalist, and editor of Jewish samizdat, recalled that a version of *Exodus* based on prison camp retelling inspired another, more explicitly Zionist version of the short samizdat text, once again omitting the romance between Ari and Kitty. It appears that several strikingly different versions of Leon Uris's novel circulated in samizdat beginning about 1963. On various versions and how we know about them, see Ann Komaromi, "Jewish Samizdat—Dissident Texts and the Dynamics of the Jewish Revival in the Soviet Union," in *The Jewish Movement in the Soviet Union*, ed. Yaacov Ro'i (Woodrow Wilson Center, 2012), 277–78.

34. Eisenstein pointed out that even if the meaning of "wide" dissemination might be debatable in the early years of print culture and in specific cases, the consequences of dissemination by print for all kinds of religious, judicial, political, and scholarly developments were enormous (Eisenstein, *The Printing Press*, 71–80).

35. Aleksandr Voronel praised the strength of typist Sara Shapiro's fingers for copying the samizdat journal he founded, *Jews in the USSR* (*Evrei v SSSR*,

Moscow, no. 1–20, 1972–79), but even she could produce only seven copies at a time. Interview with Voronel' (July 1, 2007). Konstantin Kuzminskii expressed amazement at the fact that Ester Veinger (most typists were women) typing on a Czech Consul typewriter could make eight or even nine copies. See his remarks in *Antologiia Golubaia laguna / The Blue Lagoon Anthology of Modern Russian Poetry*, vols. 1–5, ed. Konstantin K. Kuz'minskii and Grigorii L. Kovalev (Newtonville, Mass.: Oriental Research Partners, 1980–86), vol. 1: 28.

36. Leah Slovin described the photographic reproduction process as "heavy and expensive" for copies of *Exodus*. Her group took advantage of the possibility to mimeograph 300 copies. Such technology was rarely available to samizdat producers in the Soviet Union. Slovin was quoted by Leonard Schroeter, *The Last Exodus* (Seattle: University of Washington Press, 1979), 65.

37. Erofeev claimed that the manuscript of his novel *Dmitrii Shostakovich* (1972) was stolen from him on an electric train in a bag with two bottles of vermouth. See Tosunian, "Ot Moskvy." Trauberg recalled doing Borges and Ionesco translations, which were, coincidentally, also lost in an electric train (Trauberg, "Vsegda").

38. Grigorenko did not, for example, speak about the broad unwillingness of Soviet troops to fight for the Soviet system as a contributing factor. That, he knew, would have landed him in a psychiatric hospital immediately. See Petro Grigorenko, *V podpol'e mozhno vstretit' tol'ko krys . . .* (Moscow: Zven'ia, 1997), 436–37.

39. Grigorenko, *V podpol'e*, 446–47.

40. Ibid., 447.

41. Ibid., 447–48.

42. Eisenstein, *The Printing Press*, 113–26.

43. Grigorenko, *V podpol'e*, 448.

44. The first authoritative edition of Mandelshtam's works was published by émigré scholars G. P. Struve and B. A. Filippov: Osip Mandel'shtam, *Sobranie sochinenii v trekh tomakh*, ed. G. P. Struve and B. A. Filippov (Washington, D.C.: Inter-Language Literary Associates, 1967). Max Hayward and Clarence Brown helped arrange the Western publication of Nadezhda Mandelshtam's memoirs (*Hope*).

45. The trial of Vladimir Maramzin was reported in issue 35 (March 31, 1975) of the *Chronicle of Current Events* (*A Chronicle*; *Khronika*).

46. Kuz'minskii and Kovalev, *Antologiia golubaia laguna*. Krivulin described Grigorii Kovalev as one of those who preserved a special Soviet unofficial oral tradition of poetry; Kovalev could reproduce not only the words of the poet, but also his manner of reading. See Krivulin, "Zolotoi vek samizdata," in *Samizdat veka*, ed. Anatolii Strelianyi et al. (Moscow: Polifakt, 1999), 344.

47. On the autonomous field of culture, see chapter 1 of this study. See also remarks about Viktor Krivulin and his fellows in Leningrad in the conclusion.

48. The phrase comes from Osip Mandelshtam. See the introduction.

49. Johns introduced the concept of piracy as central to his study (*The Nature of the Book*, xx).

50. O'Keeffe and Szamuely, *Samizdat*, 23.

51. Ibid., 23–24.

52. Reddaway, *Uncensored Russia*, 54.

53. Revol't Pimenov, "Vospominaniia, chast' 1: Odin politicheskii protsess (1956–1958)," *Pamiat': Istoricheskii sbornik* 2 (1979): 251.

54. Grigorenko, *V podpol'e*, 448.

55. There were about fifteen instances of the description "KGB falsification—missing" (*fal'shifka KGB—otsutsvuet*) out of about 1,700 items in the NTS samizdat register of items received prior to 1987, according to the register of documents in the NTS Samizdat Collection at the Hoover Institution. Since only register numbers appeared, one wonders what the missing items were and how they were determined to have been falsified.

56. Pimenov, "Vospominaniia," 251.

57. Liudmila Alekseeva, *Istoriia inakomysliia v SSSR: Noveishii period* (Moscow: ZAO RITS "Zatsepa," 2001), 265.

58. The series *Materialy samizdata* initially comprised bulletins for internal circulation among Radio Liberty staff, though the collection of these items was later made available through libraries. The series *Sobranie dokumentov samizdata* was made available from its inception to a small number of national and university libraries in Europe and the United States ("Archival History"). The purpose of the print publications was to make samizdat documents available to Western researchers, as discussed by Boiter, "Samizdat," 282. Belles lettres were not included, since those items posed copyright issues; also, they could in principle be published elsewhere. Some other types of samizdat, including Baptist and Jewish editions, were not generally included because other outlets distributed them.

59. Radio Liberty, "Basic Information about Arkhiv Samizdata," in *Arkhiv Samizdata: Register of Documents*, enlarged and revised (Munich: Samizdat Archive Association), 1973. These publications included "primarily documents of social, political, economic or historical significance" (ibid.).

60. Interview with Galina Salova, March 28, 2008.

61. L. N. Mitrokhin, *Baptizm* (Moscow: Izdatel'stvo politicheskoi literatury, 1966), 80–81.

62. Bourdeaux's book was *Opium of the People: The Christian Religion in the U.S.S.R.* (London: Faber and Faber, 1965). Bourdeaux described his history working in this area and the sequence of events surrounding his acquaintance with Vins in an interview, July 16, 2007.

63. Interview with Bourdeaux, July 16, 2007.

64. Pimenov, "Vospominaniia," 251.

65. Natalya Gorbanevskaia said in an interview with Michael Scammell after

she had left the Soviet Union, "The importance of the *Chronicle* lies . . . in its objective tone, objective, making no judgments. . . . I have to say that this tone was not always maintained. . . . And I think that it was my own fault because I, myself, saw every issue through to its final form and did not succeed in teaching anyone how to do it." See Gorbanevskaya, "Writing for 'Samizdat,'" *Index on Censorship* 6, no. 1 (1977): 34.

66. Richard Wurmbrand, *Tortured for Christ* (London: Hodder and Stoughton, 1967).

67. The abundant and emotional imagery on the pages of *Catacombes* as well as the reliance on emotional appeals and indictments contributed to the non-academic impression this publication produces. In *Catacombes* 15 (December 15, 1972: 12), the text apparently translated from the Baptist *Bulletin of Relatives of Prisoners* 1 (1972) is oddly accompanied by an image of the *Herald of Salvation* 1 (1972) with no indication these are in fact different publications.

68. Sosin, *Sparks of Liberty*, 125–28.

69. A variety of unofficial Soviet spokespersons have commented on this phenomenon, including Aleksandr Daniel', Andrei Siniavskii, and Viktor Krivulin. I discussed these statements in Ann Komaromi, "The Material Existence of Soviet Samizdat," *Slavic Review* 63, no. 3 (2004): 611–12.

70. Efimov wrote in early 1980 to Sergei Dovlatov that it was not in fact known what Carl Proffer liked in literature. See Dovlatov's *Epistoliarnyi roman s Igorem Efimovym* (Moscow: Zakharov, 2001), 73. Dovlatov wrote to Efimov in 1984 about his work for Radio Liberty, where they refused to admit criteria of taste at all: "Radio Liberty does not allow critical reviews of works. They think that Soviet authorities already criticize emigrants severely, although I think the Soviet authorities don't give a shit" (ibid., 320).

71. See Priscilla Meyer, "Hoist by the Socialist-Realist Petard: American Interpretations of Soviet Literature," *Russian Literature Triquarterly* 1 (1971): 420. Ardis set out to recover those overlooked treasures of the early Soviet and Russian Silver Age periods. I wrote about their efforts in the article "Ardis Tamizdat Publishing: Giving Back Russian Literature," in *From Samizdat to Tamizdat*, 27–50.

72. Ellendea Proffer outlined the development of the Ardis Publishing House project in the context of Russian contacts in her essay "Ardis," in the catalog *Ardis, 25 let russkoi literatury: Biblioteka inostrannoi literatury* (Library of Foreign Literature, Moscow, May 28, 1996–June 18, 1996), 2–10.

73. Geller, "'Pamiat' i 'pamiat,'" in *Vestnik RSKhD* 128 (1979): 192.

74. "Predislovie 'Ot redaktsii' k sb. 'Pamiat,'" *Russkaia mysl'* (April 14, 1977): 5. Arsenii Roginskii, formerly editor of the collection *Memory* and now chairman of the board of directors of the International Memorial society, said he and others working on the collection heard numerous oral reports about people seeing smoke from the fires and bits of burned documents in both 1941 and 1953.

Later archival investigations confirmed that large caches of documents were burned, though details of the events have not been published. From an interview with Roginskii, April 3, 2008. Of course, voluminous archives remain and the practical problem today is more one of access to them than absence of records.

75. "Predislovie 'Ot redaktsii' k sb. 'Pamiat.'"

76. Interview with Roginskii, April 3, 2008.

77. Copies of the four issues can be found in the second issue of the publication *Evreiskii samizdat* (1974), where the title pages are reproduced.

78. Samuel Moyn, *The Last Utopia: Human Rights in History* (Cambridge, Mass.: Belknap, 2010).

79. Igor' Ratmirov, "RePatria," *Materialy samizdata* 25 (1975): 63–65. *RePatria*, the only known samizdat periodical publication of the Soviet German movement, was republished in somewhat shortened form in *Volnoe slovo* 16 (1975). Ratmirov's review appeared in number 2 of the Russian patriotic samizdat journal *Zemlia* (consulted in the Samizdat Archives, RFE/RL, Open Society Archives, AS 2060).

80. In issue 36 of the émigré journal *Kontinent* (1986), for example, the ad for issue 9 of *Nadezhda* exorted readers: "Acquire them to send to Russia. Send us your offering for the same goal."

81. Krakhmalnikova was quoted by Tatiana Goricheva in her foreword to an English-language edition of selections from *Hope* called *Cry of the Spirit: Christian Testimonies from the Soviet Union*, ed. Tatiana Goricheva (London: Fount Paperbacks, 1989), 8.

82. NTS had a long history of projects to get texts into the U.S.S.R. with the express goal of fomenting subversive political activity there. V. D. Poremskii of NTS formulated a "molecular theory" as part of his "theory of revolution in the conditions of a totalitarian regime." See *NTS: Mysl' i delo, 1930–2000*, Bibliotechka rossievedeniia series, vol. 4 (Moscow: Posev, 2000), 32–33. In an effort to reach (ideally) every single Soviet citizen individually, NTS launched a series of air balloons that between 1951 and 1957 carried 97.4 million leaflets, 7.7 million newspapers, and 930,000 brochures and journals into the Soviet Union. The Americans, from whom NTS received support, demanded that they stop in 1957, because the balloons interfered with U2 spy planes (ibid., 37).

The publications from Posev publishing, begun in 1952, included a good deal of non-political material, though some things, like the samizdat journal of poetry *Sintaksis*, published in number 58 of the Posev journal *Grani* (1965), were framed in a provocative political way that was dangerous for many writers in the Soviet Union. See details of the Posev publishing activity in M. V. Gorbanevskii et al., *Svobodnoe slovo 'Poseva.' 1945–1995* (Moscow: Posev, 1995).

83. Zoia Krakhmal'nikova, ed., *Nadezhda: Khristianskoe chtenie*, vol. 6 (Frankfurt am Main: Posev, 1981).

84. There were eight issues of *Iskusstvo kommuny* in 1962 and six more in

1963, numbered 1–6 for that year as well as parenthetically, to refer back to the edition from 1919: 19 (original issues) + 8 (issues in 1962) + 6 = 33.

85. Iurii Freidin, interview with author, April 6, 2008. Aleksandr Melamid, Natalia Gorbanevskaia, and Liudmila Petrushevskaia were all part of the group that gathered to read and discuss at evenings featuring the launch of separate issues, "Zhurnal 'IK,'" in *Parallelnaia kul'tura*, ed. V. S. Gribkov, L. A. Melamid, and V. M. Petrov (Moscow: Smysl, 1999), 4.

86. Original copies of the journal *Iskusstvo kommuny* can be found at the Historical Archive of the Forschungsstelle Osteuropa, University of Bremen, Fond 76 (V. M. Petrov, V. S. Gribkov, L. A. Melamid). The speech by Ilichev followed the meeting of Khrushchev and Ilichev with 600 representatives of the cultural intelligentsia at the Kremlin, March 7–8, 1963, the same event fictionalized by Aksenov in *The Burn*.

87. Martin Dewhirst, 2004 interview with Ia. Zykova for the Memorial Society, May 30, 2004.

88. O'Keeffe and Szamuely, *Samizdat*, 20.

89. Ibid., 20.

90. Interview with Martin Dewhirst, March 28, 2007.

91. O'Keeffe and Szamuely, *Samizdat*, 21.

92. O'Keeffe and Szamuely, *Samizdat*, 19.

93. For some indication of the extent and stakes of the involvement of intelligence agencies, so far as they are public knowledge, see Komaromi, "Ardis," 39. For a broader view of the Cold War context, including the activity of the "Congress for Cultural Freedom," see Frances Stonor Saunders, *The Cultural Cold War* (New York: New, 1999).

94. Calhoun summarized Bourdieu's forms of capital in "Habitus, Field, and Capital," 140.

95. Bourdieu wrote, "The art business, a trade in things that have no price, belongs to the class of practices in which the logic of the pre-capitalist economy lives on." The symbolic economy of cultural production functions on the basis of a "refusal" of the commercial. This is not a real negation of the "economic" interest that always haunts the most "disinterested" practices, given that symbolic capital functions as a sort of credit which "under certain conditions, and always in the long run" guarantees more material profits. Bourdieu denied, however, that this is "a simple 'dissimulation' of the mercenary aspects of the practice" (*The Field*, 74–75). The belief of the field represents its own type of labor, investing symbolic goods with value.

96. Johns argued: "A new historical understanding of print is needed. What will it look like? One immediately evident feature will be its regard for the labors of those actually involved in printing, publishing, and reading. Another will be its respect for their own representations of printing, embracing both its prospects and its dangers" (*The Nature of the Book*, 28).

97. Marcel Mauss, *The Gift: The Form and Reason for Exchange in Archaic Societies*, trans. W. D. Halls (1923–24; New York: Norton, 1990), 11.

98. Mauss, *The Gift*, 11–12.

99. Ibid., 24.

100. Editors of a special issue of *PMLA* devoted to the history of the book advocated a more material approach to that history on the basis of current critical imperatives: "Poststructuralism reinvented the articles of skepticism that bibliographers had long taken for granted: the instability of the text, the productivity of misreading, the slipperiness of authorial intention. The word *idea* in our title [the title of the special issue is "History of the Book and the Idea of Literature"] represents a bid to situate the study of material culture as a player in theoretical debates rather than as a bolt-hole from which to wait them out." "Introduction," *PMLA* 121, no. 1 (2006): 15.

101. Examples of such structuralist reading can be found in Claude Lévi-Strauss, *Introduction à l'oeuvre de Marcel Mauss* (Paris: Presses Universitaires de France, 1950); and Claude Lefort, "L'Échange ou la lutte des homes," *Temps Modernes* 6, no. 64 (1951): 1400–1417.

102. See Weber's "Préface à l'édition Quadrige," in Marcel Mauss, *Essai sur le don: Forme et raison de l'échange dans les sociétés archaïques* (Paris: Quadrige, 2007), 31.

103. Jacques Derrida, *Given Time: I. Counterfeit Money*, trans. Peggy Kamuf (Chicago: University of Chicago Press, 1992), 76.

104. Bourdieu wrote that interest as a motive for social life, including the interested "disinterest" of cultural activity, is historically contingent: "Far from being an anthropological invariant, interest is a historical arbitrary, a historical construction that can be known only through historical analysis, ex post, through empirical observation, and not deduced a priori from some fictitious—and so naively Eurocentric—conception of 'Man.'" Craig Calhoun discussed this quote in the context of cultural capital in "Habitus, Field, and Capital," 141–42.

CONCLUSION

1. The epigraph is from Sinyavsky, "Dissent as a Personal Experience," 154.

2. Bitov's narrator referred to the *stiliagi*, the early nonconformists of fashion, this way in *Pushkin House*. See chapter 3.

3. Bourdieu talked about Flaubert embarking on particular works as acting within a "space of possibles." He brought up this formulation to describe the literary field later as a set of position-takings inscribed into relationships on the field. The value of those positions is determined in some distinctive way by the field, which mediates economic and political forces exerted from outside (*The Rules*, 88, 232–33).

4. On the concerted government campaign to suppress dissidents initiated

at the end of 1979, the time of the Soviet invasion of Afghanistan, see Alexeyeva, *Soviet Dissent*, 367–68.

5. Elena Strukova cataloged the much larger range of materials with far greater circulation of the alternative press that succeeded samizdat beginning in 1987, in *Al'ternativnaia periodicheskaia pechat' v istorii rossiiskoi mnogopartiinosti (1987–1996)* (Moscow: GPIB, 2005).

6. Calhoun, "Habitus, Field, and Capital," 136–37. Bourdieu contended that there are multiple autonomous fields functioning according to their own belief and with their particular form of capital (*The Field*, 162–64).

7. There were exceptions—for example, Oskar Rabin and other nonconformist artists joined the graphic artists' section of the Moscow Artists' Union in 1975. See Leonid Talochkin's description of the period in *Drugoe iskusstvo: Moskva 1956–76* (Moscow: SP Interbuk, 1991), vol. 1: 244. In Leningrad the officially registered literary association "Klub-81" facilitated the exchange of unofficial works. See *Samizdat Leningrada. 1950-e–1980-e. Literaturnaia entsiklopediia*, ed. D. Ia. Severiukhin et al. (Moscow: Novoe Literaturnoe Obozrenie, 2003), 410–13. Both instances illustrate the kind of working compromise authorities came to with uncensored artists and writers as they sought to keep a better eye on uncensored culture by letting it go on under an official roof.

8. I catalogued samizdat periodical editions for the database *Soviet Samizdat Periodicals*, launched September 2011, http://samizdat.library.utoronto.ca. The "Subject" filter indicates the range of different groups represented among the approximately 300 titles of journals, bulletins, and periodical collections described here.

9. Moyn, *The Last Utopia*.

10. Alekseeva discussed the publicizing of the persecution of Baptist and other religious believers in the Moscow *Chronicle of Current Events* as part of a concerted effort to widen the circle of contacts of Moscow rights activists with activists in other republics and groups (*Istoriia inakomysliia*, 254).

11. Krivulin is mentioned briefly in chapter 5, where I refer to his essay "Zolotoi vek samizdata." On Krivulin and the samizdat journal *37*, see Ann Komaromi, "Modernism and the Samizdat Journal *37*," in *Essays in Honor of Stanley J. Rabinowitz*, ed. Catherine Ciepiela and Lazar Fleishman (Stanford, Calif.: Stanford Slavic Series, 2014).

12. Krivulin, "Zolotoi vek," 350–51.

13. From the editorial statement at the end of *37* no. 5 (1976), copy in the Historical Archive of the Institute for the Study of Eastern Europe, University of Bremen, F. 75 (Groys, B. E.). An electronic publication of this samizdat journal is being prepared at the University of Toronto, in association with the database *Soviet Samizdat Periodicals*.

14. Dmitrii Volchek, for example, set the playful aesthetics of his samizdat journal *Mitia's Journal* (*Mitin zhurnal*) against what he and his peers perceived

to be the dissident engagement of Viktor Krivulin and Tatiana Goricheva, a position I discuss in "'Mitin zhurnal' i sposob bytovaniia teksta," in *Vtoraia kul'tura: Neofitsial'naia poeziia Leningrada v 1970–1980-e gody*, ed. Jean-Philippe Jaccard, Violaine Friedli, and Jens Herlth (St. Petersburg: Rostok, 2013), 148. Volchek in his conversation with "Rodion" named Arkadii Dragomoshchenko as the most important poet of their time. In a footnote he summarized the further oral discussion of whom they would like to "throw overboard," including Joseph Brodsky. From Volchek, "Gde shurshat plat'e," *Teatr* 4 (2011), http://oteatre.info/2011-4/, 41, and 43, footnote 4.

15. See discussion of Brodsky's case in the introduction.

16. I included all information I could find or elicit regarding the initial number of copies of samizdat journals (Komaromi, *Soviet Samizdat Periodicals*).

17. For example, the Leningrad journal *Hours* (*Chasy*) charged readers a fee to cover typing costs. See V. E. Dolinin and D. Ia. Severiukhin, "Preodolenie nemoty," and "*Chasy*," in *Samizdat Leningrada*, 28, 463–65. Krivulin, by contrast, boasted that all who worked on the journal *37*, including typists, did so because they believed in the endeavor, and thus took no fee. See Krivulin, "37, Severnaia pochta," in *Samizdat: Sbornik materialov*, 74–81, esp. 76.

18. E. R. Romanov (Ostrovskii), founder of the Russian émigré journal *Grani* (*Facets*, 1946–), talked about a bubble of interest of foreign publishers in uncensored Russian literature in the early 1970s. Solzhenitsyn's book on the Gulag enjoyed much attention, and Vladimir Maksimov's *Seven Days of Creation* landed a huge foreign contract. Disappointing sales, the recession, and more aggressive efforts by Soviet authorities to control publishing rights combined to help dampen prices, making the economic opportunities not as great as some writers in Russia had come to think. See Romanov's interview "Missiia 'Granei,'" in *Svobodnoe slovo 'Poseva,' 1945–1995*, ed. M. V. Gorbanevskii et al. (Moscow: Posev, 1995), 68–69.

19. As seen in the samizdat journal *Exodus* (*Iskhod*), mentioned in chapter 5.

20. Voronel moved away from his democratic friends to work more specifically on Jewish concerns. His own journal came to seem too "political," so the journal *Culture* (*Tarbut*) was begun in 1975 as a more "kosher" (i.e., less potentially inflammatory to Soviet authorities) alternative. I and others discussed these topics in *The Jewish Movement in the Soviet Union*, ed. Yaacov Ro'i (Woodrow Wilson Center, 2012).

21. The 1973 Jackson-Vanik amendment linked most-favored-nation status in U.S. trade agreements to human rights, putting pressure on the Soviets to allow emigration of Jews and other groups who wanted to leave. On Sakharov's influential letter to Congress in favor of the bill with the amendment, see Gal Beckerman, *When They Come for Us We'll Be Gone: The Epic Struggle to Save Soviet Jewry* (Boston: Houghton, Mifflin, Harcourt, 2010), 299–300. Pauline Peretz also outlined the trajectory of the bill in *Le combat pour les Juifs sovié-*

tiques: Washington-Moscou-Jérusalem, 1953–1989 (Paris: Arman Colin, 2006), 236, 248. The impact of the trade reform was not as unambiguously positive as supporters hoped.

22. On Dewhirst and Ardis, see chapter 5. Edward Kline was on the board of directors of Amnesty's American chapter, and he headed up Chekhov Publishing beginning in 1968, using his own means and some U.S. government funds received through the Ford Foundation to publish works by Andrei Sakharov, Nadezhda Mandelshtam, and the Russian version of the *Chronicle of Current Events* (interview with Kline, February 2005).

23. Bourdieu, *The Rules*, 343.

24. Bourdieu, *The Rules*, 343–44. Bourdieu introduced his "Postscript" by saying, "Those I am addressing here are not all those who conceive of culture as a patrimony, a dead culture to be made into an obligatory cult of ritual piety, or as an instrument of domination and distinction, cultural bastion and Bastille . . . but rather those who conceive of culture as an instrument of freedom presupposing freedom, as a *modus operandi* allowing the permanent supersession of the *opus operatum*, of the desolate, cultured 'thing.'" He hoped they would validate the right he takes in the "Postscript" to "call for the modern incarnation of the critical power of intellectuals, a 'collective intellectual' who might be capable of making a discourse of freedom heard" (*The Rules*, 339–40).

25. In particular, Bourdieu reflected on his attachment to categories of class for critique in the foreword to the English edition of *Distinction*: "I realize how much the specificity of the French intellectual field may have contributed to the conception of this book . . . by seeking in the structure of the social classes the basis of the systems of classification which structure perception of the social world." Nevertheless, he asserted that the *method* (as opposed to the *theory*) of objectifying mental structures associated with the particularity of a social world could provide a salutary example of a critical intervention susceptible of effective translation across the boundaries of nation and social system. See his *Distinction: A Social Critique of the Judgement of Taste* (Cambridge, Mass.: Harvard University Press, 1984), xiii–xiv.

26. Roland Barthes made this claim, referring to the mythologized "Author-God" who releases a "theological" meaning, in "The Death of the Author," in *Image, Music, Text*, ed. and trans. Stephen Heath (New York: Hill and Wang, 1977), 146.

27. Bakhtin clearly distinguished dialogue from dialectics later in his career: "Dialogue and dialectics. Take a dialogue and remove the voices (the partitioning of voices), remove the intonations (emotional and individualizing ones), carve out abstract concepts and judgments from living words and responses, cram everything into one abstract consciousness—and that's how you get dialectics," in "From Notes Made in 1970–71," in *Speech Genres and Other Late Essays*, trans. Vern McGee (Austin: University of Texas Press, 1986), 147. Mor-

son and Emerson discussed the crucial distinction and explored the ways in which Bakhtin tried to think through the interaction of self and other in dialogue: not monadic entities, these subjectivities also do not resolve into a unitary synthesis. See their *Mikhail Bakhtin*, 49, 51.

28. See Morson and Emerson on Bakhtin's notion of enduring works and evolving potentials, *Mikhail Bakhtin*, 287.

29. It is worth noting that Bourdieu remained consistently interested in the status of the subject (*le sujet*) and the relationship to time, interrogating these two topics over the length of his career as sociological theorist and ethnographic researcher. See Patrick Champagne and Olivier Christin, *Mouvements d'une pensée: Pierre Bourdieu* (Paris: Bordas, 2004), 25.

30. See Edith W. Clowes, *Russia on the Edge: Imagined Geographies and Post-Soviet Identity* (Ithaca, N.Y.: Cornell University Press, 2011), 2–3.

31. Ibid., 4.

32. Joseph Frank's famous essay on "Spatial Form in Modern Literature" can be found in *The Widening Gyre: Crisis and Mastery in Modern Literature* (New Brunswick, N.J., 1963). See chapter 2 on Aksenov's intentions and a spatial view of the novel as an illuminated page of scripture.

33. I discussed the creation of alternative chronologies in samizdat as part of imagining community differently from what Benedict Anderson described as a national imagination of unified time signified by the date at the top of print periodicals, in "Jewish Samizdat," 297.

34. See, for example, Golnaz Esfandiari, "The Twitter Devolution," *Foreign Policy* (June 7, 2010), http://www.foreignpolicy.com/articles/2010/06/07/the_twitter_revolution_that_wasnt; and Malcolm Gladwell, "Small Change: Why the Revolution Will Not Be Tweeted," *The New Yorker* (October 4, 2010), http://www.newyorker.com/reporting/2010/10/04/101004fa_fact_gladwell?currentPage=all.

35. Lisa Gitelman, *Always Already New: Media, History and the Data of Culture* (Cambridge, Mass.: MIT Press, 2006), 7.

36. Henry Jenkins argued that the circulation of media content across different platforms depends on active audience participation, and that this represents a cultural shift more than a convergence of technologies, per se. See Jenkins, *Convergence Culture: Where Old and New Media Collide* (New York: New York University Press, 2006), 3. See chapter 1 of Jenkins's book on "knowledge communities" and the kind of work they do as an adjunct to the "expert paradigm" of authoritative knowledge (ibid., 52).

37. In the Jewish movement, Michael Beizer and Yuli Kosharovskii are examples of those who pursued additional training and work as historians of Jews in Petersburg or the Jewish movement in the Soviet Union, respectively. Cognate examples can be found among Lithuanian dissidents, rock music fans in the U.S.S.R., and other groups.

38. Henry Jenkins talked about "participatory culture" in *Convergence Cul-*

ture. His current research group, based at the University of Southern California and devoted to "Youth Participatory Politics" examines the relationship between participatory culture and participatory politics, as reported in the talk "From Culture Jamming to Cultural Acupuncture: Fan Activism and the Civic Imagination," Stanford Humanities Center, May 27, 2014.

39. A three-year study of the Russian Internet concluded in 2012 found a "vibrant and diverse networked public sphere that constitutes an independent alternative to the more tightly controlled offline media and political space, as well as the growing use of digital platforms in social mobilization and civic action." The authors cautioned, however, that the current degree of freedom was "in no way a prediction of the future of this contested space." See Karina Alexanyan et al., "Exploring Russian Cyberspace: Digitally-Mediated Collective Action and the Networked Public Sphere" (Berkman Center Research Publ. No. 2012–2, March 2, 2012), http://papers.ssrn.com/sol3/papers.cfm?abstract_id=2014998. The study's warning seems increasingly relevant as Russian officials threaten digital platforms. See "Zamglavy Roskomnadzora Ksenzov poluchil vygovor za Facebook i Twitter," *The Russian Times* (May 17, 2014), http://therussiantimes.com/news/10854.html.

40. Ethan Zuckerman, "Intermediate Censorship," in *Access Controlled: The Shaping of Power, Rights, and Rule in Cyberspace*, ed. Ronald J. Deibert et al. (Cambridge, Mass.: MIT Press, 2010), 71–85, http://www.access-controlled.net/wp-content/PDFs/chapter-5.pdf.

41. Gladwell, "Small Change."

42. Heather Long discussed Covergirl's "Capitol Collection" ad campaign based on inverted values taken from the Hunger Games films. Covergirl suggested that with their products a client could look like one of the corrupted elite of the capitol. See Long's "Total Misfire," *The Guardian* (November 22, 2013), http://www.theguardian.com/commentisfree/2013/nov/22/hunger-games-catching-fire-covergirl-subway-nerf-ads. By contrast, the coverage of Patagonia's campaign for corporate responsibility has been quite positive, yet buying nicely packaged luxury goods is not "participatory culture" in the grassroots sense. I am indebted to Jenkins's talk ("From Culture Jamming") and discussion for these examples.

43. See The Harry Potter Alliance, http://thehpalliance.org/.

Bibliography

Aksenov, Vasilii. "Amerikanskim pisatelem ia tak i ne stal." *Inostrannaia literatura* 1 (2003). http://magazines.russ.ru/inostran/2003/1/aksen.html.

———. "Kruglye sutki non-stop." *Novyi mir* 8 (1976): 51–122.

———. "Krylatoe vymiraiushchee." *Literaturnaia gazeta* 47, no. 5373 (November 27, 1991): 2.

———. "Mne dorogi sud'by romana." *Literaturnaia gazeta* 103 (August 27, 1963).

———. *Novyi sladostnyi stil'*. Moscow: Izdatel'stvo "Izograf", 1997.

———. *Ozhog: Roman v trekh knigakh, Pozdnie Shestidesiatye, Rannie Semidesiatye*. Ann Arbor, Mich.: Ardis, 1980.

———. "Zima trevogi nashei, ili kak marksist Nikita uchil pisatelei partiinoi pravde." *Strelets* 1, no. 65 (1991): 182–202.

Aksyonov, Vassily. *The Burn: A Novel in Three Books (Late Sixties–Early Seventies)*. Trans. Michael Glenny. New York: Random House, 1984.

———. "An Exile in Literary America." *New York Times* (April 14, 1985): A52.

———. *In Search of Melancholy Baby*. New York: Random House, 1987.

———. Interview by Don Swaim, November 1983. http://www.wiredforbooks.org/vassilyaksyonov/.

———. *The New Sweet Style: A Novel*. Trans. Christopher Morris. New York: Random House, 1999.

———. "A Soviet Émigré Takes the A-Train." *New York Times* (May 3, 1987): SM60.

———. *Surplussed Barrelware*. Ed. and trans. Joel Wilkinson and Slava Yastremski. Ann Arbor, Mich.: Ardis, 1985.

Alexanyan, Karina et al. "Exploring Russian Cyberspace: Digitally-Mediated Collective Action and the Networked Public Sphere." Berkman Center Research Publication, No. 2012–2, March 2, 2012. http://papers.ssrn.com/sol3/papers.cfm?abstract_id=2014998.

Alekseeva, Liudmila. *Istoriia inakomysliia v SSSR: Noveishii period*. Vilnius-Moscow: Vest', 1992.

Alexeyeva, Ludmilla. *Soviet Dissent: Contemporary Movements for National, Religious, and Human Rights*. Trans. Carol Pearce and John Glad. Middletown, Conn.: Wesleyan University Press, 1985.

Al'tshuller, Mark. "'Moskva–Petushki' Venedikta Erofeeva i traditsii klassicheskoi poemy." *Novyi zhurnal* 146 (1982).

Amalrik, Andrei. *Notes of a Revolutionary*. Trans. Guy Daniels. London: Weidenfeld and Nicolson, 1982.

———. *Will the Soviet Union Survive Until 1984?* New York: Harper and Row, 1970.

Andropov, Iurii. "Doklad tovarishcha Iu.V. Andropova." *Izvestiia* 213, no. 18668 (September 10, 1977): 2.

Anisimov, I. "Leningradskii dialog o sovremennom romane." *Inostrannaia literatura* 11 (1963): 246–52.

Annenkov, Iurii. *Dnevnik moikh vstrech: Tsikl tragedii*. 2 vols. Moscow: Khudozhestvennaia literatura, 1990.

Bakhtin, Mikhail. *The Dialogic Imagination: Four Essays*. Trans. Caryl Emerson and Michael Holquist, 336. Austin: University of Texas Press, 1981.

———. *Problems of Dostoevsky's Poetics*. Ed. and trans. Caryl Emerson. Minneapolis: University of Minnesota Press, 1984.

———. *Problemy poetiki Dostoevskogo*. Moscow: Sovetskii pisatel', 1963.

———. *Problemy tvorchestva Dostoevskogo*. Leningrad: Priboi, 1929.

———. *Rabelais and His World*. Trans. Helene Iwolsky. Cambridge, Mass.: MIT Press, 1968.

———. *Speech Genres and Other Late Essays*. Trans. Vern McGee. Austin: University of Texas Press, 1986.

———. *Toward a Philosophy of the Act*. Trans. Vadim Liapunov, ed. Michael Holquist and Vadim Liapunov. Austin: University of Texas Press, 1993.

———. *Tvorchestvo Fransua Rable i narodnaia kul'tura srednevekov'ia i renessansa*. Moscow: Khudozhestvennaia literatura, 1965.

Bakich, Olga Hassanoff. "A New Type of Character in the Soviet Literature of the 1960s: The Early Works of Andrei Bitov." *Canadian Slavonic Papers* 23, no. 2 (1981): 125–33.

Barthes, Roland. "The Death of the Author." In *Image, Music, Text*, ed. and trans. Stephen Heath. New York: Hill and Wang, 1977.

Bate, Jonathan. *The Genius of Shakespeare*. New York: Oxford University Press, 2008.

Bauman, Zygmunt. "Second-Generation Socialism." In *Political Opposition in One-Party States*, ed. Leonard Schapiro. London: Macmillan, 1972.

Beckerman, Gal. *When They Come for Us We'll Be Gone: The Epic Struggle to Save Soviet Jewry*. Boston: Houghton, Mifflin, Harcourt, 2010.

Belyi, Andrei. *Petersburg*. Trans. Robert A. Maguire and John E. Malmstad. Bloomington: Indiana University Press, 1978.

Bencic, Ziva. "Obraz Venichki Erofeeva." *Russian Literature* 51 (2002): 243–60.

Beraha, Laura. "Out of and into the Void: Picaresque Absence and Annihilation." In *Venedikt Erofeev's "Moscow-Petushki": Critical Perspectives*, ed. Karen L. Ryan-Hayes. New York: Peter Lang, 1997.

———. "Roll Out the Barrels: Emptiness, Fullness, and the Picaresque-Idyllic Dynamic in Vasilii Aksenov's 'Zatovarennaia bochkotara.'" *Slavic Review* 56, no. 2 (1997).

Bethea, David. *The Shape of Apocalypse in Modern Russian Fiction*. Princeton, N.J.: Princeton University Press, 1989.

Bitov, Andrei. *Piatoe izmerenie: Na granitse vremeni i prostranstva*, 224–50. Moscow: Izdatel'stvo Nezavisimaia gazeta, 2002.

———. "Pokhval'noe slovo chudakam . . ." *Literaturnaia gazeta* 7 (September 1983): 5.

———. "Posleslovie: Razgovor s knigoizdatelem." In *Dachnaia mestnost' (Dubl')*. St. Petersburg: Fond russkoi poezii, 1999.

———. *Pushkinskii dom*. St. Petersburg: Izdatel'stvo Ivana Limbakha, 1999.

———. *Pushkin House*. Trans. Susan Brownsberger. Normal Ill.: Dalkey Archive, 1998.

———. *Pushkin House*. Trans. Susan Brownsberger. Ann Arbor, Mich.: Ardis, 1990.

Bloch, Sidney, and Peter Reddaway. *Soviet Psychiatric Abuse: The Shadow over World Psychiatry*. London: Gollancz, 1984.

Bloom, Harold. *Shakespeare: The Invention of the Human*. New York: Riverhead Books, 1998.

Bogdanova, O. V. *Roman A. Bitova 'Pushkinskii dom' ('Versiia i variant' russkogo postmoderna)*. St. Petersburg: Filologicheskii fakul'tet SPGU, 2002.

Bogomolov, N. A. "Blokovskii plast v 'Moskve-Petushkakh.'" *Novoe literaturnoe obozrenie* 44 (2000): 126–35.

Boiter, Albert. "Samizdat: Primary Source Material in the Study of Current Affairs." *Russian Review* 31, no. 3 (1972): 282–85.

Bolton, Jonathan. *Worlds of Dissent: Charter 77, The Plastic People of the Universe and Czech Culture under Communism*. Cambridge, Mass.: Harvard University Press, 2012.

Bolychev, Igor'. "Umru, no nikogda ne poimu . . ." Interview with Venedikt Erofeev. *Moskovskie novosti* (December 10, 1989): 13.

Bondarenko, Vladimir. "Podlinnyi Venichka: Razrushenie mifa." *Nash sovremennik* 7 (1999): 177–85.

Boobbyer, Philip. *Conscience, Dissent and Reform in Soviet Russia*. London: Routledge, 2005.

Borden, Richard. *The Art of Writing Badly: V. Kataev's Mauvism and the Rebirth of Russian Modernism*. Evanston, Ill.: Northwestern University Press, 1999.

Bourdeaux, Michael. *Opium of the People: The Christian Religion in the U.S.S.R.* London: Faber and Faber, 1965.

Bourdieu, Pierre, *Distinction: A Social Critique of the Judgement of Taste*. Cambridge, Mass.: Harvard University Press, 1984.

———. *The Field of Cultural Production: Essays on Art and Literature*. Ed. Randal Johnson. Oxford: Polity, 1993.

———. *Les règles de l'art: Genèse et structure du champ littéraire*. Paris: Éditions du Seuil, 1998.

———. *The Rules of Art: Genesis and Structure of the Literary Field*. Trans. Susan Emanuel. Stanford, Calif.: Stanford University Press, 1992.

Bourdieu, Pierre, and Loïc J. D. Wacquant. *An Invitation to Reflexive Sociology*. Chicago: University of Chicago Press, 1992.

Bowlt, John E., and Mark Konecny, eds. *A Legacy Regained: Nikolai Khardzhiev and the Russian Avant-Garde*. St. Petersburg: Palace Editions, 2002.

Boym, Svetlana. *Common Places. Mythologies of Everyday Life in Russia*. Cambridge: Harvard University Press, 1994.

Brodskii, Iosif. *Sochineniia*. 3 vols. St. Petersburg: Pushkinskii fond, 1992–94.

Brodsky, Joseph. *On Grief and Reason: Essays*. New York: Farrar, Straus, and Giroux, 1995.

Brown, Deming. "Vasili Aksenov at 33." *Russian Literature Triquarterly* 2 (1964).

Brown, Edward. "Review of *Pushkin House*, by Andrei Bitov." *The Nation* 246, no. 10 (March 12, 1988).

Bukovsky, Vladimir. *To Build a Castle: My Life as a Dissenter*. Trans. Michael Scammell. London: André Deutsch, 1978.

Bürger, Peter. *Theory of the Avant-Garde*. Trans. Michael Shaw. Minneapolis: University of Minnesota Press, 1984.

Calhoun, Craig. "Habitus, Field, and Capital." In *Critical Social Theory: Culture, History, and the Challenge of Difference*. Oxford: Blackwell, 1995.

Champagne, Patrick and Olivier Christin. *Mouvements d'une pensée: Pierre Bourdieu*. Paris: Bordas, 2004.

Chances, Ellen. *Andrei Bitov: The Ecology of Inspiration*. Cambridge, Eng.: Cambridge University Press, 1996.

———. "The Energy of Honesty, or Brussels Lace, Mandel'stam, 'Stolen Air,' and Inner Freedom: A Visit to the Creative Workshop of Andrej Bitov's *Puskinskij dom*." *Russian Literature* 51, no. 4 (2007): 503–29.

A Chronicle of Current Events 17–63. London: Amnesty International, 1971–83.

Chudakova, Marietta. "Pasternak i Bulgakov: Rubezh dvukh literaturnykh tsiklov." *Literaturnoe obozrenie* 5 (1991): 11–17.

Clark, Katerina. *The Soviet Novel: History as Ritual*. Chicago: University of Chicago Press, 1981.

Clowes, Edith W. *Russia on the Edge: Imagined Geographies and Post-Soviet Identity*. Ithaca, N.Y.: Cornell University Press, 2011.

Cooke, Olga M., and Rimma Volynska. "Interview with Vasilii Aksenov." *Canadian American Slavic Studies* 39, no. 1 (2005): 9–36.

Cooper, Douglas. *The Cubist Epoch*. New York: Phaidon, 1971.

Dalgard, Per. *The Function of the Grotesque in Vasilij Aksenov*. Trans. Robert Porter. Aarhus: Arkona, Denmark, 1982.

———. "Some Literary Roots." In *Vasiliy Pavlovich Aksenov: A Writer in Quest of Himself*, ed. Edward Mozejko, Boris Briker, and Per Dalgard. Columbus, Ohio: Slavica, 1984.

Daniel', Aleksandr. "Istoki i smysl sovetskogo samizdata." In *Antologiia samizdata: Nepodtsenzurnaia literatura v SSSR, 1950-e–1980-e*. 3 vols. Ed. V. V. Igrunov and M. S. Barbakadze. Moscow: Mezhdunarodnyi institut gumanitarno-politicheskikh issledovanii, 2005.

Daniel', Aleksandr, and Arsenii Roginskii, eds. *Piatoe dekabria 1965 goda v vospominaniiakh uchastnikov sobytii, materialakh Samizdata, dokumentakh partiinykh i komsomol"skikh organizatsii i v zapiskakh Komiteta gosudarstvennoi bezopasnosti v TsK KPSS*. Moscow: Zven'ia, 2005.

Debreczeny, Paul. "'*Zhitie Aleksandra Boldinskogo*': Pushkin's Elevation to Sainthood in Soviet Culture." In *Late Soviet Culture: From Perestroika to Novostroika*, ed. Thomas Lahusen and Gene Kuperman, 46–68. Durham, N.C.: Duke University Press, 1993.

De Grazia, Margreta, and Peter Stallybrass. "The Materiality of the Shakespearean Text." *Shakespeare Quarterly* 44, no. 3 (1993).

De Man, Paul. *Allegories of Reading: Figural Language in Rousseau, Nietzsche, Rilke, and Proust*. New Haven, Conn.: Yale University Press, 1979.

———. "Criticism and Crisis." In *Blindness & Insight: Essays in the Rhetoric of Contemporary Criticism*. New York: Oxford University Press, 1971.

———. "Dialogue and Dialogism." In *Rethinking Bakhtin: Extensions and Challenges*, ed. Gary Saul Morson and Caryl Emerson. Evanston, Ill.: Northwestern University Press, 1989.

———. "Phenomenality and Materiality in Kant." In *Hermeneutics: Questions and Prospects*, ed. Gary Shapiro and Alan Sica. Amherst: University of Massachusetts Press, 1984.

Derrida, Jacques. *Given Time: I. Counterfeit Money*. Trans. Peggy Kamuf. Chicago: University of Chicago Press, 1992.

Dershowitz, Alan M. *Chutzpah*. Boston: Little, Brown, 1991.

Dolinin, V., and B. Ivanov, eds. *Samizdat: Materialy s konferentsii "30 let nezavisimoi pechati. 1950–80 gody."* St. Petersburg: NITs "Memorial," 1993.

Dolinin, V. E., B. I. Ivanov, B. V. Ostanin, and D. Ia. Severiukhin. *Samizdat Leningrada, 1950-e–1980-e: Literaturnaia entsiklopediia*. Moscow: Novoe literaturnoe obozrenie, 2003.

Dostoevsky, Fedor. *Memoirs from the House of the Dead*. Trans. Jessie Coulson, ed. Ronald Hingley. Oxford: Oxford University Press, 1983.

Dostoevsky, Fyodor. "Pushkin (A Sketch)." In *A Writer's Diary*, vol. 2, trans. Kenneth Lantz. Evanston Ill.: Northwestern University Press, 1994.

Dovlatov, Sergei, *Epistoliarnyi roman s Igorem Efimovym*. Moscow: Zakharov, 2001.

Drugoe iskusstvo: Moskva 1956–76. 2 vols. Moscow: SP Interbuk, 1991.

Eichwede, Wolfgang, ed., *Samizdat: Alternative Kultur in Zentral- und Osteuropa: Die 60er bis 80er Jahre*. Bremen: Edition Temmen, 2000.

Eisenstein, Elizabeth. *The Printing Press as an Agent of Change: Communication and Cultural Transformations in Early-Modern Europe*. Cambridge, Eng.: Cambridge University Press, 1979.

Elsworth, John. "Andrei Bely's Theory of Symbolism." *Forum for Modern Language Studies* 11 (1975): 305–33.

Epstein, Mikhail. "Posle karnavala, ili vechnyi Venichka." In *Vera i obraz*. Tenafly, N.J.: Ermitazh, 1994.

———. *Postmodern v Rossii: Literatura i teoriia*. Moscow: Izdanie R. Elinina, 2000.

Erenburg, Il'ia. *Liudi, gody, zhizn'*. Moscow: Sovetskii pisatel', 1961.

Erofeev (see also Yerofeev), Benedict. *Moscow Circles*. Trans. J. R. Dorrell. London: Writers and Readers Publishing Cooperative, 1981.

Erofeev, Venedikt. *Moscow to the End of the Line*. Trans. William Tjalsma. New York: Taplinger, 1980.

———. *Moskva–Petushki*. In *Zapiski psikhopata*. Moscow: Vagrius, 2000.

———. *Moskva–Petushki: Roman-anekdot*. Petrozavodsk: A/O 'KAREKO,' 1995.

———. "Proza iz zhurnala *Veche*." In *Zapiski psikhopata*. Moscow: Vagrius, 2000.

———. "Through the Eyes of an Eccentric." In *The Penguin Book of New Russian Writing: Russia's Fleurs du Mal*, ed. Victor Erofeyev and Andrew Reynolds, 126–45. London: Penguin, 1995.

———. *Zapisnye knizhki 1960-kh godov*. Moscow: Zakharov, 2005.

Eroféiev, Vénédict. *Moscou–Pétouchki*. Trans. Annie Sabatier and Antoine Pingaud. Paris: Albin Michel, 1976.

Esfandiari, Golnaz. "The Twitter Devolution." *Foreign Policy* (June 7, 2010). http://www.foreignpolicy.com/articles/2010/06/07/the_twitter_revolution_that_wasnt.

Etkind, Efim. *Zapiski nezagovorshchika: Barselonskaia proza*. St. Petersburg: Akademicheskii proekt, 2001.

Evtushenko, Evgenii. "Fekhtovanie s navoznoi kuchei." *Literaturnaia gazeta* 4, no. 5330 (January 30, 1990): 7, 13.

Fanger, Donald, and Gordon Cohen. "Abram Tertz: Dissidence, Diffidence, and Russian Literary Tradition." In *Soviet Society and Culture: Essays in Honor of Vera S. Dunham*, ed. Terry L. Thompson and Richard Sheldon, 162–77. Boulder, Colo.: Westview, 1988.

Fedotov, G. P. "The Holy Fools." In *The Russian Religious Mind*. 2 vols. Cambridge, Mass.: Harvard University Press, 1966.

Foster, Hal. "What's Neo about the Neo-Avant-Garde?" In *The Duchamp Effect*, ed. Martha Buskirk and Mignon Nixon. Cambridge, Mass.: MIT Press, 1996.

Frank, Joseph. "The Voices of Mikhail Bakhtin." In *Through the Russian Prism: Essays on Russian Literature and Culture*. Princeton N.J.: Princeton University Press, 1990.

———. *The Widening Gyre: Crisis and Mastery in Modern Literature*. New Brunswick, N.J.: Rutgers University Press, 1963.

Fraser, Nancy. "Rethinking the Public Sphere: A Contribution to the Critique of Actually Existing Democracy." In *Habermas and the Public Sphere*, ed. Craig Calhoun, 109–42. Cambridge, Mass.: MIT Press, 1992.

Frazer, James. *The Golden Bough: A Study in Magic and Religion*. New York: Macmillan, 1935.

Fried, Michael. *Absorption and Theatricality: Painting and Beholder in the Age of Diderot*. Chicago: University of Chicago Press, 1980.

———. "Art and Objecthood." *Artforum* 5, no. 10 (1967): 12–23.

Friedberg, Maurice. *A Decade of Euphoria: Western Literature in Post-Stalin Russia, 1954–64*. Bloomington: Indiana University Press, 1977.

———. *Russian Classics in Soviet Jackets*. New York: Columbia University Press, 1962.

Frolova, Nina, et al. "Neskol'ko monologov o Venedikte Erofeeve." *Teatr* 9 (1991): 74–118.

Frye, Northrop. *The Well-Tempered Critic*. Bloomington: Indiana University Press, 1963.

Gaiser-Shnitman, Svetlana. *Venedikt Erofeev "Moskva–Petushki" ili "The Rest Is Silence."* Bern: Peter Lang, 1989.

Geller, Mikhail. "'Pamiat' i 'pamiat.'" *Vestnik RSKhD* 128 (1979): 192.

Ginzburg, Aleksandr, ed. *Belaia kniga o dele Siniavskogo i Danielia*. Frankfurt am Main: Posev, 1967.

Ginzburg, Eugenia. *Journey into the Whirlwind*. Trans. Paul Stevenson and Max Hayward. New York: Harcourt, Brace, Jovanovich, 1967.

———. *Within the Whirlwind*. Trans. Ian Bolan. New York: Harcourt Brace Jovanovich, 1981.

Ginzburg, Evgeniia. *Krutoi marshrut*. Milan: Mondadori, 1967.

Ginzburg, Lidiia, "Pole napriazheniia." *Literaturnaia gazeta* 3, no. 5069 (January 15, 1986): 7.

———*Prokhodiashchie kharaktery: Proza voennykh let: Zapiski blokadnogo cheloveka*. Moscow: Novoe izdatel'stvo, 2011.

———. *Zapisnye knizhki: Vospominaniia: Esse*. St. Petersburg: "Iskusstvo-SPB," 2002.

Ginzburg, Lydia. *On Psychological Prose*. Trans. Judson Rosengrant. Princeton, N.J.: Princeton University Press, 1991.

Gitelman, Lisa, *Always Already New: Media, History and the Data of Culture*. (Cambridge, Mass.: MIT Press, 2006.

Glad, John, ed. *Conversations in Exile: Russian Writers Abroad*. Trans. Richard Robin and Joanna Robin. Durham, N.C.: Duke University Press, 1993.

Gladwell, Malcolm. "Small Change: Why the Revolution Will Not Be Tweeted," *The New Yorker* (October 4, 2010). http://www.newyorker.com/reporting/2010/10/04/101004fa_fact_gladwell?currentPage=all .

Gogol, Nikolai. *Dead Souls*. Trans. David Magarshack. London: Penguin Books, 1961.

Gombrich, E. H. *Art and Illusion: A Study in the Psychology of Pictorial Representation*. New York, 1960.

Gorbanevskaya, Natalya. "Writing for 'Samizdat.'" *Index on Censorship* 6, no. 1 (1977): 29–36.

Gorbanevskii, M. V., et al. *Svobodnoe slovo "Poseva," 1945–1995*. Moscow: Posev, 1995.

Gribanov, Aleksandr. "Samizdat According to Andropov." Trans. Masha Kowell. *Poetics Today* 30, no. 1 (2009): 89–106.

Grigorenko, Petro. *V podpol'e vstretit' mozhno tol'ko krys*. New York: Izdatel'stvo Detinets, 1981.

Groys, Boris. *The Total Art of Stalinism: Avant-Garde, Aesthetic Dictatorship and Beyond*. Trans. C. Rougle. Princeton, N.J.: Princeton University Press, 1992.

Groys, Boris, David A. Ross, and Iwona Blazwick. *Ilya Kabakov*. London: Phaidon, 1998.

Guillory, John. "Bourdieu's Refusal." In *Pierre Bourdieu: Fieldwork in Culture*, ed. Nicholas Brown and Imre Szeman. Lanham, Md.: Rowman and Littlefield, 2000.

Gushchina, Tamara, "Venedikt Erofeev. Pis'ma k sestre" *Teatr* 9 (1992): 122–44.

Habermas, Jürgen. *The Structural Transformation of the Public Sphere: An Inquiry into a Category of Bourgeois Society*. Trans. Thomas Burger with Frederick Lawrence. Cambridge, Mass.: MIT Press, 1989.

Harris, Jane Gary. "Lidiia Ginzburg: Images of the Intelligentsia." In *The Russian Memoir: History and Literature*, ed. Beth Holmgren. Evanston, Ill.: Northwestern University Press, 2003.

Hellbeck, Jochen. *Revolution on My Mind*. Cambridge, Mass.: Harvard University Press, 2006.

Hemingway, Ernest. *To Have and Have Not*. New York: Scribner, 1937.

Hesse, Petra. "K funktsii 'probela' v neofitsial'noi literature 60-kh godov: *Moskva–Petushki* Venedikta Erofeeva." *Russian Literature* 43 (1998): 221–43.

Hirsch, Marianne. "The Generation of Postmemory." *Poetics Today* 29, no. 1 (2008): 103–28.

Hopkins, Mark W. *Russia's Underground Press: The Chronicle of Current Events*. New York: Praeger, 1983.

Ignatova, Elena. "Venedikt." *Neva* 1 (1993).

Igrunov, V. V., and M. S. Barbakadze, eds. *Antologiia samizdata: Nepodtsenzurnaia literatura v SSSR, 1950-e–1980-e*. 3 vols. Moscow: Mezhdunarodnyi institut gumanitarno-politicheskikh issledovanii, 2005.

Ivanov, Viacheslav. "Besedy s Annoi Akhmatovoi." www.akhmatova.org/articles /ivanov.htm.

Jackson, Matthew Jesse. *The Experimental Group: Ilya Kabakov, Moscow Conceptualism, Soviet Avant-Gardes*. Chicago: University of Chicago Press, 2010.

Jenkins, Henry. *Convergence Culture: Where Old and New Media Collide*. New York: New York University Press, 2006.

Johns, Adrian. *The Nature of the Book: Print and Knowledge in the Making*. Chicago: University of Chicago Press, 1998.

Johnson, D. Barton. "Vasilij Aksionov's Aviary: *The Heron* and *The Steel Bird*." *Scando-Slavica* 33 (1987): 45–61.

Johnson, Priscilla, and Leopold Labedz. *Khrushchev and the Arts: The Politics of Soviet Culture, 1962–1964*. Cambridge, Mass: MIT Press, 1965.

Jones, Polly. "From the Secret Speech to the Burial of Stalin: Real and Ideal Responses to De-Stalinization," *The Dilemmas of De-Stalinization. Negotiating Cultural and Social Change in the Khrushchev Era*, ed. Polly Jones. London and New York: Routledge, 2006.

Kaganskaia, Maiia. "Shutovskoi khorovod." *Sintaksis* 12 (1984).

Karabchievskii, Iurii. "Tochka boli: O romane Andreia Bitova 'Pushkinskii dom.'" *Grani* 106 (1977).

Karpenko, G. I. "Literaturnaia kritika 1960-kh godov o tvorchestve Vasiliia Aksenova." In *Vasilii Aksenov: Literaturnaia sud'ba*, ed. V. P. Skobolev and L. A. Fink, 16–24. Samara: Izdatel'stvo Samarskii universitet, 1994.

Kayser, Wolfgang. *The Grotesque in Art and Literature*. Trans. Ulrich Weisstein. Bloomington: Indiana University Press, 1963.

Kermode, Frank. *The Sense of an Ending*. New York: Oxford University Press, 1967.

Kharkhordin, Oleg. *The Collective and the Individual in Russia: A Study of Practices*. Berkeley: University of California Press, 1999.

Kheifets, Mikhail. "Russkii patriot Vladimir Osipov: Chast' 2." *Kontinent* 28 (1981).

Kheminguei, Ernest. *Sobranie sochinenii v chetyrekh tomakh*. Moscow: Goslitizdat, 1968.

Khronika tekushchikh sobytii 1–63 (1968–83). Memorial Society. www.memo.ru/history/diss/chr/index.htm.

Khrustaleva, Anna. "Otkryt pamiatnik Erofeevu." *Nezavisimaia gazeta* 86, no. 2148 (May 13, 2000): 2.

Kind-Kovács, Friederike Labov, and Jessie Labov, eds. *From Samizdat to Tamizdat: Transnational Media during and after Socialism*, 27–50. New York: Berghahn Books, 2013.

Kittel, Gerhard, ed. *Theological Dictionary of the New Testament*. Trans. Geoffrey W. Bromiley. Grand Rapids, Mich.: Wm. B. Eerdmans, 1965), vol. 3.

Komaromi, Ann. "Ardis Tamizdat Publishing: Giving Back Russian Literature." In *From Samizdat to Tamizdat: Transnational Media during and after Socialism*, ed. Friederike Kind-Kovács and Jessie Labov, 27–50. New York: Berghahn Books, 2013.

———. "Jewish Samizdat—Dissident Texts and the Dynamics of the Jewish Revival in the Soviet Union." In *The Jewish Movement in the Soviet Union*, ed. Yaacov Ro'i. Woodrow Wilson Center, 2012.

———. "The Material Existence of Soviet Samizdat." *Slavic Review* 63, no. 3 (2004).

———. "Modernism and the Samizdat Journal 37." In *Essays in Honor of Stanley J. Rabinowitz*, ed. Catherine Ciepiela and Lazar Fleishman. Stanford, Calif.: Stanford Slavic Series, 2014.

———. "Samizdat and Soviet Dissident Publics." *Slavic Review* 71, no. 2 (2012): 70–90.

———. "Samizdat as Extra-Gutenberg Phenomenon." *Poetics Today* 29, no. 4 (2008): 629–67.

———. "Soviet Samizdat Periodicals." Database. http://samizdat.library.utoronto.ca.

———. "The Unofficial Field of Late Soviet Culture." *Slavic Review* 67, no. 4 (2007): 605–28.

———. "Vasilii Aksenov and Evgeniia Ginzburg in Magadan: Re-Conceiving Authorship Through the Gulag Experience." *Gulag Studies* (November 2013).

Krakhmal'nikova, Zoia. *Cry of the Spirit: Christian Testimonies from the Soviet Union*. Ed. Tat'iana Goricheva. London: Fount Paperbacks, 1989.

———, ed. *Nadezhda: Khristianskoe chtenie* 1–14. Frankfurt am Main: Posev, 1978–88.

Krauss, Rosalind. *The Originality of the Avant-Garde and Other Modernist Myths*. Cambridge, Mass., 1991.

Krivulin, Viktor. "Zolotoi vek samizdata." In *Samizdat veka*, ed. A. Strelianyi et al. Moscow: Polifakt, 1999.

Kulle, Viktor. Review of *Antologiia samizdata: Nepodtsenzurnaia literatura v SSSR, 1950-e–1980-e*, ed. V. V. Igrunov and M. S. Barbakadze. 3 vols.

Moscow: Mezhdunarodnyi institut gumanitarno-politicheskikh issledovanii, 2005; also in *Novyi mir* 12 (2005): 182–83.

Kustanovich, Konstantin, *The Artist and the Tyrant: Vassily Aksenov's Works in the Brezhnev Era*. Columbus Ohio: Slavica, 1992.

Kuz'minskii, Konstantin, and Grigorii L. Kovalev, eds. *Antologiia Golubaia laguna / The Blue Lagoon Anthology of Modern Russian Poetry*, vols. 1–5. Newtonville, Mass.: Oriental Research Partners, 1980–86.

Lambert, Craig. "High Type Culture." *Harvard Magazine* (November 1997). http://harvardmagazine.com/1997/11/books.html.

Lauridsen, Inger, and Per Dalgard. "Interview with V.P. Aksenov." Trans. Margaret Bradley. In *Vasiliy Pavlovich Aksenov: A Writer in Quest of Himself*, ed. Edward Mozejko, Boris Briker, and Per Dalgard. Columbus, Ohio: Slavica, 1984.

Lavrov, Vladimir. "Tri romana Andreia Bitova, ili vospominaniia o sovremennike." *Neva* 5 (1997): 186–87.

Lefort, Claude. "L'Échange ou la lutte des homes." *Temps Modernes* 6, no. 64 (1951): 1400–1417.

Levin, Iurii. "Klassicheskie traditsii v 'drugoi' literature: Venedikt Erofeev i Fedor Dostoevskii." *Literaturnoe obozrenie* 2 (1992): 159–76.

———. "Semiosfera Venichki Erofeeva." In *Sbornik statei k 70-letiiu professora Iu.M. Lotmana*, ed. A. Mal'ts. Tartu: Tartuskii universitet, 1991.

Lévi-Strauss, Claude. *Introduction à l'oeuvre de Marcel Mauss*. Paris: Presses Universitaires de France, 1950.

Levitt, Marcus. *Russian Literary Politics and the Pushkin Celebration of 1880*. Ithaca, N.Y.: Cornell University Press, 1989.

Lidskii, Iu. Ia. *Tvorchestvo E. Khemingueia*. Kiev: Naukova dumka, 1973.

Lipovetskii, Mark. "S potustoronnei tochki zreniia: postmodernistskaia versiia dialogizma." In *Venedikt Erofeev's "Moscow-Petushki": Critical Perspectives*, ed. Karen Ryan-Hayes. New York: Peter Lang, 1997.

Long, Heather. "Total Misfire." *The Guardian* (November 22, 2013). http://www.theguardian.com/commentisfree/2013/nov/22/hunger-games-catching-fire-covergirl-subway-nerf-ads.

Losev, Lev. "Tulupy my." *Novoe literaturnoe obozrenie* 14 (1995): 209–16.

Lotman, Iu. M. "Russkaia literatura poslepetrovskoi epokhi i khristianskaia traditsiia." In *Iu. M. Lotman i tartusko-moskovskaia semioticheskaia shkola*, 364–79. Moscow: Gnozis, 1994.

Lúkacs, Gyorgy. *Studies in European Realism*. New York: Grosset and Dunlap, 1964.

Maccaby, Hyam. "The Delectable Daughter." *Midstream* 16, no. 9 (1970): 50–60.

Mal'tsev, Iurii. "Review of Vasilii Aksenov, *Ozhog*, Ann Arbor, Mich.: Ardis, 1980)," *Kontinent* 29 (1981): 403–6.

Mandel'shtam, Nadezhda. *Hope against Hope: A Memoir*. Trans. Max Hayward. New York: Atheneum, 1970.

———. *Vospominaniia*. New York: Izdatel'stvo. im. Chekhova, 1970.

Mandelshtam, Osip. "Chetvertaia proza." In *Sochineniia v dvukh tomakh*. Moscow: Khudozhestvennaia literatura, 1990.

———. "Fourth Prose." In *The Noise of Time*, ed. and trans. Clarence Brown. New York: Penguin, 1993.

———. *Sobranie sochinenii v trekh tomakh*. Ed. G. P. Struve and B. A. Filippov. Washington, D.C.: Inter-Language Literary Associates, 1967.

Mann, Iurii. *O groteske v literature*. Moscow: Sovetskii pisatel', 1966.

Martin, Douglas. "George C. Minden, 85, Dies; Led a Cold War of Words." Obituary in the *New York Times* (April 23, 2006).

Mathewson, Rufus W. *The Positive Hero in Russian Literature*. Evanston, Ill.: Northwestern University Press, 1975.

Mauss, Marcel. *Essai sur le don: Forme et raison de l'échange dans les sociétés archaïques*. Paris: Quadrige, 2007.

———. *The Gift: The Form and Reason for Exchange in Archaic Societies*. Trans. W. D. Halls. New York: Norton, 1990.

McGann, Jerome. *The Textual Condition*. Princeton, N.J.: Princeton University Press, 1991.

McKenzie, D. F. *Bibliography and the Sociology of Texts*. Cambridge, Eng.: Cambridge University Press, 1999.

Men'shutin, A., and A. Siniavskii. "Davaite govorit' professional'no." *Novyi mir* 8 (1961): 248–52.

———. "Za poeticheskuiu aktivnost' (Zametki o poezii molodykh)." *Novyi mir* 1 (1961): 224–41.

Meyer, Priscilla. "Aksenov and Soviet Literature of the 1960s," and "Interview with Vasily Pavlovich Aksenov." *Russian Literature Triquarterly* 5–6 (1973).

———. "Hoist by the Socialist-Realist Petard: American Interpretations of Soviet Literature." *Russian Literature Triquarterly* 1 (1971).

Mitrokhin, L. N. *Baptizm*. Moscow: Izdatel'stvo politicheskoi literatury, 1966.

Mitrokhin, Nikolai, *Russkaia partiia. Dvizhenie russkikh natsionalistov v SSSR. 1953–1985*. Moscow: Novoe literaturnoe obozrenie, 2003.

Morrison, Simon Alexander. *The People's Artist: Prokofiev's Soviet Years*. Oxford: Oxford University Press, 2009.

Morson, Gary Saul, and Caryl Emerson. *Mikhail Bakhtin: Creation of a Prosaics*. Stanford, Calif.: Stanford University Press, 1990.

———, eds. *Rethinking Bakhtin: Extensions and Challenges*. Evanston, Ill.: Northwestern University Press, 1989.

Moyn, Samuel. "Human Rights, Not So Pure Anymore." *New York Times* (May 12, 2012).

———. *The Last Utopia: Human Rights in History*. Cambridge, Mass.: Belknap, 2010.

Mozejko, Edward, Boris Briker, and Per Dalgard, eds. *Vasiliy Pavlovich Aksenov: A Writer in Quest of Himself*. Columbus, Ohio: Slavica, 1984.

Mulrine, Stephen. "*Moscow Stations*: From Novel to Play." *Modern Drama* 41 (1998).

Murav'ev, Vladimir. "Vysokikh zrelishch zritel'." In *Zapiski psikhopata*, by Vendikt Erofeev. Moscow: Vagrius, 2000.

Nabokov, Vladimir. *Invitation to a Beheading*. Trans. Dmitri Nabokov. New York: Vintage Books, 1959.

Nathans, Benjamin. "The Dictatorship of Reason: Aleksandr Vol'pin and the Idea of Rights Under 'Developed Socialism.'" *Slavic Review* 66, no. 4 (2007): 630–63.

———. "Thawed Selves: A Commentary on the Soviet First Person." *Kritika* 13, no. 1 (2012).

———. "When Did Your Eyes Open?" *London Review of Books* 32, no. 9 (May 13, 2010): 25–26.

Nepomnyashchy, Catharine Theimer. *Abram Tertz and the Poetics of Crime*. New Haven, Conn.: Yale University Press, 1995.

———. "Andrei Siniavsky (Abram Tertz) (1925–1997)." In *Dictionary of Literary Biography*, vol. 302, *Russian Prose Writers after World War II*, ed. Christine Rydel, 296–316. Farmington Hills, Mich., 2004.

New Catholic Encyclopedia. Vol. 8. Detroit: Thomson Gale/Catholic University of America, 2003.

NTS: Mysl' i delo, 1930–2000. Bibliotechka rossievedeniia series, vol. 4. Moscow: Posev, 2000.

"Nuzhny li v literaturovedenii gipotezy?" *Voprosy literatury* 2 (1977): 82–112.

O'Keeffe, Dennis, Helen Szamuely, et al. *Samizdat, Based on a Discussion at the CRCE Led by Dennis O'Keeffe and Helen Szamuely*. London: Centre for Research into Post-Communist Economies, 2004.

Orlitskii, Iu. B. "Stikhovoe nachalo v proze Vasiliia Aksenova." In *Vasilii Aksenov: Literaturnaia sud'ba*, ed. V. P. Skobolev and L. A. Fink. Samara: Izdatel'stvo Samarskii universitet, 1994.

Orlova, E. I. "Posle skaza (Mikhail Zoshchenko—Venedikt Erofeev—Abram Terts." *Filologicheskie nauki* 6 (1996): 13–22.

Orwin, Donna Tussing. *Consequences of Consciousness: Turgenev, Dostoevsky, and Tolstoy*. Stanford, Calif.: Stanford University Press, 2007.

Ostrovskii, Nikolai. *Sochineniia v trekh tomakh*. Moscow: Izdatel'stvo TsK VLKSM "Molodaia gvardiia," 1967.

Oushakine, Serguei. "The Terrifying Mimicry of Samizdat." *Public Culture* 13, no. 2 (Spring 2001): 191–214.

Panchenko, A. M. "Smekh kak zrelishche." in *Smekh v drevnei Rusi*, ed. D. S. Likhachev, A. M. Panchenko, and N. V. Ponyrko. Leningrad: Nauka, 1984.

Paperno, Irina. "The Meaning of Art: Symbolist Theories." In *Creating Life: The Aesthetic Utopia of Russian Modernism*, ed. Irina Paperno and Joan Delaney Grossman. Stanford, Calif.: Stanford University Press, 1994.

Paperno, Irina, and Boris Gasparov. "'Vstan' i idi." *Slavica Hierosolymitana* 5–6 (1981).

Parker, Andrew, and Eve Kosofsky Sedgwick, eds. *Performativity and Performance*. New York: Routledge, 1995.

Parthé, Kathleen F. *Russian Village Prose: The Radiant Past*. Princeton N.J.: Princeton University Press, 1992.

Pasternak, Boris. *"I Remember."* Ed. D. Magarshack. New York: Meridian Books, 1960.

———. *Stikhotvoreniia i poemy*. Moscow: Biblioteka poeta, 1965.

Pawlikowski, Pawel, director. "From Moscow to Pietushki with Benny Yerofeev." BBC2 documentary (aired April 1990). http://www.youtube.com/watch?v=xxeeKDsN5Hc&feature=related .

Peretz, Pauline. *Le Combat pour les Juifs soviétiques: Washington-Moscou-Jérusalem, 1953–1989*. Paris: Arman Colin, 2006.

Perloff, Marjorie. *The Futurist Moment: Avant-Garde, Avant Guerre, and the Language of Rupture*. Chicago: University of Chicago Press, 1986.

———. *The Poetics of Indeterminacy: Rimbaud to Cage*. Princeton, N.J.: Princeton University Press, 1981.

Pimenov, Revol't. "Vospominaniia, chast' 1: Odin politicheskii protsess (1956–1958)." *Pamiat': Istoricheskii sbornik* 2 (1979).

Polikovskaia, Liudmila. *My predchuvstvie . . . predtecha . . . Ploshchad' Maiakovskogo, 1958–1965*. Moscow: Zven'ia, 1997.

Pomerantsev, Vladimir. "Ob iskrennosti v literature." *Novyi mir* 12 (1953): 18–45.

Poremsky, V. D. *NTS: Mysl' i delo, 1930–2000*. Bibliotechka rossievedeniia series, vol. 4. Moscow: Posev, 2000.

Pospielovsky, Dmitry. "From Gosizdat to Samizdat and Tamizdat." *Canadian Slavonic Papers* 20, no. 1 (1978): 44–62.

"Predislovie 'Ot redaktsii' k sb. 'Pamiat.'" *Russkaia mysl'* (April 14, 1977): 5.

Proffer, Ellendea. "Ardis." In the catalog *Ardis, 25 let russkoi literatury: Biblioteka inostrannoi literatury*. Library of Foreign Literature, Moscow, May 28, 1996–June 18, 1996.

Prudovskii, Leonid. "Sumasshedshim mozhno byt' v liuboe vremia." *Kontinent* 65 (1990): 411–30.

Pushkin, Alexander. *Eugene Onegin*. Trans. Charles Johnston. New York: Penguin Books, 1977.

Radio Liberty. "Basic Information about Arkhiv Samizdata." *Arkhiv Samizdata:*

Register of Documents, enlarged and revised. Munich: Samizdat Archive Association, 1973.

Rassadin, Stanislav. "Shestidesiatniki." *Iunost'* 12 (1960): 58–62.

———. ". . . svobody chernaia rabota." *Aprel'* 1 (1989).

Ratmirov, Igor'. "RePatria." *Materialy samizdata* 25 (1975): 63–65.

Remnick, David. "The Lush Life of a Muscovite." *The New Yorker* 71, no. 33 (October 23, 1995): 36.

———. "What's a Vassily Aksyonov?" *The Washington Post* (February 15, 1987): w20.

RePatria. *Volnoe slovo* 16 (1975).

Rogov, Konstantin, ed. *Rossiia/Russia: Issue 1[9] Semidesiatye kak predmet istorii russkoi kul'tury*. Moscow: O.G.I., 1998.

Ro'i, Yaacov, ed. *The Jewish Movement in the Soviet Union*. Washington, D.C.: Woodrow Wilson Center, 2012.

Roman, Gail Harrison, and Virginia Hagelstein Marquardt, eds. *The Avant-Garde Frontier: Russia Meets the West, 1910–1930*. Gainesville: University Press of Florida, 1992.

Ronen, Omry. "Otstuplenie." *Zvezda* 5 (2002). http://magazines.russ.ru/zvezda/2002/5/ron.html .

Rowell, Margit, and Deborah Wye, eds. *The Russian Avant-Garde Book, 1910–1934*. New York: Museum of Modern Art, 2002.

Rubinstein, Joshua, and Alexander Gribanov, eds. *The KGB File of Andrei Sakharov*. New Haven, Conn.: Yale University Press, 2005.

Rubinshtein, Lev, "Chto tut mozhno skazat' . . ." In *Indeks (po materialom rukopisnykh zhurnalov)*, ed. Mikhail Romm and E. Bogatykh. Moscow: "Efa," 1990.

———. "What Can One Say?" Trans. Gerald J. Janecek. In *Re-Entering the Sign: Articulating New Russian Culture*, ed. Ellen E. Berry and Anesa Miller-Pogacar. Ann Arbor: University of Michigan Press, 1995.

"Russian Art Goes Boom." *RA Magazine* 97 (Winter 2007). http://www.royalacademy.org.uk/ra-magazine/winter-2007/features/russian-art-goes-boom,164,RAMA.html.

Ryan-Hayes, Karen L. *Contemporary Russian Satire: A Genre Study*. Cambridge University Press, 1996.

———, ed. *Venedikt Erofeev's "Moscow-Petushki": Critical Perspectives*. New York: Peter Lang, 1997.

Safire, William. *The First Dissident: The Book of Job in Today's Politics*. New York: Random House, 1992.

Samizdat 1: La voix de l'opposition communiste en U.R.S.S. Paris: Seuil, 1970.

Sandler, Stephanie. *Commemorating Pushkin: Russia's Myth of a National Poet*. Stanford, Calif.: Stanford University Press, 2004.

Saunders, Francis Stonor. *Who Paid the Piper? The CIA and the Cultural Cold War*. London: Granta Books, 1999.

Saunders, George. *Samizdat: Voices of the Soviet Opposition*. New York: Monad, 1974.

Savitskii, Stanislav. *Andegraund: Istoriia i mify leningradskoi neofitsial'noi literatury*. Moscow: Novoe literaturnoe obozrenie, 2002.

Schroeter, Leonard. *The Last Exodus*. Seattle: University of Washington Press, 1979.

Sedgwick, Eve Kosofsky. "Queer Performativity: Henry James's The Art of the Novel." In *The Novel: An Anthology of Criticism and Theory, 1900–2000*, ed. Dorothy J. Hale. Malden, Mass.: Blackwell, 2006.

Shalamov, Varlam. *Novaia kniga: Vospominaniia, Zapisnye knizhki, Perepiska, Sledstvennye dela*. Ed. I. P. Sirotinskaia. Moscow: Eksmo, 2004.

Shaw, Kurt. "French Connections: The Three Musketeers Motif in Andrei Bitov's *Pushkinskii dom*." *Canadian Slavonic Papers* 37, no. 1–2 (1995): 187–99.

Shklovskii, Evgenii. "V poiskakh real'nosti." *Literaturnoe obozrenie* 5 (1988).

Shklovskii, Viktor. "'Evgenii Onegin' (Pushkin i Stern)." In *Ocherki po poetike Pushkina*, 197–220. The Hague: Mouton, 1969.

Shklovsky, Viktor. "Sterne's *Tristram Shandy*: Stylistic Commentary." In *The Novel: An Anthology of Criticism and Theory 1900–2000*, ed. Dorothy J. Hale. Malden, Mass.: Blackwell, 2006.

Shmel'kova, Natal'ia. "Ni tsenzor, ni den'gi, ni golod: O Venedikte Erofeeve (1938–1990)." In *Vo chreve machekhi, ili Zhizn'-diktatura krasnogo*, 9–114. St. Petersburg: Limbus, 1999.

Shmid, Wolf. "Andrei Bitov—Master 'ostrovideniia.'" In *Imperiia v chetyrekh izmereniiakh*. 4 vols. Moscow: TKO AST 1996. Vol. 1.

Shub, Anatole. "The Intelligentsia in the Fires of Stalinism." *New York Times* (November 25, 1984).

Simmons, Cynthia. "An Alcoholic Narrative as 'Time Out' and the Double in *Moskva–Petushki*." *Canadian-American Slavic Studies* 24 (1990).

———. *Their Fathers' Voice: Vassily Aksyonov, Venedikt Erofeev, Eduard Limonov, and Sasha Sokolov*. New York: Peter Lang, 1993.

Siniavskii, Andrei. "Beasts and Men." Trans. William E. Harkins. *New York Review of Books* 26, no. 21–22 (1980): 22–24.

———. "Dissidentstvo kak lichnyi opyt." *Sintaksis* 15 (1986): 131–47.

———. "Liudi i zveri" (review of Georgii Vladimov's novel *Faithful Ruslan*). *Kontinent* 5 (1975): 367–404.

———. "Odin den' s Pasternakom." *Sintaksis* 6 (1980).

———. "Perepiska Andreia Siniavskogo s redkollegiei serii 'Biblioteki poeta': Izmenenie sovetskogo literaturnogo polia." Introduction and commentary Ann Komaromi. *Novoe literaturnoe obozrenie* 71 (2005): 175–99.

———. "Poeticheskii sbornik B. Pasternaka" (review of Boris Pasternak, *Stikhotvoreniia i poemy*, ed. N. Kriuchkova [Moscow, 1961]). *Novyi mir* 3 (1962): 261–63.

———. "Poeziia i proza Ol'gi Berggol'ts." *Novyi mir* 5 (1960): 225–36.

———. "Poeziia Pasternaka." In *Stikhotvoreniia i poemy*, by Boris Pasternak. (Moscow: Biblioteka poeta, 1965.

Sinyavsky, Andrei. "Dissent as a Personal Experience." *Dissent* 31, no. 2 (1984): 152–61.

Skilling, H. Gordon, *Samizdat and an Independent Society in Central and Eastern Europe*. Columbus: Ohio State University Press, 1989.

Smirnova, E. A. "Venedikt Erofeev glazami gogoleveda." *Russkaia literatura* 3 (1990): 58–66.

Solzhenitsyn, Aleksandr. *Nobel Lecture*. Bilingual ed. English and Russian; English translation by F. D. Reeve. New York: Farrar, Straus, and Giroux, 1972.

Sosin, Gene. *Sparks of Liberty: An Insider's Memoir of Radio Liberty*. University Park: Pennsylvania State University Press, 1999.

"Stenogramma obshchemoskovskogo sobraniia pisatelei, 31 oktiabria 1958 goda." *Novyi zhurnal* 83 (1966).

Strelianyi, Anatolii, et al., eds. *Samizdat veka*. Moscow: Polifakt, 1999.

Strukova, Elena. *Al'ternativnaia periodicheskaia pechat' v istorii rossiiskoi mnogopartiinosti (1987–1996)*. Moscow: GPIB, 2005.

Tanselle, Thomas. *A Rationale of Textual Criticism*. Philadelphia: University of Pennsylvania Press, 1989.

Taubman, William. *Khrushchev: The Man and His Era*. New York: W.W. Norton, 2003.

Telesin, Julius. "Inside 'Samizdat.'" *Encounter* (February 1973): 25–33.

Terts, Abram (Andrei Siniavskii). "Anekdot v Anekdote." *Sintaksis* 1 (1978): 77–95.

———. *Sobranie sochinenii v dvukh tomakh*. 2 vols. Moscow: SP 'Start,' 1992.

Tertz, Abram (Andrei Sinyavsky). "On Socialist Realism." In *The Trial Begins, and On Socialist Realism*, trans. George Dennis. Berkeley: University of California Press, 1960.

Theological Dictionary of the New Testament. Ed. Gerhard Kittel, trans. Geoffrey W. Bromiley. Grand Rapids, Mich: Wm. B. Eerdmans, 1965.

Tihanov, Galin. *The Master and the Slave: Lukacs, Bakhtin, and the Ideas of Their Time*. Oxford: Clarendon, 2000.

Tolstoi, Aleksei. *Zolotoi kliuchik, ili, Prikliucheniia Buratino*. Moscow: Eksmo, 2002.

Tolstoy, Leo. *Anna Karenina*. Trans. Richard Pevear and Larissa Volokhonsky. London: Penguin Books, 2006.

Tosunian, Irina. "Ot Moskvy do samykh Petushkov." *Literaturnaia gazeta* (January 3, 1990): 5.

Trauberg, Natal'ia. "Vsegda li pobezhdaet pobezhdennyi? Natal'ia Trauberg o khristianskom samizdate." *Literaturnaia gazeta* (April 27–May 2, 2000): 11.

Tumanov, Vladimir. "The End in V. Erofeev's 'Moskva–Petuski.'" *Russian Literature* 39 (1996).

Uncensored Russia: The Human Rights Movement in the Soviet Union: The Annotated Text of the Unofficial Moscow Journal "A Chronicle of Current Events" (Nos. 1–11). Trans. and intro. Peter Reddaway. London: Jonathan Cape, 1972.

Ushakov, Nikolai. "Sviaz' vremen." *Literaturnaia gazeta* 24, no. 4258 (June 10, 1970): 3.

Vail', Petr, and Aleksandr Genis. *60-e: Mir sovetskogo cheloveka*. Moscow: Novoe literaturnoe obozrenie, 1996.

Vesselova, Natalia. "Venichka, Venia, Venedikt Erofeev: The Paradigm of the Narrator's Name in *Moskva–Petushki*." *Essais sur le Discours de l'Europe Eclatée* 19 (2003): 33–39.

Vest': Proza, Poeziia, Dramaturgiia. Ed. Veniamin Kaverin. Moscow: Knizhnaia palata, 1989.

Vishevsky, A., and T. Pogacar. "The Function of Conventional Language Pattern in the Prose of Vasiliy Aksenov." In *Vasiliy Pavlovich Aksenov: A Writer in Quest of Himself*, ed. Edward Mozejko, Boris Briker, and Per Dalgard. Columbus, Ohio: Slavica, 1984.

Vlasov, Eduard. "Bessmertnaia poema Venedikta Erofeeva 'Moskva–Petushki.'" In *Moskva–Petushki*, by Venedikt Erofeev. Moscow: Vagrius, 2000.

———. "Zagranitsa glazami ekstsentrika: K analizu 'zagranichnykh glav." In *Venedikt Erofeev's "Moscow-Petushki": Critical Perspectives*, ed. Karen Ryan-Hayes, 197–220. New York: Peter Lang, 1997.

Volchek, Dmitrii. "Gde shurshat plat'e." *Teatr* 4 (2011). http://oteatre.info/2011–4/.

Voronel', Nina. *Bez prikras: Vospominaniia*. Moscow: Zakharov, 2003.

Voronkov, Viktor, and Jan Wielgohs. "Soviet Russia." In *Dissent and Opposition in Communist Eastern Europe: Origins of Civil Society and Democratic Transition*, ed. Detlef Pollack and Jan Wielgohs. Burlington Vt.: Ashgate, 2004.

Vtoraia kul'tura: Neofitsial'naia poeziia Leningrada v 1970–1980-e gody. Ed. Jean-Philippe Jaccard, Violaine Friedli, and Jens Herlth. St. Petersburg: Rostok, 2013.

Wakamiya, Lisa Ryoko. *Locating Exiled Writers in Contemporary Russian Literature*. New York: Palgrave Macmillan, 2009.

White, Eric Charles. *Kaironomia: On the Will-to-Invent*. Ithaca, N.Y.: Cornell University Press, 1987.

Wolfe, Bertram D. *Khrushchev and Stalin's Ghost*. Westport, Conn.: Greenwood Press, Publishers, 1957.

Wurmbrand, Richard. *Tortured for Christ*. London: Hodder and Stoughton, 1967.

Yerofeev, Venedikt. *Moscow Stations: A Poem*. Trans. Stephen Mulrine. London: Faber and Faber, 1997.

Yurchak, Alexei. "The Cynical Reason of Late Socialism: Power, Pretense, and the Anekdot." *Public Culture* 9, no. 2 (1997).

———. *Everything Was Forever, Until It Was No More: The Last Soviet Generation*. Princeton, N.J.: Princeton University Press, 2006.

"Zamglavy Roskomnadzora Ksenzov poluchil vygovor za Facebook i Twitter." *The Russian Times* (May 17, 2014). http://therussiantimes.com/news/10854.html.

Zarzycka, Ewa Bérard. "Entretien de Ewa Bérard Zarzycka avec Andrei Bitov." *La Quinzaine Littéraire* 525 (February 1–15, 1989).

Zhukov, Iurii. "Vosem' s polovinoi krugov kinematograficheskogo ada." *Literaturnaia gazeta* 87 (July 20, 1963).

Zorin, Andrei. "Opoznavatel'nyi znak." *Teatr* 9 (1991).

———. "Prigorodnyi poezd dal'nego sledovaniia." *Novyi mir* 5 (1989): 256–58.

Zuckerman, Ethan. "Intermediate Censorship." In *Access Controlled: The Shaping of Power, Rights, and Rule in Cyberspace*, ed. Ronald J. Deibert et al., 71–85. Cambridge, Mass.: MIT Press, 2010. http://www.access-controlled.net/wp-content/PDFs/chapter-5.pdf.

UNPUBLISHED INTERVIEWS (INTERVIEW BY AUTHOR UNLESS OTHERWISE SPECIFIED)

Aksenov, Vasilii, series of conversations, April 12, 2003 (Fairfax) and Summer, 2003 (phone).

Aksenov, Vasilii (interview by D. Barton Johnson), May 20, 1990.

Bitov, Andrei, May 17, 2000.

Bourdeaux, Michael, July 16, 2007.

Dewhirst, Martin, March 28, 2007.

Dewhirst, Martin (interview by Ia. Zykova for the Memorial Society), May 30, 2004.

Freidin, Iurii, April 6, 2008.

Roginskii, Arsenii, April 3, 2008.

Salova, Galina, March 28, 2008.

Sedakova, Olga, March 2001.

PRINCIPAL ARCHIVES CONSULTED

Ardis Press Papers, University of Michigan, Hatcher Graduate Library.

Siniavskii Collection, Hoover Institution, Palo Alto, Calif.

Historical Archives, Research Center for East European Studies, University of Bremen (Forschungsstelle Osteuropa, Universität Bremen), Bremen, Germany.

Samizdat Archives, HU OSA 300–85, Records of Radio Free Europe/Radio Liberty Research Institute (RFE/RL RI), Open Society Archives at Central European University, Budapest, Hungary.

Index